# Introduction to
# Director and Lingo
## Multimedia and Internet Applications

*by Nilson Neuschotz*

Prentice
Hall

Prentice Hall, Upper Saddle River, New Jersey 07458

*For Sondra and Leah Rebecca, my beautiful wife and daughter*

**Library of Congress Cataloging-in-Publication Data**

Neuschotz, Nilson
    Introduction to Director and Lingo: multimedia and internet applications
       p.  cm.
    ISBN: 0-13-690322-3
    1. Multimedia systems. 2. Internet (Computer network). 3. Director (Computer file). 4. Lingo (Computer program language).  I. Title
    QA76.575 .N46 2000
    006.7'869--dc21                              99-055642

Acquisition editor: *Petra J. Recter*
Editorial assistant: *Sarah Burrows*
Editor-in-chief: *Marcia Horton*
Editorial/production supervision: *Barbara A. Till*
Executive managing editor: *Vince O'Brien*
Managing editor: *David A. George*
Manufacturing buyer: *Pat Brown*
Manufacturing manager: *Trudy Pisciotti*
Creative director: *Paul Belfanti*
Director of production and manufacturing: *David W. Riccardi*
Art director: *Heather Scott*

Cover designer: *John Christiana*
Production services: ***TIPS** Technical Publishing*
Copy editor: *Paulette Miley*
Compositor: *Karen Newton*
Proof readers: *Lynanne Fowle and Ellen Fussell*
Technical editor and indexer: *Robert Kern*
Lesson graphic design: *D. Garrett Nantz*
Testing: *David Newman*
Product graphic design: *Nick Kirstead*
Development services: *Motion Over Time, Inc.*
Art program: *Sarah Wood*

© 2000 by Prentice-Hall, Inc.
Upper Saddle River, New Jersey 07458

TRADEMARKS
Microsoft Windows Operating System, Apple Macintosh Operating System, Adobe Premiere, Adobe Photoshop, Adobe Illustrator, Debabilizer, Macromedia Fireworks, Macromedia Flash, Macromedia Director, Apple Quicktime, Fractel Design Painter, Lingo, MediaPaint, Hypercard, Java, SoundEdit , SoundForge, Shockwave, Strata Studio Pro, Microsoft Video for Windows, Aldus Persuassion, Microsoft PowerPoint

The New York Knicks Team identification is a trademark which is the exclusive property of the NBA Properties, Inc. and the member teams of the NBA. © NBA Properties, Inc. All rights reserved.

Printed in the United States of America

10  9  8  7  6  5  4  3  2  1

## 0-13-690322-3

Prentice-Hall International (UK) Limited, *London*
Prentice-Hall of Australia Pty. Limited, *Sydney*
Prentice-Hall Canada Inc., *Toronto*
Prentice-Hall Hispanoamericana, S.A., *Mexico*
Prentice-Hall of India Private Limited, *New Delhi*
Prentice-Hall of Japan, Inc., *Tokyo*
Pearson Education Asia Pte Ltd
Editora Prentice-Hall do Brasil, Ltda., *Rio de Janeiro*

# Contents

**CHAPTER 4**     **USING SOUND AND SYNCHRONIZING**

                     **ANIMATION TO AUDIO. . . . . . . . . . . . . . . . . . . . . 185**

# Preface

## WHY SHOULD YOU READ THIS BOOK?

Sometime in 1992 I was living in a basement I rented from a friend, 2 stories away from a bathroom and kitchen. My companions were a cat that I found on the NY subway, and a Macintosh IIci that I bought with questionable credit through a reseller that I used to work for (Windows was still quite a bit away from multimedia at the time). At the time, I was delivering Domino's pizza and video-taping weddings for a living. By chance, I came across a new magazine that was looking for contributors. The Editor-in-Chief of Imaging Magazine was kind enough to meet with me, and entertained some of my ideas for stories about video and computers. I was hopeful, but not particularly confident that this was anything other than the Editor's good deed for the day. Nonetheless, I submitted my first article to the magazine for consideration, and was published for the first time in March of 1992. It was through my tenure as a contributor for Imaging that I became acquainted with all of the big names in computer software and hardware; one of these companies was Macromedia.

One of the perks of being a technical writer was that software would show up on my doorstep daily. Besides becoming friendly with all of the overnight delivery people that toured my neighborhood, I became pretty well-versed with how software was used, and I started to lean in the direction of something that I thought had a great deal of promise—multimedia. One of the deliveries that made it to my doorstep was the Macromedia suite of products, including Director.

Initially, Director had my head spinning. I was highly motivated to learn how to use it because I was so impressed with what could be accomplished. I then received a flyer from Macromedia announcing that they were offering training in a number of cities, including Suffern NY (about 1 hour away from New York City). Although I loved the flexibility in my schedule that the type of work I did offered, and I certainly enjoyed seeing my name in print, the money wasn't good enough for me to afford food and attend training in the same month. Macromedia came through when I contacted them and said that I would like to attend the training as research for a new article. This was only partially selfish, since I was actually working on an article and I was concerned that I wouldn't be able to write much if I didn't get some help. Little did I know that this little step would change my life and begin a career.

Each morning I attended the training in Suffern, driving my girlfriend's car up the Henry Hudson Parkway in what is my favorite time of year in New York—Fall. The most important thing occurring in my life was the fact that an outline for a multimedia book I wanted to write was being considered for publication by the technical subsidiary of a large publishing house. In many ways, this week would turn out to be a major turning point for me.

The training was held at a large computer reseller that also had classrooms. There were four other people in the class. I was the only person sitting in for free. The other folks were with large corporations that planned to use this early version of Director to create simple presentations. The web was still nascent. In fact, not many people really knew about it at all, and the concept of creating a commercial CD-ROM of any type was way off. Macromedia software wasn't running on Windows yet. In fact, Macromedia had an almost entirely different product line back then. It was still a small company that generated a great deal of their revenue from a set of dedicated users-hardly the mainstream.

Even then it was easy to see Director's draw. It put a great deal of power in your hands. It allowed creative people to program and quickly and easily create animation. It seemed that the people that were interested in learning it from a business perspective would compare it to slide show software, such as Microsoft Powerpoint and Aldus Persuasion. The people that used it creatively thought Director was one of the most inventive and powerful tools ever offered. The main issue most people had with it was that it was difficult to learn and documentation could be better. In part, the training I was attending was Macromedia's response to corporate users who wanted a direct method of learning how to use Macromedia's tools. For me, the training opened my eyes.

The training started on a Tuesday. The following day I received the news that my book outline was accepted by the publisher. That evening, the class went out for drinks. Boldly, I walked up to the instructor, Bob Whitney (a man in his sixties who had been working with computers since they used tubes and was essentially the entire training force for Macromedia). I was not an extraordinary student. In fact, I was behind. But I needed to know more, and I knew that there was one way to ensure that I knew Director as best as it could be known.

"Are you looking for anyone to teach for Macromedia in New York?"

This apparently was the right question to ask, because he started telling me about how Macromedia wanted more involvement in New York and that it was expensive to travel all the way out here from San Francisco. Now, I'm sure at this point Bob was entertaining me in large part, because I wasn't showing any particular aptitude for the material. He did, however, tell me to call Macromedia for a job application. The following week, I did.

Two weeks later I called Bob from a payphone and asked if he was still interested in a trainer in New York. He asked me a simple question about Director which I answered incorrectly. At this point, my prospects weren't looking good.

Over the next two months I worked on my book and explored different software. I would occasionally review the training manuals from the Director training. Some of the concepts were still beyond me, particularly in

Lingo (Director's scripting language). Then, those concepts seemed to click. This time I called Macromedia from the basement, which I had straightened out a bit to better suit a professional author. Bob wasn't in San Francisco, he was in New York teaching another class. His assistant passed my message on to him, which to my tremendous surprise was returned less than an hour later. Bob wanted to meet me in Manhattan. He was teaching at 53$^{rd}$ street.

It turned out that Bob wasn't teaching. He was observing a new instructor who, as it turned out, was not working out. He planned to give this information to the instructor at the close of that training. Apparently my call came at an opportune moment, as Macromedia was about to be without a trainer in New York and they had already committed to another public training, as well as a private session for a group of young producers from MTV in December.

I showed Bob the article that I had written about Macromedia in Imaging following our training together. There was even a plug for Macromedia training in a sidebar. I also showed him part of the book that I was writing which included a chapter dedicated to Macromedia Director and Authorware. This seemed to be what he needed to see, because he asked if I was available the first week of December. Naturally, I was.

My first two trainings went moderately well. It was obvious to some of the students that I was new to the job, and this seemed to work in my favor. I was as equally motivated to learn how to teach as I was to learn Director, so it was a perfect job.

I continued teaching for Macromedia for the next few years. The freelance position had me travelling to such exotic locales as Atlanta, Dallas, Boston, San Francisco, and various other budding multimedia centers. At one point, I found myself in New Zealand. That alone is a story.

In 1994, my first book was published. I moved into an apartment above ground, and Macromedia asked me to come to San Francisco for a few weeks to work on the new training materials for Director 4. This was an important year for Macromedia, as the company was going to introduce a Windows version of Director, and planned to go public. Bob was certainly excited about the latter item. It was during this trip that Bob let me in on a secret. Macromedia planned to end their direct training and would leave all training to other companies. There would only be authorized training providers. At this point, I was teaching for Macromedia once a month, sometimes more. There was increased interest in me providing programming services, something I never thought would happen. It amazed me that something I enjoyed so much could actually pay bills. But this move by Macromedia meant that I needed to think about my next step. I either needed to figure out how to keep the training machine moving, or I needed to prepare to lose the biggest client I had. I decided I would keep the machine going.

At first I tried to run everything from home. I had a friend help me with calling company lists to promote our own Director training. Later I hired 2 salespeople who also worked out of their homes. This didn't work because no one knew where to return a telephone call. It was apparent that this new company was not terribly organized. Our first training happened in spite of the lack of organization. We rented a back room and computers from the facility where I was teaching Macromedia's classes. In all, I think the effort resulted in 5 students and a $100 profit. All things considered, I was in business, and it was because I knew Director.

I had actually started the company while I still lived underground using the name Motion Over Time, a name I adopted from an article on 3D animation I had written for Imaging. The office equipment I had was a phone and a chair that my girlfriend, Sondra, brought over one day as a surprise. I later married her for that and some other things that made her a valuable source of inspiration for me. I finally incorporated the business in 1994, and opened a bank account in 1995. That first class, in the summer of 1995, was the first time I accepted payment in the name Motion Over Time, Inc.

I opened the first office by subletting two rooms from a client in Manhattan. I was still essentially operating as the only resource that the company had to offer, but things would change. The purpose for the office was so that people knew which number to call if they wanted to register for a class.

Macromedia supported us in those days. They sent me on speaking engagements, gave us authorized trainer status for free, and provided us with software. Bob came by to visit once and was very impressed with the 250 square feet of room we had. There was a box for him to sit on and everything. I needed to talk to Bob, because it was hurting us to need to rent classrooms and computers. We needed a permanent solution—a bigger office with a classroom and machines in place. No one in their right mind would lend me the money and my credit was still terrible. So I asked another bold question of Bob.

"Would you let me host Macromedia's training in our new Motion Over Time facility in New York."

Of course I couldn't answer where or when this facility would be available, let alone anything about how it would be equipped and what it would look like, but Bob was good to me. He said he would consider it, but I needed to put something together for him to look at. No guarantees.

For the next few months I sent him letters, floor plans, and descriptions about how what I was putting together would be bigger, better, and more comfortable than anything that Macromedia had used to date. It would be the perfect learning environment. I really believed that Motion Over Time could do it better than anything I had seen. Of course, I needed to first find a location. During those months, there was progress and set backs. Locations found and lost. Changing timetables at Macromedia.

Demanding projects. Then it all came together. We found a location, we had a solution for computers, and I was able to answer all of Bob's "What Ifs." Then he said what I was hoping for.

"How would you like to host the next Director training in New York."

Of course I said, "It would be my pleasure."

In the coming year, we hosted Macromedia's training in New York until they stopped offering training. By then, Motion Over Time had been around long enough to be able to sustain itself. We were known for our work with Director and had a gradually increasing client base for programming and training services.

It was only four years ago that we moved into the second office, a cavernous 5000 square foot loft on 21$^{st}$ Street. More room than I ever thought we'd need along with more cost than I ever thought we could sustain. I'm happy to say that I was wrong. We're now a full service web and multimedia consulting, development, and training firm, and people actually ask me when we plan to go public. Ironically, we are also two doors away from Imaging magazine.

There are plenty of details left out, but it's time to return to the original question, "Why should you read this book?" I certainly can't guarantee that your life will be transformed, but this software is special. It allows creative people to achieve highly technical results. I was never a programmer, yet you are now holding a book on Director and Lingo that I wrote. Demand for people with Director skills is certainly on the rise. I know because we now employ plenty of them at Motion Over Time. I hope that learning this software does something different for you, too, even if all you are doing is enhancing an already successful career. The most important personal achievements I've made were marrying Sondra and the birth of our daughter, Leah, but following the fork in the road labeled "Director" was one of the best professional moves I could ever have made. I remember something about that each time I look at my old Domino's Pizza nametag which now sits on my desk. That is why you should read this book and any other you can get your hands on about this software.

## NOTES AND WARNINGS

Notes are helpful hints and highlights from the lesson that are particularly useful, as well as information that extends the material taught in the lesson. Warnings indicate situations to avoid. Both will be presented in gray boxes throughout the book. It will be important to read all notes and warnings as they are designed to help avoid confusing situations as well as provide helpful hints.

## HOW TO FOLLOW INSTRUCTIONS IN THIS BOOK

Most instructions are explicit, such as "click the OK button in the Alert dialog window." They are usually presented with a figure that gives a graphic representation of the instruction. Menus are treated a bit differently; for example "select New from the File menu" is presented as "choose file>new." This is particularly helpful when an item must be selected from a submenu, such as "select Properties from the Movie submenu in the Modify menu," which becomes "choose Modify>Movie>Properties." Many of the menu selections are also accompanied by figures that offer a graphic representation.

## HOW THIS BOOK IS STRUCTURED

Each chapter of this book will lead you through part of the process of developing a multimedia presentation that we have named the Billionaire's Shop. The Billionaire's Shop is an imaginary on-line store that makes all of the most valuable and rare items on Earth (and off-Earth) available us. The Shop allows you to browse these items and update the inventory as new products become available on the Internet. The lessons in this book will teach you how to plan the project, assemble the parts of the presentation, and write the scripts that will make it work. To accomplish this, each lesson teaches gradually advancing material that is designed to move the project along while giving you important information that you can later use on your own. The subjects in this book are separated into four general categories: project planning, animation, Lingo, and Hybrid scripting.

Chapter 1 presents part of the project planning process that we employ here at Motion Over Time, Inc. The examples in this chapter use the Billionaire's Shop lesson in the book as the subject of a planned project.

Chapters 2 through 4 cover basic and advanced animation techniques along with the use of digital video. These are also the chapters that teach the navigation of Director's interface.

Chapters 5 through 8 cover Lingo scripting. Basic scripting covers the programming of buttons and creating a nonlinear presentation. This means that the presentation is controlled by user interaction, as opposed to a linear presentation, which is designed to only play from beginning to end with no user interaction. The more advanced scripting features show you how to control screen features, such as programming a slider control in the presentation that changes volume settings. We also work with new features such as auto-puppeting and Behavior scripts, which have made some of the more difficult programming issues in Lingo much easier to accomplish for the beginner.

In chapters 9 through 11 we work with Hybrid scripts, which allow Director to retrieve information from the Internet. We first work with downloading and reading text files, which will cause different things to occur in

The Billionaire's Shop project based upon the text contained in the document retrieved. We then work with downloading graphic file types, which is how we update the products displayed through The Billionaire's Shop. Finally, we prepare our project for delivery on a CD-ROM, along with adding an email feature to the presentation that allows Director's Hybrid scripts to send information to an email account on the Internet.

## ACKNOWLEDGMENTS

The following people have provided much needed support and patience in the development of this work. My good wishes and sincerest thanks to them all.

### PROJECT DEVELOPMENT TEAM

Development Services: Motion Over Time, Inc.
Lesson graphic design: D. Garrett Nantz
Product Graphic Design for The Billionaire's Shop: Nick Kirstead
Proof Reading and Testing: David Newman

### PRODUCTION TEAM

Production Services: *TIPS* Technical Publishing
Technical edit and index: Robert Kern
Art program: Sarah Wood
Copy editor: Paulette Miley
Compositor: Karen Newton
Proof reader: Ellen Fussell and Lynanne Fowle

### PRENTICE-HALL

Publisher: Alan Apt
Editorial Assistant: Toni Holm
Senior Acquisitions Editor: Petra Recter
Editorial Assistant: Sarah Burrows

### REVIEWERS

Michael Ascroft (University of Iowa)
Karen Duda (Youngstown State University)
Ann Kellerman (SUNY at Binghampton)
Robert Kern (*TIPS* Technical Publishing)
Louise Moses (Mount Union College, OH)
Carol Race (Truman State University)
Tracey Temple (Ohio State University)

Special thanks to Macromedia for continually producing good products.

*—Nilson Neuschotz*

# CHAPTER 1

# THE MULTIMEDIA
# DEVELOPMENT PROCESS

# 1 The Multimedia Development Process

In this chapter, you will learn how to:

- Plan and organize the development of a multimedia project
- Plan and organize a project developed with Macromedia Director
- Use the Billshop CD
- Locate and launch the Director Help and interactive Lingo Dictionary files
- Write a script for a multimedia project
- Storyboard the animation in a Director movie
- Plan the programming and interactive elements of a project using a Logic Flowchart
- Track the progress of a project's development using a media inventory
- Open a Director file
- Use the Control Panel to play a Director movie
- Determine the needs for testing and delivering a multimedia project

Also in this chapter:

- Learn about the Trial version of Director
- Get an overview of the features of Macromedia Director along with a brief history of what has made it popular

## THE IMPORTANCE OF PLANNING

Multimedia development, like any production process that involves the coordination of multiple skills, can be fairly detailed. Careful planning can help to ensure that your project moves along smoothly and efficiently. The overall objective of the planning process is to accurately assess the time, resources, and costs associated with a project. Most producers (whether a boss or a client) appreciate and need this information, with the same motivations: supporting a schedule or controlling expenses. There are many variations for how to plan a project that are useful no matter which tool you are using (of course our focus here is using Macromedia Director). In this chapter we cover the part of the project planning process that we use here at Motion Over Time.

The planning process occurs in stages intended to progressively evolve a project esthetically and technically. The first stage is the development of a project description, or *proof of concept*, which is a written description of the project. A good proof of concept is useful for consolidating and directing the ideas for a project before any complex computer work is started. It is usually a good idea to have a proof of concept included with any contracts you submit to a client. This way both you and the client know what the expectations are for the project. In our opinion, the area of greatest potential for misunderstanding is proof of concept. Prior to this point, all expression of the project is usually verbal, and no one can really tell what another person is thinking based on words alone. This explains why the next stage of project planning is the development of a storyboard and a logic flowchart, which are explained next.

A *storyboard* is a visual representation of the project using images and descriptions to give the proof of concept a tangible form that can be discussed and viewed by anyone involved. After images are introduced, you will be able to determine if your ideas about screen layout, color, and other esthetic concerns are truly the direction that you want to take. The complexity of the storyboard is really dependent upon the complexity of the project. If all the storyboard describes is an animation, then it will only contain drawings; if it involves video, it will contain drawings accompanied by the sounds and voices that should occur when the images appear on screen.

A *logic flowchart* is a storyboard for the interactive parts of a project. Interactivity in a presentation involves the parts of the presentation in which the viewer can participate. For example, you might want to provide the viewer with a screen that contains buttons and a menu of the parts of your presentation so that they can access the items they want to view in the order in which they want to view them. A classic example of an interactive presentation is an Automated Teller Machine; the screens that let you enter your password and choose checking or savings are interactive screens. At some point, the developers needed to produce a logic flowchart to determine what should happen when different buttons were clicked. If your presentation does not contain interactivity, then it is not necessary to create a logic flowchart.

The flowchart itself resembles a family tree, with shapes and lines that show how one part of the project relates to and leads to others. Later in this chapter we will review a logic flowchart that is designed for the project that we will work on throughout this book.

Once all of the planning has been made for the design of a project, attention can be placed on planning and creating the elements that will actually be included in the project. This not only helps organize the project, but also helps determine the software needed. For example, if your project will include video, you will need a method to capture that video onto a computer as well as software to edit the video. The types of graphics or images that you choose to include in your project determine the type of graphics or image editing and creation software that you use. Many clients request a list of the tools that you will work with. Therefore, when you prepare the proof of concept, and any later documentation that you will deliver with the project, it is a good idea to list the software (with version numbers), hardware, and operating system versions that you plan to use to develop the project.

Part of the process of organizing the media for a project is developing the *inventory*, a list of all of the media needed. The idea is to create a record and reference that members of the development team can use to be aware of what is happening in other parts of the project. An inventory typically contains the name, media type, and location in the project of each item used in the project. Besides serving as an organizational tool, the inventory can also serve to put into stark perspective the scope of what is required to create the project. Speaking from my own experience, every project seems easier than it turns out to be. The inventory can present facts such as the number of images that will need to be created for each scene. The fact that a project seems minor in scale because it has only five or six screens might not mean that the project won't take much time to produce. Those screens might require hundreds of individual elements, each needing to be designed, created, named, and incorporated into the project. There also needs to be time to correct any media that does not meet your expectations within the project. It's these small details that are the most time consuming and that have the greatest potential for error. Being organized from the beginning is the best way to navigate through production later. The inventory is not only a list of file names, it is a production tool.

The next step in the process of project development is the actual execution of the project. This is where all of the plans and ideas are given digital form. Programmers work with the inventory and logic flowchart to create the shells for the project. *Shells* are programs that use temporary media and allow the programmer to create the functions of the project while the final elements of the project are being developed by an artist.

While the programmers are working, the artists can design final media using the storyboards. As the artists create elements for the project, the programmers can incorporate those elements so that the project slowly begins to approach its final form. This also gives the artists the opportunity to see their designs in the context of being on screen. If anything isn't working out the way they planned, it can be modified at an early stage. Depending upon the size of a project, there might also be a Project Manager, who essentially oversees the scheduling and progress of the project at its multiple stages from concept to delivery. Some projects also have a Media Manager, who keeps track of all of the media elements of the project, what has been created as final media, what is still in progress, and scheduling for handoff of new media elements.

At some point, the project is tested on the types of computers that the final project will be viewed upon. This is very important because the computers that developers work with are usually much more powerful than the computers that the project will be used on. Also, it's important to test special features of the project. For example, if your project will be delivered over a network through an intranet, then it is a good idea to test the project over a network and make any adjustments before the project is delivered. This is where the technical documents of the proof of concept are extremely helpful, because they identify the target platform and eliminate many of the variables that can make testing before delivery difficult.

Including user support documentation along with your project can be extremely helpful to the end user. This support documentation serves as a manual for your project. Even if your project is very simple, it's useful and appreciated by most people to have some form of documentation that outlines your project and the contents of what you are delivering. This information includes how to use it, the types of computers it is intended for, any special operating requirements (such as special plug-ins for Web browsers), and who developed the project, with contact information. The complexity of this documentation will vary depending upon the requirements of the client, so it might also be necessary to include the design documents that you created the project with along with the final digital files and media. Many large companies need all this information to satisfy their record-keeping standards.

The size of your team should not affect the effort that goes into planning and documenting the project. Even one-person teams benefit from thorough tracking and documentation. An excellent reason is that this keeps the project organized so as not to hinder the creative process with maintenance details or lost materials, while providing a good reference for future development on the same project or one of similar design. This can be particularly useful in maintaining consistency if a project will be worked on at a later date and possibly by other people. Also, good organization in a project can make it possible for a small team to manage multiple projects simultaneously. This is the rule by which we have managed at Motion Over Time.

As we step through the project-planning process we will develop the blueprint for the project that will be built in this book. Our project is a Hybrid Internet project, meaning it will consist of local multimedia files and files that are located on the Internet. The end result will be a fictitious online store called The Billionaire's Shop where you can buy extraordinarily expensive products such as water from the Fountain of Youth or even the Empire State building. The Hybrid part of the project uses scripts in Director to check the Internet for the most recent inventory for The Billionaire's Shop. If the files on your hard drive are up to date, then the viewer will be sent a message to this effect enabling the viewer to browse the shop. If the inventory is not up to date, then The Billionaire's Shop will automatically update itself by downloading the new inventory from the Internet. It is easy to see how this feature of Director can help extend the life of a CD-ROM project.

## WHY DIRECTOR IS POPULAR

Macromedia Director was originally designed to be an animation tool for video productions. In fact, the application's original name was VideoWorks. The first version of the application was developed at a time before the existence of color monitors, large hard drives, CD-ROM, or even computer memory. Considering how fast and dynamic multimedia projects can be, it's clear to see that the application has taken several steps in its evolution.

The interface was designed for video developers. It contains a timeline window that is used to lay animations out one frame at a time, just as traditional animations have been developed for years. Initially, this is all the application was used for, creating simple animations for onscreen presentations and video.

Later versions of Director introduced Lingo, the scripting language that can be used to add interactive elements, such as buttons, to a presentation. Lingo also allows us to add intelligence to a Director movie, such as the ability to keep track of a student's performance in an interactive exam, with the capability of determining different reactions from the program based on how well the student has done. Initially, the interactive features of Director were very basic, so it was not used to create anything as complex as the games that are developed with it today. It was still primarily used for onscreen presentations, such as business presentations. The popularity of Director at this point was because of its roots—it was designed for graphic artists. To create an interactive presentation any other way, a developer would need to work with another application, called HyperCard, which was limited in its animation capability and required a greater amount of programming to create a complete presentation. The only other option was to work with traditional programming languages, such as Pascal or C. Director made it possible for designers to work within an environment in which they felt comfortable, allowing them to focus more on the visuals of a project as opposed to the programming.

Director's animation interface has remained largely unchanged since its earliest versions. The most significant changes have appeared in Version 7 and are covered in this book. Most of the modifications have appeared around the scope of interactivity in the application through the expansion of Lingo. As Director has matured, the scripting language has taken on many of the features of traditional programming languages. It can now be used to develop more involved presentations, such as highly interactive games and computer-based training modules. It has taken many of its original users along with it through the versions, helping many designers develop programming skills through the gradual introduction of scripting features. Many of the Director users today, including the author of this book, had absolutely no programming background before Director. Director was the tool that made it possible.

Now the animation and interactive feature set of Director is such that developers are using it with a programming background or an animation background. Computer speeds are such that Director can be used as an alternative to many projects that previously required the use of traditional programming languages. Director has also proved to be stable and well supported, so developers can feel comfortable that learning how to use Director is a skill that will be given room to evolve as new features are added with changing technology.

One large example of Director's ability to evolve is its integration with the Internet. The Internet was primarily intended as a method to deliver text-based information. Animation and graphics were later introduced, but were a challenge for the technology infrastructure and network behind the Internet. Animations on the Web were considered largely inefficient and impractical for the Web because they would take too long to view and would play too slowly. In many ways, this was the challenge originally answered by Director in the early days of color and graphics on desktop computers. Director was successfully modified to play over the Internet using Shockwave technology, which permits the playback of Director movies through Web browsers. Continual efforts to design smaller file sizes for the web led Macromedia to introduce the use of Flash assets in Director. Flash assets are small animations that use technology from another Macromedia application, Flash. This allows Director movies to remain very small, but still have the same level of interactivity.

Another remarkable marriage between Director and the Internet is portrayed in the Hybrid scripting methods that are covered in this book. These methods allow Director developers to create their projects for delivery on media such as a CD-ROM, but contain features that are downloaded from the Internet, just like a standard Web-browsing application such as Netscape Navigator or Microsoft Internet Explorer. Now we can take advantage of the ability to have highly dynamic animations and interactions on a CD-ROM, with little attention paid to file sizes, and have elements change frequently in the presentation by changing the source files on the Internet, just like updating a Web site. In the examples in this book, we will use Hybrid scripts to update the inventory of The Billionaire's Shop project.

Before we begin the lessons in the book, let's first load Director onto the computer.

## INSTALLING DIRECTOR

As is the case with most software, Director is upgraded on a regular basis. The best way to be certain that you have the most current version is to go to the developer's Web site. In this session we will download the latest trial version of Director so that we can begin our lessons. The trial software is time-limited and feature-crippled, but you will be able to view all files and follow along in the lessons just as if you were working with the commercial version of Director. If you have the commercial version of Director, then use that.

1.   Log onto the Internet and visit http://www.macromedia.com. This is Macromedia's Web address and is where you will be able to find the trial version of Director.

2.   Locate and download the trial version of Director from Macromedia's Web site. Macromedia's Web site changes frequently, so the location of the trial version of Director moves from time to time. If you have difficulty locating the trial version, contact Macromedia and ask for advice.

3.   After you have downloaded the Director installer, launch it to begin the installation process.

4.   Follow the directions presented by the installation software.

If you do not currently have the Quicktime extension installed on your machine, it can be installed using this software. Follow the options offered by the software. Quicktime is software that allows you to view digital video on your computer. You will need Quicktime to view some of the files in the lessons, so it must be installed before you can proceed properly.

Now that we have installed Director, let's view the completed version of The Billionaire's Shop. After that, we can look at the files used to plan The Billionaire's Shop.

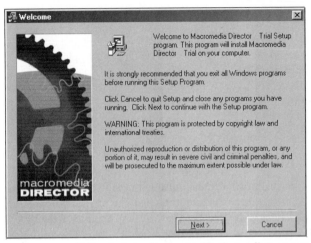

**FIGURE 1.01** *Follow the instruction presented by the installation program for the trial version of Director.*

## VIEWING THE COMPLETED VERSION OF THE BILLIONAIRE'S SHOP

The CD-ROM that accompanies this book contains all of the lesson files that we will be using to develop The Billionaire's Shop. The lesson files are organized in folders named for each chapter number and contain the incomplete lesson files, as well as the completed version of the lesson. The files for chapter 1 are intended to serve as a reference to the project development process for The Billionaire's Shop. The completed project is in a folder named TheShop. We will play this file to see the project that we will build together in the upcoming chapters.

The completed version of The Billionaire's Shop will download files from the Internet that must be saved to a hard drive to be used in the project. As a result, we must copy the completed project to the hard drive, because files cannot be saved to a CD-ROM. To do this we will drag the folder named Billshop from the Billshop CD to the hard drive.

1.  **Open the Billshop CD on your computer.**

2.  **Locate and copy the folder named Billshop from the CD-ROM to your hard drive. The Billshop folder is located along the following directory path on the CD-ROM: ...lessons/chaptr1/**

**FIGURE 1.02** *Copy the directory named Billshop from the chapter 1 folder on the Billshop CD to your hard drive.*

3. **Log onto the Internet. Use any Internet dial-up service to log onto the Internet. You must be connected to the Internet to view the full capability of The Billionaire's Shop.**

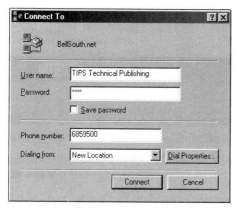

**FIGURE 1.03** *Log onto the Internet using the software that you would ordinarily use, such as America Online or a local access Internet service provider.*

4. **Launch Director. When Director opens you will see several windows from the interface. We will work with each of these windows in detail in upcoming lessons. For now, we will only open The Billionaire's Shop project and preview what we will be building.**

**FIGURE 1.04** *Locate and launch Director to view the sample files.*

5. **Choose File>Open... This will present you with the Open dialog box which we can use to open Director Movie and Cast files. We will use it to locate and open the project.**

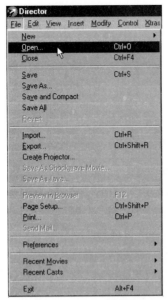

**FIGURE 1.05** *Choose File>Open... to access the Open dialog box, which we can use to locate and open the Director files that we will be working with.*

6. In the Open dialog box, navigate to the Billshop directory, which you dragged to your hard drive earlier. This directory contains the files that we will want to play back.

7. Locate and select the file named Billshop.dir in the Billshop directory on your hard drive. When the file is selected, the Open button should become available.

8. Click the button labeled Open in the Open dialog box. The Billshop movie will load into Director. You will see the windows in Director's interface fill up with the content of The Billionaire's Shop project. Because we only want to view the project and not edit it, we can close most of the windows. A quick way to do this is to choose Stage from the Window menu.

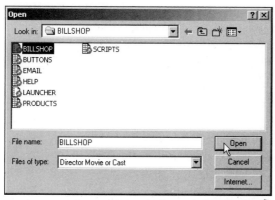

**FIGURE 1.06** *Locate and open the file named Billshop.dir, which is located in the Billshop directory that we dragged to the hard drive earlier.*

9. **Choose Window>Stage. Selecting Stage will cause the Stage window to move in front of any other windows that are open. Selecting this menu item when the Stage is already in front of the other windows will cause the Stage to close. Next we will open the window that is used to play Director movies, which is called the control panel. This time we will use a keyboard shortcut.**

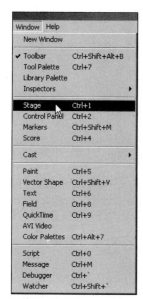

**FIGURE 1.07** *Choose Window>Stage to place the Stage window in front of any other open windows.*

10. Open the control panel by clicking Command+2 (Macintosh)/
Control+2 (Windows).This will open the control panel. This window is designed with many of the same symbols that appear on a
VCR. You can play the movie by clicking the button that is
labeled with a single arrow pointing to the right.

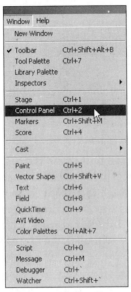

**FIGURE 1.08** *Open the control panel by pressing Command (Macintosh) / Control
(Windows) + 2 on the keyboard. You can also open the control panel by selecting
Window>Control Panel. The control panel will give us access to buttons that will allow us
to control the playback of the Director presentation in this file.*

11. Click the Rewind button on the control panel. This is the button
labeled with a double arrow pointing to the left. The movie is
probably already at the very beginning, but this will make sure of
it in case you accidentally advanced the movie by clicking a button or clicking in one of the other windows.

12. Click the Play button. This is the button labeled with a single
arrow pointing to the right. When this button is clicked the
movie will begin playing, showing you a screen that asks if you
are currently connected to the Internet.

**FIGURE 1.09** *Use the buttons on the control panel to control the playback of a Director
movie.*

13. Click the button labeled No on the screen. If we had clicked Yes, then The Billionaire's Shop would automatically update itself. We want to see what the shop is like before being updated. The movie will play through an opening animation and eventually will stop at a screen that contains several buttons and a display window for the products in the shop. Let's browse through the products.

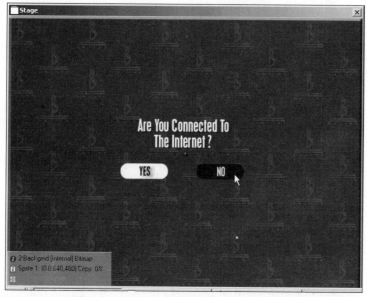

**FIGURE 1.10** *When the movie begins playing you will be presented with a screen that asks if you are connected to the Internet. Click No even though you are connected to the Internet. This will allow us to use other features of The Billionaire's Shop later in this chapter.*

14. Click the right-arrow button on the screen. This will advance you through the products in the shop. The window on the left displays a graphic, and the window on the right displays the product description and price. Now we will update the inventory of the shop.

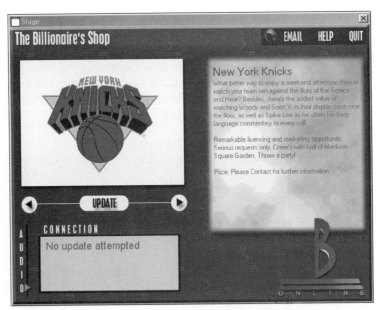

**FIGURE 1.11** *Use the arrow buttons beneath the Product Display area to channel through the products on the Interactive Product Browsing screen of the shop.*

15.  **Click the button labeled Update on the screen. You should be connected to the Internet at this point. If you aren't, clicking Update will produce errors in the movie. Although you can certainly view this project offline by clicking the No button at the very beginning, it is advisable to view it online so that you can see everything that the movie is capable of doing.**

   After you have clicked the Update button, the shop will begin checking the Internet for an update to the inventory. There is an update available, so after a short time you will see information in the Status window that indicates the status of the inventory update. Temporary graphics appear in the product display and description areas of the screen as place holders until the download is complete. When the download is finished, you can click through the products to see if there is anything new. There will be three new products that were downloaded from the Internet! All of this was automatically accomplished by the scripts in this movie, which are the same scripts that we will be learning to write in the upcoming lessons. When you are finished previewing The Billionaire's Shop, you can stop the movie.

   The Interactive Product Browsing area of the shop with the temporary graphics signals an update in progress. An arrow identifies the Update button.

> **If you attempt to update The Billionaire's Shop without a live connection to the Internet, you might receive error messages, and the shop will not update. You must first be connected to the Internet to view the full capability of this project. If you have difficulty playing back this project, visit www.motionovertime.com and send us an email with a description of the difficulty you are having.** **WARNING**

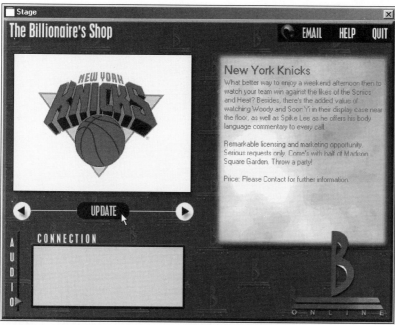

**FIGURE 1.12** *Click the Update button to update the products in the inventory of The Billionaire's Shop.*

16. **Click the Stop button on the control panel. This will stop the presentation. Now we will look at how this movie was planned. We will no longer need to be connected to the Internet in this chapter, so you can log off the Internet until later if you choose.**

## ABOUT THE HELP WINDOW

Like most applications, Director comes with a help window that contains a great deal of useful information about subjects such as interface elements and the Lingo scripting language. The help window is actually an application that runs separately from Director and can remain open even if Director is not running. You can open the help window by selecting

Help>Director Help. You can also open an interactive reference for the Lingo scripting language by selecting Help>Lingo Dictionary.

**FIGURE 1.13** *Director comes with an interactive help reference that you can access by selecting Help>Director Help.*

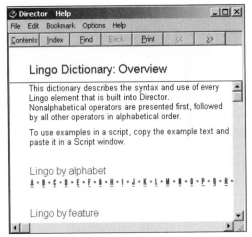

**FIGURE 1.14** *Another useful resource is the interactive Lingo dictionary, which you can access by selecting Help>Lingo Dictionary.*

## VIEWING THE PLANNING FILES FOR THE BILLIONAIRE'S SHOP

In this session we will play a movie that simply serves as a slide show for the files that were used in the planning of The Billionaire's Shop. You can use these as a reference to the description of the planning process in the following pages.

1.  **Choose File>Open... This will present the Open dialog box again.**

2.  **Locate and select the Director movie named Planning.dir on the CD-ROM in the following directory: ...lessons/chaptr1/. This is the movie that we will use to view the files used to plan The Billionaire's Shop.**

3.   Click the button labeled Open in the Open dialog box. This will
     load the Planning.dir movie.

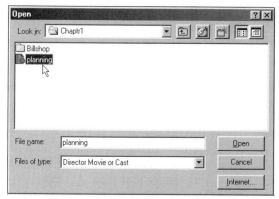

**FIGURE 1.15** *Locate and open the movie named Planning.dir, which is located in the
following directory on the Billshop CD: ...lessons/chaptr1/*

4.   Click the Rewind button on the control panel. This is to make
     certain that the movie begins from the first frame.

5.   Click the Play button on the control panel. This will start the
     movie that will allow you to view the files used to plan The Bil-
     lionaire's Shop. As you read the text in the rest of this chapter
     you will be given instructions to visit different parts of this
     movie to view the corresponding files.

## CONCEPT DEVELOPMENT AND SCRIPTING THE PROJECT

A well written description can help define a smooth-running project. It can
also help identify and avoid any obstacles to completion. One common
example is developing a project without considering the computers that
the project must be able to run on. This is particularly true for projects
that are to be developed for general distribution, such as games, and
projects developed for large corporations, which might have a wide variety
of machines that were purchased at different points of computer development. Defining the least capable computer for your project's playback is
called identifying the *lowest common denominator platform*.

Defining the lowest common denominator for playback is important
for any project. It will help define what can be included in the project, such
as whether or not the machines are capable of running presentations that
contain video. How large can the video files be? Do the computers contain
sound cards? These and other computer playback capabilities can force a
project into serious reworkings if they are not clearly defined up front.

The next important step is identifying the *target audience*, the demographic analysis of the type of computer user the project is designed for. Among the information that should be identified are age, computer experience, education, and existing knowledge of subject in presentation. This will help define the design of the interface—how in depth any Help features should be. It will even help to define the type of music and graphics that should be used. Clearly a project designed for first graders will have a different look, sound, and feel than a project designed for engineers at General Motors. Keep in mind, however, that at this point we are only looking for basic concept development and a written description. Actually designing the look, sound, and feel of the project comes at a later step in a project's development.

Once you have defined the basic design and technology for the project, you can develop a more in-depth description of the project, which includes a description of what the user's experience will be. An important part of beginning the description process is keeping it very basic—as clearly understandable as possible to someone who has no experience with multimedia. Keeping the description simple will help you evolve your idea without getting distracted by the details of how the project will be put together. When the written description is complete, you can compare what is written with what the technology and the delivery platform will permit (making adjustments in later drafts).

Here is the script for The Billionaire's Shop project that we will be building in the upcoming lessons:

1.  **Click the right-arrow button. This is the basic description for The Billionaire's Shop project.**

    **Project:** The Billionaire's Shop online hybrid project for the book on the subject of Macromedia Director for hybrid Internet applications. Nilson Neuschotz, Author. Prentice-Hall, Publisher. Motion Over Time, Developer.

    **Synopsis:** A multimedia store that allows the user to browse through expensive and mythological items such as Aladdin's Lamp. Each product is presented with an image and a description. The store is linked to the Internet and automatically updates the products available in the shop using the Lingo scripting language in Director.

    **Target Audience:** Students using the book on the subject of Macromedia Director for hybrid Internet applications. This group includes new users to Director who have basic experience with computer operating systems (Macintosh or Windows). Some experience with other graphic or multimedia software is helpful, but not necessary. Target audience also includes users of previous versions of Director who are interested in updating to the most recent version of Director and users interested in Hybrid Internet applications for Director.

2.  **Click the right-arrow button. The scrolling text field on this screen contains the detailed script for The Billionaire's Shop.**

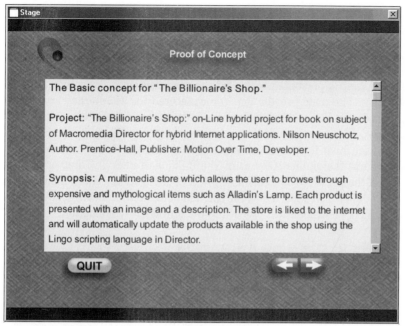

**FIGURE 1.16** *The basic concept for The Billionaire's Shop.*

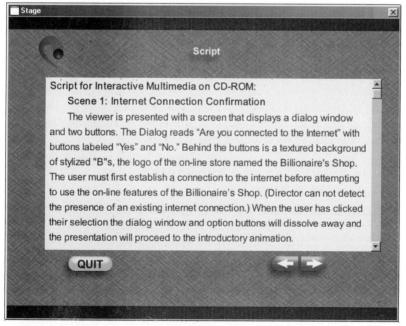

**FIGURE 1.17** *The detailed script for The Billionaire's Shop project. Use the scrolling arrows for the text field to see the rest of the script.*

## SCRIPT FOR INTERACTIVE MULTIMEDIA ON CD-ROM:

### SCENE 1: INTERNET CONNECTION CONFIRMATION

The viewer is presented with a screen that displays a dialog box and two buttons. The dialog reads "Are you connected to the Internet?" with buttons labeled Yes and No. Behind the buttons is a textured background of stylized "B"s, the logo of the on-line store named The Billionaire's Shop. The user must first establish a connection to the internet before attempting to use the on-line features of The Billionaire's Shop. (Director can not detect the presence of an existing internet connection.) When the user has clicked their selection the dialog box and option buttons will dissolve away and the presentation will proceed to the introductory animation.

### SCENE 2: OPENING ANIMATION

Five Icons of Wealth animate around on the screen: a dollar sign, yacht, sports car, mansion, and airplane. The background is the same textured logo background that was the backdrop of scene 1. In the background is music with a game-show feel.

　　At a moment of change in the music the Icons of Wealth dissolve from their current positions and reappear at positions along the right edge of the screen. A caricature of a billionaire animates from the distance in the lower left corner and grows to full size to fill the left lower quarter of the screen. The billionaire animation is synchronized to a rapid chord played on a xylophone or piano.

　　When the billionaire graphic has reached its final position a title that reads "The Billionaire's Shop" appears above it. The title's appearance is presented with a sound effect that will be appropriate for the animation. Almost immediately following the appearance of the title, the billionaire graphic winks at the viewer and, after a brief pause, the presentation proceeds to the interactive browsing area of the shop.

### SCENE 3: INTERACTIVE BROWSING AREA OF THE BILLIONAIRE'S SHOP

Embedded in the textured logo background is a display window for the products in the upper left corner of the screen. A similar, but narrower and taller window, displays the product descriptions on the right side of the screen. The products include expensive items, such as the Empire State Building and a bottle of water from the Fountain of Youth. A connection to the internet will automatically update the inventory of The Billionaire's Shop if new products are available. If the viewer clicked the No button in scene 1 (indicating that they are not connected to the internet), then no update will be attempted and the shop will use a set of default products that are already part of the built in inventory.

Viewers can browse through available products by clicking left and right pointing arrow buttons. With each click the product changes along with the description on the right side of the screen. The arrow buttons will only page to the first and last available products. If the user reaches the end, they must page back in the opposite direction to see the other products.

A text display window in the lower left area of the screen is labeled Connection and reports the current status of the shop's connection to the internet. If The Billionaire's Shop detects that there is an available update then the product and descriptions change to Stand-by graphics which serve as place holders until the new inventory is downloaded. The Connection display field will report each stage of the download with statements such as "A new inventory is available!" or "Downloading new inventory."

To the left of the Connection field is a vertical volume slider which controls the volume of the background music. Dragging the slider's knob toward the top increases volume, while dragging it down decreases volume. The background music consists of a simple music loop with a more relaxed, but similar style to the music that played behind the introductory animation. The loop duration is approximately 15 seconds.

Elsewhere on the screens are four buttons labeled Update, Help, Email, and Quit. Clicking the update button is a alternative way to cause The Billionaire's Shop to check the internet for an update to the inventory. Clicking the Help button will activate a Help feature which will produce information balloons to appear over various features of the interface when they are rolled over with the mouse. Clicking the Help button a second time will deactivate the feature. Clicking the Email button will cause the shop to present the viewer with an Email screen that is described in scene 4 below. Clicking the Quit button will cause the shop to present the Quit screen which is described in scene 5 below.

Also on the screen is the stylized logo for The Billionaire's Shop. All buttons will present a change in appearance when they are rolled over with the mouse or clicked. This graphic change is intended to signal that the button is active.

## SCENE 4: E-MAIL SCREEN

Again using the stylized "B" logo background, this screen presents the user with four text entry windows where they can enter information about themselves and comments that they would like to send to Motion Over Time. The text entry windows are labeled Name, Address, email address, and Comments from top to bottom. Below the text entry windows is a display window labeled Connection which will present the current state of any email that has been sent with messages such as "Sending email to Motion Over Time" and "Your email has been successfully sent."

Elsewhere on the screen are two arrow buttons, one pointing left, the other right. The right pointing arrow is labeled Send and will send the entered email information to Motion Over Time. The left pointing arrow is labeled "Return" and will bring the viewer back to the Interactive Browsing area of The Billionaire's Shop. (Scene 3). The Motion Over Time logo is in the upper right corner of the screen. The background music is the sound loop of scene 3.

## SCENE 5: QUIT SCREEN

A dialog box superimposed over the dollar sign texture background presents the message "Are you sure you want to quit?" Below the dialog are two buttons: Yes and No. The No button will return the viewer to the Interactive Browsing area of The Billionaire's Shop (Scene 3). The Yes button will exit The Billionaire's Shop and cause the project to close on the computer. The background music is the sound loop of scene 3.

## STORYBOARDING

The storyboard is the first visual representation of the project. It translates the images described in the script into a form that all team members can see and is used as a blueprint for the development of the graphics and other visual elements of the project. Besides serving as a guide, the storyboard can also serve in determining the effectiveness of the graphic design described in the script.

The storyboard consists of a series of images that show moments of change in the project. It describes the action in the scene, such as the path of animations in the presentation, and where a scene changes. It also contains information about when sound is present and what the sound is, such as music or voiceover. The key to taking full advantage of a storyboard is to develop the project's graphic description as completely as possible before beginning to work with the software that will be used to create the actual images. Remember that the storyboard is intended to be used as a map, so you will want it to be as detailed as necessary to work for everyone who will be using it.

As an example, here is the storyboard for The Billionaire's Shop:

1.  **Click the right-arrow button. This is the storyboard sketch for Scene 1, the "Internet Connection Confirmation" of The Billionaire's Shop.**

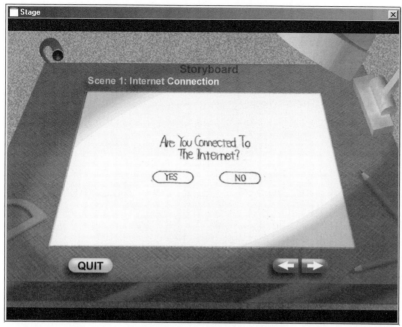

**FIGURE 1.18** *Scene 1: Internet Connection Confirmation.*

## DESCRIPTION:

Screen that allows the user to determine if they are connected to the Internet. Project programming will cause different features to activate based upon the button that is selected.

## ANIMATION:

None.

## TRANSITION:

Center-out wipe.

## INTERACTIVITY:

Yes button: Permits user to determine that they are connected to the Internet.

No button: Permits user to determine that they are not connected to the Internet.

## AUDIO:

None.

2.    **Click the right-arrow button. This is the storyboard sketch for scene 2, part 1, the Opening Animation, Icons of Wealth animation of The Billionaire's Shop.**

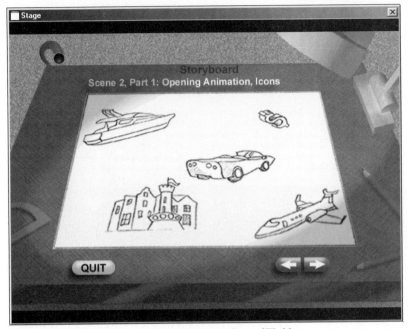

**FIGURE 1.19** *Scene 2, Part 1: Opening Animation, Icons of Wealth.*

**DESCRIPTION:**

Five Icons of Wealth animate around. In the background is game-show style music.

**ANIMATION:**

Five Icons of Wealth animate in a repeating pattern. The icons are: a sailboat, a sports car, a mansion, a rotating dollar sign, and a jet.

**TRANSITION:**

Center-out wipe.

**INTERACTIVITY:**

None.

**AUDIO:**

Game-show tune.

3. **Click the right-arrow button. This is the storyboard sketch for scene 2, part 2, the Opening Animation, Billionaire Animation of The Billionaire's Shop.**

**FIGURE 1.20** *Scene 2, Part 2: Opening Animation, Billionaire Animation.*

**DESCRIPTION:**

A dissolve positions the five Icons of Wealth on the right side of the screen. Then a caricature of a billionaire animates from the lower left corner of the screen to full size. The full-size graphic is flush with the left and lower edges of the screen.

**ANIMATION:**

The Billionaire graphic animates from small to large from the lower left corner of the Stage.

**TRANSITION:**

Dissolve bits.

**INTERACTIVITY:**

None.

**AUDIO:**

A rapid piano or xylophone chord.

4.    **Click the right-arrow button. This is the storyboard sketch for scene 2, part 3, the Opening Animation, Title Animation of The Billionaire's Shop.**

**FIGURE 1.21** *Scene 2, Part 3: Opening Animation, Title Animation.*

**DESCRIPTION:**

The words The Billionaire's Shop appear as a stylized graphic over the head of the Billionaire. The Title animation is accompanied by a sizzle sound.

**ANIMATION:**

A digital video animation appears superimposed over the background of the intro animation. All audio and transition effects are contained within the digital video animation file.

**TRANSITION:**

Contained within the digital video file.

**INTERACTIVITY:**

None.

**AUDIO:**

A sizzle sound effect embedded within the digital video file.

5. **Click the right arrow button. This is the storyboard sketch for scene 2, part 4, the Opening Animation, Billionaire Wink of The Billionaire's Shop.**

**FIGURE 1.22** *Scene 2, Part 4: Opening Animation, Billionaire Wink.*

**DESCRIPTION:**

The Billionaire's eye winks at the viewer. The graphic effect is accompanied by a chime.

**ANIMATION:**

The Billionaire graphic on the screen transforms to wink one of the Billionaire's eyes.

**TRANSITION:**

None.

**INTERACTIVITY:**

None.

**AUDIO:**

A chime accompanies the wink animation.

6.   **Click the right-arrow button. This is the storyboard sketch for Scene 3, the Interactive Product Browsing area of The Billionaire's Shop.**

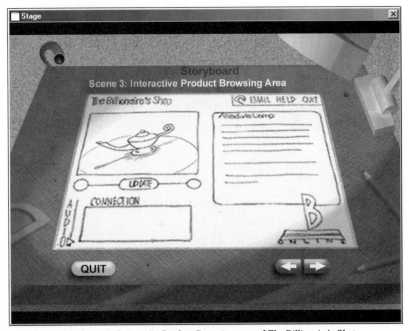

**FIGURE 1.23** *Scene 3: Interactive Product Browsing area of The Billionaire's Shop.*

**DESCRIPTION:**

A static interactive screen with buttons that allow the viewer to browse through the features of The Billionaire's Shop. The upper left corner contains the product display area. Beneath this display area are two arrow-shaped buttons, one pointing right, the other left. These buttons will channel through the available products in The Billionaire's Shop. The upper right corner contains the product description area. Both areas are framed with a gold-colored border with a black background. The lower left corner of the screen contains an Internet connection status display area. The lower right contains three buttons: Update checks for available updates to the inventory and will download any new inventory items, Help activates a Help Balloon feature, which presents a graphic balloon describing the interactive features on the screen. The balloons appear when the Help Balloon feature is active and the pointer is rolled over the button or other interactive feature. The third button is Quit, which will exit The Billionaire's Shop.

Beneath the three buttons is the stylized title: The Billionaire's Shop. This is positioned over a button labeled with the Motion Over Time logo and the words Contact Motion Over Time. This button will activate an email feature that will allow the viewer to send a message to Motion Over Time. At the center toward the bottom of the screen is a volume control slider that can be clicked and dragged to modify volume settings for the background music.

### ANIMATION:

Button rollover and pressed states.

Volume slider click/drag action.

Help Balloon switch for rollover states of interactive screen elements and other specific non-interactive elements, such as the Product display area. Help Balloons are only active when the Help button is clicked.

Products switch in the Product Display and Product Description areas on the screen. The product switch animation is active when the viewer clicks the left- and right-pointing arrow buttons beneath the Product Display area.

### TRANSITION:

Dissolve Bits on initial entry.

### INTERACTIVITY:

Left-arrow button: Channels backward through available products. Channel action ceases when the last product is reached.

Right-arrow button: Channels forward through available products. Channel action ceases when the first product is reached.

Volume slider: Can be clicked and dragged along a vertical track, increasing volume toward the top and decreasing it toward the bottom.

Update button: Checks for new products in The Billionaire's Shop. Automatically triggers download of new products.

Help button: Activates Help Balloon feature. Clicking the button a second time deactivates the Help Balloon feature. Items that produce a help balloon when the feature is active: Product Display area, Product Description area, Internet Connection Status area, Volume slider, and Update, Help, Quit, and Logo email buttons. Note all buttons produce a rollover and down state. Non-button features, such as the Product Display area, only produce a rollover graphic when the Help feature is active.

Quit button: Exits The Billionaire's Shop.

### AUDIO:

Background looping music that is similar in style to the Game Show opening theme of the intro animation.

7.    **Click the right-arrow button. This is the storyboard sketch for scene 4, The Email screen of The Billionaire's Shop.**

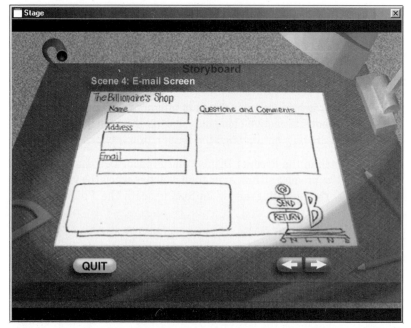

**FIGURE 1.24** *Scene 4: Email screen.*

### DESCRIPTION:

Four text-entry areas allow viewers to enter their name, address, email address, and comments for an email that is sent to Motion Over Time. A fifth text area displays the status of the email in the sending process. Two buttons allow the viewer to send an email, or return to the interactive product-browsing screen.

### ANIMATION:

Button rollover and pressed states for the Send and Return buttons. Help Balloon switch for button rollover states. (Only active if Help button is clicked on the interactive product-browsing screen.)

### TRANSITION:

Dissolve Bits.

### INTERACTIVITY:

Send button: Triggers an email script that sends data entered in text fields to Motion Over Time.

Return button: Returns the viewer to the interactive product-browsing screen.

**AUDIO:**

Background looping music used in the interactive product-browsing screen.

8. **Click the right-arrow button. This is the storyboard sketch for scene 5, the Quit screen of The Billionaire's Shop.**

**FIGURE 1.25** *Scene 5: Quit screen.*

**DESCRIPTION:**

A graphic dialog box presents the question "Are you sure you want to quit?" Below the dialog box are two buttons labeled Yes and No.

**ANIMATION:**

Button rollover and pressed states for the Yes and No buttons.

Help Balloon switch for button rollover states. (Only active if Help button is clicked on the interactive product-browsing screen.)

**TRANSITION:**

Dissolve Bits.

**INTERACTIVITY:**

Yes button: Confirms decision to quit and exits The Billionaire's Shop.

No button: Returns the viewer to the interactive product-browsing screen.

**AUDIO:**

Background-looping music used in the interactive product-browsing screen.

## LOGIC FLOWCHART

The object of a logic flowchart is to graph the interactive elements of a project. Through this map we can identify which parts of a project are interactive, which parts are animations, and where interactive elements lead. Just as the storyboard helps to present the graphic vision of the project, the logic flowchart helps to present the technical side.

The primary use of the logic flowchart is to serve as a guide for project programmers. It also facilitates having multiple programmers work on the same project because the flowchart identifies how different parts of a project interconnect and therefore permits programmers to work separately as long as the interconnecting elements are common. Because programming is usually the most highly technical and complex part of a project, it is very important for a good plan to be in place for all involved.

Another excellent use for the logic flowchart is to identify patterns in the project's design. This can serve to allow programmers to write scripts that can be reused in different parts of a project by creating a Shell, a programmed template that can be reused by minor scripting modifications or changing the media used in the structure. For example, a project might contain ten separate screens that are composed of a paragraph of text and three buttons. Such a basic design could easily be replicated without requiring the reprogramming of each screen. The programming could be redesigned to change to a new screen simply by changing the graphics on the screen.

Using a logic flowchart to identify and program for patterns in a project design frequently calls for some cooperation in how the project is graphically designed. For example, the graphics needed for the 10 screens mentioned earlier might need to comply with certain graphic sizes and placements to truly support a common programming template. The buttons might need to be the same size, and/or the area covered by the text might need to be in a specific area of the screen and use a certain font type and size with a word-count maximum. As you can see, no one part of the project planning process needs to stand alone. By combining the different stages of development, a developer can help to economize time and effort. This will become even clearer when we reach the steps that cover the programming of a project along with the design and incorporation of media.

In The Billionaire's Shop we use some recycled scripts, particularly on all of the buttons. Each button exhibits common behaviors: they each have an up or inactive state, they each highlight when the pointer is rolled over them, and they each appear depressed when the mouse pointer is clicked over them. The differences in their appearance at each of these states is caused by switching out the graphic used to display the button at the appropriate time. Each button needs to be programmed to detect the presence of the mouse pointer and then to switch the graphic onscreen to the highlighted version of the same graphic. Instead of programming each button individually, we wrote a single script that will work for all of them. This script appears in chapter 6 and is described in greater detail there.

Here is the logic flowchart for The Billionaire's Shop:

9. **Click the right-arrow button. This is the logic flowchart that describes the programming plan for The Billionaire's Shop.**

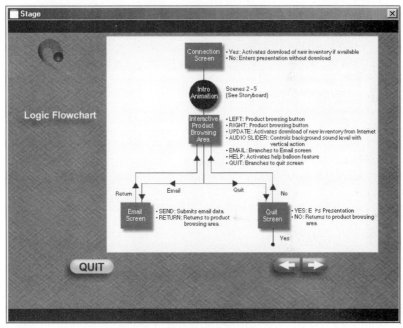

**FIGURE 1.26** *The Logic Flowchart for The Billionaire's Shop.*

## INVENTORY

A project's inventory is a listing of all the media elements that will be used in the project. In addition to the type of media element, each item in the inventory should also list a file name for the element and the use and location in the project where it will be used. Some inventories also contain detailed information such as file size, the dimensions of graphics, or the sample rate of a sound file.

In addition to keeping a project organized and allowing the artist to keep track of what has been completed, the inventory is extremely helpful in connecting the program and design end of a project. Programmers frequently begin development of a project using Dummy media, which are temporary graphics used for placement that will only later be replaced with the final media. This allows the programmer to begin the job while allowing the designers to remain on their own schedule. By having a concise inventory, the programmers and graphic artists know what to name different media elements so that temporary media can easily be replaced with the final media.

10. **Click the right-arrow button. This is the inventory of media for The Billionaire's Shop.**

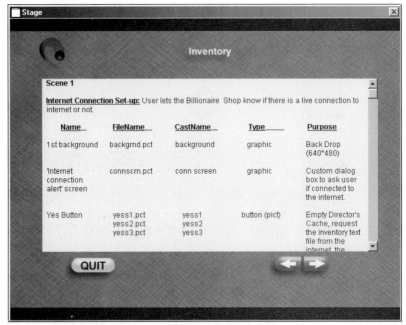

**FIGURE 1.27** *The Inventory of media for The Billionaire's Shop.*

## PROGRAMMING

After you complete the process of developing a project's plans on paper, the computer work can begin. Using the inventory, logic flowchart, and storyboards, the programmers should be able to build the interactive parts of the project using temporary media that will later be replaced with final media from the art developers. The overall objective is to have the technical and artistic aspects of the projects developed concurrently.

We usually have programmers develop their part of the project using graphics and other media that are maintained externally. This means that the media are not embedded within the Director file, but are maintained in external directories that are linked to the Director file. This allows the temporary media to be replaced with the final media simply by replacing the external files. The only important element in making this media swap simple is that the final media have the same file names and are located in the same directories as the temporary media that they replace. This is the support that the inventory gives because it lists file names that can be referenced and used by both the artists and the programmers.

The final step in the media swap is to embed the files into the Director project. This is necessary because Director files are more efficient with media handling and memory when the files are all internal. It is also helpful to maintain media internally because it results in fewer files to maintain on a hard drive or CD-ROM. The only exception to internalizing media is digital video, which cannot be embedded into a Director file.

11.  **Click the right-arrow button. This is a scene from The Billionaire's Shop that uses temporary media, which allows the programmers and the artists to develop their parts of the project separately. Later, the temporary media will be replaced with the final media.**

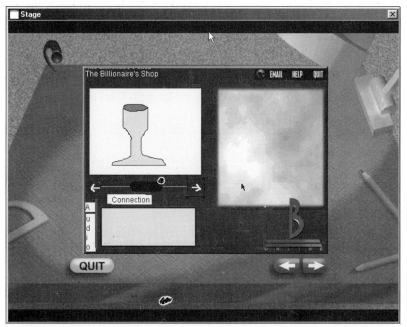

**FIGURE 1.28** *Using the storyboard and inventory, the programmer can begin developing the technical end of a Director project using temporary media. The temporary media will later be replaced by final media provided by the artists on a separate, but concurrent, development schedule.*

## DEVELOPMENT OF GRAPHICS AND OTHER MEDIA

While the programmers are developing the technical format for the project, the artists can develop the visuals using tools such as Adobe Photoshop and Strata StudioPro. The programmers are not dependent upon the artists' completion of artwork to develop their end of the project; therefore, the artists have independence in experimenting with different approaches to layout. The only information that needs to be identified are the basic screen elements, such as the number of interactive elements, number of text objects, and the presence of a digital video file on the screen. The programmers can tell by the storyboards if something the artists are developing will affect the programming; this allows changes to be made early in the project when the elements are the most flexible. The artists can change screen elements as frequently as they need to while they are looking for the right combination of color and placement on the screen.

This method of flow of media from the artist to the programmer also allows the artist to produce media in any order and still allow the media to be incorporated into the project smoothly. For example, the artist can produce all of the backgrounds at once and the buttons later, or any combination that helps them work quickly and efficiently. It's akin to filming a movie in the order of what is most efficient: if the same sets are used in scene 1 as in the last scene of a movie, then it makes sense to shoot the first and last scenes together.

12. **Click the right-arrow button. Final media is gradually introduced to The Billionaire's Shop as the artists develop it. The programmers simply replace temporary media with final media.**

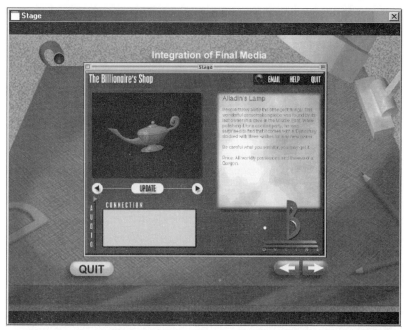

**FIGURE 1.29** *As the artists develop final media, they can deliver it to the programmer in pieces as they are completed. The programmer can incorporate the final media by replacing the temporary media. This allows the programmer and artist to see and alter parts of the project as it is developed.*

## TESTING AND DELIVERY

It is absolutely critical to test the project at all stages of development, especially if there is a special technical requirement for the presentation. For example, The Billionaire's Shop connects to media on the Internet. It was important for us to address the development issues around this part of the project as early as possible because it involved various types of technology: networks, the Internet, Macintosh, and Windows. In that case testing helped determine if any of the technology for the project needed to be changed. It also helped make certain that playback was consistent and the graphics appeared the same on all machines.

The main method of testing a project is to play it on the delivery platform that is the least capable machine the project is designed for. This machine is called the *lowest common denominator*. This is where you establish requirements such as minimum RAM requirements and processor speed for your project. Naturally, you want your machine to play on all available machines, but that might simply be impossible for older computers.

If your project is intended for playback using a method other than a computer's hard drive, then it is also important to test the project using the intended delivery medium. For example, if your project is intended for use on the Internet as a Shockwave movie, then it is important to convert your movie into a Shockwave movie, place it on a server, and view it through a browser over the Internet. This will let you know what the project's performance is like on the Internet, or over an intranet. If your project is intended for playback from a CD-ROM, then it is helpful to have a CD-ROM burner to create a disc for testing. You can then try the project on different computers using different CD-ROM drives and speeds. There is also CD-ROM emulation software that will allow you to test the playback of a project at different settings without the requirement of actually creating a disc. This isn't as reliable as actually creating your own CD-ROM, but it is a big saver of time and money. Whatever the technical requirement, incorporate it into your testing process to ensure the smooth and timely scheduling of your project.

Now that many projects are delivered over the Web, it is important to incorporate the Web into testing environments as well. The Web is a very complex environment with many variables that could affect your project's playback. There are plug-ins for browsers that are required, some multimedia features will not play back on older browsers, and clients might have protective firewalls on their networks, which could inhibit access to certain files. All of these questions must be answered and tested for because the issues will only arise when it's time for delivery. The project will probably work well as long as it is running through the software on your desktop computer. The delivery machine and environment, however, are what matter for playback.

After all development and testing are completed, it is time to prepare the project for delivery. The important part of this process is to determine that all necessary files and the arrangement of files are present in the packaged project. Remember that much of the project's development will have occurred on machines that contain all of the source files and will also have their own directory structure. Make sure that every file and organizational structure for the project is present in whatever shape the project takes in delivery to the end user.

In the case of The Billionaire's Shop there were files that needed to be organized into directories for each chapter in this book on a CD-ROM. The CD-ROM also needed to run on both Macintosh and Windows computers with files that were specialized for either platform. We needed to be certain that files for Windows were only visible when the CD-ROM was running on a Windows machine and that the same was true for Macintosh computers. In all, making sure that the delivery structure of your project is easy to understand and navigate will ease the use of your project.

13.    **Click the right-arrow button. This is the directory structure for the files on the Billshop CD that accompanies this book and contains the progressive lessons for creating The Billionaire's Shop.**

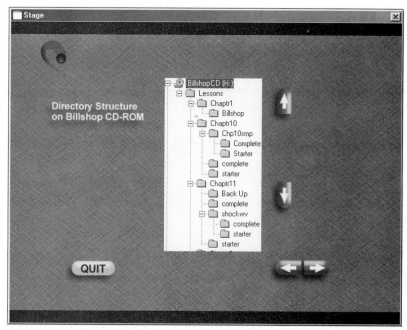

**FIGURE 1.30** *The directory structure for the lessons in this book as delivered on the Billshop CD.*

14. Click the right-arrow button again. This is the directory structure for the files that are located on the Internet. These files are used as part of the Hybrid Internet scripting lesson in this book. They are the files that contain the new inventory to update The Billionaire's Shop.

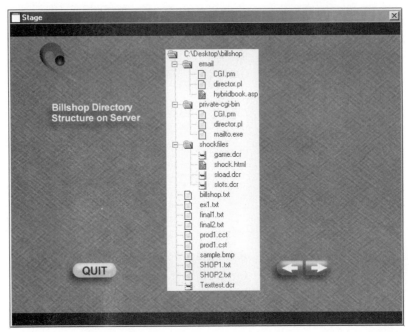

**FIGURE 1.31** *The directory structure for the files on the Internet that complement the Hybrid scripting lessons in this book.*

## TECHNICAL DOCUMENTATION

As discussed earlier, the documents that are delivered with a project vary in complexity depending upon the needs of a project. Usually all that is required is a simple manual for your project that outlines the content of your project, computer system requirements for playback, and how to install and use your project.

15.  Click the right-arrow button again. This is technical documentation that outlines the contents of The Billionaire's Shop CD-ROM project and how to use it.

16.  Click the Exit button. This will exit the project development demonstration file for chapter 1. Now we are ready to begin building The Billionaire's Shop.

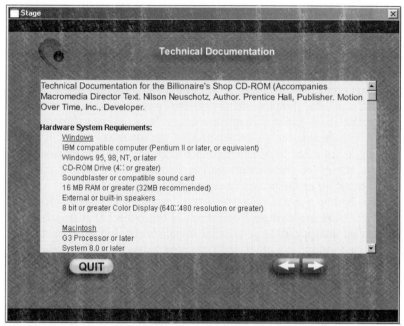

**FIGURE 1.32** *The technical documentation for The Billionaire Shop CD-ROM.*

## SUMMARY

Macromedia Director is a tool originally designed by artists for artists that later had programming elements incorporated into the interface. Director has never lost its design as an artist's tool and is therefore an excellent option for anyone interested in developing interactive presentations. Over the years the scripting language that is part of Director, named Lingo, has become extremely sophisticated and is now very attractive to programmers as well as artists. This detail in Director has made it a very popular application that is continually modified with current industry demands. Two prime examples of Director's evolutionary nature are Shockwave and the Hybrid scripting technology that is covered in this book, both of which take advantage of the Internet as a delivery method for multimedia. Director's visual interface makes it an excellent tool to learn with, as well as to demonstrate concepts such as the multimedia development process covered in this chapter.

The multimedia development process is very methodical and can be taken from project to project, regardless of the software used or the intended end result for the project. Through meticulous planning and documentation, we can plan the project's schedule and anticipate any special needs the project might have. Following careful planning, we can follow a systematic process of implementing programmed and designed elements to progressively develop and test the project while it is being worked on.

The overall intention is to coordinate the project in a way that allows many people to work together simultaneously, cooperatively, and synchronously. The development process can also help small teams, even one-person teams, develop projects quickly and efficiently.

The planning methodology in project development is designed to support team project development, as well as to anticipate any special considerations for the project. Most of the project-planning process is accomplished on paper through the use of a script, storyboards, flowcharts, and an inventory. Although most of the paper-based part of project planning is intended to be accomplished prior to actual development, the process should be considered ongoing because many project considerations can arise as the project is executed.

The first step in planning a project is developing a project concept and a script. These are written descriptions of the project that go into detail about what images will be seen, what sounds heard, where interactive elements are located, and other description considerations. This description is helpful in determining that all team members have the same concept in mind and have the same foundation to work from.

The next step in project planning is the development of a storyboard. This is a series of sketches that show the visual concepts for the project. This step is helpful in determining if scenes that are described in the script are also effective as images. The storyboard also serves as a guideline for the project designer's developers.

The third step is the development of a logic flowchart. This is a diagram that maps out the interactive elements of a presentation. The logic flowchart is particularly useful in serving as a guide for all involved programmers, as well as indicating areas of a project that are similar and could possibly share the same programming.

The fourth step is the development of a project media inventory. The inventory is a documentation of all of the media used in a project. It includes the names of source files and their use and location within the project. The inventory allows the programmers to begin their work using temporary files that use the actual names that the final media will use. This allows the designers to work on a separate, but synchronous, schedule with the programmers helping to encourage overall efficiency. Although the inventory is listed as the last step in the project-planning process, it is actually intended to be started during the earlier stages and developed as new information comes to light during the rest of the planning process.

Following project planning, the development of the project can begin. This is where the programmers begin the development of interactive parts using temporary media, and the designers begin development of the final media. As final media is completed, it can be passed on to the programmers who can use it to replace the temporary media. When all development concerns are completed, the project can go into final testing and preparation for delivery. The testing process should be a part of the entire process, including identifying and testing the project at various stages of development on the least capable computer intended for the project. The process for identifying the least capable machine is known as determining the lowest common denominator for playback.

When the project is ready for delivery, it is usually a good idea to provide technical documentation outlining the use and computer-system requirements of your project. This documentation serves as a reference manual just like the manuals that accompany any software that you might buy. The complexity of the documentation you provide will vary depending upon the needs of the client and the type of project you are documenting, but it should contain a brief description of the project, computer system requirements, installation instructions, and contact information in the event that any questions arise.

## QUESTIONS

1. What are the four stages of the project-development process? What are the purposes for each step?

2. Why is it useful and efficient to have an artist deliver final media as it is completed to the programmer, as opposed to waiting for all media to be completed, then delivering it to the programmer?

3. How does the media inventory serve as a guide for both the artist and programmer?

4. Why is Hybrid scripting a powerful tool for multimedia development?

5. What is the lowest common denominator, as it is referred to in the multimedia development process?

**EXERCISES**

1.  Write a script that describes a project that includes three animations. One animation will play immediately. At the end of this animation there will be two buttons, each of which will lead to another animation. At the end of each of the new animations, there should be a return button that will jump back to the first animation. As we work through the lessons in this book, you will learn all of the skills required to create this animation.

2.  Using the examples in this chapter, draw a storyboard of an animation that you can later use to create the animation in Director. By chapter 4 you will know how to create this animation.

3.  Add two buttons to the last screen of the animation in exercise 1. Then create two new storyboards of the animations that these buttons will jump to when clicked. At the end of the two new animations, add a button that will jump back to the first animation. By chapter 6 you will know how to add these buttons.

4.  Using the examples in this chapter, create a logic flowchart that diagrams the programming of the project you have planned so far in exercises 1 and 2.

# Chapter 2

# Overview of Director's Interface

# 2 Overview of Director's Interface

**In this chapter, you will learn to:**

- Control settings for the Stage and general movie properties
- Use Cast files
- Import graphics, sounds, and other media elements into a Director movie
- Create a sprite
- Modify the duration of a sprite
- Use the Library palette
- Create a basic animation
- Use the sprite overlay and change sprite preferences

Director's interface is based upon three central windows: the Stage, the Cast window, and the Score. Understanding the uses of these features and their relationship with each other is critical to working in Director. In this chapter, we will tour Director's interface as we examine a completed copy of the project we build in this book: The Billionaire's Shop.

There is an obvious theatrical theme in the naming of these windows that aids in the understanding of their purposes. The first of the three central features, the *Stage*, is the display area on which the presentation plays. The second, the *Cast* window, is where all of the media elements of the presentation are stored, much like a library or database. The final feature, the *Score*, is Director's construction window, where the scenes and animations in the presentation are assembled. The fact that a file created with Director is also called a movie supports the analogy.

This chapter is the most elementary and most important step in your work with authoring using Director. Director is based upon your understanding the relationships among the features in the program. This begins with Director's windows themselves and evolves to the Lingo scripts that you will eventually work with in later chapters. Pay careful attention here, because these basic concepts are the foundation that you will repeatedly return to, even in the most complex Director projects.

NOTE    There are several terms that can be used to refer to work created with
         Director. Although these terms can be used interchangeably in many
         cases, they also have specific definitions: *Movie*—a file created with
         Director; *Presentation*—one or many Director files and Casts that together
         compose a complete work; and *Project*—the process of developing a
         Director presentation, including the planning process and the development
         of media in other applications, such as images and audio.

Let's open a completed version of The Billionaire's Shop and tour the interface.

## VIEWING THE BILLIONAIRE'S SHOP

In chapter 1 we previewed The Billionaire's Shop to see the end result of the work we will do with this book. We can use this completed project to examine Director's interface. Later, we will create a new file in which we will build our own version of The Billionaire's Shop.

If you previewed the project in chapter 1, you might have already copied The Billionaire's Shop to your hard drive. This will allow you to experiment with various features and save versions of The Billionaire's Shop. You can also choose to run the project directly from the CD-ROM. In either case, you will need to create a directory on your hard drive in which to place any work that you do with this book.

## CREATING A DIRECTORY FOR YOUR WORK

This will be the location for all of the work that you do for The Billionaire's Shop.

1.  **Choose and open the hard drive where you will place the directory for your project work. Choose a hard drive with about 20MB of hard-disk space; this will be more than enough for the complete version of The Billionaire's Shop as well as for the version that you will build in upcoming lessons.**

2.  **Create a new directory at the root level of the hard drive.**

    Root level means that the directory is one of the folders that are seen as soon as you open the hard drive. No other folders or directories should need to be opened to access this new directory. This is for simplicity purposes, because you will be frequently returning to this directory to access parts of your work. The easier these files are to reach, the more efficient your work with this book will be.

3.  **Name the new directory Billshop.**

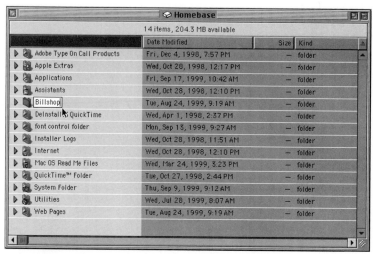

FIGURE 2.01 *This is an example of a Directory created at the root level on a Macintosh.*

Billshop

FIGURE 2.02 *This is an example of a directory created at the root level on a computer running Windows 98.*

## COPYING THE COMPLETED VERSION OF THE BILLIONAIRE'S SHOP TO THE NEW DIRECTORY

If you copied The Billionaire's Shop to your hard drive in chapter 1, then you do not need to follow these steps.

1.   **Place the CD-ROM that accompanied this book in your CD-ROM drive. The CD-ROM is located in a sleeve in the back cover of this book.**

2.   **Locate and open the CD-ROM drive in your computer.**

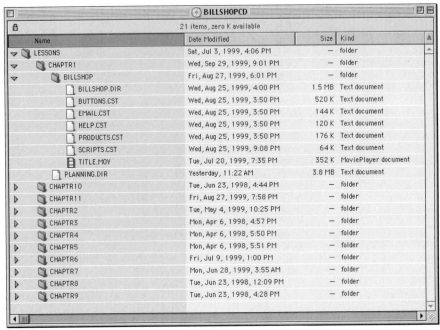

**FIGURE 2.03** *This is what the open CD-ROM directory looks like on the Macintosh.*

3. **Open the directory named Lessons.**

4. **Locate and open the directory named Chaptr1. This is the same directory that we used for chapter 1. We will use the same file because it contains everything that we need for this lesson as well. In all future lessons, we will work with files that are located in the directory named for that chapter.**

5. **Copy the files in the directory named Billshop to the Billshop directory that you created earlier.**

Now, we will open the presentation and tour the interface.

**NOTE** If you copied a Billshop directory to your hard drive in chapter 1, you might want to consider moving it to the Billshop directory that you created in this lesson. This will consolidate your files, and your directory will match the images of the directories that you will see in this lesson.

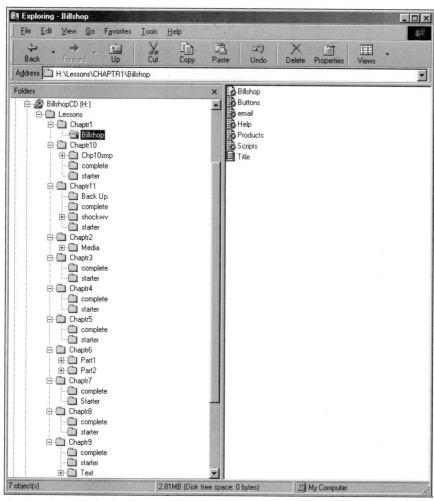

**FIGURE 2.04** *This is what the open CD-ROM directory looks like on a computer running Windows 98.*

## REVIEW OF THE BILLIONAIRE'S SHOP PROJECT

The Billionaire's Shop is designed to provide clear examples of each step in the development of a project in Director. The first part of this project contains animation, synchronized audio, and digital video, subjects of a lesson in this book. The later chapters introduce Lingo scripting and Hybrid Internet capabilities. In this session we will see how all of these features come together into a completed project.

1.   **Establish a connection to the Internet. The Billionaire's Shop automatically searches for update information from the Internet. The first screen of the project presents the end user with the**

option of viewing The Billionaire's Shop without an Internet connection, but you will be missing some of the new and powerful capabilities of Director and its Internet capabilities.

Your Internet connection is established by using the software that you usually use to log onto and browse the Internet. It is not necessary to launch an Internet browser such as Microsoft Internet Explorer or Netscape Navigator; simply use the Dial Up software that you were provided with by your Internet Service Provider. If you are an America Online or CompuServe subscriber, then you can establish a connection to the Internet.

2.  **If it is not already open, launch Director.**

3.  **Choose File>Open... This will present you with the Open... dialog box.**

4.  **Use the Open... dialog box to locate the file named Billshop.DIR on your hard drive. If you copied the file to your hard drive in this lesson, then you will find this file in your Billshop directory.**

5.  **Select the file named Billshop.DIR in the Open... dialog box.**

6.  **Click the button labeled Open. This will load the completed version of The Billionaire's Shop into Director. Now we can preview what we will build together.**

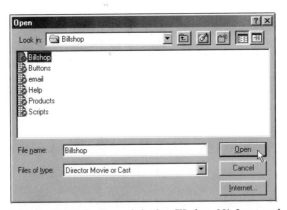

**FIGURE 2.05** *The Open... dialog box (Windows 98). Locate and select the file named Billshop.DIR, then click the button labeled Open.*

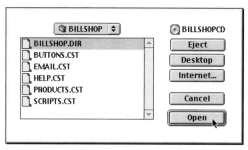

**FIGURE 2.06** *The Open... dialog box (Macintosh). Locate and select the file named Billshop.DIR, then click the button labeled Open.*

## PREVIEWING THE BILLIONAIRE'S SHOP AND INTRODUCING THE STAGE

The *Stage* is the display area of the presentation and will contain any movie activity that should be visible to the end user. By positioning images on the Stage, you create the screen compositions of your movie. Although the Stage is technically classified as a window and can be moved by clicking and dragging the title bar at the top of the Stage window, it contains no buttons or tools. It is essentially a blank projection screen waiting for you, the author, to put something on it.

1.  **Close any windows in Director's interface that are currently open on the screen.**

2.  **If the Toolbar is not currently open, choose Window>Toolbar. The Toolbar is the strip along the top of the screen that contains several buttons. These buttons can be used to perform system functions, such as creating new files or cutting and pasting. Other buttons on the Toolbar are used to play presentations and open or close other windows in Director's interface.**

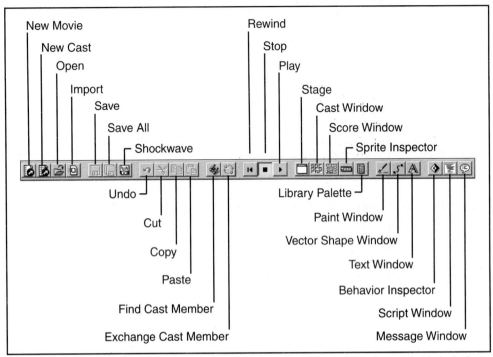

**FIGURE 2.07** *The Toolbar provides buttons that control different parts of Director's interface and the playback of presentations.*

3.  Click the Play button on the Toolbar. The presentation will begin playing. You will immediately be presented with a screen that asks if you are currently connected to the Internet.

4.  Click the Yes button if you are currently connected to the Internet; click the No button if you are not. After you click your choice, the presentation will play. First, there are several animations with background music. Then you enter The Billionaire's Shop, where you can toggle through a variety of products. A Status area displays information about any activity that The Billionaire's Shop is engaged in on the Internet. Experiment with the buttons in the shop to see what they are programmed to do.

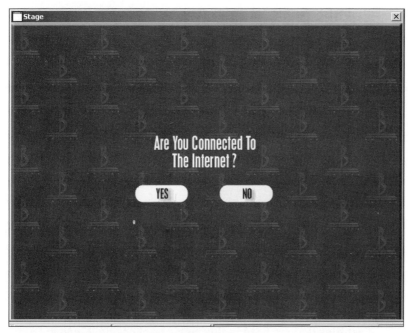

**FIGURE 2.08** *The first screen of The Billionaire's Shop allows you to confirm that you are currently connected to the Internet.*

5.    **Click the Stop button on the Toolbar.**

Now we will examine how other parts of Director's interface were used to develop The Billionaire's Shop, a Director presentation.

You can temporarily make all of the windows in Director's interface, except the Stage, invisible by selecting View>Full Screen. This will maximize the playback area so that nothing obscures your view of the movie while it is playing. The menus will also become invisible, but if you move the mouse to the top of the screen and click, the menu that would normally be in that area will appear. You can also press Control+Alt+1 (Windows)/ Command+Option+1 (Macintosh). Choosing this key combination will toggle the full-screen feature on and off.    **NOTE**

## THE CAST

The *Cast* is the storage location for all of the media in this Director movie. When images and other media, such as text, are created or imported into Director, they become *Cast members*. Cast members can then be integrated into the movie as frequently as necessary simply by clicking and dragging them to the desired location.

Each Director movie has an internal Cast window by default. You can also create other Cast windows that you can use to categorize different types of media. For example, you might want to keep all of your images in one Cast window and all of your sounds in another. This is for convenience purposes and is not a necessary step because each Cast window can contain up to 32,000 Cast members, easily maintaining all of the media for even the largest Director projects. The trial version is limited to 2 casts and 1,000 cast members per cast.

Director also allows you to create external Cast files that can be shared with multiple Director movies. This facilitates keeping project sizes small because you will not need to re-import media into every movie that uses the same files. External Cast files can also be transported separately from Director movies, making it easier for people working together on a project to share media.

1.   **Click the Cast button on the Toolbar. This will open the default Internal Cast file. This Cast file contains the images and sounds that we heard in the opening animation of the presentation. Several other Cast files are used in The Billionaire's Shop. You can view the other Cast windows by selecting from the Choose Cast menu at the upper left of the Cast window. You can also choose Cast files that are used in this movie by choosing Window>Cast> (selected Cast).**

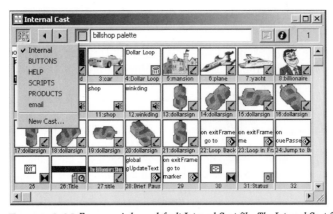

**FIGURE 2.09** *Every movie has a default Internal Cast file. The Internal Cast file in The Billionaire's Shop contains the images and sound files that are used in the opening animation of the presentation. You can create new Cast files by choosing New Cast.... You can also create new Cast files by clicking the New Cast button in the button bar.*

2.   **Choose Buttons from the Choose Cast menu. This Cast file contains the images for the backgrounds and buttons used in the interactive areas of The Billionaire's Shop. When other Cast files are selected from the Choose Cast menu, the new Cast replaces the old Cast in the window on the Stage.**

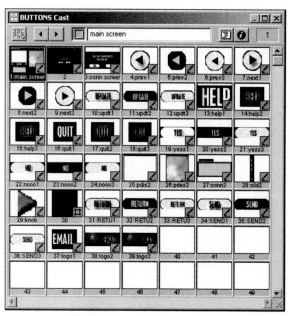

**FIGURE 2.10** *Each Director movie can contain multiple Cast files. This one contains the images for the background and buttons used in the interactive parts of The Billionaire's Shop.*

3.    **Choose Window>Cast>Scripts. If you select a Cast file from the Window menu, the selected Cast file will open in addition to the Cast window that is already on the Stage. This step will open the Cast file that contains many of the scripts used in The Billionaire's Shop.**

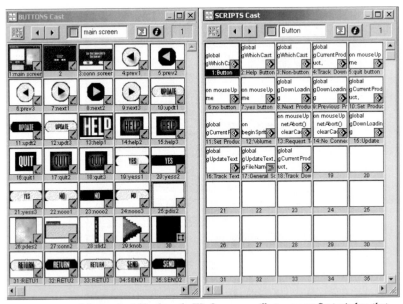

**FIGURE 2.11** *Selecting Cast files from the Window menu will open a new Cast window that displays the selected Cast file.*

4.   Choose File>Preferences>Cast.... This will open the Cast Window Preferences dialog box for the currently selected Cast file. You can use the menus in this dialog box to modify how the Cast members in the Cast window are displayed.

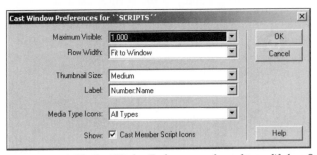

**FIGURE 2.12** *The Cast Window Preferences can be used to modify how Cast members are displayed in the Cast.*

5.   Click the OK button in the Cast Window Preferences dialog box. Each Cast window can be distinguished by its name as well as its content. The Cast Properties dialog box allows you to name each Cast file, including renaming the default internal Cast file.

6.   Choose Modify>Cast Properties.... The Cast Properties dialog box will open. This window allows you to name the Cast file and indicates if it is an internal or external Cast file; it also shows information about the collective size of all of the media contained in that Cast. The menu at the bottom of the dialog box allows you to determine when the Cast members in that Cast file are loaded into memory for the movie. WHEN NEEDED is a progressive loading of the members in that Cast based upon when the members appear in the movie. BEFORE FRAME 1 will load the entire Cast file as soon as the movie is launched. This is a good choice if you know that the Cast members in a Cast file will be needed immediately because it will make the loading of the Cast file be part of the startup of the entire movie. AFTER FRAME 1 is a good choice if you know that the members in that Cast file are used later in the movie and you want the movie to begin as quickly as possible.

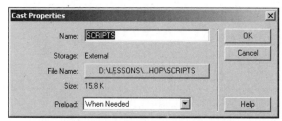

**FIGURE 2.13** *The Cast Properties dialog box can be used to name a Cast file and provides other useful information, such as the size of the media in that Cast file.*

7.   Click the button labeled OK. This closes the Cast Properties dialog box.

8.   Choose Modify>Movie>Casts.... This will open the Movie Casts dialog box. Besides creating new internal and external Cast files in Director, you can add existing Cast files as new internal and external Cast files by linking them to the current movie, using this dialog box. All of the Cast files that are currently used in this movie are listed here.

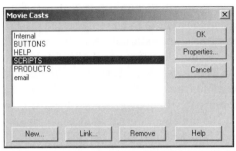

**FIGURE 2.14** *The Movie Casts dialog box lists all of the Cast used in the movie that is currently open. You can also use this window to link your movie to new Cast files.*

9.  **Click the button labeled OK. We will be using these windows to modify the content of Cast files as well as the Cast files used in our version of The Billionaire's Shop Director project throughout the lessons in this book. The next window for us to examine is the Score.**

## ABOUT THE LIBRARY PALETTE

Director comes with a collection of pre-made Cast libraries that contain scripts, graphics, sounds, and other types of media that are ready to be inserted into your movies. You can access these libraries through the Library palette located at Window>Library palette. You can use items from that Library palette by dragging them directly into your movie. You will learn more about using Cast members later in this chapter. Only items that are used from a library become part of your movie, so you don't need to be concerned about deleting the other items.

Any Cast library can be placed into the Library palette, so it is possible to create your own. Later we will learn how to create a Cast library. The libraries can be internal to a movie, or they can be independent external files used by multiple movies. The external files can be added to the Libs folder in the Director directory on your hard drive. All Cast files that are located in this folder are automatically added to the items listed in the Library palette. This provides for an extremely convenient way to share media with different people.

The thumbnail graphics that illustrate each item in the Library palette are customizable. There will be more on how this is accomplished in the section titled "About Customizing The Thumbnail Graphic For A Cast Member," later in this chapter.

**FIGURE 2.15** *The Library palette gives you access to pre-made media libraries that come with Director. You can also create your own customizable palettes.*

## THE SCORE

The *Score* is Director's construction window. This is where you set up different scenes in your presentation, similar to the scenes in a film production.

1.  **Choose Window>Score. This opens the Score. Time passes from left to right in the Score and is measured in *frames*. The numbers on the bar along the top of the Score are frame numbers. The images, sounds, and other features of the scenes in your project are located in *channels*, which are positioned from top to bottom in the Score. The numbers along the left side of the Score represent *sprite channels*. This is where you will place any visible element in your presentation, such as images and text. There can be up to 1,000 sprite channels (the trial version is limited to 24 channels and 500 frames). The number of channels displayed is set in the Movie Properties dialog box, which will be covered later in this chapter.**

    The channels at the top of the Score are the *effects channels* and are where you would locate sounds, transitions, and other settings that enhance the scenes of your presentation. The point where a channel crosses a frame is called a *sprite cell*.

---

The effects channels at the top of the Score might be hidden when you first open the Score by using the Hide/Show Effects Channels button on the right side of the Score. See figure 2.16.    **NOTE**

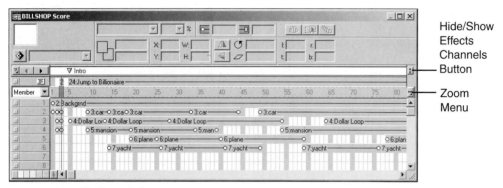

Hide/Show
Effects
Channels
Button

Zoom
Menu

**FIGURE 2.16** *The Score window.*

The horizontal bars in the Score are the different elements of the movie. If you click on something on the Stage while the movie is not playing, you will see the corresponding bar highlight in the Score. These are called *sprite objects*.

When a sprite object is selected, the Score will display information in the windows along the top about that sprite's positioning as well as other settings applied to it.

2.   **Click on any sprite object in the Score. You will see numbers appear in the windows in the upper right area of the Score. You might also notice that a small window, called the *sprite overlay*, that contains information about the selected sprite will appear over the sprite. Later in this and other chapters, we will work with controlling some of these settings.**

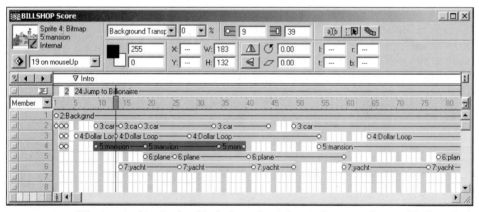

**FIGURE 2.17** *When a sprite object is selected in the Score, the windows in the upper right area of the Score display information about the settings applied to that sprite.*

The items in the Score extend beyond the visible area of the Score because of the length of the animations and other scenes in the presentation. You can zoom in or out in the Score by using the Zoom menu on the right side of the Score. This allows you to see the entire composition of your movie at a glance, or zoom into the objects of the Score so that they can be seen in greater detail.

3. **Choose 200% from the Zoom menu on the right side of the Score. This will double the visible area of the Score composition for The Billionaire's Shop. See figure 2.16 for the location of the Zoom menu in the Score.**

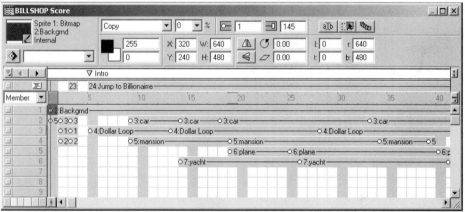

**FIGURE 2.18** *Use the Zoom menu to increase or decrease the visible area of the Score. Zoom set to 200%.*

4. **Choose 100% from the Zoom menu. This will return the view of the Score to its original setting.**

5. **Choose Window>New Window. You can use the Zoom menu at your convenience. Considering that you might frequently change settings, such as the view of the Score, Director has the capability of having more than one view of the Score visible on Stage at once. This step will display another Score window on the screen. You can create as many views as you like and change anything about them. All Score windows on the Stage display information about the same movie, but their views can be changed independently. For example, you can change the zoom setting for each Score displayed, but if you move to another frame, it will move to the same frame in all Score windows.**

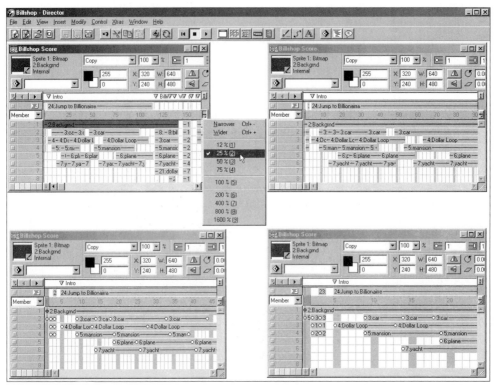

**FIGURE 2.19** *You can add multiple Score windows to the work environment. This will provide you with multiple views of the Score.*

**NOTE**   You can access each new Score window that you add to the movie by choosing Window>Score>(Selected Score window).

6.   Close all new Score windows that you have created. All new Score views are only temporarily maintained, so as you close the new windows they will be removed from the movie. The only Score window setting that will remain will be the original one. Now we will look at the other windows that can be used to change settings for the Score.

7.   Choose File>Preferences>Score.... This will open the Score Window Preferences dialog box. This can be used to make general settings for the Score. If you are a Director 5 user, you can choose the Director 5 Style Score Display option to return to the old-style Score.

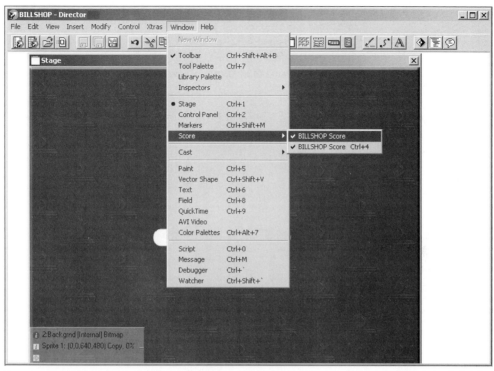

**FIGURE 2.20** *You can bring the different Score windows to front on the Stage by choosing Window>Score>(selected Score window).*

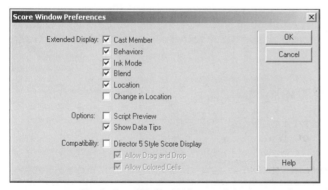

**FIGURE 2.21** *Use the Score Window Preferences dialog box to make general settings for the Score in your movie.*

8.    Click the button labeled OK. This will close the Score Window Preferences dialog box. If you have made changes to the Score Window Preferences dialog box and are not certain what the original settings were, you can click the Cancel button or use the settings that appear in figure 2.21.

**WARNING** **Do not change any of the default settings in the Score Window Preferences dialog box while you are working on the Billionaire's Shop. Any changes could cause significant differences between the images in this book and those on your screen.**

## EXAMINING THE STAGE AND WORKING WITH SPRITE OBJECTS

So far we have examined the Cast and Score in Director's interface by viewing the completed version of The Billionaire's Shop. Now, we will look at the settings for the Stage and learn how to create and manipulate a sprite object. First, however, we will start a new Director file so that we can begin creating our version of The Billionaire's Shop.

## THE STAGE

Earlier in this chapter, we learned that the Stage is the display area of the presentation and contains any movie activity that we want to be visible to the viewer. There are three aspects of the Stage that you can modify: dimensions, color, and location. All three can be changed through Director's Movie Preferences dialog box, which can be reached from the Modify menu.

## CHANGING DIRECTOR'S MOVIE PROPERTIES

1.    Choose File>New>Movie.

**WARNING** **If you inadvertently made changes to The Billionaire's Shop movie, Director will prompt you to save those changes before opening a new file. Do not save the changes.**

This opens a new Director movie with a blank Stage. You can see that the Cast and Score are empty. General settings are carried over to a new movie, so the color, size, and position of the Stage will be precisely what they were for the completed version of The Billion-aire's Shop. Now we can freely alter the Stage, experiment with basic sprite manipulation, and create a simple animation.

2.   **Choose Modify>Movie>Properties. This will open the Movie Properties dialog box. The settings here reflect the current set-ting for the Stage. Its dimensions are 640 pixels wide and 480 pixels high; it is positioned in the center of the screen and is black.**

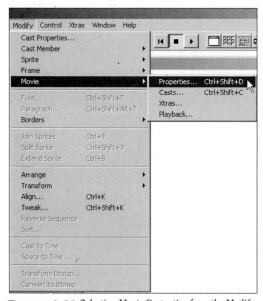

**FIGURE 2.22** *Selecting Movie Properties from the Modify menu.*

The Movie Properties dialog box gives you preset menu options for the size, location, and color of the Stage as well as entry areas for custom settings. It allows you to determine which color palette the presentation will use if no specific palette is entered elsewhere in the presentation. A *color palette* is a selection of 256 colors that the movie will use to display images. Director is programmed with sev-eral palettes already installed; however, you can import palettes that are optimized for the images in your presentation. Using a palette designed specifically for the images in your movie will ensure that your images look their best. If you are familiar with advanced con-trol of color in graphics applications such as Adobe Photoshop, you can use hexadecimal values to determine specific colors.

3.   Type 320 in the box labeled Width and 240 in the box labeled Height. This changes the dimensions of the Stage visible onscreen when the Movie Properties dialog box is closed.

4.   Choose Upper Left from the pop-up menu beside Stage Location. After we enter all of the new settings and click the OK button, this setting will move the Stage to the upper left corner of the screen so that it is flush against the top and left of your monitor's display area. Note that the numbers in the boxes labeled Left and Top both now contain the number 0. This is where the pixel point of the upper left corner of the Stage is located on the Screen. Both numbers will increase if the Stage is moved to the right and down; for example, a setting of 50 in the box labeled Left indicates that the Stage is 50 pixels away from the left edge of the monitor's display area. The same is true for a number typed in the box under the label Top, indicating the number of pixels away from the upper edge of the monitor's display area.

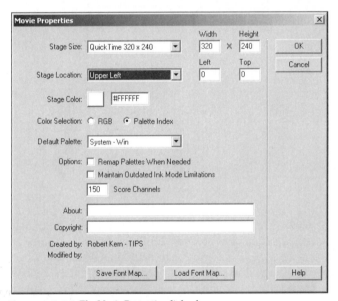

**FIGURE 2.23** *The Movie Properties dialog box.*

NOTE    As mentioned earlier, the Score is capable of displaying up to 1,000 sprite channels. The text entry window in the center of the Movie Properties dialog box is where you can indicate how many channels are visible at once. We will leave The Billionaire Shop at Director's default setting of 120 channels; this will be more than enough for what we will need for The Billionaire's Shop (the trial version only supports 24 channels).

**Do not use a setting for the number of Score channels that is lower than the number of channels that are used in the movie. Lower settings will delete channels that are higher than the setting in your Movie's properties.**   **WARNING**

5.   Click and hold the mouse pointer over the colored square beside the words Stage Color. This will bring up the currently active palette in your Director presentation. Choosing a color from the color palette is similar to selecting an option from a menu. You can click and release on a color for a new selection.

A palette is the selection of colors that are available to be used in your movie to create and display images. Color computers are capable of displaying an unlimited number of colors, but they can only display a small selection of colors at any given time. The number of colors can be limited by the amount of memory installed in the computer and the capability of the computer's display adapter. The True Color setting on a Windows machine will display millions of colors, while the high-color setting will display thousands. You have probably noticed that the larger display resolutions from which you can choose (i.e., 640x480, 800x600, etc.) become limited as you display more colors. This is because it requires more power on the part of the computer to process the higher number of colors.   **NOTE**

On Apple computers the number of colors for display is described as 16, 256, thousands, or millions. These settings will also show up as their bit values. A bit is a measure of computer memory, so the higher the bit value, the more colors are displayed. For example: 4 bits = 1 color, 8 bits = 256 colors, 16 bits = thousands, and 24 bits = millions. Many computers are now capable of displaying 32 bits and will almost certainly be higher than that before very long.

Although many new machines can display a high number of colors, and Director is capable of displaying and animating graphics that use millions of colors, the lowest capability that is still commonly used is 8-bits, or 256 colors. Most computers have difficulty displaying color combinations that use more than 256 colors. The safest way to make certain that your movie will be viewable on the widest selection of machines is to develop it using images and graphics that can be displayed well under 8-bit settings.

Using software such as Macromedia Fireworks and Adobe Photoshop, you can set your images to be displayed under 256 colors. This will remove some of the color information from the images so that they will look as natural as possible under the limited number of colors available for 8-bit color. Director's palettes allow you to have multiple selections of 256 colors, so that you are not limited to the same 256 colors throughout your movie. You can jump around to different palettes as the movie plays. The movie can have a default palette set for it, but this palette can change by using the palette channel, which we will learn about when we work more with the Score.

6.  **Click to select a different color from the palette. Release the mouse button when you have reached the color you want. This new color will be applied to the Stage when you close the Movie Properties dialog box.**

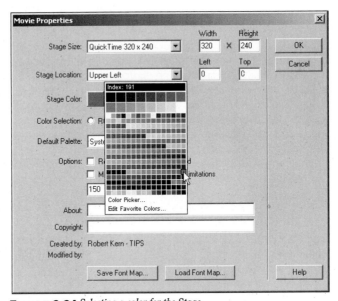

**FIGURE 2.24** *Selecting a color for the Stage.*

A palette is not recognized as an independent file type by Director. However, Director is intelligent enough to know if your images are designed with a custom palette and will give you the opportunity to extract the palette from an image as it is imported. The images we will use for The Billionaire's Shop use a custom palette, so you will have the opportunity to see how Director creates a palette when we import them.

Most image applications, such as Adobe Photoshop, allow you to create a customized palette for your images. The images in The Billionaire's Shop were created in Strata StudioPro, a 3D images application. Because the images created with a 3D application are always rendered using millions of colors, but can later be saved as images that use only 256 colors,

3D applications typically include a customized palette for images created in them.

Once a custom palette has been imported and used in the movie, it will become available in all menus where a palette can be selected, such as the Default Palette option in the Movie Properties dialog box. You can then select from your custom palette the color of the Stage.

7. **Click the button labeled OK in the Movie Properties dialog box. You can now see that the Stage has reduced in size and is snugly positioned at the upper left corner of your monitor screen.**

When you create a *Projector*, a Director movie that has been packaged as **NOTE** an application that no longer requires the Director application to play, you will have the option of having your movie play full screen. This means that the desktop area of your monitor will be blanked out by a solid color while your Director movie is playing. The color that is used for the area behind your movie is determined by the color of the Stage. If you use an image that covers the entire Stage as a background, the Stage color no longer has an effect on the movie's esthetic results. However, it will have an impact when the Projector is made. Keep this in mind when you choose the color for your Stage and before you create a Projector. We will cover how to create a projector in chapter 11.

Using a smaller Stage is an excellent way of reducing the file size of your **NOTE** Director movie. Smaller file sizes help improve movie playback speed as well as reduce download time of Shockwave movies on Web pages. Changing the color of the Stage is also an efficient way of adding color to a Director movie while not increasing overall file size.

## RESETTING THE STAGE FOR THE BILLIONAIRE'S SHOP PROJECT

We can very easily change the size, positioning, and color of the Stage. Color and size can be used for esthetic purposes, but positioning can also serve to design your desktop work environment. You might simply find that having the Stage positioned in the upper left or lower right of your screen gives you more room to position Director's other windows. You can change the positioning of the Stage at any time without affecting the other aspects of the movie. When we later create a Projector, you will have the option to determine if you would like your movie to always play in the center of the viewer's screen; selecting this option will supersede any existing Stage positioning in the Movie Properties dialog box.

1.  Choose Modify>Movie>Properties. This once again opens the Movie Properties dialog box. You can see the settings we made earlier to change the color, position, and size of the Stage.

2.  Type 640 in the box labeled Width and 480 in the box labeled Height. These are the Stage settings for The Billionaire's Shop project.

*Director 8*
*File*
*↳ Preferences*
*↳ General*

3.  Choose Centered from the pop-up menu beside Stage Location. This relocates the Stage to the center of your monitor's display screen. Note that the entry boxes beside the Stage Location pop-up menu now have numbers greater than 0 in them. This will vary depending upon the size of the monitor on which your movie is playing; in fact, the number will remain at a setting of 0 if you happen to be working with a monitor that has a resolution setting of 640x480 pixels. The Centered setting will always position your presentation in the center of the screen, even if the movie is transferred to a computer that has a different sized monitor.

4.  Click and hold the mouse pointer over the colored square beside the words Stage Color. The color of this square is the current color of the Stage. We will change this color to black for The Billionaire's Shop.

5.  While still holding the mouse button down, drag to select the black square at the lower right corner of the color palette. As noted earlier, the Stage color can be used to block out the desktop when your movie is playing as a projector. In the case of The Billionaire's Shop we will use images that cover the entire Stage, but using black will create a dramatic effect around the movie's display area when we have completed authoring the presentation.

*For this area:*
*1. Select Modify..Movies,*
*2. In the Property Inspector*
*   a. you can set the size of the stage.*
*   b. by clicking the down arrow next to the offset*
*      parameters, you can center the stage.*
*   c. you also set the color of the stage.*

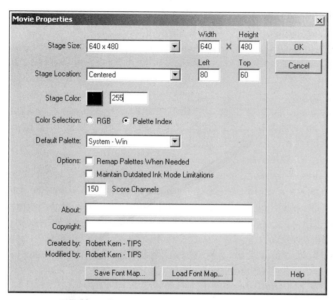

**FIGURE 2.25** *Movie Property settings for The Billionaire's Shop project.*

6.   **Click the button labeled OK in the Movie Properties dialog box. You now see that the Stage has increased in size and is centered on your monitor's screen.**

It is recommended that you save your work frequently. As mentioned in chapter 1, the lessons in this book are designed to progressively build The Billionaire's Shop. At the beginning of each chapter, you will be able to work with the file that you created in the earlier chapters. We have also included partly completed files at the beginning of each lesson so that you can pick up where you left off in the last chapter.

**NOTE**

## MORE ON THE MOVIE PROPERTIES DIALOG BOX

1.   Reopen the Movie Properties dialog box.

### THE FONTMAP BUTTONS

At the bottom of the Movie Properties dialog box are two buttons: Save Font Map and Load Font Map. The *font map* is a text file that Director uses to determine which fonts it should use when a file is *cross-platform* (transferred from a Macintosh to a PC and vice versa). For example, if you use the Helvetica font in a Director movie created on the Macintosh, Director will automatically use the Arial font when the movie is played on a PC.

Director automatically uses the file named Fontmap.txt, which is located in the same folder as the Director program. Viewing and changing this file is accomplished outside Director, using any text-editing application such as Microsoft Word or Claris Works. If you would like to make any modifications to the fonts that Director will substitute for cross-platform files, you can open the file, change the names and other settings for the fonts indicated, then re-save the file with a new name so that you don't overwrite the original file. You can then use the button labeled Load Fontmap... in the Movie Properties dialog box to locate and select the new font map on your hard drive.

The button labeled Save Fontmap... will give you the opportunity to save and name a duplicate of the currently used font map to your hard drive (by default this is the file named Fontmap.txt). This accomplishes the same thing as opening Fontmap.txt in a word processor and saving it with a different name to the hard drive so that you can make changes to the new file without affecting the original. This action is also useful if Fontmap.txt is lost or damaged somehow because it will extract the font map loaded into any Director file to your hard drive.

We will not need to change anything about the font map for The Billionaire's Shop, but there is detailed information in the manuals that come with Director if you are interested in learning more.

### REMAP PALETTES WHEN NEEDED

This checkbox gives Director permission to create a common palette and remap all images on the Stage that have a different palette, without changing the images permanently. Although this is an easy way to solve the problem of images created using different palettes, it is unpredictable and not recommended. You will serve the quality of your presentation best by controlling the palette through an image-editing program such as Macromedia Fireworks or Adobe Photoshop. You can also use an application designed specifically for creating custom palettes, such as Debabelizer. This application allows you to select all of the images that you would like mapped to the same palette before they are imported into Director, and then create a super palette, which creates an average of all of the colors used and remaps all of the images to this palette.

2.    **Close the Movie Properties dialog box.**

NOTE    You can make adjustment to the general settings for Director by using the General Preferences dialog box. You can access the General Preferences dialog box by choosing File>Preferences>General....

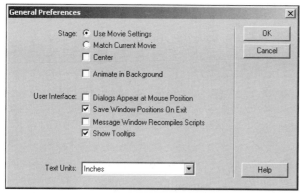

**FIGURE 2.26** *Use the General Preferences dialog box to make general settings for Director, such as activating Tooltips. Tooltips present small windows that identify many of the features in Director's interface when they are rolled over with the mouse pointer.*

## CREATING A NEW CAST MEMBER

Now that we have started a new Director movie, we can experiment with creating Cast members and sprite objects. Director's interface does not provide you with any Cast members to work with immediately, so you must either create them within Director or create them in another application and import them. In most instances, you will use the latter method because there are many tools available, such as Macromedia's Fireworks and Adobe Photoshop, that are designed specifically for the development of images—others, such as SoundEdit 16 (Macintosh) and Sonic Foundry's SoundForge (Windows), are designed for sound. All of the media in The Billionaire's Shop were created outside of Director and imported.

In this session, we will create a simple image using Director's Paint window. The Paint window has many tools that are similar to other digital paint applications, such as Fractal Design Painter. For example, there's a paintbrush, a spray can, and a paint bucket. In addition to creating new images in the Paint window, you can open imported images and modify them. This is particularly helpful if you have an image that you would like to separate into different parts so they can be animated independently. We will not be using the Paint window to create any of the media in The Billionaire's Shop, but it is a useful tool to preview the images that we will import.

## USING THE PAINT WINDOW

1.   **Choose Window>Paint. This will open the Paint window. The Paint tools are along the left side of the Paint window. The buttons toward the top of the Paint window are used to manipulate**

images, such as flipping or rotating. Our next step is to create a simple image.

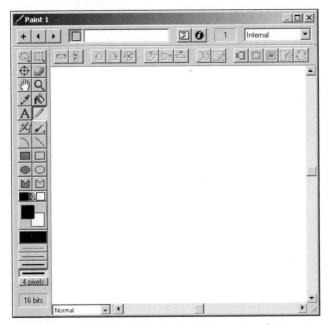

**FIGURE 2.27** *The Paint window. Use this tool to create or edit images.*

2.  Create a small, simple image. You can choose different colors by selecting from the foreground color chip and selecting the tool you want to work with. You select a color from the foreground color chip in the same manner in which you selected a different color for the Stage; click and drag to the color you want. The image in figure 2.28 was created using the Filled Ellipse tool. The Filled Ellipse and other shape tools are used by clicking and dragging in the work area. Make certain that your image is only about 2x2 inches so it will fit on the Stage and can be animated.

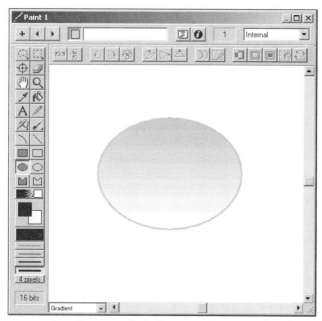

**FIGURE 2.28** *Create a small, simple image in the Paint window. This image was created using the Filled Ellipse tool.*

3. Close the Paint window. After we have created the image, it can be used in the movie.

4. Open the Cast window. Notice that when the Cast window is opened there is a Cast member in Cast position 1. Anything created in Director becomes a Cast member. Any media element that can be used in Director is stored in the Cast: images, sounds, transitions, and so forth.

5. Double-click on Cast member 1 in the Cast window. This automatically opens the Paint window. Any image that is imported into the Cast or created in Director will launch the Paint window when it is double clicked. This is a useful feature for quickly making modifications to images in your presentations.

6. Close the Paint window. Our next step is to add our new Cast member to the presentation.

You can use the Paint Window Preferences dialog box to make settings for the tools in the Paint window. You can access the Paint Window Preferences dialog box by choosing File>Preferences>Paint.    **NOTE**

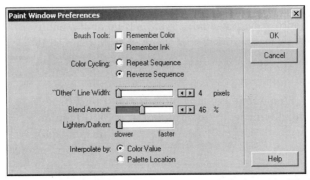

**FIGURE 2.29** *Use the Paint Window Preferences dialog box under File>Preferences to adjust settings for the tools in the Paint window.*

## CREATING A SPRITE OBJECT

After you create a Cast member, you can incorporate it into your presentation by dragging it to the Stage. This will create an instance of the Cast member called a *sprite object*. A sprite object has all of the properties of the original Cast member, but it does not increase the size of the presentation because it is only a projection of the Cast member onto the Stage. This feature allows you to use a Cast member multiple times without affecting the file size of your presentation.

**NOTE**   Controlling the size of the media in your Cast controls the overall file size of your Director presentation. This is especially important in the development of Director movies that you will convert into Shockwave presentations for playback over the Internet.

1.   **Open the Score window.**

2.   **Click the frame bar above the number 1 in the Score. This moves the playback head to frame 1 of the presentation.**

3.   **Click Cast member 1 in the Cast window. This is the simple image that you created earlier in the Paint window.**

4.   **While holding the mouse button down, drag Cast member 1 directly to the Stage. You will see that as you drag the Cast member, your mouse pointer is followed by an empty square. This square indicates where the Cast member will appear when you release the mouse button.**

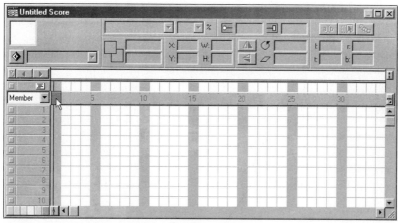

**FIGURE 2.30** *Move the playback head to frame 1 of the Score.*

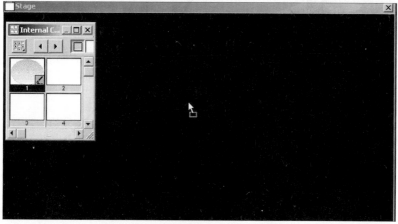

**FIGURE 2.31** *Cast member 1 being dragged to the Stage.*

5.    Release the mouse button while the Cast member is over the
      Stage. The positioning square of the dragged Cast member will
      be replaced by a sprite of the Cast member with a white square
      surrounding the image. This bounding square is called the
      sprite's ink effect. The *sprite overlay* for this sprite should also
      appear at this time. If Director's sprite overlay feature is deacti-
      vated, then it will not be visible. We will learn how to activate
      the sprite overlay in the next few steps. Next we will learn how
      to control the sprite's ink effect.

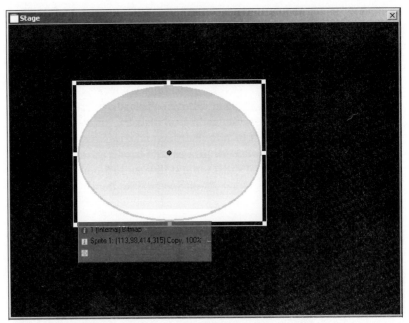

**FIGURE 2.32** *When you release the mouse button, an instance of the Cast member, a sprite object, appears on the Stage.*

## CHANGING THE SPRITE'S INK EFFECT

1.  Return to the Score. There is now a bar in channel 1 that
    extends from frame 1 to frame 28. This is the sprite object that
    was generated when we dragged Cast member 1 to the Stage.
    This image now exists in 28 consecutive frames. Notice that
    there is information about the sprite object displayed in the win-
    dows at the top of the Score. There is also a pop-up menu at the
    top of the Score that can be used to change the sprite's ink
    effect.

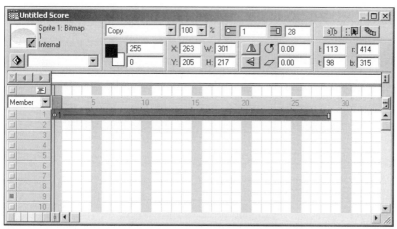

**FIGURE 2.33** *The windows at the top of the Score will display information about any selected sprite.*

2. **Make certain that the sprite in channel 1 is selected. You can select the sprite by clicking directly on the sprite on the Stage, or by clicking anywhere along the center of the sprite object in the Score.**

Sprites can be selected by clicking directly on them or by dragging and selecting them. This is especially useful for selecting multiple sprites on the Stage or in the Score. You can also hold down the Shift key while clicking on sprites in the Stage or the Score to select multiple sprites. If you hold the Option/Alt key down, you can select multiple sprites in the Score that occupy non-contiguous frames.

**NOTE**

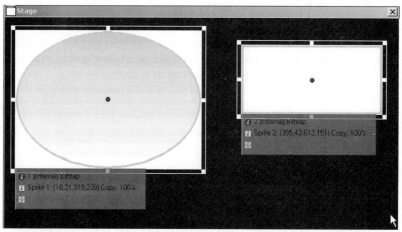

**FIGURE 2.34** *You can quickly select multiple sprites on the Stage by clicking and dragging a selection rectangle around the sprites you want.*

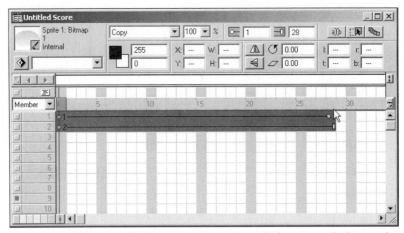

**FIGURE 2.35** *The same method that you can use to select multiple sprites on the Stage can be used in the Score by clicking and dragging a selection rectangle around the desired sprite objects.*

*Director 8*

*1. Right Click on Sprite*
   *↳ properties*

*2. Copy dropdown button from the*
   *Property Inspector.*

*3. Background Transparent.*

3.   Choose Background Transparent from the Ink pop-up menu at the top of the Score. This will cause the sprite's white background to disappear. The original setting was Copy, meaning that the sprite appears on the Stage the way that it appears in the Cast, including the area surrounding the image. Background Transparent causes all parts of the image that are the same color as the background color to disappear. In a later lesson we will work with the Matte ink effect setting, which renders only the background area of the image transparent, but not the areas within the sprite that are the same color as the background. For example, Background Transparent will render the white areas around the edges of a cartoon character transparent and will also make the whites of the character's eyes transparent. Matte will only render the white areas around the character transparent, leaving the whites of the character's eyes opaque. The other ink effects are generally used for special effects because they dramatically modify the appearance of a sprite.

Two other locations in Director's interface to find information and make settings for a sprite, in addition to the windows and menus at the top of the Score, are the sprite inspector and the sprite overlay.

## THE SPRITE INSPECTOR

1.   Choose Window>Inspectors>Sprite. This will open the sprite inspector. This window displays information about any selected sprite in your presentation. You will see that the windows and menus at the top of the Score are also available in the sprite

inspector. The purpose of this window is to adjust settings for a sprite without requiring the presence of the Score, helping to conserve the workspace on your monitor. The dimensions of the sprite inspector can be adjusted in three different ways on the Macintosh by clicking the button in the upper right corner of the sprite inspector's title bar. Changing the dimensions of the sprite inspector could reduce the clutter on your screen.

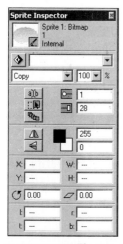

**FIGURE 2.36** *The sprite inspector displays information about a selected sprite.*

2.    Click the button in the upper right corner of the sprite inspector's title bar (Macintosh only). This will change the sprite inspector to a horizontal layout (see figure 2.37).

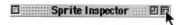

**FIGURE 2.37** *Clicking on the button in the upper right corner of the sprite inspector will cause it to convert to a horizontal layout (Macintosh only).*

3.    Click the button in the upper right corner of the sprite inspector's title bar again (Macintosh only). This will change the sprite inspector to a vertical layout (see figure 2.38).

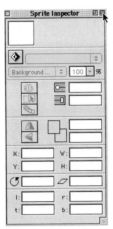

**FIGURE 2.38** *Clicking on the button in the upper right corner of the sprite inspector while it is in a horizontal layout will cause it to convert to a vertical layout (Macintosh only).*

4.   **Click the button in the upper right corner of the sprite inspector's title bar one more time. This will return the sprite inspector to its square layout.**

5.   **Close the sprite inspector. In later chapters, we will use the sprite inspector as a convenient method for adjusting the setting for the sprites in The Billionaire's Shop.**

## THE SPRITE OVERLAY

When a sprite is selected on the Stage, there is a box superimposed over the sprite that displays information about it. This is called the sprite overlay and can be used to access information and dialog boxes that are associated with the selected sprite. If this box does not appear when you select a sprite on your Stage, then the sprite overlay feature is not activated. In this session we will learn how to turn on this feature and examine how this feature impacts the development environment.

1.   **Choose View>Sprite Overlay>Show Info. This option activates the box that displays information about the selected sprite. The Show Info option for the sprite overlay is activated and deactivated by selecting the same option from the View menu. The arrow beside the Show Info menu item indicates that this option is turned on. If the arrow is present and you select the Info menu item, then the arrow will disappear and this option will be turned off.**

2.    **Choose View>Sprite Overlay>Show Paths. This will activate the feature of the sprite overlay that displays the animation path of the sprite. We will use this feature later in this chapter.**

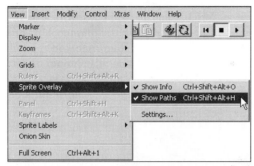

**FIGURE 2.39** *Activate Director's Sprite Overlay feature by choosing Show Info and Show Paths. These features are active when a check mark appears beside them.*

3.    **Select the sprite on the Stage. If the sprite overlay did not appear before, it should appear now. Now we will look at the preference setting for the sprite overlay feature.**

4.    **Choose View>Sprite Overlay>Settings.... The Sprite Overlay Settings dialog box will appear. Use this box to determine when you would like the sprite overlay to appear: when the sprite is rolled over with the mouse pointer, when selected, or to be visible simultaneously for all sprites selected or not. You can also choose the color for the text that is displayed in the sprite inspector.**

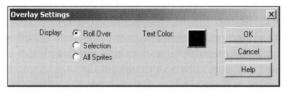

**FIGURE 2.40** *Use the Sprite Overlay Settings dialog box to determine when the Sprite Overlay feature appears over the sprites in your movie.*

5.    **Click the button labeled OK in the Sprite Overlay Settings dialog box.**

6.    **Display the Stage and select the sprite. The sprite overlay will appear. There is a small line on the right edge of the sprite overlay that can be used to change the transparency of the sprite overlay.**

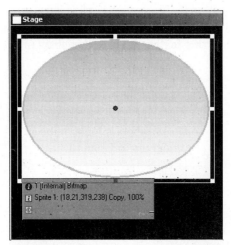

**FIGURE 2.41** *Drag the transparency bar up or down to change the transparency of the sprite overlay.*

7.  Click the line on the right edge of the sprite overlay and drag it toward the top of the window. This will cause the background of the sprite overlay to become transparent, preventing it from obscuring your view of any sprites that appear behind it.

8.  Click the line on the right edge of the sprite overlay and drag it toward the bottom of the window. This will cause the background of the sprite overlay to become opaque, making it appear clearly over anything else on the Stage.

9.  Drag the line on the right edge of the sprite overlay to the middle of the right edge of the window. We will maintain a neutral setting for this feature. The three lines of information on the sprite overlay provide information about different aspects of the sprite. The first line displays information about the Cast member used to create the sprite. The second line displays information about the sprite itself, such as the channel it occupies and the dimensions and location of the sprite on the Stage (see the section titled "The Score" earlier in this chapter, for more information about channels). The last line displays information about any behaviors that are applied to the sprite. *Behaviors* are Lingo scripts that we will work with in upcoming chapters. You can access the dialog box that will allow you to change the settings that appear in the sprite overlay.

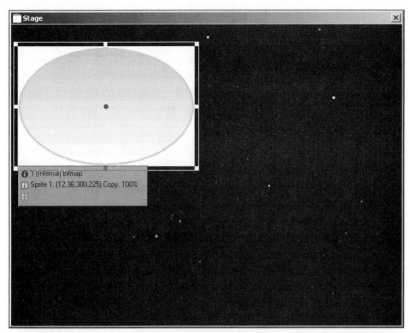

**FIGURE 2.42** *The sprite overlay displays information about the Cast member used to create the sprite, the sprite itself, and any scripts that have been applied to the sprite.*

10.    Click the blue *i* on the left side of the sprite overlay. This will open the Cast Member Properties dialog box for the selected sprite. You can make adjustments, such as naming the Cast member, in this box.

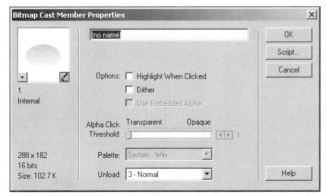

**FIGURE 2.43** *Clicking the blue i button on the sprite overlay will open the Cast Member Properties dialog box for the Cast member that was used to create that sprite.*

11.   **Click the button labeled OK. This will close the Cast Member Properties dialog box.**

12.   **Click the red *i* on the left side of the sprite overlay. This will open the Sprite Properties dialog box for the selected sprite. You can make adjustments to the sprite, such as changing the dimensions and location of the sprite on the Stage in this box.**

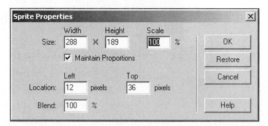

**FIGURE 2.44** *Clicking the red i button on the sprite overlay will open the Sprite Properties dialog box for the selected sprite.*

**NOTE**   The blend feature that appears in the Sprite Properties dialog box, as well as in the sprite inspector and at the top of the Score, is used to change the overall transparency of the sprite. This is not the same as making an adjustment to the ink effect of the sprite. You can use this feature to create effects such as a transparent stained-glass window in a house.

13.   **Click the button labeled OK. This will close the Sprite Properties dialog box.**

14.   **Click the green triangle on the left side of the sprite overlay. This will open the behavior inspector. We will use this window to add interactivity to The Billionaire's Shop.**

15.   **Close the behavior inspector.**

The sprite inspector and the sprite overlay features make it possible to accomplish much of what would otherwise require the Score and Cast windows. This will help to keep your work environment open and clear. Now we will look at one other location for sprite settings.

## ABOUT CUSTOMIZING THE THUMBNAIL GRAPHIC FOR A CAST MEMBER

Earlier in this chapter we discussed the Library Palette and the fact that the thumbnail graphics for each item can be customized. The thumbnail graphic is the image that is used to represent the Cast member in various preview windows, such as the Cast Member Info dialog box and the Cast window. Anywhere the Cast member can be used can have a representation of the Cast member as a thumbnail somewhere. Customizing this graphic is accomplished through the Cast Member Info dialog box, which can be opened by clicking on the *i* button in the upper right corner of the Cast window.

There is a small downward-pointing arrow in the lower left corner of the preview window in the Cast Member Info dialog box. This arrow is a menu that has three selections: Copy Thumbnail, Paste Thumbnail, and Clear Thumbnail. Using this menu you can copy a thumbnail used by one Cast member and paste it into another Cast member, or you can clear the thumbnail altogether, in which case the Cast member will use a miniature of the Cast member itself. In the case of scripts and text, the thumbnail will become the first few words in the script or text. You can also create your own thumbnails by copying a graphic from another program or from Director's Paint window. After selecting Copy Thumbnail, choose a new Cast member; when you choose Paste Thumbnail, the graphic will become the new thumbnail. If the original graphic was larger than the thumbnail window, then the graphic will be resized automatically to fit. All thumbnails require the same amount of memory in the file, so it does not matter what the original size of the graphic was.

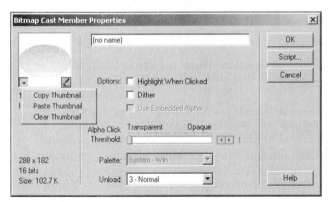

**FIGURE 2.45** *The thumbnail edit window allows us to copy, paste, or clear customized thumbnail graphics for Cast members.*

## SETTING SPRITE PREFERENCES

1.  **Choose File>Preferences>Sprite.... This will open the Sprite Preferences dialog box. You can use this window to make settings such as the number of frames that a sprite occupies when it is created. The default setting for this feature is 28.**

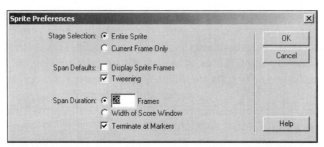

**FIGURE 2.46** *The Sprite Preferences dialog box can be used to adjust sprite settings such as the number of frames a sprite occupies when it is initially added to the Score.*

2.  Click the button labeled OK on the Sprite Preferences dialog box. This will close the Sprite Preferences dialog box. Besides the Span Duration setting in the Sprite Preferences dialog box, there are other ways to modify the duration of a sprite in the Score.

## MODIFYING THE DURATION OF A SPRITE

1.  Open the Score and select the sprite. One method for modifying the duration of a sprite in the Score is to click directly on the endpoints of the sprite and drag them to a new position in the Score. We will use this method first.

2.  Click the endpoint at frame 28 for the sprite in channel 1 and drag the endpoint to frame 35, then release the mouse button. The duration of the sprite is now extended to frame 35 of the Score. Now we will look at another method for modifying the sprite's duration.

3.  Move the playback head to frame 45 of the Score. Move only the playback head. Leave the endpoints for the sprite object at their current positions.

4.  Choose Modify>Extend Sprite. The endpoint for the sprite will jump over to frame 45. We have just extended the duration of the sprite 10 frames. If there were multiple selected sprites in this movie, they would all be simultaneously affected by selecting Modify>Extend Sprite. This menu option can also be used to reduce the duration of the sprite object.

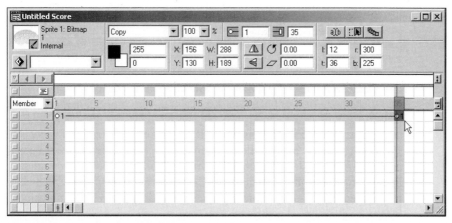

**FIGURE 2.47** *You can change the duration of a sprite in the Score by dragging its endpoint to a new location.*

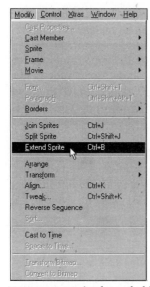

**FIGURE 2.48** *Another method for changing the duration of a sprite in the Score is selecting Modify>Extend Sprite.*

5. **Move the playback head to frame 40 in the Score. Leave the endpoints for the sprite object at their current positions.**

6. **Choose Modify>Extend Sprite. The endpoint for the selected sprite will move to frame 40.**

Now we will look at how to animate a sprite using the sprite's path.

## INTRODUCTION TO A SPRITE'S PATH AND ANIMATING A SPRITE OBJECT

When we activated the sprite overlay, we used two separate settings: Show Info and Show Paths. Show Info is the setting that activates the box that displays information about the sprite. Show Paths activates a feature that allows you to see the animation path of a sprite on the Stage. The red and green dots at the center of a selected sprite are the endpoints of the animation path. If the endpoints of the path are not dragged away from the sprite, then the sprite will not animate. In this session we will extend the sprite path of the sprite on the Stage.

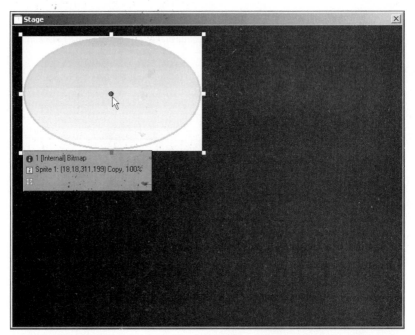

**FIGURE 2.49** *The dots at the center of a selected sprite are the endpoints of that sprite's path.*

1.  Move the playback head to frame 1. We will animate the sprite from frame 1.

2.  Select the sprite on the Stage. The sprite overlay will appear. Notice that there is also a dot at the center of the image. This is the endpoint of the sprite.

3.  Click on the dot at the center of the selected sprite on the Stage and drag it away from the sprite. You will see that a red dot follows the mouse pointer as you drag it. Along with the red dot,

the sprite's path extends away from the sprite. When we play this move, the sprite will animate along this path.

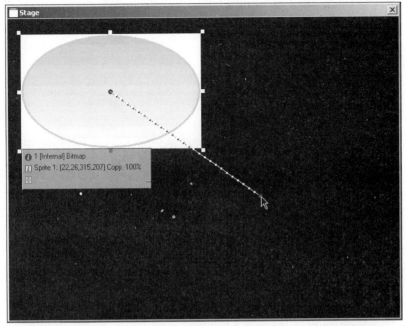

**FIGURE 2.50** *Clicking and dragging the path of a sprite will extend and define that sprite's animation path.*

4. Click the Play button on the toolbar. The sprite will animate continuously along the path that you defined on the Stage.

5. Click the Stop button.

This is the simplest and most immediate method for animating a sprite. We will work further with this and other animation methods in chapter 3. Now we will look at alternative methods for playing a Director presentation.

## ALTERNATIVE METHODS FOR PLAYING A DIRECTOR PRESENTATION

The toolbar has Play, Stop, and Rewind buttons that can be used to play a Director presentation. These are convenient, but other methods for playing a presentation will allow you to customize your working environment and temporarily close all windows in Director's interface from the Screen while a movie is playing. The first method we will look at is the control panel.

1.  Choose Window>Control Panel. The control panel is a movable palette that has movie playback tools. It is useful for its mobility and compact design. It also contains more detailed information about location and tempo settings in the movie.

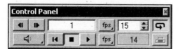

**FIGURE 2.51** *The control panel is a movable palette that provides movie control features such as Play and Rewind buttons.*

2.  Click the Play button on the control panel. These tools function just as the tools on the toolbar did. Notice that the Play button on the toolbar will appear depressed along with the Play button on the control panel.

    Click the Stop button on the control panel.

Another alternative for playing a Director presentation is a keyboard combination.

1.  Press Command+Option+P (Macintosh)/ Control+Alt+P (Windows) on the keyboard. This will cause the movie to play while keeping all of Director's windows open on the screen. Notice that the Play buttons on the Control Panel and the toolbar appear depressed. Make certain that you press all of the keys indicated simultaneously, otherwise this keyboard shortcut will not work.

2.  Press Command+Period (.) (Macintosh) / Control+Period(.) (Windows). This will stop the movie. Now we will look at a method for playing a Director presentation while temporarily eliminating all open windows on the Stage.

3.  Press Command+Option+Shift+P (Macintosh)/ Control+Alt+ Shift+P (Windows) on the keyboard. Adding the Shift key to the combination will cause the movie to play, closing all open windows in Director's interface. This way you can have an unobstructed view of the Stage and your presentation.

4.  Press Command+Period (.) (Macintosh) / Control+Period(.) (Windows). This will stop the movie.

Using these keyboard methods will help you be more efficient in your work with Director.

Now we will begin developing The Billionaire's Shop. Our first step is to create a new file and import the images that we will need for the next few chapters.

## CREATING A NEW FILE AND IMPORTING MEDIA FOR THE BILLIONAIRE'S SHOP

1.   **Choose File>New>Movie. This will close the movie that we have been working with and open a new one. You will be presented with a dialog box that asks if you would like to save changes to the movie. We will not be returning to this movie, so there is no need to save it.**

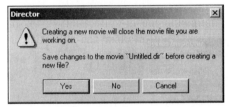

**FIGURE 2.52** *Director will present the Save Movie... dialog box when you attempt to create a new movie.*

2.   **Click the button labeled No.**

3.   **Choose File>Import.... If the Cast window is not currently open, then it will open automatically when you select Import.... The Import Files Into... dialog box will appear. The name that follows Import Files Into... is the name of the Cast file that the media is being imported into; in this case, the Cast file is named Internal.**

    This Import Files Into... dialog box allows you to browse the directories in your hard drive and locate all of the media that you would like to import into your Director file. As you select the files you want in the upper window, they will be added to a list of files in the lower window. Then you can use the button labeled Import to bring all of the media into Director simultaneously.

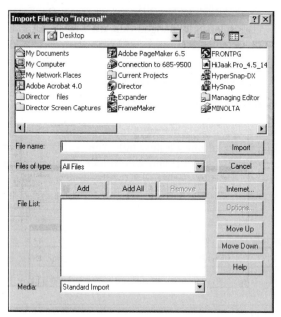

**FIGURE 2.53** *Use the Import Files Into... dialog box to select the files that you would like to add to your Director movie.*

4.    Use the Directory menu at the top of the Import Files Into... dialog box to locate the CD-ROM in your computer. The files that we need are located on the CD-ROM that accompanies this book. If the CD-ROM is not currently inserted into your computer's CD-ROM drive, insert it now, then repeat this step.

5.    Locate and open the folder named Lessons on the CD-ROM. This contains all of the media and partly completed and completed files for the lessons in this book.

6.    Locate and open the folder named Chaptr2 in the Lessons folder. This folder contains the completed version of the file that we are currently creating as well as the folder that contains the media we are about to import.

7.    Locate and open the folder named Media in the Chaptr2 folder. This folder contains the sound and images that we want.

8.    Locate and open the folder named Backgrnd in the Media folder. This folder contains the background image that we will use to cover the Stage.

9.  Locate and select the file named Backgrnd.pct in the Backgrnd folder. This is the background image. When it is selected, the Add button will become active. We will add this file to the list of files that we want to import.

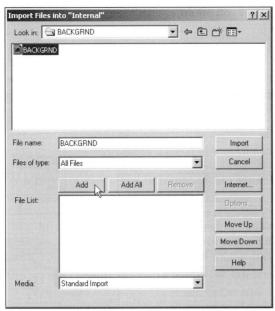

**FIGURE 2.54** *Locate and select the files that you want in the upper window of the Import Files Into... dialog box. Then click the Add button to add the files to a list of files that will be imported into your movie simultaneously.*

10. Click the button labeled Add. The Backgrnd.pct file is added to the window in the lower part of the Import Files Into... dialog box.

**NOTE**

You can specify the type of media that you would like to import into your Director presentations by choosing the media type from the Files ofType: pop-up menu. The Import dialog box will only display the files that match the media type that you specify. This is helpful if you have files of different media types located in the same directories in your computer. Using the All Files setting will display any file types that can be imported into Director.

**FIGURE 2.55** *You can specify the media types that you would like to import into Director by choosing from the list of available options in the Files of Type: menu. The Import Files Into... dialog box will then only display files that match that media type.*

11.  Using the Look in: pull down menu in the Import Files Into... dialog box, return to the folder named Media. There are other files here that we want to import.

12.  Locate and open the folder named Icons in the Media folder. This contains the files for the Icons of Wealth animation that appears first in The Billionaire's Shop.

13.  Click the button labeled Add All. We want to import all five files. Clicking Add All will add all of the files that appear in this directory to the list of files in the lower part of the dialog box.

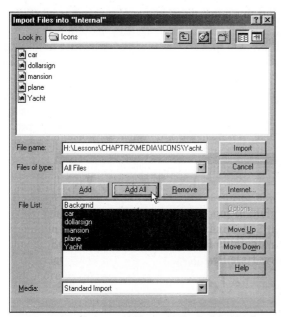

**FIGURE 2.56** *If you would like to include all of the files that are located in a specific folder to the list of files to import, click the Add All button.*

14. Using the Look In: menu in the Import Files Into... dialog box, return to the folder named Media. Now we will import the sound files that we will use in The Billionaire's Shop.

15. Locate and open the folder named Sounds in the Media folder. There are three files in this folder. We will add them all.

16. Click Add All. Notice that we can choose any combination of media types to import into Director simultaneously.

17. Return to the Media folder. Now we will import the Billionaire.

18. Locate and open the folder named Billion. There are two files here that we want, so we can once again use the Add All button. Both of these files are Flash Assets, which are files created with Macromedia Flash that have been saved in Shockwave format. These files are created using vector graphics, which makes them much smaller than bitmaps and easier to animate in certain ways.

There are some special things you need to know about Vectors and the Vector window. **NOTE**

Vector graphics are files that describe pictures using calculations (as opposed to bitmaps, which describe images by maintaining information about each pixel in the image). The major difference in appearance between the two is that bitmaps can contain much richer content, such as photographs, and vectors generally look like illustrations. Director includes a simple graphics window, called the Vector window, that can be used to create vector graphics of different shapes. It permits the creation of one graphic at a time and allows us to create very small graphics for Director movies.

Unlike the Paint window, the Vector window will only allow us to create images; it does not permit images that are imported to be edited. We will not be using the Vector window in The Billionaire's Shop, but if you are interested in exploring it on your own you can access it by choosing Windows>Vector.

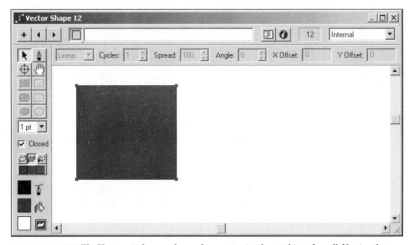

**FIGURE 2.57** *The Vector window can be used to create simple graphics of small file size that can easily be animated and resized.*

19.    **Click Add All. We now have most of the media that we need for the first few chapters of this book listed in the lower part of the Import Files Into... dialog box. Now we will finish the import.**

20.    **Click the button labeled Import. The Import Files Into... dialog box will close to be replaced by the Import Options For... dialog box. This window will appear if you attempt to import an image into Director that uses a custom palette. These images use a custom palette, so we must choose to import this custom palette or allow Director to modify the images so that they use a default palette that is already within Director. We will import the palette.**

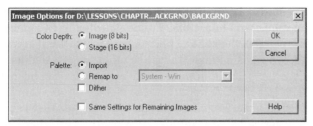

**FIGURE 2.58** *The Import Options dialog box will appear if you attempt to import images that use a custom palette.*

21. Select the Radio button beside the Image (8 bits) option beside the words Color Depth. These images are designed to look good when displayed using only 256 colors. There is no need to import them at higher resolution, which would be more memory-intensive.

> Director will automatically attempt to import files at a color depth equal to your monitor's setting, unless you specify something different. **NOTE**

22. Select the Radio button beside the Import option next to the word Palette. This tells Director that you want to import the palette with which this image was created. This palette will appear in the Cast (we will examine the custom palette later in this chapter). The dither option lets Director smooth the edges of the image as it is imported. In this case, this is unnecessary because the edges of these images were smoothed in the program in which they were created.

23. Click the checkbox beside the statement Same Settings for Remaining Images. All of the images that we are importing use the same palette, so we can prevent this dialog box from appearing for each image by allowing Director to apply these settings to all of the other images that we are importing.

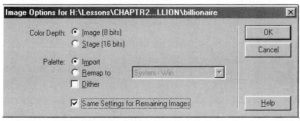

**FIGURE 2.59** *The images for The Billionaire's Shop use a custom palette, so use the settings of the Import Options dialog box.*

24.  Click the button labeled OK. All of the files will appear sequentially in the Internal Cast file. Notice that the first Cast member that is created is the custom palette with which the images were created. We can also import and use other images that use a different custom palette; however, only one palette can be used on the Stage at a time. If we attempt to display images that use different palettes on Stage at once, only the images that use the currently active palette will display properly. The other images will appear distorted.

**FIGURE 2.60** *All of the files that we selected in the Import Files Into... dialog box are added to the Cast when we click Import. The first Cast member is the custom palette that was used to create the images for The Billionaire's Shop.*

**NOTE**   You can choose to import files so that the Cast members they create are still linked to the original files on the hard drive. This will allow you to edit the files using external programs without needing to re-import the file. You can choose this option by selecting it from the pull-down menu at the bottom of the Import Files Into... dialog box. You can also set Director to allow you to launch other applications to edit media inside your Cast by using the Editor Preferences dialog box located at File>Preferences>Editors.... You can select an editor for each file type that Director can import. Take a look!

25.  Double click on Cast member 1. This will open the Color Palettes window. We can use this window to make changes to palettes in Director, create new palettes, or simply preview the colors in a palette. The currently displayed palette is the custom palette that we imported with the images. You can use the pop-up menu in the upper left of the Color Palettes dialog box to preview the other palettes in this movie.

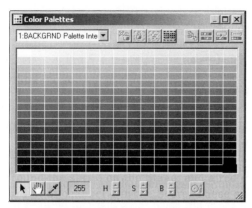

**FIGURE 2.61** *Double clicking on a palette Cast member will open the Color Palettes window. You can use this window to modify Director's palettes or create new ones.*

26. Close the Color Palettes window. You can double-click on any of the other Cast members that we imported into Director and preview them. Sounds will open the Cast Member Info dialog box and allow you to play the sound; images will open in the Paint window, in which you can edit them if you choose. We will not be making any changes to these images for The Billionaire's Shop, so do not make any permanent changes if you choose to experiment.

27. Choose File>Save. You can use the partly completed version of the files that is provided in each lesson. The Starter file for each lesson begins where the last lesson finished.

28. Name the file Billshop.dir.

29. Locate and open the directory you created earlier named Billshop. This is where we placed all of our earlier files.

30. Click the button labeled Save. We are now ready to begin building The Billionaire's Shop!

## SUMMARY

Director's interface is based upon a theatrical theme that uses a window called the Stage as the display area for the presentation. All media used in a presentation are located in a window called the Cast, which serves as a database for sounds, images, text, and any other media that you can use in a Director presentation. The design for the presentation is developed in the Score, where all animation sequences, sounds, and other presentation elements are positioned along a timeline. Director produces movie files and Cast files, further supporting the theatrical theme.

A Director movie can contain multiple Cast files, each capable of containing up to 32,000 Cast members. Cast members are incorporated into Director presentations when they are dragged from the Cast to the Stage or to the Score. When a Cast member is dragged to the Stage or the Score, an instance of the Cast member is created called a sprite object. A sprite object has the appearance of the original Cast member, but does not duplicate the file size of the original Cast member. Each Cast member can be used multiple times throughout a presentation without increasing the overall size of the movie. The files that are used as Cast members are generally created outside of Director in tools such as Adobe Photoshop and SoundEdit 16, although there are some tools that can be used to create Cast members within Director, such as the Paint window for images.

By changing the position of a sprite over time, you can create animations in Director. You can change the location of a sprite over time by using the sprite's path. The sprite path is a line that can be pulled away from the sprite to define the direction of the sprite. You can modify other sprite features, such as duration within the presentation and the dimensions of the sprite, by using Director's sprite inspector and sprite overlay features. Sprites can also be directly edited within the Score.

Understanding Director's interface is rooted in understanding the relationships between the different parts of the program. For example, a sprite on the Stage is dynamically linked to the Cast member that was used to create it. Any changes that are made to the Cast member will be immediately apparent in any sprites that are created using that Cast member. Another example is the relationship between the composition in the Score and the sprite on the Stage. The Score, together with the Stage, can only display a single moment in time within your presentation, but the Score also contains all other points in time in your presentation. As a result, it is possible to edit a part of a Director presentation without the presence of the affected part visible on the Stage. Understanding that what you do in any one location within Director could yield results in several other locations within your movie, and learning how to predict and control these ulterior results, are the keys to understanding and ultimately excelling with Director.

## QUESTIONS

1.   How many sprite channels are there in the Score?

2.   What is a color palette?

3.   What are the three categories of information that are displayed in a sprite overlay?

4.   How many Cast members can be contained in a single Cast file?

5.   What is the keyboard shortcut for playing a Director movie while causing all open windows to temporarily close?

6.   Besides containing a large number of Cast members, why is it useful to use more than one Cast file in a Director movie?

## EXERCISES

1.   Start a new movie. Then, using the tools in the Paint window, create four Cast members. Drag the new Cast members to the Stage to create four sprites.

2.   Create four new views for the Score. Using the Zoom In/Out menu, set the different Score views to different settings.

3.   Start a new movie, then create two new Cast windows. Import the airplane image from the CD-ROM into the internal Cast, the car into one of the new Casts, and the boat and mansion into the other.

# CHAPTER 3

# BASIC ANIMATION
# AND EDITING THE SCORE

# 3 Basic Animation and Editing the Score

In this chapter, you will learn how to:

- Extend and edit a sprite's path
- Use the Sprite Tweening dialog box
- Perform step recording
- Perform real-time recording
- Edit and animate a sprite's rotation using the sprite inspector
- Edit and animate a sprite's skew angle
- Use the Paint window to create a sequence of images for an animation
- Create a film loop
- Use the Cast to time command
- Use the behavior inspector

One of Director's most powerful features is the ability to generate animations quickly and easily. This ability to produce the movement of images on the Stage can be used for entertainment purposes, such as in a game or presentation; for illustration purposes, such as an arrow moving to highlight different parts of a technical diagram; or simply to tell a story. The movement of images in your presentations will keep the viewer's attention and is a valuable means of artistic expression.

Any image used as a sprite on the Stage is equipped with a sprite path that can be extended to define a direction of movement and a destination. This path can also be edited to create a more detailed path of movement. There are also other animation techniques that can be used for greater precision, such as generating an animation frame by frame. In this chapter we will learn some of the different animation methods that are available in Director, and we will create the opening animation for The Billionaire's Shop.

## Viewing the Completed File

1.    If it is not already open, launch Director.

2.    Choose File>Open.

3.    Locate and select the file named Chp3cmp.dir, which is located
      on the CD-ROM in the directory Lessons/Chaptr3/Complete/
      Chp3cmp.dir.

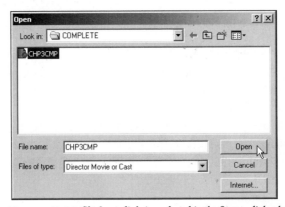

**FIGURE 3.01** *Chp3cmp.dir being selected in the Open... dialog box.*

4.    Click Open and then play the movie. You can use the Play button
      on the Toolbar or on the Control Panel. You can also use the key-
      board shortcut: Command+Option+P (Macintosh) or Con-
      trol+Alt+P (Windows). If you add the Shift key to either
      keyboard combination, any open windows in Director's interface
      will temporarily close. Command+Period (.) (Macintosh) or Con-
      trol+Period(.) (Windows) will stop the presentation and reopen
      the temporarily closed windows in Director's interface. This
      movie contains the opening animation for The Billionaire's Shop.
      The five icons representing wealth that we imported in chapter 2
      move around the screen. One icon, the dollar sign, spins around
      as it moves around the screen. In this session we will create this
      animation.

5.    Stop the movie.

**FIGURE 3.02** *The Icons of Wealth animation that we will create in this lesson.*

## OPENING THE PARTLY COMPLETED FILE

1. Choose File>Open. The Open... dialog box will appear.

2. Open the file named Chp3inc.dir, located in the directory Lessons/Chaptr3/Starter/ on the CD-ROM, or you can continue working with the file you created in chapter 2.

> Remember to save your work frequently because the end result of each **NOTE** lesson is the beginning of the next lesson. We have also supplied you with the partly completed version of each lesson on the CD-ROM so that you can work with the working copy of Director that is on the CD-ROM.

## EXTENDING A SPRITE'S PATH

The simplest technique for creating an animation in Director is the sprite path. This is the path that is displayed when the sprite's overlay is present on the Stage. When the sprite's path is not extended, it appears as a dot at the center of the sprite on the Stage. To experiment with this technique, we will create a sprite that has one of the images currently in the Cast.

1.  If the Cast and the Score are not currently open, open them. You can open the Cast and the Score by clicking on the Cast or Score buttons on the toolbar. You can also choose Windows>Cast for the Cast and Windows>Score for the Score. Notice that the Cast currently contains the images that we imported in chapter 2.

2.  Move the playback head to frame 1. You can move the playback head to frame 1 by clicking above the number 1 on the frame bar. In chapter 2 we changed the color of the Stage to black for The Billionaire's Shop. That is still the color we want for The Billionaire's Shop, but we will temporarily change the color to white for the experimental parts of this lesson. This way the sprites and their paths show with greater contrast against the Stage.

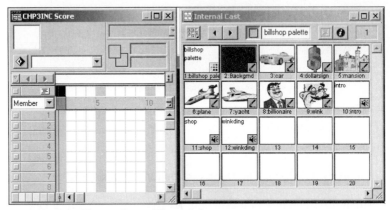

**FIGURE 3.03** *The open Cast and Score windows.*

3.  Choose Modify>Movie>Properties.... This will open the Movie Properties dialog box.

4.  Change the color of the Stage to white (if it is not already white). Later we will change the color of the stage back to black.

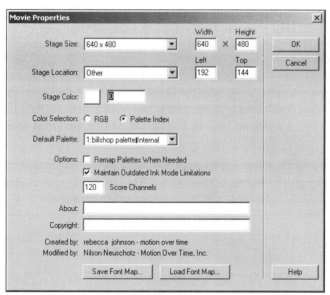

**FIGURE 3.04** *Change the color of the Stage to white.*

5.  Click the button labeled OK in the Movie Properties dialog box. This will close the Movie Properties dialog box and change the color of the Stage to white.

6.  Drag Cast member 3 (the car) to the left side of the Stage. After you drag the car to the Stage, a sprite will appear on the Stage and in the Score in channel 1, frames 1 to 28.

    The sprite overlay that we activated in chapter 2 should appear over the sprite while it is selected.

NOTE

The image Cast members in this movie were created with a custom palette that will automatically appear in the palette channel, which is located with the other effects channels at the top of the Score. This palette is located at Cast position 1 in the Cast window and was created when the images for The Billionaire's Shop were imported. Now that this palette is in the palette channel of the Score, any images that use this palette will display properly. You also have the option of using other palettes later in the palette channel. Each palette will change the appearance of the images from the point in the Score where the palette appears on to the next palette that appears in the Score. We will be using only one palette in The Billionaire's Shop. Only images that use the currently active palette will display properly. Any images that use a different palette will remap to the currently active palette and will likely appear distorted. Use the Show/Hide Effects Channels button on the Score to make the effects channels visible.

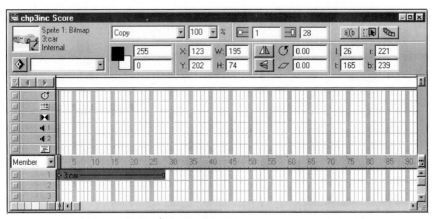

**FIGURE 3.05** *The revealed effects channels of the Score.*

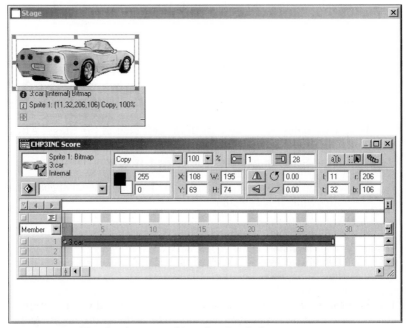

**FIGURE 3.06** *The selected car sprite object selected on the Stage.*

**NOTE**  If the sprite overlay is not currently visible when the sprite you created is selected, follow the directions in the section entitled "Activating the Sprite Overlay," in chapter 2.

7.     **Click and Drag the sprite path for the car sprite to the right side of the Stage. Release the mouse pointer when you reach the right side of the Stage. As you drag the sprite path endpoint, you will see a line extend away from the car sprite along with the mouse pointer. The dots that appear along the sprite path represent the frames that this sprite passes through. For example, this sprite passes through 28 frames, so there are 28 dots along this sprite's path.**

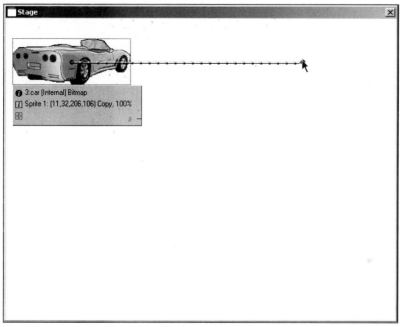

**FIGURE 3.07** *The extended sprite path.*

The quickest method for animating a sprite is extending its sprite path.

8.     **Play the movie. The car sprite will travel along the sprite path that we extended across the Stage. The differences in position from frame to frame are what produces the illusion of movement when the movie plays.**

If the car animation stops after playing once, then the Loop setting is not activated. You can activate the Loop setting by clicking the Loop button in the upper right of the control panel. You can open the control panel by choosing Windows>Control Panel.

**NOTE**

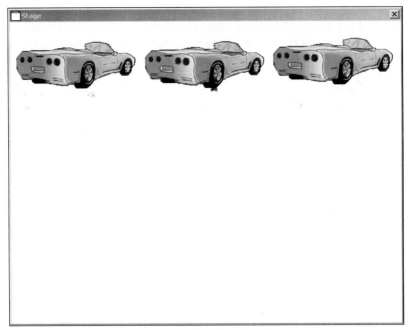

**FIGURE 3.08** *Images of the car sprite traveling along the path.*

Extending the sprite path for the car changes the position of the car in all of the frames it passes through. This difference in position from frame to frame is what produces the illusion of movement when the movie plays.

9.    **Stop the movie. Now we will edit the sprite's path.**

## EDITING THE SPRITE'S PATH

When the car sprite is selected, its path will be visible. At this point the path is a straight animation that moves directly from the starting point to the ending point. You can also edit a sprite's path so that it travels along a curved path.

1.    **Select the car sprite on the Stage. Its path will become visible.**

2.    **Hold down the Option (Macintosh) or Alt (Windows) key on your keyboard. Holding down this key will allow us to edit the points along the animation path of the sprite. If the path disappears as your cursor leaves the overlay frame, click View/Sprite Overlay/ Settings and select the Selection Display option.**

3.    **While holding down the Option or Alt key, click on any of the dots along the sprite's path and drag the point away from its current position. You will see that, as you drag the point, the entire**

animation path becomes modified to accommodate the new position for that point. Notice that a circle will appear in the Score at the point along the sprite object's animation path where the change was made. This new circle is called a *keyframe*, which is a point of change in the animation of a sprite. By making changes at keyframes, Director modifies the rest of the animation to accommodate the change. In this case, Director will change the position of all points along the car sprite's animation path to include the position of the new keyframe. This automatic updating is one of the reasons Director is so powerful for creating animation.

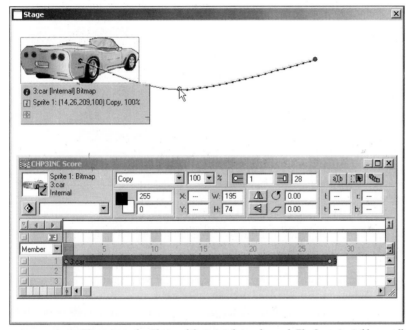

**FIGURE 3.09** *The sprite path with one of the points being dragged. The Score is visible as well, with the cursor identifying a new keyframe present on the sprite object.*

You can modify the direction of the sprite's path by holding down the Option (Macintosh) or Alt (Windows) key while you click and drag the points along the sprite's path. A keyframe will be created in the sprite object in the Score.

4.  **Play the movie. You will see that the car sprite will travel along the newly curved path.**

5.  **Stop the movie.**

Now we will look at another method for modifying the sprite's path.

## USING THE INSERT KEYFRAME COMMAND

We have already looked at how to add a keyframe and modify a sprite path in a single step. Now we will learn how to add a keyframe without immediately changing the sprite's path. This allows us to add several keyframes to a sprite path, then edit them together on the Stage.

1.  **In the Score, click a point along the sprite object you created earlier that is not a keyframe. The areas of the sprite object that are not keyframes are any points that contain a line and not a circle. When the sprite is selected, the sprite's path is visible on the Stage.**

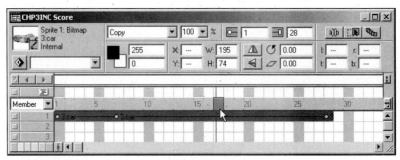

**FIGURE 3.10** *The Score with the frame being placed in a frame that does not contain a keyframe.*

Move the playback head to a frame that does not contain a keyframe for the sprite object in channel 1.

2.  **Choose Insert>Keyframe. A new circle will appear on the sprite Object in the Score. This is a new keyframe. You will also see that a circle appears along the sprite path that is visible on the Stage. The only points that can be clicked directly and moved are keyframes. Any other point will move the entire sprite path, not just the point.**

    The sprite object is visible in the Score with the new keyframe at the selected position. Choose Insert>Keyframe to place a new keyframe at the position that you selected.

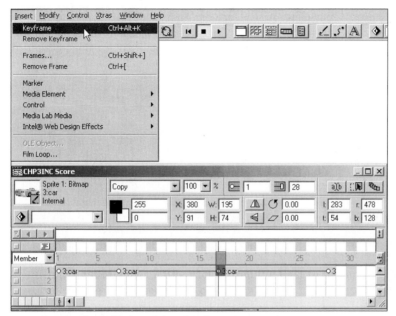

**FIGURE 3.11** *Insert>Keyframe being selected.*

3. Click the new keyframe point along the sprite's path on the *Stage*, then drag the point to a new position. The animation path for the sprite will alter to accommodate the new keyframe position. The first and last frames of an extended sprite path automatically become keyframes.

4. Drag the new keyframe to a different position along the sprite object in the *Score*.

You can remove a keyframe from a sprite's animation path by selecting the keyframe on the Stage or in the Score, then choosing Insert>Remove Keyframe. **NOTE**

5. Play the movie. You will see now that the animation path has changed to accommodate the new keyframe.

6. Stop the movie.

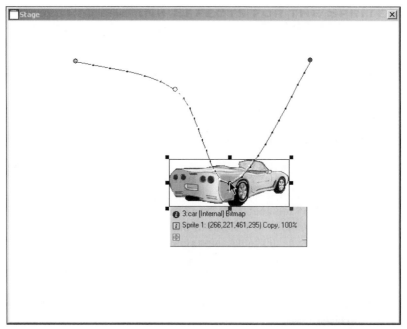

**FIGURE 3.12** *The new keyframe being dragged to a different position along the sprite object in the Score.*

## USING SPRITE TWEENING OPTIONS

The animation that we have created so far is a curved animation, which will probably serve most of our purposes, but there might be times in which you will want the animation path for a sprite to travel along very straight lines. We can accomplish this by using the Sprite Tweening dialog box. When you create an animation using a sprite path, Director will automatically add some curvature between the sprite's keyframes. This curvature can be increased or decreased in intensity by using options that are available in the Sprite Tweening dialog box. *Tweening* refers to Director's automatic modification of a sprite's path based upon changes made to keyframes. The term tweening is used because this updating occurs be*tween* the sprite's keyframes.

1.    Select the sprite on the Stage. The sprite animation path will become visible on the Stage. The animation path is currently curved along the path that is defined by the keyframes that we created earlier.

2.    Choose Modify>Sprite>Tweening.... This will open the Sprite Tweening dialog box where we can make adjustments to the animation settings for the selected sprite's path.

3. Drag the Curvature: arrow all the way to Linear on the left edge of the drag bar. You will see as you drag the arrow that the thumbnail representation of the sprite path on the left will change to reflect the changes you have made to the setting. The Curvature setting will determine the level of curve that is incorporated in the frame between keyframes in the animation. The other settings can be used to make an animation speed up or slow down, or to animate different features of an animation, such as the size of a sprite (or the blend, which is the transparency of the sprite).

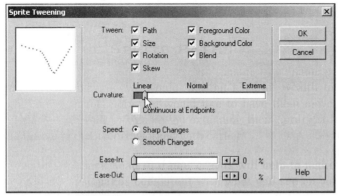

**FIGURE 3.13** *The Sprite Tweening dialog box—arrow is being dragged to the left.*

4. Click the button labeled OK. This will close the Sprite Tweening dialog box.

5. Play the movie. Now you will see that the sprite moves along the animation path directly from keyframe to keyframe. There is no curvature along the animation path.

6. Hold down the Control key (Macintosh) or use the right-mouse button (Windows) while clicking on a sprite object in the Score to access a menu with different options for editing that sprite, including the Sprite Tweening dialog box.

> You can access the Tweening Properties dialog box as well as many of the **NOTE** other dialog boxes that are used to modify aspects of a sprite by using the Control key (Macintosh) or the right-mouse button (Windows) and clicking down on the sprite you would like to edit. This will produce a menu that contains many of the options you need, including the Sprite Tweening option.

**FIGURE 3.14** *The pull-down menu that appears when a sprite object is clicked while the Control key (Macintosh) or right-mouse button (Windows) is held down.*

## EDITING THE KEYFRAME POSITIONS AND THE DURATION OF A SPRITE OBJECT (INCLUDES ANIMATION BEHAVIOR)

Each of the keyframes along a sprite's path can be edited separately, not just in their location on the Stage, but in their position in time. This allows you to modify the speed at which different parts of your animation will play at different times throughout your movie.

1.   **Select the sprite object you created earlier in the Score. The animation path will become visible on the Stage. You can see that the number of dots between the keyframes is equivalent to the number of frames between the keyframes. If we change the location of the keyframes in the Score, then the number of frames will be different. We will see this change in the number of dots between keyframes on the Stage.**

     In the Score, click on one of the keyframes that you created earlier for this sprite. Notice that when you click directly on a keyframe, only that cell highlights. Also, there is a single-lined box surrounding the sprite on the Stage. When the entire sprite object is selected, this box has a double line. This is another visual cue that you can make changes to an individual keyframe.

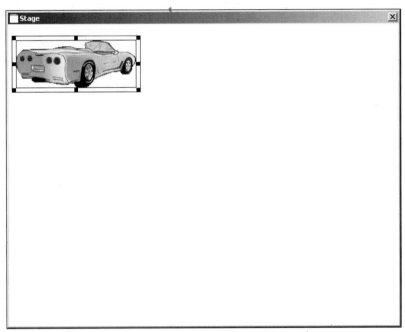

**FIGURE 3.15** *The selected sprite object that was created earlier for illustration purposes.*

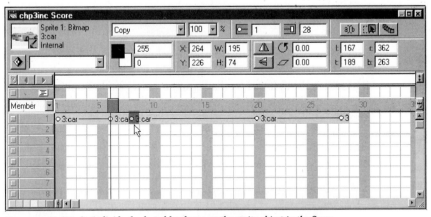

**FIGURE 3.16** *An individual selected keyframe on the sprite object in the Score.*

If you click directly on a keyframe, you will only highlight that single frame on the sprite object. This will isolate that keyframe so that you can make changes without affecting the entire sprite object.

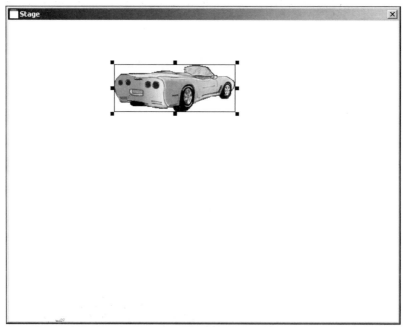

**FIGURE 3.17** *The isolated selected keyframe on the Stage.*

When a keyframe is directly selected in the Score, the selected sprite on the Stage will indicate that you are only making changes to that isolated keyframe by displaying a single-lined selection box as opposed to the double-lined selection box that appears when an entire sprite object is selected.

2.   **Drag the selected keyframe close to one of the keyframes before or after it in the Score. You will see that the line between the keyframes will change to reflect the new position. When you release the keyframe, the number of dots between the keyframes on the Stage will change to reflect the new positions of the keyframes in the sprite object.**

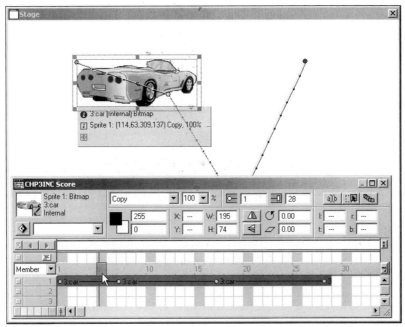

**FIGURE 3.18** *One of the keyframes dragged to a different position in the Score. The sprite path is visible on the Stage.*

When you drag a keyframe to a new position, the number of dots between the modified keyframes will reflect the new number of frames between the keyframes.

3.  **Play the movie. You will see that the animation has changed to reflect the new keyframe positions. You can make this type of change to the sprite's animation path at any time. Changing the position of a keyframe between the first and last keyframes only affects the duration of playback between those frames but does not change the overall duration of the entire sprite object. To do this you must change the first or last keyframes.**

4.  **Stop the movie. Now we will change the duration of the animation.**

5.  **Click the sprite endpoint at frame 28 in channel 1 of the Score. This is the last keyframe on this sprite's path.**

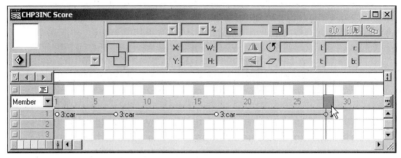

**FIGURE 3.19** *The selected endpoint for the sprite object.*

We can change the overall duration of the entire sprite object by moving the sprite's endpoint keyframe.

6.    **Drag the endpoint 15 frames to the right in the Score. Notice that as you drag the endpoint, the other keyframes will move as well. The distance between the keyframes will change in proportion to the overall duration of the sprite object. Now this sprite will last for a longer period of time in the presentation.**

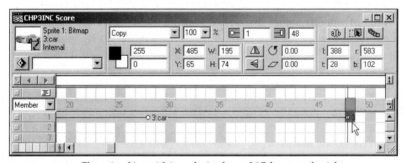

**FIGURE 3.20** *The sprite object with its endpoint dragged 15 frames to the right.*

When the endpoint of the sprite is dragged, the keyframes along the sprite object will change relative to the new endpoint position. Moving the position of the sprite's endpoint changes the overall duration of the entire sprite object.

7.    **Play the movie. You will see that the entire sprite path has changed to accommodate the new position for the sprite's endpoint.**

8.    **Stop the movie. Now that we have examined the tweening methods for animating a sprite using its path, let's learn some other animation techniques.**

## ANIMATING A SPRITE'S ROTATION AND SKEW ANGLE USING THE SPRITE INSPECTOR

The sprite inspector is the window that allows us to view and edit information about a sprite on the Stage. Part of this information is the rotation and skew angle of the sprite. These settings can be used to change the appearance of the sprite on the Stage. If the settings are different in different keyframes, then this will result in an animation from one appearance of the sprite to another. This can have a morph-like effect for skew settings, or it can produce a rotation animation for the rotate setting.

1. Open the sprite inspector by choosing Window>Inspectors>Sprite. The sprite inspector will appear.

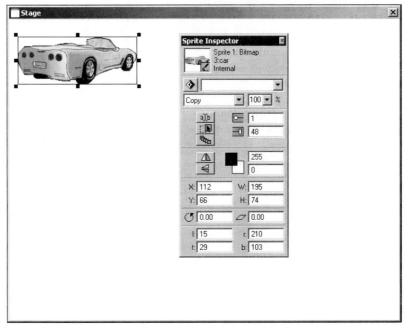

**FIGURE 3.21** *The sprite inspector open over the Stage with the current sprite displayed.*

The sprite inspector gives us access to features of a sprite that can be animated, such as rotation and skew angle.

2. Select the sprite object you created earlier in the Score. The animation path will become visible on the Stage. You will also see that the windows in the sprite inspector are now populated with the settings for this sprite. To create our animation, we will change the setting in the sprite inspector.

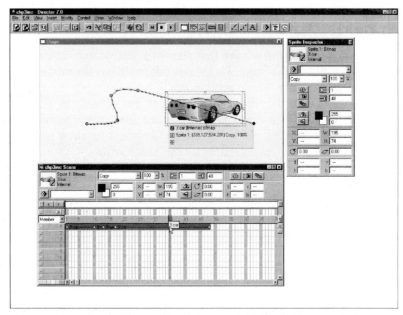

**FIGURE 3.22** *The selected sprite object that was created earlier for illustration purposes.*

3.   In the Score, click on one of the keyframes that you created for
     this sprite. Notice that when you click directly on a keyframe,
     only that cell highlights. You will also see that the sprite inspec-
     tor has more information in its windows. This is because some
     of the information, such as the specific position of a sprite, can
     only be determined when a single frame is selected.

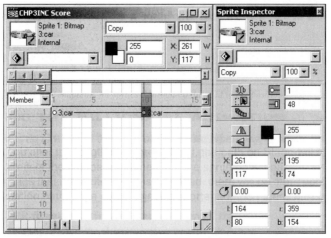

**FIGURE 3.23** *An individual selected keyframe on the sprite object in the Score.*

When a single sprite frame is selected, the sprite inspector can display more information, such as the exact coordinates of the sprite on the Stage.

4. **In the sprite inspector, enter the number 90 in the Rotation Angle window (labeled with a circle with an arrow at one end). This will enter a setting of 90 degrees clockwise for the sprite. We will see the results in a moment when we press the Return (Macintosh) or Enter (Windows) key.**

5. **In the sprite inspector, enter the number 15 in the Skew Angle window (labeled with a diamond on its side). This edits the skew angle of the sprite. The skew angle will shift the top and bottom of the sprite so that it looks slanted.**

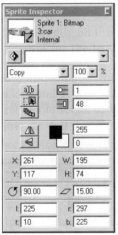

**FIGURE 3.24** *The settings identified in steps 4 and 5 above entered into the sprite inspector.*

After you have selected a keyframe for the sprite on the Stage, enter these settings into the sprite inspector.

6. **Press the Return (Macintosh) or Enter (Windows) key. The settings we have entered will now change the sprite on the Stage.**

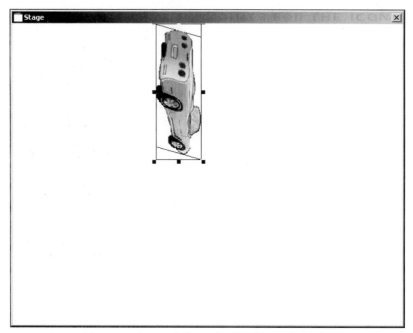

**FIGURE 3.25** *The sprite on Stage with the rotation and skew settings applied.*

7.  **Play the movie. You will see that the sprite rotation and skew angle are now animated between the keyframes where the new settings were made. Try different settings to see what other combinations you can produce.**

8.  **Stop the movie. Now we will look at how to animate a sprite one frame at a time.**

## STEP RECORDING

*Step Recording* is a procedure that allows you to create an animation frame by frame. You position a sprite on the Stage, then advance the movie one frame at a time. With each advance you move the sprite to a new position. The usefulness in this animation technique is that the results are irregular. The tweening methods evenly distribute the distance between the different positions of the sprite over time divided by the number of frames that the sprite passes through. With step recording, you can define the distance between each position with each frame. The results can be a more human or hand-drawn effect. This technique can also be used to fine tune an animation.

1.  **Open the Score.**

2.  **Drag select the sprite object in channel 1 of the Score.**

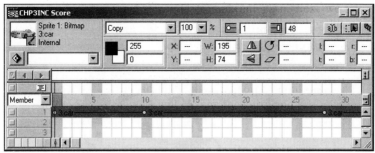

**FIGURE 3.26** *The selected sprite in the Score.*

3.  **Choose Edit>Clear Sprites. This will eliminate all of the sprites that are currently in the Score. We will start with a fresh Stage and Score.**

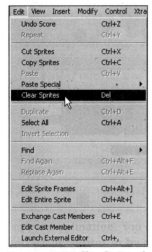

**FIGURE 3.27** *Clear Sprites selected from the Edit menu.*

4.  **Place the playback head in frame 1. Making certain that the playback head is in frame 1 will help ensure that your screen looks like the images on these pages.**

5.  **Drag Cast member 3 (the car) to the left side of the Stage. We will work with this Cast member again. You can choose a different Cast member if you like.**

6.    Open the control panel. We will need the Step Forward button on the control panel. You can open the control panel by choosing Window>Control Panel.

7.    Select the Sprite on the Stage. We are now set to begin step recording.

8.    Choose Control>Step Recording. Notice that the rectangle around the selected sprite changes. This is an indication that step recording has been activated. In the Score, an icon will appear at the far left of channel 1 in the Score. The icon is the label for the Step Forward button on the control panel.

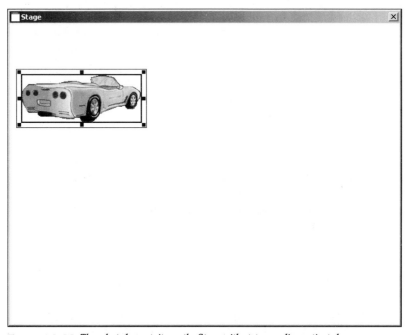

**FIGURE 3.28** *The selected car sprite on the Stage with step recording activated.*

9.    Click the Step Forward button on the control panel. This will advance the playback head one frame; it will also make the next frame on the sprite object in the Score a keyframe. Now we need to define this frame in the animation.

10.   Click on the sprite on the Stage and drag it to a new position. You will see that the sprite's path extends with the sprite on the Stage.

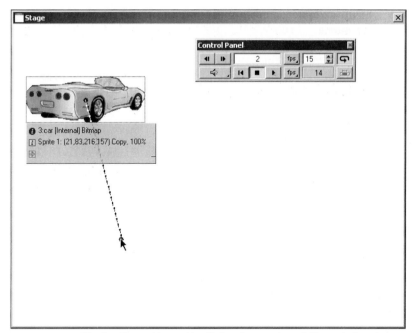

**FIGURE 3.29** *The Step Forward button identified on the control panel. The sprite is actively being dragged to a new position.*

11.   Click the Step Forward button on the control panel again. Once again, this will advance the playback head one frame. Step recording will duplicate the current frame of the sprite to the next frame.

> If you would like the sprite to stay in the same position for a number of frames, just continue clicking the Step Forward button through all the frames in which you would like the sprite to be stationary. This will duplicate the sprite position in each frame, but will not change the sprite's position unless you choose to click and drag the sprite to a new position.
>
> **NOTE**

12.   Drag the sprite on the Stage to a new position. Each time you step forward in the Score, you create a new frame for this animation. Each new frame starts as a duplicate of the last frame in the animation. You can then change the position of the sprite in the duplicate frame, creating a new frame.

13.   Repeat steps 8 and 9 at least 10 more times. In order to create a well-defined animation, we will need to create multiple frames.

When we are finished, we can preview the animation by playing the movie.

14. Play the movie. You can see that an animation path created using step recording is a bit irregular when compared to an animation created using a tweening method.

15. Stop the movie.

Now we will look at another animation technique called *real-time recording.*

## REAL-TIME RECORDING

Real-time recording allows you to create an animation by clicking and dragging a sprite along a path while the movie is playing. You can base the animation upon the real-time movement of the other sprites in your presentation. This animation technique is very closely related to the playback speed of your presentation as each frame of the animation is generated as the playback head passes from frame to frame. For example, if your movie is set to play at 1 frame per second, then you will generate only 1 frame of animation for each second that you drag the sprite. It will probably be sporadic in its result. On the other hand, a setting of 15 frames per second will generate 15 frames of animation per second. It will appear smoother because there are more images to contain the detail of the animation.

1. Drag select any sprites that are currently in your movie. Once again, we will start with a fresh Stage and Score.

2. Choose Edit>Clear Sprites. This will clear the Score and the Stage.

3. Place the playback head in frame 1. As in our earlier examples, we will have our real-time recording begin at frame 1.

4. Drag Cast member 3 (the car) to the left side of the Stage. As before, you can choose a different Cast member if you like.

5. If the control panel is not currently open, open it. We will use the control panel to set the frame rate for this movie.

6. Use the Tempo setting entry area on the control panel to set the tempo to 15 frames per second. This will produce 15 frames of animation for each second that you hold down the mouse button and drag the sprite around the Stage.

**FIGURE 3.30** *The control panel with the cursor over the Tempo setting.*

7.  Select the sprite on the Stage. We are now set to begin real-time recording.

8.  Choose Control>Real-Time Recording. A red square will appear around the sprite on the Stage, and a red dot will appear at the far left of channel 1 in the Score. These signals indicate that real-time recording has been activated.

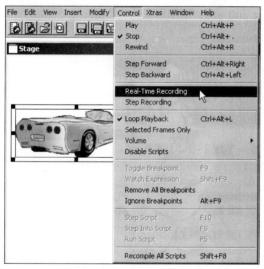

**FIGURE 3.31** *The selected sprite on the Stage with Control>Real-Time Recording selected.*

9.  Click the car sprite and drag it around the Stage for about 2 seconds. Release the mouse button when you are finished. As soon as you click on the sprite on the Stage, the playback head will begin to move across the Score. Director is now recording your movements. When you release the mouse button, the movie will continue playing so that you can preview the animation you just made. You can see in the Score that a keyframe appears at every frame where you moved the sprite to a new position. If you held the mouse button down for more than two seconds, then the sprite will extend beyond the end of the current sprite object, extending the endpoint of the sprite object.

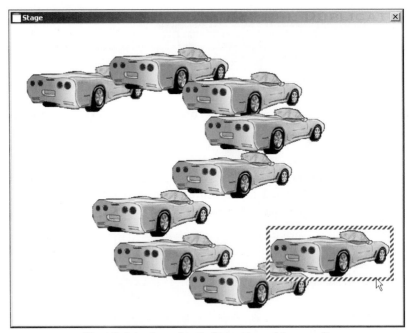

**FIGURE 3.32** *The sprite being dragged on the Stage using real-time recording.*

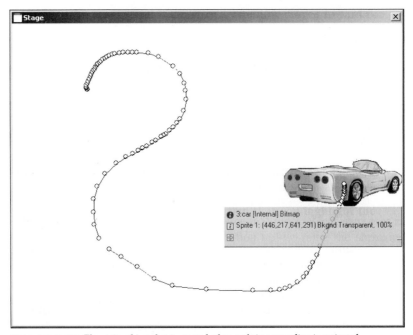

**FIGURE 3.33** *The sprite object that is created when real-time recording is activated.*

> If you would like a sprite to stay in a stationary position for a number of frames during real-time recording, allow the playback head to pass through the desired number of frames without changing the position of the sprite.

**NOTE**

10. **Stop the movie.**

## CREATING A ROTATING ANIMATION AND USING CAST-TO-TIME

Now we will look at how to animate a sprite so that it rotates on the Stage. This will be the first step in creating the rotating dollar sign for the opening animation of The Billionaire's Shop. In the completed version of this lesson, the five Icons of Wealth move around the screen. One of them, the dollar sign, rotates as it moves around the Stage. To create this rotation, we must create a series of Cast members that depict the dollar sign at different degrees of rotation. This is because a sprite cannot be rotated directly on the Stage. This sequence of rotated Cast members can then be grouped into a new type of Cast member, called a *film loop*, which is a sequence of images grouped into a single Cast position. The usefulness of a film loop is that you can use techniques such as tweening and real-time recording to animate the entire sequence around the Stage, just as if you were working with a single image. We can create the series of Cast members that we need for a film loop in the Paint window using a technique called *Auto Distort*. First, we will clear out the current movie so that we can start with a fresh Stage.

1. **Drag select any sprites that are currently in the Score.**

2. **Choose Edit>Clear Sprites.**

3. **Place the playback head over frame 1. Now we will create the sequence of rotating Cast members.**

4. **If the Cast is not currently open, open it. The dollar Cast member is in Cast position 4.**

5. **Double-click the dollar Cast member. This will launch the Paint window.**

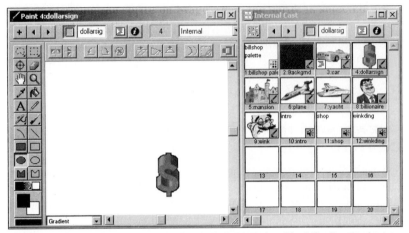

**FIGURE 3.34** *The Cast window is open beside the Paint window. The dollar Cast member is displayed in the Paint window.*

6.　Click and hold the mouse pointer over the Marquee tool at the top of the Tool palette on the left side of the Paint window. After a moment a menu will appear at the Marquee tool. The Marquee tool is used to select images in the Paint window. The options in this menu are used to select settings for the Marquee tool.

7.　Choose Shrink from the Marquee tool menu. This will cause the selection that you make with the Marquee tool to shrink to the smallest square that will fit around the selected area of the image.

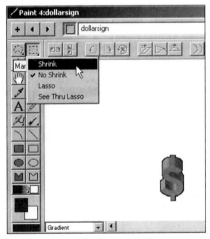

**FIGURE 3.35** *The Marquee Settings menu open over the Marquee tool.*

8.   With the Marquee tool selected, click and drag a selection rect-
     angle around the dollar image in the Paint window. Drag the
     selection rectangle so that it encloses the entire image. When
     you release the mouse button, the rectangle will shrink to the
     smallest rectangle that will fit around the dollar image. Now we
     will rotate the image.

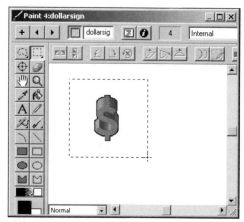

**FIGURE 3.36** *A marquee selection dragged around the dollar Cast-member image.*

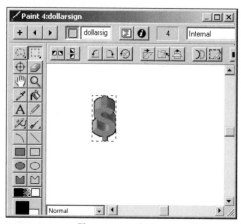

**FIGURE 3.37** *The marquee selection shrunken around the dollar image.*

9.   Click the Free Rotate tool at the top of the Paint window. This
     will cause the selection around the dollar image to become ani-
     mated. Four control points will also appear at the four corners of
     the selection. These control points can be clicked and dragged to
     rotate the image.

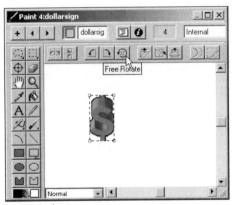

**FIGURE 3.38** *The dollar image with Free Rotate activated.*

10.  Click and hold the mouse button over the control point in the upper right corner of the selection rectangle around the dollar image. We will drag to rotate this image so that we can create the rotation animation.

11.  Rotate the Dollar image about 350 degrees clockwise. Initially, you will only see the rectangle rotate with the mouse. When you release the mouse button, the image will alter to fit the degree of rotation at your final position. Director will remember the original position and will rotate the dollar on the stage from the first position to the position that we drag it to now.

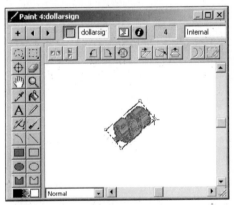

**FIGURE 3.39** *The dollar image in the process of being rotated.*

12.  Choose Xtras>Auto Distort.... This will present you with the Auto Distort dialog box.

**FIGURE 3.40** *Auto Distort selected from the Xtras menu.*

13.    Type 8 in the Generate: entry window. This will cause Director to create eight new Cast members, which will bring the dollar image from the original position to the current position.

14.    Click the button labeled Begin. Director will now generate the 8 new Cast members. You will see them actively created in the Paint window. They will also appear in the Cast because they are generated. The new Cast members will appear at the next 8 available positions in the Cast, which are positions 13 through 20. The original dollar Cast member will remain at position 4 in the Cast. Now we will reorganize the Cast window so that the dollar Cast members are all together.

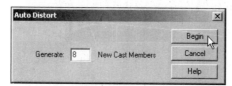

**FIGURE 3.41** *The Auto Distort dialog box. An 8 is displayed in the Entry window. The pointer is over the button labeled Begin.*

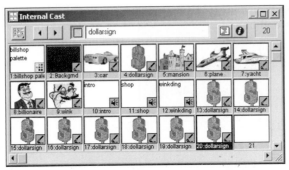

**FIGURE 3.42** *The new Cast members in the Cast window.*

## REARRANGING THE CAST

When we created the series of rotated Cast members, the original Cast member was separated from the newly generated Cast members. This is because Director will position the new Cast members at the next available positions in the Cast. It will be much easier to keep track of all of our Cast members if related Cast members are kept together. This type of organization can also save hours of development time wasted on locating needed Cast members at different locations in the Cast of a movie.

1.  In the Cast, click and drag Cast member 4 over Cast position 13. You will see that a purple line will appear and flash on and off between Cast positions 12 and 13. This indicates that the Cast member we are dragging will appear at Cast position 13.

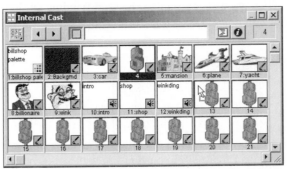

**FIGURE 3.43** *Cast member 4 in the process of being dragged over position 13.*

2.  Release the mouse button. The original dollar Cast member will now be placed at Cast position 13. All of the Cast members from positions 13 to 20 are moved to positions 14 to 21. We will leave the empty space left behind by Cast member 4. Later we

will place the film loop Cast member that we are about to create at that position.

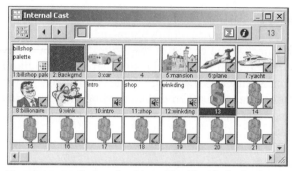

**FIGURE 3.44** *Cast member 4 in position 13 with all other Cast members shoved to the right.*

## BUILDING THE FILM LOOP

Now that we have created the rotated dollar-image Cast members, we can create the dollar-film loop. The first step is to create an animation using the sequence of Cast members on the Stage. Then we will take this animation and group it together into a film loop.

1.  Select Cast member 13. This is the first dollar-image Cast member.

2.  Hold down the Shift key and select Cast member 21. This will select the range of Cast members from position 13 to position 21.

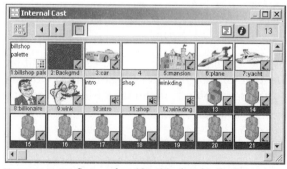

**FIGURE 3.45** *Cast members 13 to 21 selected in the Cast.*

3.  If the playback head is not currently in frame 1, move it to frame 1 now. As in the earlier examples, we will have the animation begin in frame 1.

4.  Choose Modify>Cast To Time. All of the selected Cast members will be placed in sequence on the Stage and in the Score as a single sprite object at the center of the Stage. This would serve if the animation needed to play only once, but we would like it to repeat as many times as necessary while the movie is playing, so we will take the additional step of converting this animation into a film loop. Before we take this step, let's preview the animation at this point.

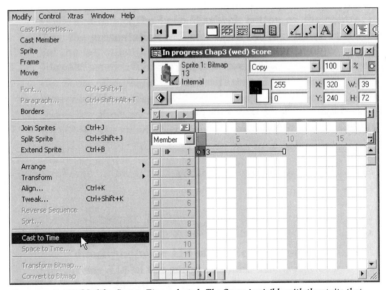

**FIGURE 3.46** *Modify>Cast to Time selected. The Score is visible with the sprite that is generated.*

5.  Play the movie. You can see now that the entire animation is contained within this single sprite object. You can extend the endpoint of the sprite object; it will take a little longer to play, but it will still only play once.

6.  Stop the movie. Now we will create the film loop.

7.  Select the new sprite object in channel 1.

8.  Choose Background Transparent from the Ink menu at the top of the Score. Before we convert this animation into a film loop, we

will change its ink effect to Background Transparent. This needs to happen now because the ink effect of a film loop cannot be changed. Changing the ink effect will not have a visible effect at this point because the color of the Stage is currently white. But it will be important later when this animation is placed over the background for The Billionaire's Shop. Now we can convert this animation into a film loop. First, we will make certain that the new film loop will be positioned as Cast position 4.

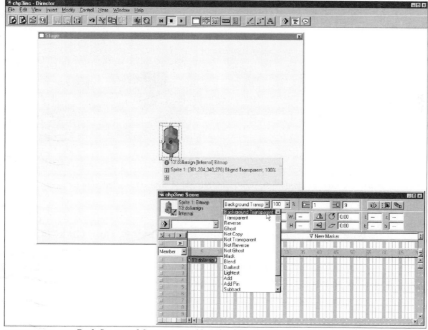

**FIGURE 3.47** *Both Score and Stage are visible. The selected sprite is on the Stage, and a transparent background is selected from the Ink: pull-down menu at the top of the Score.*

9.  Select the empty Cast position at position 4 in the Cast. Director will automatically seek the next available Cast position for the new film loop. This is really a precautionary measure.

10. Click on the sprite in the Score. The Score must be active for the film loop option to be available.

11. Choose Insert>Film Loop.... This will open the Create Film Loop dialog box, which will allow us to name the new Cast member that the film loop will occupy.

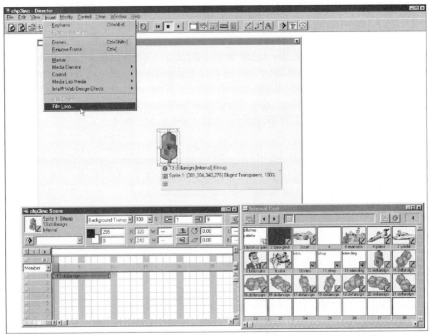

**FIGURE 3.48** *The selected empty Cast position at position 4. The sprite selected in the Score. Insert>Film Loop... is selected.*

12. Type Dollar Loop in the Name entry window, then click the button labeled OK. This will name the Cast member dollar loop and place the new film loop Cast member at Cast position 4. This Cast member can now be animated just as any other in this movie. The only difference is that this single Cast member contains the entire dollar rotation animation!

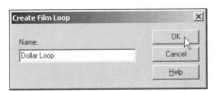

**FIGURE 3.49** *The Create Film Loop dialog box. Dollar Loop is typed into the Name entry area. The pointer is over the OK button.*

## ANIMATING THE FILM LOOP

Now that we have generated the dollar-loop Cast member, we will quickly preview how it can be animated using its sprite path.

1.     Select the sprite that is currently in the score and choose Edit>Clear Sprites.

2.     Drag Cast member 4, the dollar-loop Cast member, to the Stage. It will generate a sprite object just as any other Cast member would.

3.     Drag the sprite path for the dollar-loop sprite across the Stage. The path will extend as it has in the earlier examples. The sprite object crosses 28 frames, so there are 28 points along the path. You can edit the path further if you like using the Option (Macintosh) or Alt (Windows) key to drag any of the points to new locations.

4.     Play the movie. The dollar loop will follow the path you created, rotating as it moves along. This simple film-loop procedure has greatly enhanced the entertaining quality of this animation.

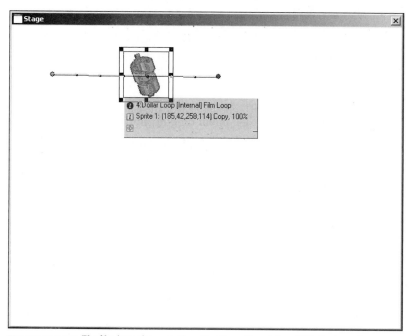

**FIGURE 3.50** *The film loop along a path on the Stage. One of the middle Cast members is visible.*

5.     Stop the movie. Now that we have experimented with all of these methods, we are ready to create the opening animation for The Billionaire's Shop!

**NOTE**    A film loop requires the presence and original Cast positions of the original Cast members used to create it in order to operate properly. If any of the Cast members are altered or removed, then the film loop itself will be altered as well. This is because the film loop only references the Cast members that were used to create it; it does not duplicate them.

## RESETTING THE MOVIE PROPERTIES FOR THE BILLIONAIRE'S SHOP

To create the opening animation, we will use the sprite paths for the Icons of Wealth. We will also change the endpoints of the sprites' animations to have them move at different rates around the screen.

We are going to move forward with creating The Billionaire's Shop. All work that we do in this movie will lead us toward the completion of this project from here on through the rest of the lessons in this book. The first thing we will do is reset the color of the Stage.

1.  **Clear the Score.**

2.  **Choose Modify>Movie>Properties.... This will open the Movie Properties dialog box. We will change both the color of the Stage as well as the default palette that this movie uses.**

3.  **Change the Stage Color to black. Black will help to add drama to The Billionaire's Shop.**

4.  **Choose 1:Billshop Palette from the Default Palette menu in the Movie Properties dialog box. This will have Director automatically use the custom palette that was created when we originally imported the images for The Billionaire's Shop. This palette was already added to the palette channel when we dragged the car Cast member to the Stage. We will not change this, but explicitly making this setting makes the presence of the Billshop palette in the Score unnecessary unless we also intend to use other custom palettes at different points in the Score.**

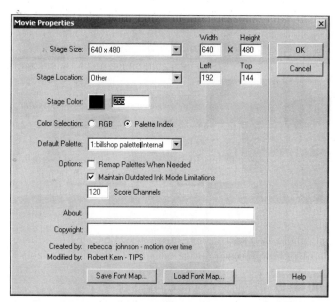

**FIGURE 3.51** *The Movie Properties dialog box with black selected for the Stage color and the default palette set to Billshop Palette.*

5.    Click the button labeled OK. This will close the Movie Properties dialog box.

## ADDING THE SPRITES FOR THE BILLIONAIRE'S SHOP OPENING ANIMATION TO THE STAGE

1.    Click and Drag Cast Member 2 (the background) directly to frame 1, channel 1, of the Score. When this member is dragged directly to the Score, the sprite it creates will appear at the exact center of the Stage. Because this is the background image and is intended to cover the stage from end to end, it serves us perfectly. Sprites that are created by dragging a member directly to the Stage will be positioned wherever you release the mouse.

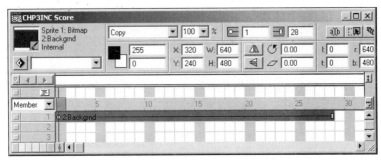

FIGURE 3.52 *The sprite information area at the upper left of the Score.*

NOTE    If you accidentally miss frame 1, channel 1, you can drag the sprite object
        you created to the correct position by moving the pointer over the selected
        sprite object in the Score and clicking and dragging to the correct position.

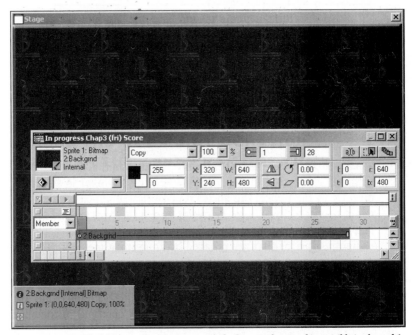

FIGURE 3.53 *The background on the Stage with the Score and sprite object visible in channel 1.*

2.    **Drag Cast Member 3 (the car) from the Cast to the center left
      side of the Stage.**

> When an image that uses a custom palette is dragged into a presentation, **NOTE** the palette is automatically placed in the Palette channel of the Score. If the effects channels of the Score are not currently visible, you can click the Hide/Show Effects Channels button on the right side of the Score (see figure 3.05). The palette channel is the second channel from the top of the Score.

3.  **Drag Cast Member 4 (the dollar loop) from the Cast to the upper right side of the Stage.**

4.  **Drag Cast Member 5 (the mansion) from the Cast to the lower center of the Stage.**

5.  **Drag Cast Member 6 (the airplane) from the Cast to the lower right side of the Stage next to the mansion.**

6.  **Drag Cast Member 7 (the yacht) from the Cast to the upper left side of the Stage above the car.**

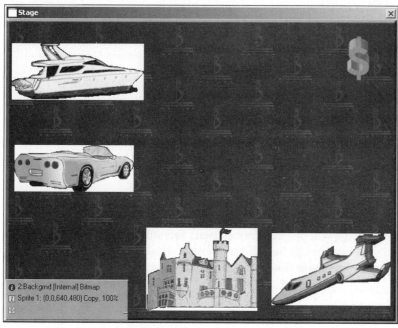

**FIGURE 3.54** *Cast members at their starting positions.*

## CHANGING THE INK EFFECTS FOR THE SPRITES TO BACKGROUND TRANSPARENT

Our next step is to change the ink effects for all of the sprites to Background Transparent. The ink effect of the sprites currently on the Stage is set to Copy, which we learned earlier means that there is no special treatment applied to the sprite, so the sprite looks the same as the Cast member that was used to create it. So far we have changed the ink effect of only individual sprites. We can change the ink effect of multiple sprites by selecting and modifying them together.

1.  **Drag Select all of the sprite objects currently in the Score. This includes channels 1 to 6 in the Score. You can drag-select them by clicking an area of the Score that does not contain a sprite object and dragging up and to the left to enclose all of the sprites in the selection rectangle. All of the sprites will highlight when they are selected.**

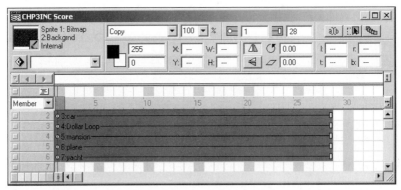

**FIGURE 3.55** *The selected sprites in channels 2 through 6.*

2.  **Choose Background Transparent from the Ink pull-down menu at the top of the Score. All of the white areas of the sprites on the Stage will become transparent. You will be able to see the background image behind the Icons of Wealth on the Stage. Next we will animate the sprites using their paths.**

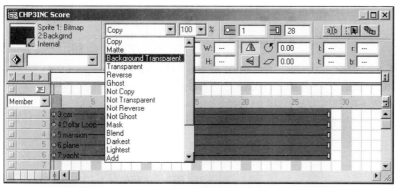

**FIGURE 3.56** *Background Transparent being selected from the Ink pull-down menu.*

## ANIMATING THE SPRITE PATHS

Currently all of the sprites on the Stage will remain in the same position while the movie is playing. We would like the Icons of Wealth to move across the Stage; furthermore, we would like to have them move along curved paths. We can do this easily by extending their sprite paths and using the tweening method we worked with earlier.

1. Move the playback head to frame 1. This will help to make the images on these pages consistent with what you see on your screen.

2. Click directly on the car sprite on the Stage. The sprite overlay for the car will appear.

3. Click and drag the sprite path for the car across the Stage. Use figure 3.57 as a reference.

4. Repeat steps 2 and 3 above for the mansion, plane, yacht, and dollar-loop sprites. Use figure 3.58 as a reference. When you have finished placing the sprites and extending their paths, we will preview the animation.

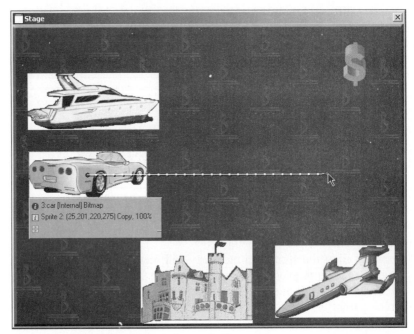

**FIGURE 3.57** *Sprite 2's path dragged across the Stage.*

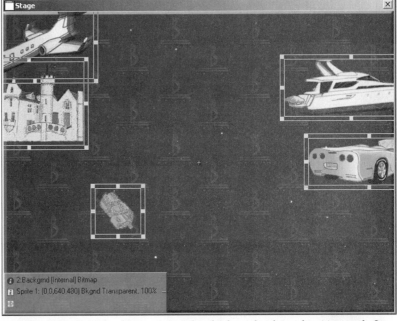

**FIGURE 3.58** *The paths of Sprites 2, 3, 4, 5, and 6 dragged to their end positions on the Stage.*

5.  Play the movie. All five of the Icons of Wealth will now animate along their paths. The dollar-loop sprite will spin as it animates across the screen.

6.  Stop the movie.

## MAKING A TEMPO SETTING

Now we will add a tempo setting to the movie that will cause the movie to play at the same rate on any machine The Billionaire's Shop is played on. Keeping consistent with the theatrical metaphor that Director's interface is based upon, frame rates in the Score are called *tempo settings*, just as the playing speed of a musical score for a movie or other theatrical presentation is called the tempo. Director can play movies at any speed up to 500 frames per second. Part of what determines the actual speed playback is the complexity of the animation and the capability of the computer that the movie is playing on. The animation that we are creating will play best at 15 frames per second, so in this session we will set the speed of the presentation to that setting. This will ensure that the movie will play no faster than 15 frames per second on any computer.

1.  Make the effects channels of the Score visible. The effects channels of your Score might already be open. If not, then click on the Show/Hide Effects Channels button on the right side of the Score. The tempo channel is at the top of the effects channels and is labeled with a small clock icon.

2.  Double-click frame 1 of the tempo channel. This will open the Tempo Settings dialog box. You can use this window to set the speed of the movie or a period of delay before proceeding. We will explore the available settings in the Tempo Settings dialog box in upcoming sessions throughout the chapters of this book. Right now we are interested in the actual playback frame rate.

3.  Drag the Frame Rate slide bar to a setting of 15 frames per second (fps). You can also use the arrows next to the number that represents the frame rate to change the tempo one fps at a time.

Tempo channel
  Palette channel                          Hide/Show Effects Channels button
  Transition channel

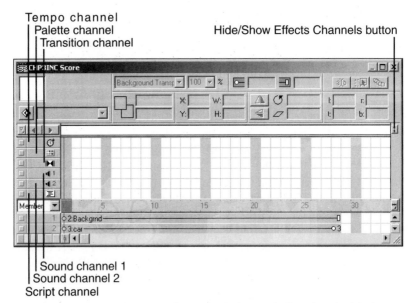

Sound channel 1
Sound channel 2
Script channel

**FIGURE 3.59** *The top of the Score. Arrows identify the special effects channels of the Score. Each effects channel is labeled, as is the Hide/Show Effects Channels button.*

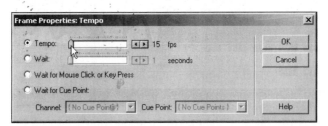

**FIGURE 3.60** *The Tempo Settings dialog box. The pointer is over the drag bar for the tempo settings.*

4.  **Click the button labeled OK. This will close the Frame Properties: Tempo dialog box and leave a setting at frame 1 of the tempo channel. The thumbnail at the top left of the Score will present the current tempo setting.**

NOTE     You can place multiple tempo settings in any one Director movie. This allows you to accommodate different presentations without being concerned about whether they are all designed to play at the same frame rate.

Next we will enhance the opening animation by moving the endpoints of the sprites' paths past the edges of the Stage. This will make the sprites appear to enter the Stage from an offstage location as opposed to suddenly appearing at their first position.

## MOVING THE ENDPOINTS OF THE ANIMATION PATHS OFF THE STAGE

Director's Stage has wings, just like a real-world stage, which means that something can be present in the presentation, but not visible to the viewer because it is off one of the Stage's sides, in the wings. This can be used to enhance a presentation by having sprites enter or leave by passing the Stage's edges. In this session we will drag the endpoints of the Icons of Wealth sprites so that they animate on and off the Stage.

1.   If the toolbar is currently visible, close it. You can do this by choosing Window>Toolbar. Removing the toolbar from the display area will make it easier to move the sprites that are near the top of the Stage. If you are using a monitor that is larger than your Stage's display area, then you do not need to follow this step because the toolbar does not interfere with the Stage.

2.   Click directly on the cell in frame 1, channel 2, of the Score. This is the car sprite. This will select only this keyframe on this sprite. This is very important for this procedure, because we only want to move the very first point of the animation. If we highlight the entire sprite object, we will move the entire animation path.

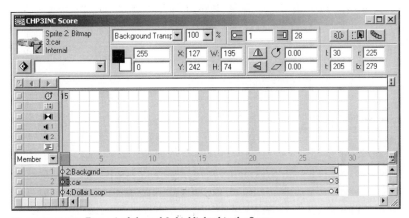

**FIGURE 3.61** *Frame 1 of channel 2, highlighted in the Score.*

**NOTE**   You can only highlight a single cell along a sprite object if it is a keyframe. These are the frames that contain a circle or the very end of a sprite object, which might contain a rectangle. Clicking on any cell in a sprite object that contains part of the connecting line between keyframes will result in highlighting the entire sprite object.

3.   Using the arrow keys on your keyboard, nudge the sprite completely off the edge of the Stage. When a sprite is selected in the Score, you can use the arrow keys to move the sprite one pixel at a time. Because we have already positioned the sprites as close to the edges as we could by using the mouse pointer, we must use the arrow keys to move them completely off. By selecting only the very first cell of the sprite object, we will only move that one point on the sprite's path. Note that the entire sprite object path changes relative to the location of the first keyframe on the Stage.

4.   Click directly on the cell in frame 28 of channel 2 of the Score. This is the last point on the animation path of the sprite object in the channel.

5.   Using the arrow keys on your keyboard, nudge the sprite completely off the edge of the Stage. Now this sprite will move on and off the Stage.

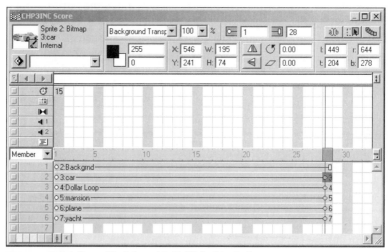

**FIGURE 3.62** *Frame 28 of channel 2, highlighted in the Score.*

6.  Repeat steps 2 through 5 above for sprites 3, 4, 5, and 6. This will move the starting and ending points for all of the remaining sprite objects off the Stage.

7.  Choose Window>Toolbar. This is an optional step that will reopen the toolbar if it is currently closed.

8.  Play the movie and then stop it. All of the Icons of Wealth should animate on and off the Stage. Now we will further enhance the animation by changing their entry and exit points in time.

## CHANGING THE EXIT POINTS FOR THE ICONS OF WEALTH SPRITES

Currently all of the sprites in our animation enter and leave the Stage simultaneously. We can make a much more interesting animation if the sprites enter at different points in time. The nature of the Score allows us to edit when a sprite enters and leaves a presentation very easily. First we will edit the exit points for the animations.

1.  Click directly on frame 28, channel 2 in the Score. This is the endpoint of the animation path for the sprite object in channel 2 (the car).

2.  While holding the mouse button, drag the endpoint to frame 40 in the Score. The entire sprite object extends along with where you drag the endpoint. This sprite will still animate along the same path on the Stage, but it will now take 40 frames to reach the end of the animation instead of 28. The other sprites in the animation will have completed their animations and will no longer be visible when the playback head reaches frame 28. The sprite in frame 2 will still have a few frames to go.

3.  Repeat steps 1 and 2 above for sprites 3, 4, 5, and 6, dragging their endpoints to frames 50, 35, 55, and 45, respectively.

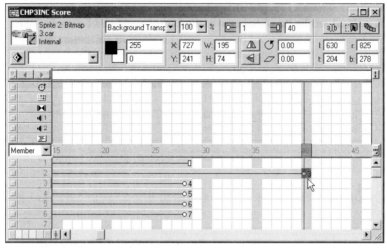

**FIGURE 3.63** *Sprite 2's endpoint being dragged to frame 40.*

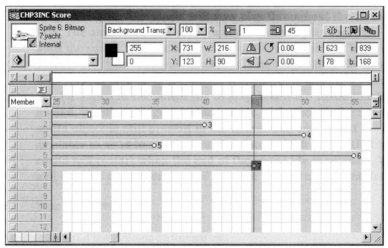

**FIGURE 3.64** *The endpoints for sprites 3 through 6 dragged to the positions indicated in step 3 above.*

**NOTE**   When you alter the length of a sprite object, the path on Stage will also alter to reflect the number of frames that the sprite object passes through. This means that if a sprite object is extended, there will be more dots along its animation path; if the sprite object is shortened, then there will be fewer dots.

4. **Play the movie. You can see now that the animation paths remain the same, but some of the sprites are taking longer than others to reach the end of their animation paths. The sprites also make their exits at different times. Now we will edit when the sprites enter the animation. Notice also that the background disappears when the playback head passes frame 28. This is because this sprite needs to be extended to the end of the animation.**

5. **Stop the movie.**

## EXTENDING THE BACKGROUND SPRITE OBJECT

Currently the background sprite object is only present up to frame 28. If we want the background to be visible for the duration of the animation, we will need to extend its endpoint to the end of the animation in the Score.

1. **Click directly on the cell in frame 28 of channel 1. This is the endpoint for the background sprite.**

2. **Drag the endpoint for the sprite object in channel 1 to frame 55 in channel 1. Now the background will remain on Stage until the last of the Icons of Wealth reach the end of their animations. Now we will modify the entry points for the Icons of Wealth.**

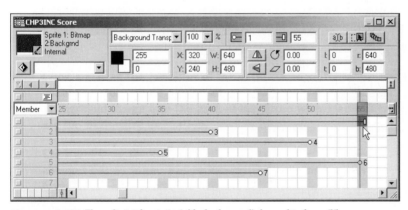

**FIGURE 3.65** *The endpoint for sprite 1 (the background) dragged to frame 55.*

## CHANGING THE ENTRY POINTS FOR THE ICONS OF WEALTH SPRITES

The sprites all now leave the Stage at different times, but they still enter the presentation simultaneously. We can drag the starting point of a sprite object just as we can the endpoint, which allows us to quickly and easily alter when a sprite appears.

1.  **Click directly on the cell in frame 1 of channel 2. This is the starting point of the car sprite.**

2.  **Holding the mouse button down, drag the starting point of the sprite object in channel 2 to frame 5. Now this sprite will not appear until the playback head reaches frame 5.**

3.  **Repeat steps 1 and 2 above for sprites 3, 4, 5, and 6 as follows:**

    Sprite 3: Leave unchanged

    Sprite 4: Drag to frame 5

    Sprite 5: Drag to frame 15

    Sprite 6: Drag to frame 10.

    **Now all of the sprites will enter the Stage at different points in time (see figure 3.66).**

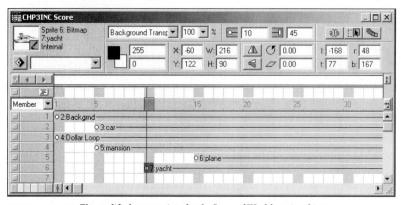

**FIGURE 3.66** *The modified entry points for the Icons of Wealth sprite objects.*

4.  **Play the movie. The animation is a bit more interesting now. The Icons of Wealth now enter and leave the Stage at different points, and they also move at different rates of speed.**

5.  **Stop the movie.**

We have completed the first part of the opening animation.

## DUPLICATING THE ANIMATION

In the completed version of this lesson, the sprites in the animation passed across the Score twice, each time along a different path. Next we will duplicate the animation that we have created, then we will modify the animations so that all of the sprites travel along different paths. An important and powerful feature of the Score is the ability to copy and paste existing animations. This allows us to quickly reproduce work, saving time and energy. In this session we will add a duplicate of our existing animation further along in the Score, then we will change the entry and exit points of the duplicate animation to make it slightly different.

1.   **Click and drag a selection around the sprite objects in channels 2 through 6 in the Score. Be careful not to include the background in channel 1. The sprites in channels 2 through 6 become highlighted. We can also shift-click to select multiple sprites just as we were able to select multiple Cast members.**

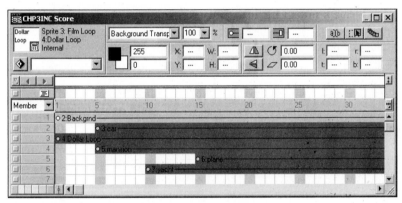

**FIGURE 3.67** *The sprites in channels 2 through 6 selected in the Score.*

2.   **Copy the animation. You can accomplish this by choosing Edit>Copy Sprites or by clicking the Copy button on the toolbar. Either of these methods will copy these sprites in their current position to your system software's Clipboard. The Clipboard serves as a temporary storage location that will retain the last item copied. You can then paste the item using the Paste command. Each time the Copy command is used in a program, it replaces the content of the Clipboard with the newly copied item.**

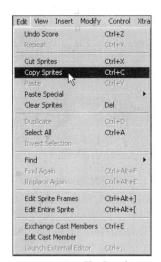

**FIGURE 3.68** *The Copy button on the toolbar and the menu selection Edit>Copy in a composite image.*

**NOTE**   Dragging and selecting multiple sprites in the Score can also be accomplished by dragging and selecting multiple sprites directly on the Stage.

3.   **Click directly on frame 60 of channel 2. This will move the playback head to frame 60. Now we will paste a new copy of the sprites from the animation we created earlier.**

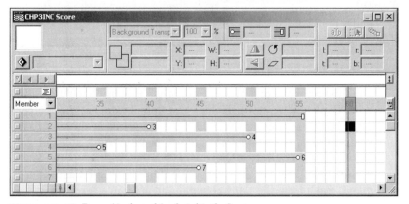

**FIGURE 3.69** *Frame 60, channel 2 selected in the Score.*

4.  **Paste the sprites into the Score. We can accomplish this by choosing Edit>Paste, or by clicking the Paste button on the toolbar. After the sprites are pasted, they will appear on the Stage and in the Score, but the Background image will no longer be visible. We will correct this shortly.**

> When sprites are pasted into the Score, they will appear from the first point selected in the Score. By selecting a cell in channel 2, we ensure that the duplicate will appear in channels 2 through 6.                    **NOTE**

So far we have learned that we can reuse animations in other locations in the Score. We have also learned that we can have different objects in the same channels of the Score at different points in time.

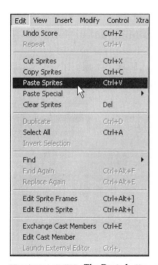

**FIGURE 3.70** *The Paste button on the toolbar and the menu selection Edit>Paste Sprites.*

> If you attempt to paste sprites into frames that are already occupied, you will be presented with the Paste Options dialog box. These options will allow you to determine how you would like the new sprites to be incorporated into the Score.                    **NOTE**

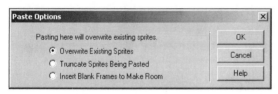

**FIGURE 3.71** *The Paste Options dialog box.*

The Paste Options dialog box will give you three options for how to paste sprites into frames that are already occupied. Overwrite Existing Sprites will replace the sprites in the selected cells with the new sprites; Truncate Sprites Being Pasted will paste sprites only in the unoccupied area of the selected area of the Score; and Insert Blank Frames To Make Room will divide the sprites that are currently in the Score, placing one-half before the pasted sprites and the other half after the pasted sprites.

## SCROLLING AND ZOOMING IN THE SCORE

After pasting the second set of sprites, you will find that you can no longer see the end of the animation all at once in the Score. You can scroll the Score left or right to see Score elements that occur at different points in time. You can also zoom into the Score, which will reduce or increase the display area of the Score.

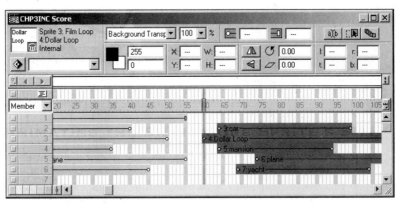

**FIGURE 3.72** *The Score zoomed at 75%.*

An arrow identifies the Zoom pull-down menu. Click and drag this box to view different areas of the Score. Another arrow identifies the Center Current Frame button with the copy: The Center Current Frame button will send you over to the frame in which the playback head is currently located.

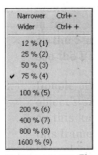

**FIGURE 3.73** *The selected Zoom pull-down menu.*

## CHANGING THE ENTRY POINTS FOR THE DUPLICATE SPRITES

By adding the duplicate of the animation later in the Score, we have extended the animation. Now let's change some of the entry points of the new sprites so that they appear when the sprites of the earlier parts of the animation disappear.

1.   Drag the entry point for the sprite object in channel 2, frame 64, to channel 2, frame 45. This will cause this sprite object to appear earlier in the animation. We will leave the entry point for the sprite object in channel 3 as it is and continue with the sprite object in channel 4.

2.   Drag the entry point for the sprite object in channel 4, frame 64, to channel 4, frame 50. This will cause this sprite to appear earlier in the animation, but still after the sprite in channel 2. We will skip channel 5 and continue with channel 6.

3.   Drag the entry point for the sprite object in channel 6, frame 69, to channel 6, frame 55.

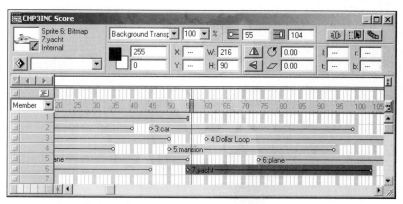

**FIGURE 3.74** *The Score detailing the modified entry points for the duplicate sprite objects.*

4.   Play the movie. Some of the second animation sprites enter the Stage while the sprites from the earlier part of the animation are still visible. However, the background disappears when the playback head passes frame 55.

5.   Stop the movie.

## ADDING THE BACKGROUND TO THE DUPLICATE ANIMATION

Next we will correct the disappearing background issue. We have already learned that we can drag an endpoint to extend a sprite in the Score. We can save a few steps by using another option, called Extend Sprite, under the Modify menu. We can also directly insert frame numbers for a sprite in the Start Frame and End Frame boxes on the Score.

**FIGURE 3.75** *Modify>Extend Sprite button.*

**FIGURE 3.76** *The Start Frame and End Frame Sprite fields on the Score.*

1.  Click on the background image, the sprite in channel 1, at the beginning of the Score. Make certain that you highlight the entire sprite object.

2.  Scroll forward in the Score and click the frame bar at frame 114. It is important that you click on the frame bar and not on a cell in the Score. This way the sprite object in channel 1 will remain highlighted. If you click elsewhere in the Score, you will highlight that part of the Score and deselect the sprite in channel 1. Now only the playback head will move over to frame 114.

3.  **Choose Modify>Extend Sprite. Now the background sprite will extend to the end of the animation.**

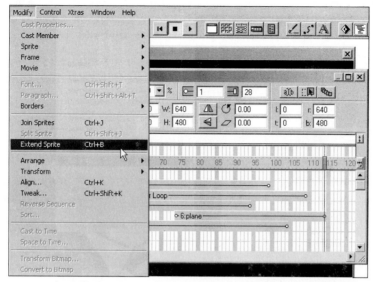

**FIGURE 3.77** *The Score set up to extend the background to frame 114. Modify>Extend Sprite is selected from the menus.*

4.  **Play the movie. The background is now visible throughout the animation.**

5.  **Stop the movie.**

## ANIMATING THE SPRITES ALONG CURVED PATHS

Next we will enhance the animation by adding curves to the sprites' paths. Extending a sprite object's path produces an animation that brings the sprite directly from the first point to the last point. While this can serve many purposes, there are also times in which you might want a sprite to travel a more irregular path, such as with the flight of a butterfly or the falling of a leaf from a tree. Earlier we learned that we can modify the path of a sprite directly on the Stage so that it travels along a curved path. In this exercise we will modify the paths of the Icons of Wealth so that they travel along curved paths.

1.  **Click on the first sprite located in channel 2 of the Score. Be certain that you have selected the entire sprite object by clicking on an area that contains a line and not a circle. You can also click**

directly on the sprite on Stage. Once the sprite is selected, its animation path is visible.

2.  Hold down the Option key (Macintosh) or the Alt key (Windows). We will use the Option/Alt key to drag the points on the sprite's animation paths to new locations on the Stage.

3.  Click and drag the fifth dot along the sprite's path to a new location. The change will result in the modification of the sprite's path.

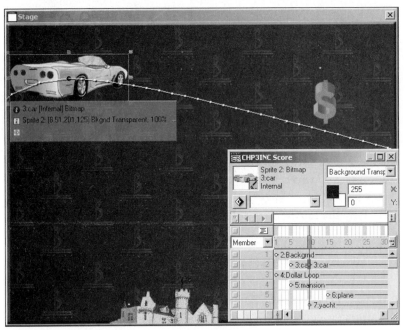

**FIGURE 3.78** *Fifth dot on Sprite 2's animation path being dragged. An arrow shows the path of drag from the original location to the destination point.*

Also visible in figure 3.78 is the sprite object in the Score. You can see the new keyframe in channel 5. When a point on a sprite's path is moved, it becomes a circle in the Score to let you know where the change has taken place.

4.  Use the Option (Macintosh) or Alt (Windows) key to click and drag the 20th dot along the sprite path to a new location. Drag this point in the opposite direction of the first point you dragged; this will produce a curve in the opposite direction. If you drag

the point in the same direction as the first point, it will result in a more exaggerated curve in one direction.

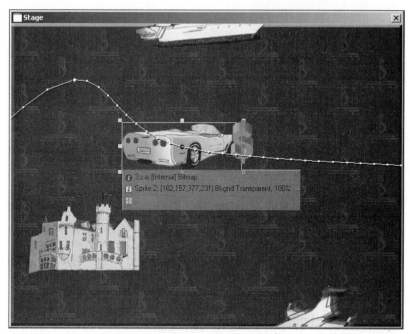

**FIGURE 3.79** *The 20th dot on Sprite 2's animation path being dragged.*

5. **Repeat steps 1 through 6 above for remaining sprites in the animation.**

Move two or more points along each sprite's path. It isn't important which points you move. Remember that there are two sprites in each channel, so there are a total of 9 more sprite paths to modify. You can select multiple sprites and edit their paths on Stage, or you can work with each one at a time, whatever is your preference. If you accidentally deselect the sprite, just reselect it in the Score or on the Stage, and its path will reappear. When you have finished modifying the sprite paths, play the movie to preview your results. Our next step is to add loops to the animation paths.

Figure 3.80 shows the first set of sprites on Stage in the intro animation. They are all selected, so their paths are all visible. The beginning of the score is also visible, so the highlighted sprite objects are also visible.

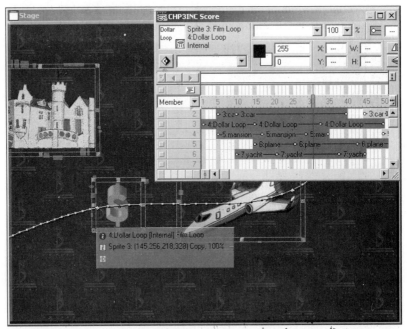

**FIGURE 3.80** *The curved paths of the intro animation in The Billionaire's Shop completed project.*

## CREATING A LOOPED PATH

In the completed version of this lesson, we saw that some of the sprites looped in their animation paths. This can be accomplished by crossing the points of an animation path on the Stage. We will use the first instance of the car animation as an example of how to accomplish this.

1. Select the first car sprite that appears on the Stage and in the Score. This sprite is located toward the beginning of the Score in channel 2.

2. Hold down the Option (Macintosh) or Alt (Windows) key.

3. Click on one of the points toward the beginning of the car sprite's path on the Stage.

4. Drag the point at an angle away from the sprite's path. This will produce a curved path toward the point that is dragged.

5. Click on a point toward the end of the car sprite's path and drag this point toward and past the first point. By dragging beyond the first point, we will force the animation path to become a loop that crosses over all of the points in this sequence.

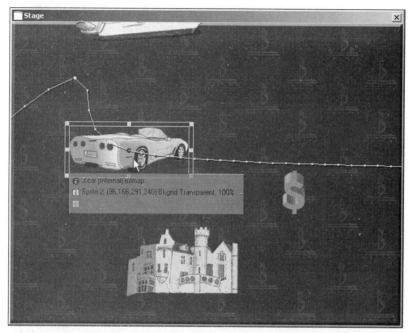

**FIGURE 3.81** *A point on a single sprite's animation path being dragged at an angle away from the sprite's path.*

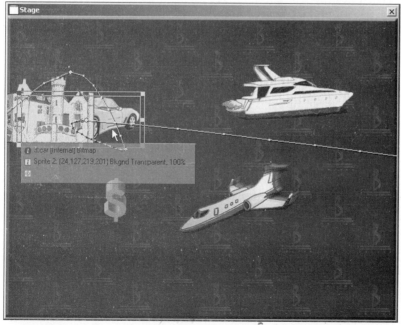

**FIGURE 3.82** *The second point being dragged past the first point to produce a loop.*

6.  Play the movie. You will see that the car sprite will animate along a loop on the Stage. You can modify other sprites in the opening animation using this technique as well.

7.  Stop the movie.

### ADDING A MARKER TO THE SCORE

A useful feature of Director's Score is the ability to label different areas so that they are easy to identify with a glance. Next, we will label this area of the Score. These labels are called *markers* and are added simply by clicking toward the top of the Score and typing the chosen name. We will now add a marker to the opening animation.

1.  Click anywhere in the white marker display area between the effects channels and the data display area of the Score. An inverted triangle will appear with a text entry area immediately to the right. The text area will read New Marker.

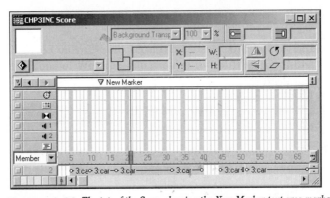

**FIGURE 3.83** *The top of the Score showing the New Marker text area marker.*

2.  Type the word Intro. This now becomes the name of the marker.

3.  Drag the marker to frame 1 of the Score. The animation begins in frame 1, so this is where we want our marker. A marker can be moved to any point in time in the Score whenever you choose. To remove a marker, click and drag the marker above or below the marker display area. Next we will add a command to the end of the animation that will cause it to loop.

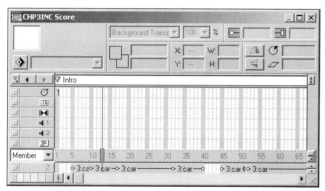

**FIGURE 3.84** *The top of the Score. The new marker has been relabeled Intro and has been dragged to the beginning of the Score.*

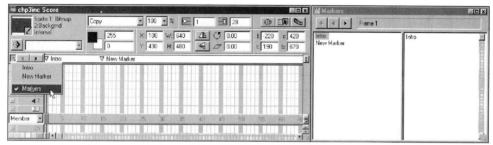

**FIGURE 3.85** *The open markers menu. Any markers that are added to the Score are also added to the markers menu at the upper left of the Score.*

## INTRODUCING THE BEHAVIOR INSPECTOR TO LOOP THE ANIMATION

The *behavior inspector* is a simple Lingo script generator that is used to add scripts to a movie in a very quick and intuitive manner by allowing you to choose settings as opposed to creating your own scripts from scratch. This means that you can add Lingo to a presentation without typing a single line of code! The behavior inspector allows you to choose a combination of settings, save that combination with a name, and reapply it elsewhere if appropriate. The settings are based on selecting an *event* (the action that will activate the behavior, such as a mouse click or a keypress) and an *action* (the result produced by the behavior, such as moving a sprite or playing a sound). Each event can have multiple actions associated with it. One or more of these event-action groups are what define a behavior. Basically, the behavior inspector has made Lingo programming, which was once considered advanced in proficiency, easy for an absolute beginner to add to their presentations. We will do more in-depth work with Lingo in the upcoming chapters. For now, let's look at how simple using the behavior inspector is for adding a looping script to a presentation.

The intro animation repeats because of a temporary setting that we have in Director's control panel. When we deliver a presentation as a projector, we must use Lingo scripts to control the playback head. If we don't, then the movie will simply end when the last frame of the score is reached. We can use the behavior inspector's scriptless authoring capability to add a behavior that will tell the playback head to return to the beginning of the animation. Our first step is to deactivate the loop setting in the control panel.

1.    **If the control panel is not currently open, open it. You can open the control panel by choosing Window>Control.**

2.    **Click to deselect the Loop Playback button on the control panel. Now the presentation will end when the last frame is reached.**

3.    **Play the movie. When the animation reaches the last frame of the Score, the playback head will stop. This is how the presentation would have played had we packaged this movie into a projector for playback on a computer that does not have Director installed. The movie has stopped, so it is not necessary to click the Stop button. Now we will add the loop behavior.**

4.    **If the effects channels of the Score are not currently visible, then click the Hide/Show Effects Channels button on the right side of the Score. See figure 3.59 for the location of the Hide/Show Effects Channels button.**

5.    **Click directly in frame 114 of the Script channel. This will highlight frame 114 of the script channel. The script channel is the first channel above the frame bar. Frame 114 is the last frame of the animation.**

6.    **Click the Behavior Inspector button at the top of the Score. This will open the Behavior Inspector window.**

Window
  ↳ Inspector
       ↳ Behavior

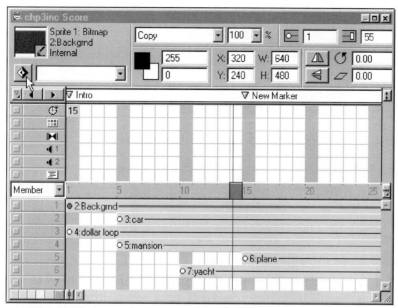

**FIGURE 3.86** *The Score with the cursor identifying the Behavior Inspector button.*

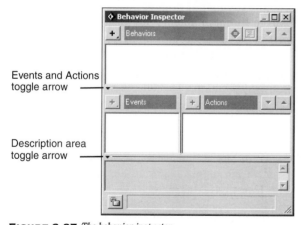

**FIGURE 3.87** *The behavior inspector.*

Figure 3.87 exhibits the Behavior, Action, and Event pull-down menus. Labels identify the toggle arrows that can be used to make the lower parts of the behavior inspector visible. The upper arrow is used to expand and collapse the event and action areas. The lower arrow is used to expand and collapse the behavior description area.

7.   **Choose New Behavior from the + button at the upper left of the behavior inspector. This will open the dialog box that will allow you to name your new behavior.**

**FIGURE 3.88** *The selected Behaviors pull-down menu, with New Behavior selected.*

8.  **Name the behavior Loop Back, then click OK. The name is actu-
    ally just an identifier for you. You can name the behavior any-
    thing you want; it will work just the same. Generally, it's a good
    idea to name behaviors after what they are intended to accom-
    plish, for organizational and clarity purposes. Now that we have
    named the behavior, we can add features to it.**

**FIGURE 3.89** *The Name Behavior dialog box with Loop Back typed in the Behavior
Name text-entry area.*

9.  **If the lower part (event and action areas) of the behavior inspec-
    tor is not visible, click the toggle arrow on the middle left of the
    behavior inspector (see figure 3.87).**

10. **Click on the + button next to the Event menu. An event is some-
    thing, such as a mouse click or key press, that occurs in Director
    that activates a script. For example, Mouse Down will activate a
    script when the mouse button is pressed. Because the behavior
    that we are creating should activate when the playback head
    passes through frame 114, we will use Exit Frame as an event.**

11. **Choose Exit Frame. The new event is added to the event area of
    the behavior inspector. Now you can associate an action with
    this event.**

**FIGURE 3.90** *The selected + button in the Event menu, with Exit Frame selected.*

You can add one of each event in the Event pull-down menu to each behavior. You can add any appropriate combination of actions under the Actions menu. This results in a great deal of flexibility in each behavior. **NOTE**

12. **Click on the Actions pop-up menu.**

13. **Choose Navigation>Go to Marker.... The Specify Marker pull-down menu appears.**

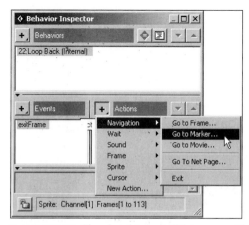

**FIGURE 3.91** *The selected Action pull-down menu with Navigation>Go to Marker selected.*

14.  **Choose Intro from the Specify Marker menu.**

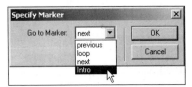

**FIGURE 3.92** *The Specify Marker dialog box with Intro selected.*

15.  **Click OK. Our loop behavior is created!**

16.  **Close the behavior inspector.**

17.  **Highlight frame 114 of the script channel right above the frame bar. Our next step is to add the script to frame 114 of the script channel.**

18.  **Choose Loop Back from the Behavior pull-down menu at the top of the Score. This will place the Loop Back behavior into frame 114 of the script channel.**

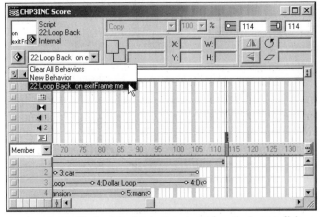

**FIGURE 3.93** *The Loop Back behavior selected from the Script pull-down menu at the top of the Score.*

19.  **Play the movie. Now we can test our work so far. When the playback head reaches frame 114, it will jump back to the marker labeled Intro. Our new behavior works. We added Lingo without typing a single line of code!**

20.  **Stop the movie.**

We will work more with Lingo in later lessons. First there is much more to learn about animation and other presentation methods in Director, such as the use of digital video. In the next chapter we will work with synchronizing animations to sound files.

## SUMMARY

Animating sprites is accomplished in a variety of ways. The most direct is dragging the sprite's path from the center of the sprite to the destination of the animation. The sprite's path is part of the sprite overlay and is represented by a dot at the center of the sprite on the Stage.

This extended sprite path automatically results in a direct line from the starting point of the animation to the endpoint. We can add detail to the sprite's path, such as curves and loops, by holding down the Option (Macintosh) or Alt (Windows) key and dragging points along the path to different positions on the Stage. The sprite's path will alter to accommodate the new positions.

A sprite's path can also be edited by selecting the desired sprite and changing settings in the Sprite Tweening dialog box. For example, the Sprite Tweening dialog box can be used to determine the extremity of curves that are added to a sprite's path. The Sprite Tweening dialog box can be accessed by choosing Modify>Sprite>Tweening.

There are two other methods for animating sprites besides directly editing a sprite's path. Step recording allows us to create an animation frame by frame, and real-time recording allows us to create an animation by recording the movements that we make moving a sprite on the Stage. These methods can be used to create irregular animation paths, such as the flight of a butterfly or the falling of a leaf.

We can use all of the mentioned methods for animating sprites to change the position of a sprite on the Stage over time. In chapter 4 we will learn that we can also use these techniques to animate the size of a sprite over time. The only aspect of a sprite's dimension that cannot be directly animated is rotation. To animate a sprite's rotation, we must create a series of Cast members that depict different stages of the sprite's rotation. These must then be grouped together into a Cast member type called a film loop. We used the Cast-to-Time command to bring multiple sprites to the Stage simultaneously to generate the animation that we later grouped into a film-loop Cast member, using the Film Loop command from the Insert menu.

We created the sequence of images that we used for the film loop with the Auto Distort command in the Paint window. We first defined the degree of rotation of the dollar image using the Free Rotate tool in the Paint window. Then we used Auto Distort to define the number of new Cast members we wanted to use to create the sequence of rotated Cast members.

Placement and management of Cast members is a critical aspect of authoring using Director. The Cast members in a movie can change and multiply just through the use of standard Director tools, such as Auto Distort. Taking the time to rearrange the Cast to keep like members together will save time and energy in the development process.

We briefly worked with the behavior inspector, which allows us to automatically generate Lingo scripts to a movie without requiring knowledge of Lingo programming. The behavior inspector provides us with commonly used Lingo scripts that are useful for authors who are beginners; it permits them to add simple interactive elements, such as buttons, to their Director movies without advanced knowledge of Lingo. This feature of Director is called *scriptless authoring* and will be covered at greater length in upcoming chapters, particularly chapter 6.

## QUESTIONS

1. Does a film loop require the presence of the Cast members used to create it? Explain.

2. What are the dots that appear along a sprite's path?

3. Can the number of dots that appear along a sprite's path be changed? How would this be accomplished? Why would this be useful? And what are the results that would be generated if this were possible?

4. What is the procedure required to generate a step recording, and what is the result of using this technique?

5. What is the procedure required to generate a real-time recording? What is the result of using this technique?

6. What is the procedure required to generate a rotating animation using a film loop?

## EXERCISES

1. Create an animation of three sprites using the sprites' paths.

2. Create an animation, using step recording, of the car sprite moving in a circle.

3. Create a film loop of the car rotating.

# CHAPTER 4

# USING SOUND AND SYNCHRONIZING ANIMATION TO AUDIO

# 4 Using Sound and Synchronizing Animation to Audio

**In this chapter, you will learn how to:**

- Animate a sprite's size
- Add a sound to the Score
- Create a custom behavior
- Use the cuePassed event to synchronize sounds to animations
- Access a behavior's Lingo scripts
- Add a transition to the Score
- Control script coloring

Sound is an important medium to use in any presentation. It can serve to entertain in place of animation, or to enhance it. Audio can be used also as an invaluable story-telling tool in the form of voiceovers, or as the audio track in digital video files. Sound can be used to add sound effects to a presentation, helping enhance buttons and other user interaction by providing audio feedback to the user along with any visual feedback. Overall, sound can be used to establish mood.

Sounds that are imported into Director can be added to either of the two sound channels in the effects channels of the Score. Sounds in the sound channels take the form of sprite objects, just like the image sprite objects we worked with in chapter 3. The major difference is that sounds in the Score are not visible on the Stage; they are only represented as sprite objects and will play in the frames that the sprite object occupies. You can drag the endpoints of sound sprite objects so that they extend across as many frames as desired.

A powerful feature of sound in Director is the use of *cue points*, which are labels within the sounds that can be used to synchronize the sound to animations and other activities in Director. Cue points are similar to the markers in the Score that we worked with in chapter 3, but they are added to the sound files in other applications, such as Macromedia's SoundEdit 16 (Macintosh) and Sonic Foundry's SoundForge (Windows). Cue points can be added at appropriate points in a sound, then you can use Lingo scripts to read the cue points as the sound plays through Director. For example, you can label when certain subjects are mentioned in a voiceover sound file and synchronize those cue points to animations that emphasize the mentioned subject.

In this chapter we will add a sound to the opening animation in The Billionaire's Shop. We will also add the part of the animation in which the Billionaire moves onto the screen. The distinguishing characteristic of this animation is that it occurs when the background music reaches a certain point. This is accomplished by using a Lingo script that instructs the playback head to jump to this animation when a cue point is reached in the background sound file. Although we will work more extensively with Lingo in later chapters, we must learn this very small bit of Lingo here to make use of this new and remarkably powerful feature of animation with audio synchronization in Director.

**NOTE**   To create sound files that contain cue points on the Macintosh, use Macromedia SoundEdit; to create sound files in Windows, use Sonic Foundry's SoundForge. Files created on either platform can be used in Director for Macintosh or Windows.

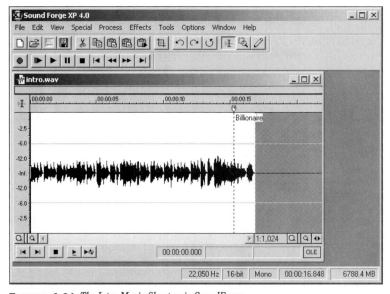

**FIGURE 4.01** *The Intro Music file open in SoundForge.*

## VIEWING THE COMPLETED FILE

1.  If it is not already open, launch Director and choose File>Open.

2.  Locate and select the file named Chp4cmp.dir, which is located on the CD-ROM in the directory Lessons/Chaptr4/Complete/ Chp4cmp.dir.

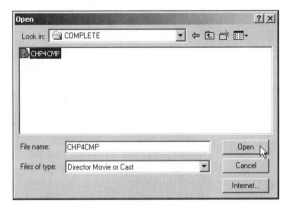

**FIGURE 4.02** *Locate and open the file named Chp4cmp.dir in the CD-ROM's directory Lessons/Chaptr4/Complete/Chp4cmp.dir.*

3.  Click Open.

4.  Play the movie.

This file contains the animation that we created in chapter 3, with the addition of music. When the music reaches a certain point, we see an animation of the Billionaire's face zooming toward us. The effect that has all of the Icons of Wealth dissolve away to be replaced by the Billionaire is called a *transition*. It is a visual effect that enhances the switch from one scene to another. We will add the audio file as well as the Billionaire animation. We will also learn how to add transitions to a presentation.

**NOTE**

In chapter 3 we learned several ways to play a Director presentation, such as the Play button on the toolbar or on the control panel, or using the following keyboard shortcuts: Command+Option+P (Macintosh) or Control+Alt+P (Windows). If we add the Shift key to either keyboard combination, any open windows in Director's interface will temporarily close. Command+Period (.) (Macintosh) or Control+Period (.) (Windows) will stop the presentation and reopen the temporarily closed windows in Director's interface.

### 5.    Stop the movie.

Now we will work with the partially completed file.

**FIGURE 4.03** *The Billionaire animation that we will create in this lesson.*

## OPENING THE PARTLY COMPLETED FILE

1.    **Choose File>Open and open the file named Chp4inc.dir, located in the directory Lessons/Starter/Chaptr4/ on the CD-ROM.**

The Open... dialog box will appear. You can use the starter file, or you can continue working with the file that you created and saved in chapter 3.

**NOTE**    Remember to save your work frequently because the end result of each lesson is the beginning of the next lesson. We have also supplied you with the partly completed version of each lesson on the CD-ROM so that you can work with the working copy of Director that is on the CD-ROM.

> Sound files that are in the Cast become platform independent. For      **NOTE**
> example, WAV files are designed specifically for Windows applications, so
> they must be imported into a Director movie that is running within the
> Windows operating system. This Director movie can then be transferred to
> Director on a Macintosh, where the sound file will play normally. Director
> effectively bridges the gap between platform-specific file types. In order for
> this to work properly, the sound Cast member cannot be an externally
> linked Cast member.

## SHOCKWAVE AUDIO

Shockwave is the technology developed by Macromedia that prepares multimedia and audio files to be used more effectively from a Web page on the Internet. This technology helps bridge the gap of low bandwidth over networks by using Shockwave compression and playback to keep file sizes small without harshly diminishing quality. Another benefit that Shockwave brings to the playback of multimedia files over the Internet is *streaming* capability, which means that the file will begin to play as soon as the first pieces of the file are downloaded from the network. This allows for a more immediate experience when viewing multimedia over a network, because we don't need to wait for the entire file to download before we hear or see it begin to play.

Local projects, like The Billionaire's Shop, do not need Shockwave, but projects that are local can take advantage of Shockwave compression by applying it to files that are to be downloaded for playback locally. For example, some of the updates for The Billionaire's Shop have Shockwave compression applied to them so that they are smaller and will require less time to reach The Billionaire's Shop from our Web site. There will be more on how to create Shockwave files and the different methods of playback for Director movies in chapter 11.

## ADDING SOUND TO THE OPENING ANIMATION

We can add sound to a presentation much the same way we have added images. We import the sound file, we can then drag the resulting Cast member to the Score, and then we can drag the sprite object to occupy the frames that we would like the sound to play in. In this session we will add a sound to the Intro animation.

1.     **Make the effects channels of the Score visible. The effects channels of your Score might already be open. If not, then click on the Show/Hide Effects Channels button on the right side of the Score (see figure 4.04).**

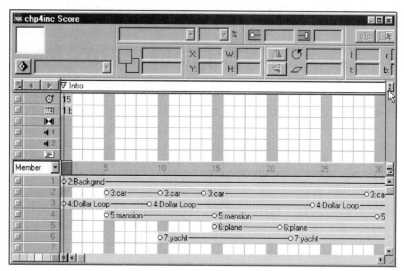

**FIGURE 4.04** *The Score, with the cursor identifying the Hide/Show Effects Channel button on the right side of the Score.*

2.   If the Cast window is not currently open, open it. You can use the Cast button on the toolbar or choose Window>Cast.

3.   Double-click on Cast member 10 (Intro Music) in the Cast. The Sound Cast Member Properties dialog box will open.

4.   Click the button labeled Play. This will play the Intro Music Cast member.

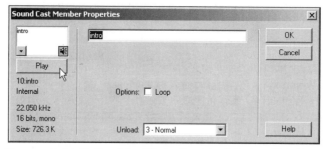

**FIGURE 4.05** *The Sound Cast Member Properties dialog box. Click the button labeled Play to preview the sound.*

5.   Click the button labeled OK. This will close the Sound Cast Member Properties dialog box.

6.  Drag Cast member 10 (Intro music) from the Cast directly to frame 1 of sound channel 1 in the Score. This will create a sprite object in sound channel 1 in the effects channels of the Score. The sprite object will span frames 1 through 28.

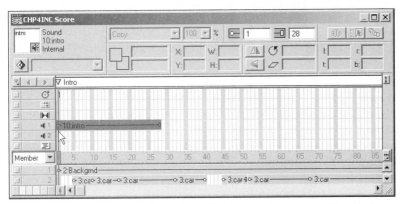

**FIGURE 4.06** *Sound Cast member 10 dragged into frame 1 of sound channel 1 in the Score.*

7.  Play the movie. The sound we have added to the Score will now play during the opening animation we created in chapter 3. When the playback head reaches frame 28, the sound ends abruptly because the playback head passes through frames that do not contain the sound. This lets us know that sound sprite objects must occupy all of the frames that we would like the sound to play in. Next we will extend the Intro sound sprite object to the end of the animation so that it will continue to play for the duration of the movie that we have created so far.

8.  Stop the movie.

## EXTENDING THE INTRO SOUND TO THE END OF THE ANIMATION

Now we will extend the sound sprite object so that it plays for the duration of the animation we created in chapter 3. Earlier we learned that a sound must be present in all of the frames that it is intended to play. The sound that we placed in sound channel 1 only plays through frame 28 because that is the last frame that it occupies. The rest of the animation occupies frames 1 through 114. In this session we will extend the sound sprite object in sound channel 1 so that it will play through to the end of the animation.

1.  Drag the endpoint of the sound sprite object in sound channel 1 to frame 114. The sound is now present in all of the frames that the animation occupies.

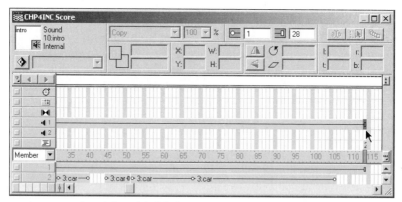

**FIGURE 4.07** *Sound channel 1 of the Score.*

2.  Play the movie. The music will now play throughout the animation. The animation and sound will continue to play together until the sound file reaches the end of the music in it. The animation will then continue because it is no longer than the sound file. This teaches us that a sound will only play as long as there is information in the sound file to play. When the sound reaches its end, it will no longer produce music, even though the sound sprite object is still present in the Score. One option that is available to us is to set the sound to loop, which means that the sound will restart when the end of the sound file is reached. We will use this option for a sound file that we will use in chapter 6.

3.  Stop the movie.

Now we will add the Billionaire animation.

## ADDING THE BILLIONAIRE ANIMATION

Our first step is to label the area of the Score where we will create the Billionaire animation. This label will help us keep track of where we are in the Score and can later be used in a behavior script to tell the playback head where to go.

1.  Click frame 120 in the Marker area of the Score. A marker appears with a flashing cursor beside it.

2.  Name the marker Billionaire. This is how we will identify where our new animation is located. Our next step is to extend the background and sound sprite objects so that they occupy the frames that the Billionaire animation will occupy.

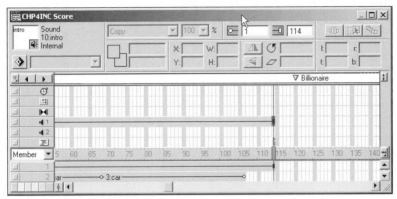

**FIGURE 4.08** *A marker added to frame 120 of the Score labeled Billionaire.*

## EXTENDING THE BACKGROUND AND SOUND SPRITE OBJECTS

By adding the background image and music to the area that the Billionaire animation will occupy, we will create a sense of continuity. The background will remain the same, while the images over the background change.

1.  Click and drag the endpoint of the background sprite object in channel 1 from frame 114 to frame 130. This will extend the background image into the area of the Score where we will create the Billionaire animation.

2.  Click and Drag the endpoint for the sound sprite object in sound channel 1 from frame 114 to frame 130. Now the sound will be heard in the area where we will locate the Billionaire animation. Now we will add the Billionaire images.

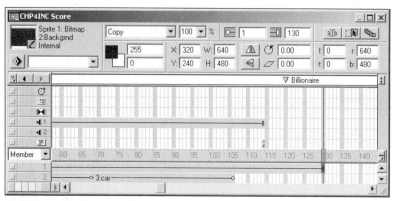

**FIGURE 4.09** *The extended background and sound sprite objects.*

## ADDING THE BILLIONAIRE ANIMATION

In the completed version of this lesson, the Icons of Wealth animation repeats until a cue point in the background sound file is reached. When the cue point is reached, the next animation we see is the face of the Billionaire approaching from the distance. Our next step is to create this Billionaire animation.

1.  Move the playback head to frame 120. This is where we have placed the Billionaire marker.

2.  Drag Cast member 8 (the Billionaire) from the Cast to frame 120, channel 2. The Billionaire will appear at the center of the Stage. We will adjust its placement in the next few steps. The sprite object will span frames 120 through 147. We will only need frames 120 through 130 for the Billionaire animation, so our next step is to drag the endpoint for the Billionaire animation back to frame 130.

3.  Set the ink effect for the Billionaire sprite object to Matte. This will cause the white areas surrounding the Billionaire to disappear.

4.  Move the endpoint for the Billionaire sprite object in frame 147 of channel 2 to frame 130 of channel 2. Now the Billionaire sprite object terminates in the same frame as the music and background sprite objects.

Our next step is to animate the Billionaire. First we will use the Selected Frames Only setting, so that we can preview the Billionaire animation without also seeing the Icons of Wealth animation each time.

**FIGURE 4.10** *The Billionaire Cast member dragged to frame 120 of channel 2. The Billionaire image is visible on the Stage.*

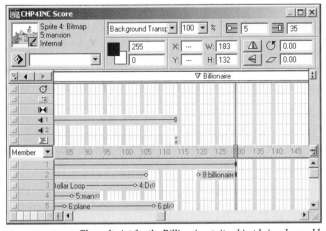

**FIGURE 4.11** *The endpoint for the Billionaire sprite object being dragged back to frame 130.*

## USING THE SELECTED FRAMES ONLY SETTING

Now that we have added the sprites for the Billionaire animation to the Score, we can take the steps necessary to animate the Billionaire. As we proceed, we will want to preview the animation as it is developed, but we don't necessarily need to see the Intro animation each time we play the movie. In this session, we will set Director so that it will only play the frames that the Billionaire animation will occupy (frames 120 to 130).

1.  **Select the Billionaire sprite object in channel 2. To restrict the range of operation of the playback head, we must first select the desired range of frames. The Billionaire sprite object is located in precisely the frames that we need, so highlighting the Billionaire serves the purpose of selecting the appropriate frames. You must, however, make certain that the entire Billionaire sprite object is highlighted. If you click directly on a sprite's keyframe, you will only select a single frame. You can make certain that the entire sprite object is selected by clicking on a frame that contains a line and not a circle.**

2.  **Open the control panel. The Selected Frames Only setting can be activated from the control panel.**

3.  **Click the Selected Frames Only button on the control panel. A green line will appear along the top of the Score at frames 120 through 130. This line indicates that the Selected Frames Only setting has been activated. Now when we play this movie, the playback head will be restricted to the range from frame 120 through 130.**

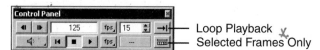

FIGURE 4.12 *The control panel. Arrows identify the Selected Frames Only and Loop Playback buttons.*

4.  **Make certain that the Loop Playback button is selected. As we preview the selected frames, it will be helpful if the playback head loops so that we don't need to click the Play button over and over.**

5.  **Play the movie. The playback head remains between frames 120 and 130. Of course, nothing moves on the Stage because we have not yet animated the Billionaire sprite object. We will do this next.**

6.  **Stop the movie.**

Now we will animate the Billionaire using its sprite path. It is no longer necessary to keep the control panel or Cast window open, so to conserve workspace you can close these windows if you choose.

## EXTENDING THE BILLIONAIRE SPRITE'S PATH

In chapters 2 and 3 we learned that every sprite has an animation path that can be extended away from the sprite to produce a direction of movement. We also learned that we can designate control points along this path, called keyframes, to produce curves and loops. In addition to being able to change a sprite on the Stage by changing its location, we are also capable of changing a sprite's size by resizing the sprite in different keyframes. In this session we will produce this animation for the Billionaire, creating the illusion that the Billionaire is approaching from the distance. Our first step is to extend the sprite's path.

1.   **Click in the middle of the sprite object located in channel 2 between frames 120 through 130 (the Billionaire). This will highlight the Billionaire sprite on the Stage.**

2.   **Move the playback head to frame 130 of the Score. Make certain that you click frame 130 of the frame bar; otherwise, you will remove the highlight that we have applied to the Billionaire sprite.**

3.   **On the Stage, click and drag the sprite path for the Billionaire down and to the left about 2 inches. This will animate the Billionaire from its starting position down and toward the left corner of the Stage. It will also result in creating a keyframe for the Billionaire sprite in frame 130 of the Score. Later we will adjust the animation so that the Billionaire moves away from the corner and changes size.**

4.   **Play the movie. The Billionaire moves toward the corner of the stage. Note that the playback head only plays between frames 120 and 130.**

5.   **Stop the movie.**

Next we will animate the size of the Billionaire.

**FIGURE 4.13** *The Billionaire sprite object with the pointer dragging the path endpoint.*

## ANIMATING THE BILLIONAIRE SPRITE'S SIZE

In the completed version of this animation, we saw that the Billionaire not only moves across the screen, but also increases in size. Director allows us to easily change a sprite's size over time, just as we can change a sprite's position. We will change the Billionaire sprite object's size at one of its keyframes so that it will change its size over time. Because the Billionaire is a flash asset, it will resize smoothly and easily because one of the features of vector graphics is that they can be any size without increasing file size. They look the same when they are small as they do large, with minimal distortion to the image.

1.   Make certain that the Billionaire sprite is selected on the Stage in frame 120. We will edit the Billionaire sprite object directly on the Stage instead of the Score, so we will need to be able to see the Billionaire sprite's animation path.

2.   Double-click on the red dot at the end of the Billionaire sprite object's path. This produces the same result as clicking directly on this keyframe in the Score. The playback head will jump to this frame, and the Billionaire image will appear to jump over to the selected point along its path. The playback head is now located in frame 130, which is the last point in the Billionaire

animation. Notice that the sprite on the Stage is framed by a single lined square; this indicates that only this keyframe is selected. This will allow the changes that we apply to this sprite to be isolated to only this frame.

3.  Click on the control point at the upper right of the selected Billionaire sprite object. We can drag these control points to resize the sprite.

4.  Drag the control point down and to the left to reduce the size of the Billionaire Sprite object. As you drag the sprite's control point, it will resize on the Screen. Now we can preview the animation.

**FIGURE 4.14** *The pointer over the red endpoint of the Billionaire sprite object's animation path on the Stage.*

**FIGURE 4.15** *The Billionaire sprite object selected on stage, with the pointer over the control point at the sprite's upper right corner.*

5.    **Play the movie. The Billionaire sprite now moves toward the lower left corner of the Stage and shrinks in size.**

6.    **Stop the movie.**

Our next step is to reverse this animation so that the Billionaire increases in size. We will also reposition the starting and ending points for the Billionaire image on the Stage so that it appears in the same positions as the completed version.

## REVERSING THE BILLIONAIRE ANIMATION

So far we have animated the Billionaire sprite so that it shrinks in size while it moves toward the lower left corner of the Stage. In the completed version of The Billionaire's Shop, the Billionaire sprite object increases in size. We can accomplish this same animation by reversing the shrinking animation in the Score, using a technique called *reverse sequence*.

1.    **Select the Billionaire sprite object in the Score at channel 2, frames 120 through 130. The entire sprite object should be highlighted.**

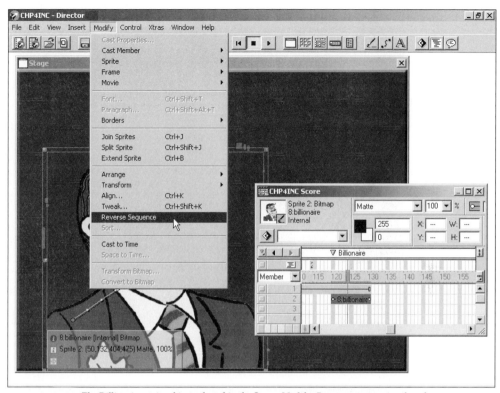

**FIGURE 4.16** *The Billionaire sprite object selected in the Score. Modify>Reverse sequence is selected.*

2.  Choose Modify>Reverse Sequence. This will cause the order of the changes along the sprite object to reverse in the Score. Now the first frame of the sprite object contains the smallest point in the animation, and the last frame contains the largest point.

3.  Click directly on frame 120 of sprite channel 2. This is the first point on the Billionaire sprite object. This keyframe is also its smallest point in size.

4.  On the Stage, drag the selected Billionaire sprite so that it is located flush against the bottom left corner of the Stage. Our next step is to reposition the Billionaire sprite at its largest point in size.

5.  Click directly on frame 130 of sprite channel 2. This is the last point on the Billionaire sprite object.

6.  On the Stage, drag the selected Billionaire sprite so that it is positioned flush against the bottom and left edges of the Stage.

**FIGURE 4.17** *The Billionaire sprite object on the Stage positioned in the lower left corner.*

**FIGURE 4.18** *The Billionaire sprite object at its final animation position.*

7.   Play and then stop the movie. The Billionaire sprite now animates up from the lower left corner of the Stage and increases in
size as it moves. The animation loops at this point because we
have loop playback set in the control panel.

## ADDING A LOOP BEHAVIOR TO THE BILLIONAIRE ANIMATION

Our next step is to add a behavior to the end of the Billionaire animation in
the Score that will keep the playback head in frame 130 when it is
reached. This way we will see the animation play only once. To accomplish
this, we will add a looping behavior to the last frame of the Billionaire animation. As the Billionaire animation plays, we will want to see it only once
during the course of the opening animation. In this session we will add a
behavior to the last frame of the Billionaire animation that will keep the
playback head at the last frame after the animation has played once.

1.   Highlight frame 130 of the script channel. This is the last frame
of the animation in the Score.

2.   Click on the Behavior Inspector button at the top of the Score.
This will open the Behavior Inspector window.

3.   Click on the + button in the upper left corner of the Behavior
Inspector window. Our first step is to create and name our new
behavior.

4.   Choose New Behavior... from the Behavior pop-up menu at the
upper left of the Behavior Inspector window. This will open the
Name Behavior dialog box.

**FIGURE 4.19** *The Behavior Inspector window.*

5.   **Name the Behavior Loop in Frame. This name will make it easy to identify the purpose of this behavior if we want to use it elsewhere.**

**FIGURE 4.20** *The Name Behavior dialog box with the name Loop in Frame typed into the entry window.*

*Property Inspector*
*↳ Script*
*Window*

6.   **Click on the Event pop-up menu at the middle left side of the Behavior Inspector window. Like the behavior we created for the Intro animation, we will want this behavior to be activated when the playback head passes through this frame.**

*Alphabetical Lingo*
*Categorized Lingo*

7.   **Choose Exit Frame from the Event pop-up menu. This will instruct Director to activate this behavior when the playback head passes this frame. Now we are ready to choose the action that we would like to have when Exit Frame occurs.**

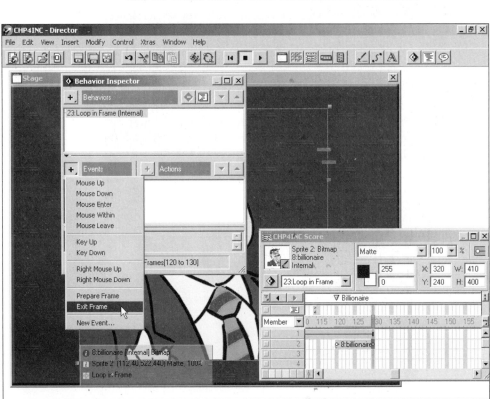

**FIGURE 4.21** *The behavior inspector. Exit Frame is being selected from the Events menu.*

8. Click on the Actions pop-up menu at the center of the behavior inspector. This will produce the menu of preset actions that we can choose from.

9. Choose Wait>On Current Frame from the Actions pop-up menu. This will cause the playback head to stop in this frame, but the movie will continue playing.

10. Close the behavior inspector. The behavior we just created is located in the Cast at position 22. Now we will apply it to the script channel at frame 130.

11. Make certain that frame 130 of the script channel is still high-lighted. This is where we want to position the new behavior.

12. Choose Loop in Frame from the Sprite Script pop-up menu at the top of the Score. This menu contains all of the scripts that can currently be used in the Score in this movie. You can see that one of the options in this menu is the Loop Back behavior that we created in chapter 3.

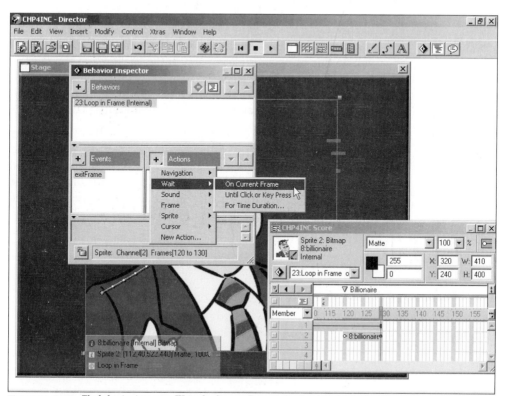

**FIGURE 4.22** *The behavior inspector. Wait>On Current Frame is being selected from the Actions menu.*

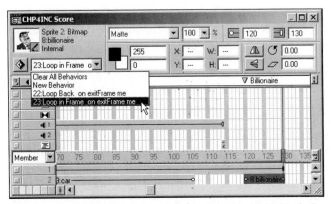

**FIGURE 4.23** *Frame 130 of the sprite Script channel highlighted in the Score.*

13.   **Play the movie. Now the animation will play only once, and the playback head will wait in frame 130. The movie is still playing, because we can still hear the music. If the control panel or toolbar is visible, you will see that the Play button is depressed.**

14.   **Stop the movie.**

15.   **Choose Control>Selected Frames Only. Our next step is to link the Icons of Wealth animation to the Billionaire animation. We will do this by using the cue point in the background sound file to synchronize a jump from the Icons of Wealth to the Billionaire, just as it occurs in the completed version of this lesson. Our first step is to deactivate the Selected Frames Only setting.**

Currently the Selected Frames Only option under the Control menu has a check mark beside it. After selecting it, the check mark should disappear. This has the same result as deselecting the Selected Frames Only button on the control panel. Notice that the green line along the frame bar from frame 120 to 130 disappears. This also indicates that this feature has been disconnected.

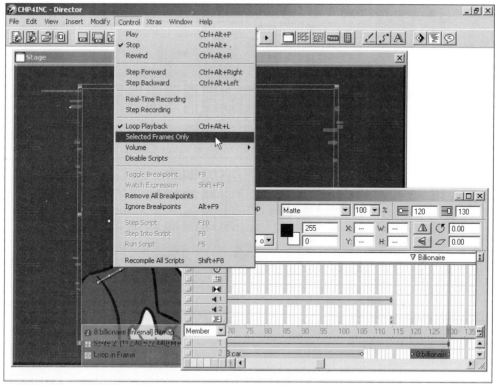

**FIGURE 4.24** *Selected Frames Only selected from the Control menu.*

## ADDING THE ICONS OF WEALTH TO THE BILLIONAIRE SCENE ANIMATION

In the next few steps we will synchronize the Billionaire animation to the Icons of Wealth animation; but first, let's finish the Billionaire animation screen by adding the Icons of Wealth to their positions there. In the completed version of this lesson, the Icons Of Wealth all dissolve to positions to the right of where the Billionaire image appears at its final position. In this session we will add the Icons of Wealth to these positions in the Billionaire area of the Score.

1.  **Move the playback head to 120. This is the beginning of the Billionaire animation.**

2.  **Drag Cast members 3, 5, 6, 7, and 13 (be sure to skip Cast member 4) to frame 120 in channels 3, 4, 5, 6, and 7, respectively. These are the Icons of Wealth: the car, mansion, airplane, yacht, and dollar sign. We used Cast member 13 instead of 4 for the dollar sign because we do not want the dollar sign to move dur-**

ing the Billionaire animation. Cast member 13 is one of the original Cast members that we used to create the dollar loop that now resides at Cast position 4.

3.   Move the playback head to frame 130 in the Score and then position the Icons of Wealth sprite objects on the Stage as they appear in figure 4.27. We moved the playback head to frame 130 so that we are in the frame where the Billionaire is at full size. This gives us a more accurate point of reference for positioning the Icons of Wealth sprite objects on the Stage.

4.   Drag select all of the Icons of Wealth sprite objects that are located in the Billionaire area of the Score. The settings that we are going to apply to the Icons of Wealth sprite objects can be applied to them all simultaneously.

5.   Set the ink effect for the Icons of Wealth sprite objects to Background Transparent. With all of the sprites selected, you can simply select Background Transparent from the Ink: menu at the top of the Score.

**FIGURE 4.25** *The Icons of Wealth positioned on the Stage beside the Billionaire.*

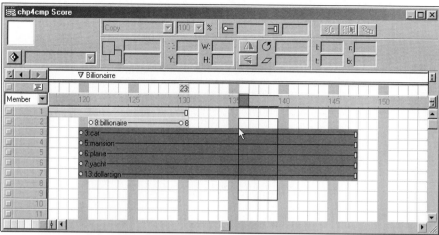

**FIGURE 4.26** *The Icons of Wealth in the Billionaire area of the Score being drag-selected.*

6. **Move the playback head back to frame 130, then click the Extend Sprite button of the Toolbar, or choose Modify>Extend Sprite. Make certain that you move the playback head by clicking the number 130 on the frame bar. This way the Icons of Wealth sprite objects will remain highlighted. Using Extend Sprite will bring the endpoints for all of the Icons of Wealth sprite objects that are in the Billionaire area of the Score from frame 147 back to frame 130.**

Now that we have finished creating the animation and adding the image elements that we want in the Billionaire area of the Score, we can synchronize the Billionaire animation to the Icons of Wealth using the cue point in the background music file.

**FIGURE 4.27** *The Icons of Wealth sprite objects with their endpoints relocated to frame 130.*

## OPENING THE INTERMEDIATE LESSON FILE AND SYNCHRONIZING THE ANIMATION USING A CUE POINT

The cue point that we placed in the sound is positioned at precisely where we would like to see the Billionaire animation appear. All we need to do is create a behavior to detect this cue point as it passes and then to send the playback head to the Billionaire animation at the right time.

1.  Click in frame 1 of the script channel. The behavior we are about to create will be located in frames 1 to 113 of this channel.

2.  Open the behavior inspector. You can open the behavior inspector by clicking the Behavior Inspector button at the top of the Score.

**FIGURE 4.28** *Behavior Inspector button.*

3. Create a new behavior and name it Jump to Billionaire. You can create a new behavior by choosing New Behavior... from the Behaviors pop-up menu. You will then be presented with the Name Behavior dialog box, where you can type Jump to Billionaire (see figure 4.20).

4. Choose Events>New Event.... New Event... is at the bottom of the Events pop-up menu. This will present you with the Name Event dialog box.

5. Name the new event cuePassed. The cuePassed event name is actually an existing Lingo script that is activated when a cue point in a sound is encountered.

**FIGURE 4.29** *The Name Event dialog box with cuePassed entered.*

6. Choose Actions>Navigation>Go to Marker.... We want the playback head to jump to the Billionaire area of the Score when the cue point in the sound is encountered.

> Lingo is not case sensitive in most situations. This means that you can type any combination of upper and lower case letters in a Lingo script. You must, however, obey any syntax issues, such as including spaces between Lingo terms. The only exception to the non-case sensitivity rule is Property Lists, which are a method for sorting information used in a Lingo script. **NOTE**

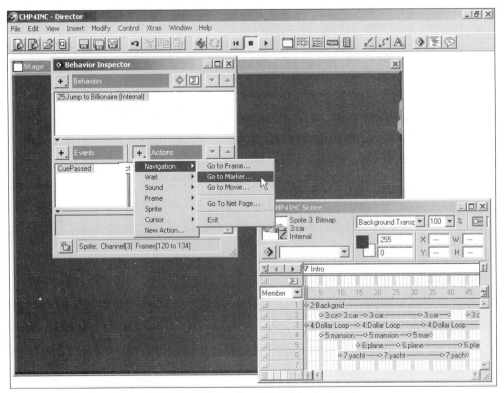

**FIGURE 4.30** *Actions>Navigation>Go to Marker... selected in the behavior inspector.*

7.  **Choose Billionaire from the Specify Marker dialog box. This is the marker that we want to jump to. Any other markers we add to the Score will be added to the menu in the Specify Marker dialog box. This allows us to easily create behaviors that will send the playback head anywhere we label in the Score.**

8.  **Click OK and close the behavior inspector. This will close the Specify Marker dialog box.**

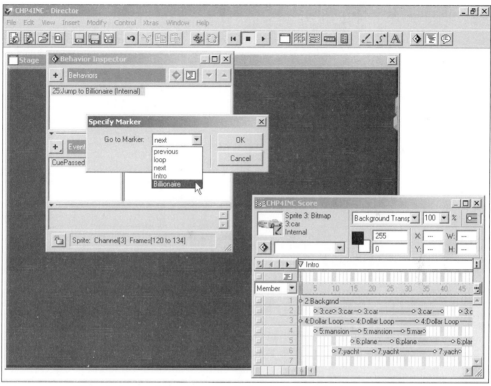

**FIGURE 4.31** *Billionaire is selected from the menu in the Specify Marker dialog box.*

9.  Highlight frames 1 through 113 in the script channel of the Score. Be sure you do not also select frame 114. Now we're ready to add this behavior to the Score. These are all of the frames, with the exception of the last frame, in the Intro part of the opening animation.

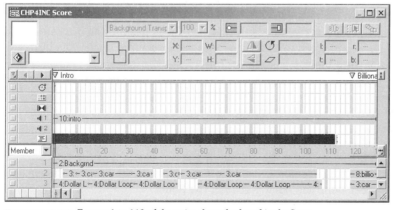

**FIGURE 4.32** *Frames 1 to 113 of the script channel selected in the Score.*

10.   **Choose Jump to Billionaire from the Sprite Script pop-up menu at the top of the Score. This will place the new behavior in all of the selected frames. Now we can test our new behavior.**

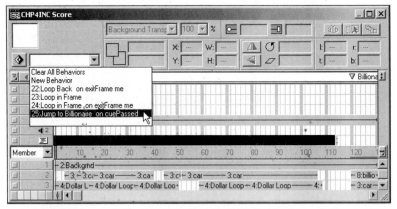

**FIGURE 4.33** *Jump to Billionaire selected from the Sprite Script menu on the Score.*

11.   **Play the movie; then stop it.**

The Intro animation loops, and the music plays in the background. When the cue point in the Intro Music sound file is encountered, the playback head jumps over to the marker labeled Billionaire. Our behavior works!

## ADDING THE CUE POINT BEHAVIOR TO THE SCRIPT IN THE LAST FRAME OF THE ICONS OF WEALTH ANIMATION

Although our behavior works, the cuePassed script is not in the very last frame of the Intro animation. To truly be thorough, we should place the cuePassed script in frame 114 as well. The behavior in frame 114 is the looping behavior that sends the playback head back to the marker labeled Intro. We still need this behavior because we want to stay in the Intro animation until the cue point in the Intro music file is reached. Frame scripts can only contain a single behavior, so we will need to add the cuePassed behavior to the Loop Back behavior that is already there. In this session we will copy the cuePassed script from the Jump to Billionaire behavior and paste it into the Loop Back behavior.

1.   **Click on any of the cells in the script channel of the Score between frames 1 and 113. This is where the Jump to Billionaire behavior has been placed in the Score.**

2.   **Open the behavior inspector. You can use the Behavior Inspector button at the top of the Score.**

3.   **Click the Script Window button at the top of the behavior inspector. Clicking this button will open the Script window and display the Lingo script that is used in the selected behavior.**

**FIGURE 4.34** *The Script Window button at the top of the behavior inspector.*

**FIGURE 4.35** *The open Script window with the script from the Jump to Billionaire behavior in it.*

```
on cuePassed me
    go to "Billionaire"
end
```

What we see here is the Lingo script that was created when we used the behavior inspector to create the Jump to Billionaire behavior. The behavior inspector really is just an easy way to create scripts by choosing simple options. Director then automatically creates a Lingo script in one of the Cast positions in the Cast Window. For example, the Jump to Billionaire behavior is located at Cast position 23.

The Script Window button allows us to jump into the script behind a behavior so that we can customize and edit it in ways that the behavior inspector is not designed to do. Lingo is a very rich scripting language and has many options available to it. In upcoming sessions we will do work with customizing behaviors by creating our own Lingo scripts.

All Lingo scripts have the same basic structure:

```
on (script name)
    lingo statements
end
```

This basic structure is called a *handler.* We will work more with handlers in chapters 7 through 11.

## WHAT DOES "ME" MEAN AFTER THE HANDLER'S NAME?

The word "me" as it appears in the scripts that we have worked with is actually part of an advanced method of programming called *object-oriented programming.* Behaviors can be used to generate scripts using this method, so Director automatically adds the word "me" to the end of each handler that is created in the behavior inspector. The work that we will be doing with Lingo in this book does not include object-oriented programming, so the "me" element is unnecessary for us.

### ABOUT THE COLORS IN THE SCRIPT TEXT

Scripts in Director can be color-coded according to the roles that different parts of a script play. This can be helpful as you learn more about Lingo and your scripts become longer and more complex. The organization is already established within Director with the Script Window Preference dialog box, which can be accessed by selecting `File>Preferences>Script…`.

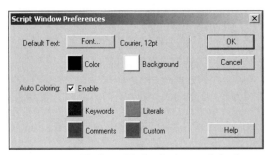

**FIGURE 4.36** *The Script Window Preferences dialog box.*

The button at the top of the window will allow you to choose which font will be used to display the text. The colored squares beneath the Text button allow you to change the color that is used for each category. The first two selections will change the color that is used for the text and background of the script window. The four color chips at the bottom of the window control the color used in different parts of the body of the script. These categories are defined in chapter 7, where there is greater detail on the structure of Lingo. The checkbox in the center of the window toggles the color coding for scripts on or off.

4.    **Highlight the on cuePassed script. You can highlight the text in the Script window the same way you can highlight text in a word processor. Simply click and drag across the text that you want to highlight.**

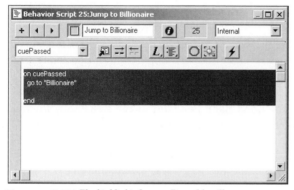

**FIGURE 4.37** *The highlighted on cuePassed handler.*

5.    **Copy the script. We can copy the script by choosing Edit>Copy Text, or by clicking the Copy button on the toolbar. The script will then be copied onto the system's Clipboard, from which it can be pasted later.**

6.    **Close the Script window. Now we will add this script to the Loop Back behavior.**

7.    **Select frame 114 in the script channel of the Score. This is where the Loop Back behavior is located.**

8.    **Click on the Behavior Inspector button at the top of the Score. This will bring the behavior inspector back to front.**

Behavior Inspector button

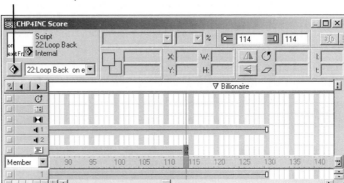

**FIGURE 4.38** *Frame 114 of the script channel selected in the Score. An arrow identifies the Behavior Inspector button.*

9.    **Click on the Loop Back behavior in the Behaviors window. This is the behavior that we want to add the cuePassed script to.**

10.   **Click the Script Window button at the top of the behavior inspector. This will open the Script window again with the behavior that sends the playback head back to Intro.**

**FIGURE 4.39** *The open Script window containing the script.*

```
on exitFrame me
    go to "Intro"
end
```

11.   **Click in the Script window below the exitFrame handler. The flashing text entry cursor will appear toward the bottom of the window. Now we can paste the cuePassed script. You can also**

place a few empty lines below the exitFrame handler by pressing the Enter key on your keyboard.

12. **Paste the cuePassed script into the Loop Back behavior script. The on cuePassed handler will be added to the bottom of the Script window.**

Although frame scripts cannot contain more than one behavior at a time, each behavior can contain more than one script. Now, the Loop Back behavior will send the playback head back to Intro, unless there is a message sent that a cue point has passed from a sound file that is playing. When the cue point in the opening music passes, then Loop Back will respond by sending the playback head on to Billionaire. Now the Icons of Wealth animation is completely synchronized with the Intro music file.

**FIGURE 4.40** *The on cuePassed handler pasted below the on exitFrame handler in the Script window for the Loop Back behavior.*

13. **Play, then stop the movie.**

Every frame of the Icons of Wealth animation will now be synchronized to the music and will branch to Billionaire when the cue point is reached. Now that we have successfully added the Intro music sound file and synchronized it to the opening animation using its cue point, we can add some final touches to the animation.

## ADDING A TRANSITION TO THE BILLIONAIRE ANIMATION

When the playback head jumps to Billionaire, the visual change is abrupt. All of the Icons of Wealth suddenly disappear, to be replaced by the Billionaire animation. Earlier in this session you learned that a transition can be used to make the switch from one scene to another smoother. In this session you will learn how to add a transition to a presentation.

1. **Double-click frame 120 of the transition channel. The transition channel is the third effects channel down from the top of the Score. If the effects channels of your Score are not currently visible, click the Hide/Show Effects Channels button at the top right of the Score (figure 4.41). When you double-click in the transition channel, the Frame Properties:Transition dialog box appears (figure 4.42).**

**NOTE**   You can also access the Frame Properties:Transition dialog box by choosing Modify>Frame>Transition....

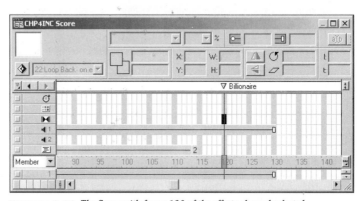

**FIGURE 4.41** *The Score with frame 120 of the effects channel selected.*

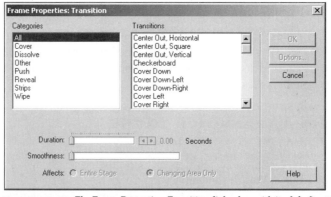

**FIGURE 4.42** *The Frame Properties: Transition dialog box with its default settings.*

There are 52 transitions that are built into Director. The All category on the left side of the Frame Properties: Transition dialog box displays all available transition effects in a window to the right. The other options listed under Categories include an organization of the different transitions into sets of similar effects. We will apply the transition Dissolve Bits.

> **NOTE**
>
> Additional transitions can be added to a Director movie by adding Transition Xtras to the Xtras folder in the Director application folder. Xtras are program add-ons to Director's features. They are available from Macromedia as well as other companies. Check Macromedia's Web site at Macromedia.com. Transitions Xtras that are added to Director can be accessed and placed in the Score through the Frame Properties>Transition dialog box under the Modify menu.

2.  **Click Dissolve in the Categories window on the left side of the Frame Properties: Transition dialog box. The Dissolve category is third from the top. This will cause all of the transitions that are dissolves to list in the Transition display area on the right side of the dialog box.**

3.  **Choose Dissolve, Bits from the Transition area on the right side of the Frame Properties: Transition dialog box. Dissolve, Bits is the first option in the Transition display area in the dialog box.**

4.  **Click and drag the arrow on the meter beside the word Duration: until you reach a setting of 1.00 seconds. We can also change the duration setting to .25 seconds at a time by using the arrows beside the duration setting. We will leave the other settings as they are.**

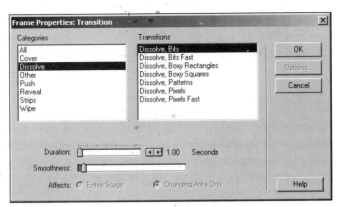

**FIGURE 4.43** *The Frame Properties: Transition dialog box with Dissolve Bits selected and a tempo setting of 1.00 second.*

5.    Click the button labeled OK. This transition will now be applied to frame 120 of the transition channel. Let's take a look at the effect it has on our presentation. When a transition is added to a movie, it creates a transition Cast member at the next available position in the Cast window. For example, this new transition is located at position 24. Because transitions create Cast members, we can use this transition again if we want the same settings for the same transition effect at another point in the movie.

6.    Rewind and play the movie. The animation plays and jumps at the right time synchronized with the music. Now the Icons of Wealth disappear gracefully, to be replaced by the Billionaire animation. The only problem is that the very first frame of the Billionaire sprite is visible as the transition occurs. We can enhance the animation further if we have the Billionaire appear one frame later, so that it appears to originate from somewhere way off in the distance.

7.    Stop the movie.

## REMOVING THE BILLIONAIRE SPRITE FROM THE FRAME THAT CONTAINS THE TRANSITION

Our next step is to remove the Billionaire sprite from the transition frame.

1.    Click and drag the starting point of the Billionaire sprite object in channel 2 from frame 120 to frame 121. Now the Billionaire will make his appearance after the transition has removed all of the Icons of Wealth.

Let's preview the change:

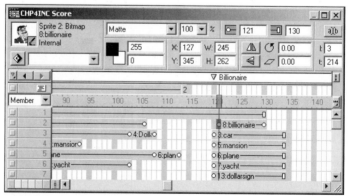

**FIGURE 4.44** *The starting point of the Billionaire sprite object in channel 2, frame 120, being dragged to frame 121.*

2. **Rewind and play the movie. As before, the animation plays and jumps at the right time with the music, and the Icons of Wealth then disappear and are replaced by the Billionaire animation. However, now the Billionaire does not appear until the transition is fully completed, producing a grander entrance for our deliriously wealthy fellow.**

3. **Stop the movie.**

We have now explored the use of sound and cue points in a presentation. We have also worked a little more with the behavior inspector and the effects channel of the Score. In the next chapter we will continue working with these and other Director features while we learn about playing digital video files in a Director presentation.

## SUMMARY

Digital sounds that are recorded or created in sound editing applications, such as SoundEdit 16, can be saved as files (such as AIF and WAV) that can be imported and used in Director movies. The sound files reside in the Cast and are incorporated into a Director movie when dragged to the sound channels of the Score. There are two sound channels, which are located among the effects channels at the top of the Score. The sound sprite objects must be located in all of the frames that sound should play.

Animation and other activity within Director can be closely synchronized with sound files. This synchronization is accomplished with cue points, which are tags placed within the sound file in the sound editing application that was used to create them. SoundEdit 16 and Sound Forge can be used to add cue points to sound files. These cue points are recognized by Lingo scripts, which can be used to trigger events, such as jumping to different parts of an animation when certain markers occur within a sound.

Changing the sprite's dimensions at keyframes along the sprite's path will animate a sprite's size. Director automatically interpolates the change in size from one keyframe to the next, so that the sprite grows or shrinks over time. This animation technique can also be used to produce the illusion that a sprite is receding into or approaching from the distance.

Transitions can be added to a Director presentation to create an added visual interest to the changes between scenes. There are 52 different transitions that are included with Director. We can add other, custom transitions by using Xtras, which are program add-ons that add to Director features. All transitions are added to Director through the Frame Properties: Transition dialog box. This dialog box can be accessed by double-clicking a cell in the transition channel of the Score or by choosing

Modify>Frame>Transition.... Transitions that are added to the Score also generate Cast members, which can be reused.

Scripts generated by the behavior inspector create Lingo script Cast members, which can then be directly accessed and edited to create custom scripts for a behavior. These scripts can be accessed by double-clicking directly on the behavior script Cast member, or by clicking the Script Window button at the top of the behavior inspector. Events that are added to a behavior directly through the Script window are listed in the behavior inspector as custom Lingo scripts.

## QUESTIONS

1.  How can we directly access the Lingo statements generated when a script is created with the behavior inspector?

2.  What is the name of the event handler that detects the passing of a cue point in a sound that is playing in Director?

3.  What is the procedure for animating a sprite's size?

4.  To animate a sprite's size, does a sprite's animation path need to be extended away from the sprite on the Stage? Why?

5.  Why is the Selected Frames Only setting useful?

6.  How can a sprite's animation sequence be reversed?

## EXERCISES

1.  Create an animation of the dollar sign, making it start small at the left of the Stage and grow large as it moves to the center of the Stage.

2.  Add a marker to the beginning of the Dollar Sign animation from exercise 1, then use the behavior inspector to create a behavior at the end of the animation that will cause the playback head to jump back to the beginning of the animation.

3.  Add a sound to the Score that will play for the duration of the Dollar animation. Set the sound to loop so that it will replay when the end of the sound is reached.

4.  Use the storyboards that you created in chapter 1 to create three animations in Director. We will add the interactive elements that you designed into the storyboards and flowchart in a later lesson.

# CHAPTER 5

# ADDING DIGITAL VIDEO TO THE BILLIONAIRE'S SHOP

# 5 Adding Digital Video to The Billionaire's Shop

**In this chapter, you will learn how to:**

- Use digital video in a Director movie
- Use a tempo channel setting to control the playback head in relation to a digital video file in the Score
- Use the tempo channel to wait for the end of a sound to finish playing in the Score
- Bypass the behavior inspector to directly enter a script in the script channel of the Score

**Also in this chapter:**

- Technical information about the creation and playback of digital video files
- Details of some methods used to record and edit digital video files

Digital video is a series of images and optional sound contained together in a single file. These files are created and edited in programs such as Adobe Premiere and are saved using different types of compression, called *Codecs* (*co*mpression/*dec*ompression), to reduce their file sizes and make them easier to play on a computer. One of the ways these Codecs work is to remove and combine parts of images in different frames that are similar. For example, a video of a talking head against a still background contains very little that changes from frame to frame. The person's expression changes, perhaps the head moves a bit, but the background doesn't change from frame to frame. What a Codec might do is use the same background across multiple frames and change only the areas of the image that are different. In this chapter we will add the Title movie that appears over the Billionaire's head in the completed version of The Billionaire's Shop (see figure 5.01).

**FIGURE 5.01** *The Title animation that we will create in this lesson.*

Programs capable of playing digital video files are actually cooperating with software-system extensions that have been installed to work with the computer's operating system, such as Microsoft's Video for Windows (Windows) and Apple's QuickTime (Macintosh and Windows). This software must be present and working with the computer's operating system in order for the digital video to play in your presentation. Generally, if you use digital video in a Director project, it's a good idea to distribute the software needed for the operating system along with your project.

Digital video files are created by using add-on hardware, called *digital video capture devices,* to bring sequences of images in from external video sources, such as video-tape recorders, although many applications will allow you to create synthetic, digital video files with animations and images. For example, animations created in Director can be saved as digital video files that can then be used in other applications that are compatible with digital video. This allows you to use Director to add titles and images to digital video files that you are editing in a digital video editing program such as Adobe Premiere. You can save your Director animations as digital video files by choosing File>Export... (see figures 5.02 and 5.03). The Title animation was created in Strata MediaPaint. When Director is used in this way, the digital file that is created is only a sequence of images and cannot contain interactive features. By using this optional method of output for a Director movie, you can use Director's powerful animation capability to enhance a digital video project.

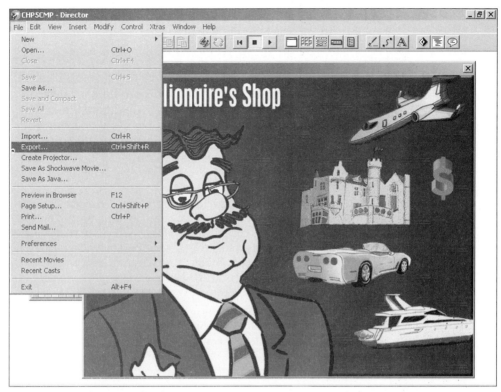

**FIGURE 5.02** *File>Export selected.*

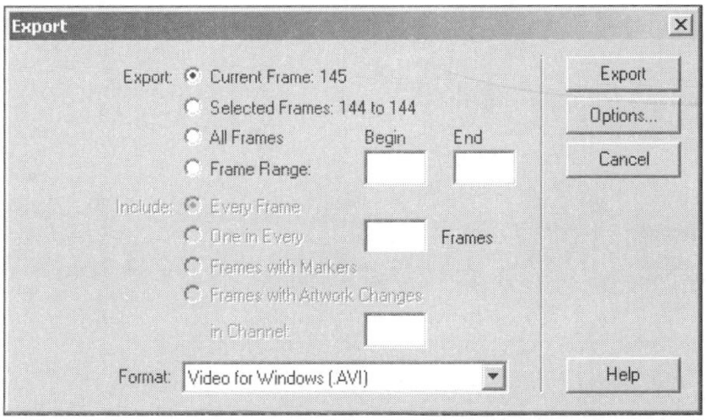

**FIGURE 5.03** *The Export dialog box. The Video for Windows movie option is selected from the Format menu.*

**NOTE**   Director projects that are saved as digital video files lose any interactive
capabilities that are generated using Lingo.

**WARNING**   **Digital video files used in Director projects are always linked to
the originating file, at its original location on the hard drive or
CD-ROM. You must always distribute original digital video files
with presentations that use them. Organize the video that you
plan to use in a single directory before importing, then include
this directory along with your presentation.**

**NOTE**   You can synchronize animations in Director to the sound in digital video by
adding cue points to the audio in the digital video file using SoundEdit 16
(see figure 5.04). At the time this book was written, SoundEdit 16 was the
only program that included this feature, and it was only available for the
Macintosh. Files created with SoundEdit 16 can be used both on
Macintosh and on machines running Windows.

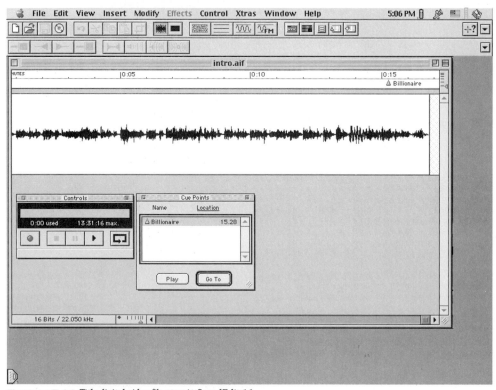

**FIGURE 5.04** *Title digital video file open in SoundEdit 16.*

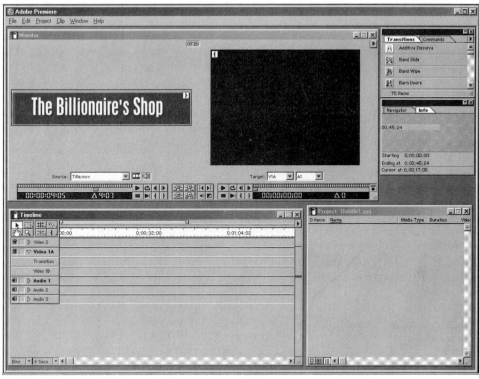

**FIGURE 5.05** *The Title digital video file open in Adobe Premiere.*

**NOTE**

Applications such as Adobe Premiere (see figure 5.05) allow audio files to be saved in digital video format. This allows these audio files to be played in places where digital video files can play, but they only contain sounds and no images. This can be useful within Director, which has only two channels dedicated to audio and 120 channels dedicated to images and other visual sprites, such as digital video. You could save an audio file as a digital video file in another application, then import it into Director and place it in one of the sprite channels. Now you can have three sounds playing at once. You can have more sounds playing at once if you use more of the sprite channels with audio files that are saved in digital video format.

## INSTALLING QUICKTIME

If you are using a Macintosh computer, you probably have QuickTime already installed in your system software. If you are using a Windows machine, this is less likely. QuickTime is installed with the Commercial version of Director. If you are using the Academic or Trial version of Director, or if you don't think the current version of QuickTime is installed on

your computer, then go to ***http://www.apple.com/quicktime***, download the
current version of Quicktime, and run the installer

## VIEWING THE COMPLETED FILE

1.   **If it is not already open, launch Director.**

2.   **Choose File>Open.**

3.   **Locate and select the file named Chp5cmp.dir, which is located
     on the CD-ROM in the directory Lessons/Chaptr5/Complete/
     Chp5cmp.dir.**

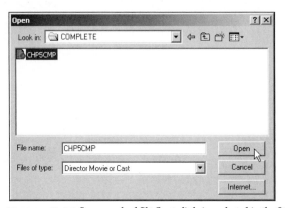

**FIGURE 5.06** *Screen grab of Chp5cmp.dir being selected in the Open... dialog box.*

4.   **Click Open and play the movie.**

     The opening presentation is the same. The Icons of Wealth anima-
     tion moves around the screen, and the Billionaire animation moves
     onto the screen in synchronization with the music. Following what
     we have accomplished so far is the animation of an image that con-
     tains the words The Billionaire's Shop, with its own attached sound
     effect. This is a digital video file that can contain both image and
     sound in the same file. After the digital video file finishes playing,
     the Billionaire winks with a sound effect. In this session we will add
     these new elements, completing the opening animation.

5.   **Stop the movie.**

## PLACING THE DIGITAL VIDEO FILE ON YOUR HARD DRIVE

One of the unique characteristics of digital video files in Director is that they cannot be embedded into Cast files. A digital video file can be imported, and a Cast member will be created, but the file itself will always exist as an external file to which the Cast member is linked. Playing a digital video file is a collaboration between the Director application that the digital video file is played in and system software extensions, such as QuickTime and Microsoft Video for Windows. These extensions perform functions that decompress digital video files and play them directly from a storage device, such as a hard drive. Another reason for the external location of digital video files is their size, which can typically be rather large. One 10-second digital video file with a display area of 320x240 pixels can easily be a minimum of 10MB in size. Having the file decompressed in sections and played from a hard drive is far more economical with computer memory then having the entire digital video file loaded into memory when the application launches.

The playback quality of digital video files is subject to several parameters, such as the size of the file, which determines how much of the file can be read into memory at once; the amount of memory installed in the computer, which determines the size of the file that the computer can support with each read; and the speed of the storage device that contains the video file, which determines how quickly the file can be read from the drive to memory. Hard drives are generally faster than CD-ROM drives, so copying the digital video file that we will use in this chapter to your hard drive will help ensure optimal performance. Another good reason to copy the video file to your hard drive is that the location of the video file on your computer is remembered by the Cast member that was created with that video file. As a result, if you import a file from a CD-ROM drive, the file you create with Director will require the presence of that CD-ROM disc on the computer where the Director movie is playing. Copying the file to the same directory as your Director application means that you can transport the Director file and the video file together as a unit without the original CD-ROM.

1. **Locate the Billshop CD.**

2. **Locate the file named Title.mov, which is located on the CD-ROM in Lessons/Chaptr5/Complete/Chp5cmp.dir.**

3. **Copy the file named Title.mov from the CD-ROM to the directory you created in chapter 1 named Billshop.**

Now we are ready to add the digital video file to The Billionaire's Shop.

**NOTE**    The extension for QuickTime movies for Windows is .MOV. Other extensions are .AVI for Video for Windows and .MPG for digital video compressed using the Mpeg compression method . Using the extension name is not necessary for digital video files on the Macintosh, but it is a good idea for Macintosh developers to maintain a naming convention that uses extensions, because this will allow your movie to be easily transported to a Windows computer if necessary.

**FIGURE 5.07** *The Title.mov file displayed through system software (Windows).*

**FIGURE 5.08** *The Title.mov file displayed through system software (Macintosh).*

## OPENING THE PARTLY COMPLETED FILE

1. Choose File>Open. The Open... dialog box will appear.

2. Open the file named Chp5inc.DIR in Lessons/Starter/Chaptr5/ on the CD-ROM. If you are working with a commercial version of Director, you can continue working with the file that you created and saved in chapter 4. If you are copying the partly completed file to your hard drive, you also need to copy the Title.mov digital video hard drive to the same directory. Follow the directions in the section below titled Importing the Digital Video File.

> Remember to save your work frequently because the end result of each   **NOTE**
> lesson is the beginning of the next lesson. We have also supplied you with
> the partly completed version of each lesson on the CD-ROM so that you
> can work with the working copy of Director that is on the CD-ROM.

## IMPORTING THE DIGITAL VIDEO FILE AND THE TITLE IMAGE

You will need to import the Title.mov and Title files if you are working with the file that you created in chapter 4.

1. Open the internal Cast file. We want to make sure that the Title.mov file is imported into the internal Cast file. We can do this by making the internal Cast file the active Cast. You can open the internal Cast file by choosing Window>Cast>Internal, or by choosing the internal Cast file from the Choose Cast menu in the upper left corner of the Cast window.

2. Choose File>Import.... This will open the Import Files Into... dialog box.

3. Locate and select the file named Title.mov that you copied to your Billshop directory earlier in this chapter.

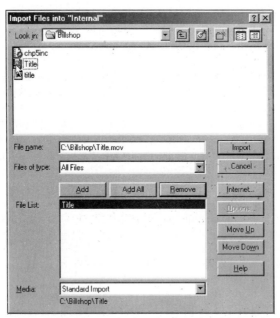

**FIGURE 5.09** *The Import Files Into... dialog box with the Title.mov file displayed in the Billshop directory.*

4.  Click the button labeled Add. This will add the Title.mov file to the list of files to import. Now, we will add the Title.pct image.

5.  Locate and select the file named Title.pct that is located in Lessons/Chaptr5/Starter/ on the CD-ROM.

6.  Click the button labeled Add. This file will also be added to the list of files to be imported. Now we will bring the files into the Cast.

7.  Click the button labeled Import. This will place the Title.mov digital video file at Cast position 26, and the Title.pct image into position 27. The Title.pct image is actually a still image of the last frame of the Title.mov digital video file. Digital video files are not affected by transitions in the Transition channel. To allow the end of this part of the opening animation to dissolve to the next scene in The Billionaire's Shop (that we will create in chapter 6), we will use Title.pct to replace the Title.mov file in the last frames of the animation we are creating in this chapter.

8.  When the Title.pct file is imported, it will cause the Image Options dialog box to open. This window gives us the opportunity to modify the image to more closely match other images

that are already in the Cast. The first option allows us to determine if we would like the image to retain the same bit depth, which is the feature that determines the number of colors that are used to display the image. An image source might have a different bit depth than the images that are already in a movie. For best results, it is generally preferable to have all of the images in a movie share the same bit-depth setting. The second option allows us to determine if we would like to import a custom palette for the image, or if we would like to remap the image to a palette that is already in the movie. For the purposes of this lesson, we will select the 8-bit option for Color Depth; this will make the Remap To: menu available. Select the option labeled Billshop Palette Internal; this will remap the colors in the image so that it uses the colors that are in the other images in The Billionaire's Shop.

## PREVIEWING THE NEW VIDEO FILE

We can open and play digital video files that are in the Director Cast by using the Video window.

1. Open the internal Cast file. The Title.mov file is located at position 26 in this Cast window. We can directly open the Video preview window by double-clicking the digital video Cast member.

2. Locate and double-click Cast member 26. This will open the Video window. At the bottom of this window is a play button that you can use to preview the selected digital video Cast member.

3. Click the play button at the bottom of the video window. This animation was created using Strata StudioPro to create the three-dimensional text and movement of the letters. The audio was added with SoundEdit 16.

4. Close the Video window.

Play button —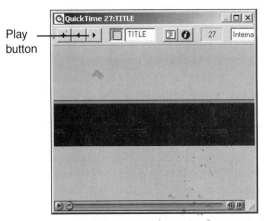

**FIGURE 5.10** *The Video window with an arrow pointing to the Play button.*

**NOTE**
**(WINDOWS ONLY)**

The digital video file used in this lesson was created using the QuickTime format. It is also possible to use video files that were created using the Windows AVI format. Director has an additional window that allows us to preview and play AVI movies on Windows computers.You can open the AVI preview window by double-clicking on an imported AVI digital video Cast member, or by selecting Window>AVI Video.

## ADDING THE DIGITAL VIDEO TO THE SCORE

In this session we will create a new area of the Score where we will locate the digital video animation. It will appear in a frame that is identical to the last frame of the Billionaire animation.

## ADDING THE TITLE MARKER

1.  Click the Marker channel at frame 135. This will produce a marker at frame 135 with a flashing cursor.

2.  Name the marker Title. This will be the location for the digital video animation. First let's add the other elements that will also be seen on the screen.

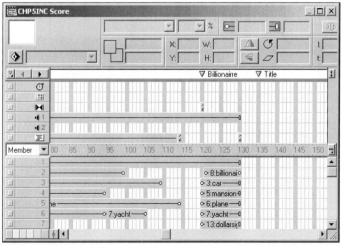

**FIGURE 5.11** *The Title marker at frame 135.*

## ADDING THE BACKGROUND, BILLIONAIRE, AND ICONS OF WEALTH SPRITE OBJECTS TO THE TITLE AREA OF THE SCORE

1.  Click and drag the endpoint for the Sprite Object in channel 1, frame 130 to channel 1, frame 145. This will add the background image to the Title area of the Score. We have an interesting situation with dragging the endpoint for the Billionaire across, because the last frame of the Billionaire is part of an animation. If we just click and drag the endpoint, we will extend the entire Billionaire animation into the Title area of the Score. We want to keep the animation isolated to the Billionaire area, so we just want a duplicate of the last frame in the Title area.

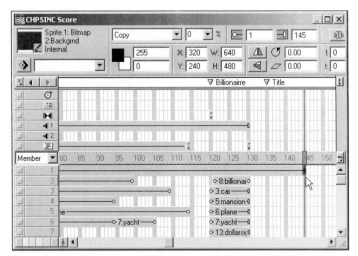

**FIGURE 5.12** *The endpoint of the background sprite object dragged from frame 130 to frame 145.*

2.  Hold down the Option/Alt key, then click and drag the endpoint for the sprite object in channel 2, frame 130 to channel 2, frame 145. The last key frame of the Billionaire sprite object will remain in frame 130 while the pointer drags a duplicate to frame 145. Now the animation will remain as it was, and we have a copy of the Billionaire sprite object in frame 145.

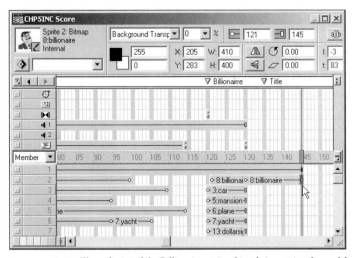

**FIGURE 5.13** *The endpoint of the Billionaire sprite object being option-dragged from frame 130 to frame 145.*

3.  Drag-select the sprite objects in channels 3 through 7 in the Billionaire area of the Score. These are the Icons of Wealth at their displayed positions during the Billionaire sprite's appearance.

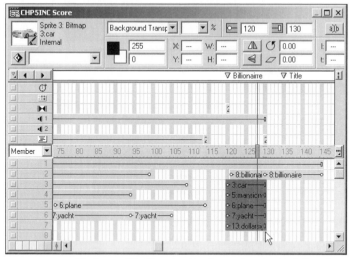

**FIGURE 5.14** *The Icons of Wealth sprite object being selected in the Billionaire area of the Score.*

4.  Move the playback head to frame 145 of the Score. Make certain that you move only the playback head at this point. Do not click in any of the channels of the Score because this will remove the highlight on the selected sprite objects in the score.

5.  Choose Modify>Extend Sprite. This will cause the Icons of Wealth sprite objects to extend across the Title area to frame 145 of the Score.

**FIGURE 5.15** *The playback head moves to frame 145 of the Score with Modify>Extend Sprite selected.*

## PLACING THE VIDEO CAST MEMBER
## ON THE STAGE

Now that we have added the background elements for the Title area of the Score, we can add the digital video file.

1.    Drag Cast member 26 (the digital video member) to frame 135 of channel 8 in the Score.

2.    Position the Title digital video sprite on Stage to the position pictured in figure 5.16. You can also use the arrow keys on your keyboard to adjust the placement of the digital video file on the Stage.

**FIGURE 5.16** *The Title digital video file dragged to channel 8 of frame 135 of the Score.*

3.  **Drag the endpoint of the sprite object in channel 8 (the digital
    video sprite) from frame 163 back to frame 145. Now all of the
    sprites in the Title area of the Score end in the same frame. Our
    next step is to adjust the end of the Billionaire animation so that
    it matches the Title animation.**

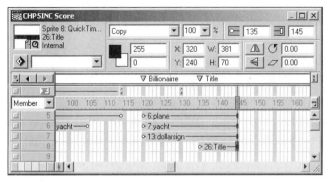

**FIGURE 5.17** *The endpoint for the digital video sprite object dragged from frame 163 of
channel 8 to frame 145 of channel 8.*

## USING A TEMPO CHANNEL SETTING TO CONTROL THE PLAYBACK HEAD

Video can play in one frame of the Score or in multiple frames. All of the information in the digital video sprite is contained in a single file, as opposed to images spread out across the Score. We will work with the video sprite across the first five frames of the Title, because it will be easier to work with and select the sprites in the Score as we proceed. We will add a setting to frame 139 that will keep the playback head in that frame until the digital video file has completed, then we will allow the playback head to proceed to the Wink animation that we will create later in this chapter.

In previous chapters we used a behavior to loop the playback head in a frame; video offers us a second option, a tempo setting. In addition to allowing us to control the frame rate of the movie, settings in the Tempo channel let us wait for the video sprite object in channel 8 to finish playing. Our next step is to add this tempo setting to frame 139.

1.    **Double-click in frame 139 of the tempo channel, the first channel that is labeled with a clock icon. This will open the Frame Properties:Tempo dialog box.**

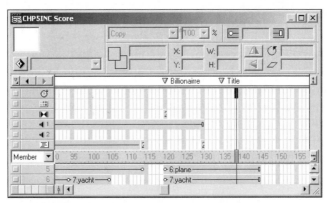

**FIGURE 5.18** *Frame 139 of the tempo channel selected.*

2.    **Select the radio button beside the words Wait for Cue Point:. This will cause the playback head to wait until the digital video file is finished playing. The only option available is the digital video file in channel 8. If there were any other sounds or video in this frame in the Score, they would be available from the Channel: pop-up menu. There are no cue points in this video file, but we can choose the default setting of {End} from the Cue Point: pop-up menu to have the playback head wait for the digital video file in channel 8 to finish playing before proceeding.**

3.   Choose {End} from the Cue Point: pop-up menu. Now the play-
     back head will remain in frame 139 until the digital video file in
     channel 8 has finished playing.

**FIGURE 5.19** *The Frame Properties:Tempo dialog box with Title selected from the Channel menu and {End} selected from the Cue Point menu.*

4.   Click the button labeled OK. This will close the Frame Proper-
     ties:Tempo dialog box.

## PREVIEWING THE TITLE

We have created enough of Title animation to begin previewing what we
have accomplished. First, let's set the playback head to play Selected
Frames Only so that we will only see the frames that contain the video file.

1.   Click on the sprite object in channel 8 between frames 135 and
     145. This is the digital video sprite. It spans all of the frames
     that we want to preview, so if it is highlighted it can be used to
     define the frames for Selected Frames Only.

2.   Choose Control>Selected Frames Only. A green line appears on
     the frame number bar that defines the frames that we have
     restricted playback to. The green line should be located between
     frames 135 and 145 (see figure 5.22).

3.   Play the movie. We now see the Title video animation play. The
     playback head waits for the video to finish in frame 139, then
     continues to frame 145, where it loops back to frame 135. Note
     how the video file remains onscreen with the last frame of the
     video visible, even though the playback head is playing through
     frames that contain the video sprite. This is because there are
     no more frames of video to play, and we have not set the video to
     loop in its property dialog box (see figure 5.23).

4.   Stop the movie.

Now we will add the Wink character animation.

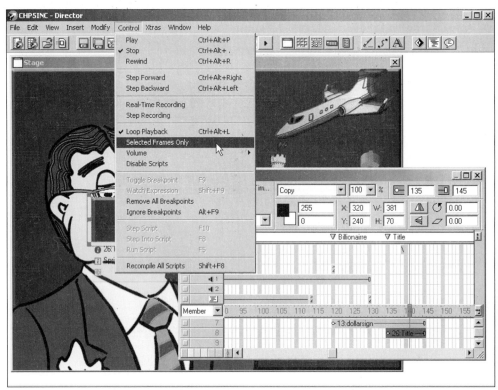

**FIGURE 5.20** *The digital video sprite selected in channel 8 and Control>Selected Frames Only chosen from the Control menu.*

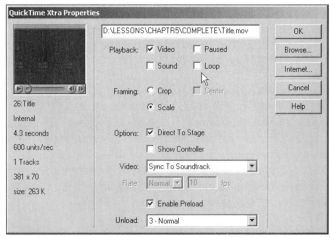

**FIGURE 5.21** *The Digital Video Cast Member Info dialog box with the cursor pointing to the Loop checkbox.*

## ADDING THE WINK

In this session we will add the part of the animation where the Billionaire winks. This type of animation is called *character animation*, a more traditional animation technique where variations of an image representing a character are presented sequentially to produce the illusion of movement. A character swinging its arms as it walks across the street is an example of a character animation. Here we will change the Billionaire's expression so that he appears to wink. We will start from another partly completed file that contains all of the work that has been added up to this point.

1. Click the Marker channel of the Score at frame 140. This is where we will place the Wink character animation.

2. Name the new marker Wink.

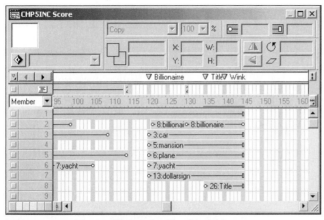

**FIGURE 5.22** *The new Wink marker placed in the Score.*

## ADDING THE WINK IMAGE

1. Drag Cast member 9 (the Wink image) to frame 140 of channel 9 in the Score. You can make certain that the image starts in frame 140 by first placing the playback head in that frame. If you miss frame 140, you can drag the starting point of the sprite object to frame 140.

2. Drag the endpoint of the sprite object in frame 167 back to frame 142. Now that the wink has been placed, we have completed the image part of the opening animation. There are only a few more steps left.

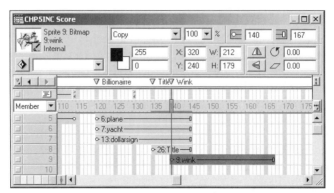

**FIGURE 5.23** *The Wink sprite object in channel 9 of the Score in frames 140 through 167.*

3.  While the Wink sprite object is selected on the Stage, select the Background Transparent ink effect from the Ink menu at the top of the Score. This will allow the graphics in the background to be visible behind the Wink graphic. Now it will be easier to position the sprite.

4.  Position the Wink image over the Billionaire's face as it appears in figure 5.24. By superimposing the Wink image over the Billionaire's eye, we can make him appear to wink when the playback head passes through these frames.

**FIGURE 5.24** *The Wink image over the Billionaire's face.*

## ADDING A SOUND TO THE WINK ANIMATION

We will synchronize the Billionaire's wink to the sound Cast member named Winkding (Cast member 12) by placing it in the same frames in the Score and using a tempo setting to wait for the sound to complete before proceeding through the Score.

1.  Drag Cast member 12 (the Winkding sound) to frame 140 in sound channel 1. Currently the new sound sprite object extends well beyond the Wink animation. We will change its endpoint next.

2.  Drag the endpoint of the sprite object in sound channel 1 from frame 167 to frame 142. Now the Winkding sound lasts as long as the Wink animation. Our next step is to have the playback head wait for the Winkding sound to finish playing before proceeding through the Score. We will use a tempo channel setting to accomplish this.

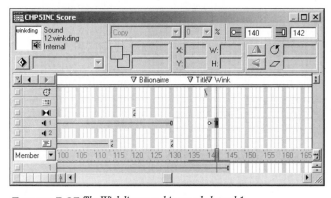

**FIGURE 5.25** *The Winkding sound in sound channel 1.*

## ADDING A TEMPO CHANNEL SETTING TO SYNCHRONIZE THE WINK ANIMATION AND SOUND

We will want the playback head to wait for the Winkding sound to finish playing before proceeding though the Score. We will use the same tempo setting that we used to hold the playback head while the digital video sprite that we created with the Title.mov Cast member finished playing. The exception will be the file that we select from the Channel: menu.

1.  Double-click frame 142 of the tempo channel. This will open the Frame Properties:Tempo dialog box.

2.    Select the radio button beside the words Wait for Cue Point: The
      Channel: and Cue Point: menus will become active.

3.    Choose Sound 1: Winkding.Aif from the Channel: menu. This is
      the sound we just placed in sound channel 1 of the Score.

4.    Choose {End} from the Cue Point: menu. There are no cue points
      in this sound, so we only have {Next} and {End} to choose from,
      which in this case are one and the same. By choosing {End} we
      are indicating that we want the playback head to wait until the
      default cue point at the end of the file is reached.

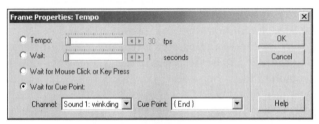

**FIGURE 5.26** *The Frame Properties:Tempo dialog box with Sound 1:Winkding selected
from the Channel: menu and {End} selected from the Cue Point menu.*

5.    Play the movie. When the video has completed playing, the Bil-
      lionaire winks with the Winkding sound. When the sound fin-
      ishes playing, the Billionaire reopens his eye and the playback
      head continues, looping back to the beginning of the Title area
      of the Score.

6.    Stop the movie.

Now we will add a few finishing touches to the opening animation for
The Billionaire's Shop.

## DELAYING THE PLAYBACK HEAD
## USING A BEHAVIOR AND A TEMPO SETTING

The last frame of the Wink animation is the last frame of the opening animation. In this session we will create a few seconds of delay to keep the
playback head in the last frame before looping back to frame 1. This will
give us a moment of pause after all of the active animation and sound have
completed.

1.    Highlight frame 145 of the script channel. This is the very last
      frame of the presentation so far.

2. **Open the behavior inspector. You can access the behavior inspector by clicking the behavior inspector button at the top of the Score, or by choosing Window>Inspectors>Behavior.**

3. **Choose New Behavior... from the Behaviors pop-up menu. This will open the Name Behavior dialog box.**

4. **Name the new behavior Brief Pause, then click the button labeled OK. The Brief Pause behavior will now be added to the list of behaviors in the behavior inspector.**

**FIGURE 5.27** *The Name Behavior dialog box open with Brief Pause typed into the entry window.*

5. **Choose Events>Exit Frame from the Events pop-up menu in the behavior inspector. This will cause the Brief Pause behavior to be activated when the playback head is leaving frame 145.**

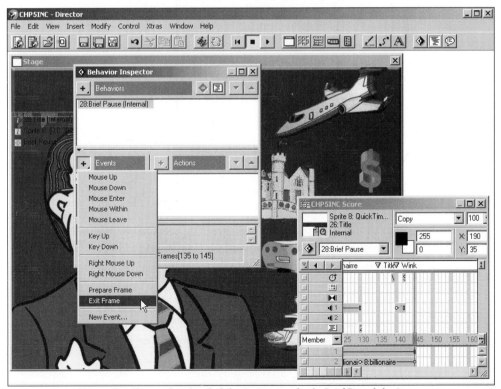

**FIGURE 5.28** *Events>Exit Frame selected in the behavior inspector for the Brief Pause behavior.*

6. Choose Actions>Wait>For Time Duration... in the behavior
   inspector. The Specify Time Duration dialog box appears.

7. Drag the arrow on the slider beside the words Delay (seconds):
   in the Specify Time Duration dialog box to a setting of 5.00.
   Now the playback head will remain in this frame until 5 seconds
   pass.

**FIGURE 5.29** *The Specify Time Duration dialog box with a setting of 5 seconds.*

8. Click the button labeled OK. Displayed in the Actions area of the
   behavior inspector is Wait for Time Duration 300. This refers to
   Director's measurement of time which is in Ticks, 1/60 of a second. 300 ticks is the equivalent of 5 seconds.

**FIGURE 5.30** *The behavior inspector with the settings for the Brief Pause behavior.*

9. Close the behavior inspector. The behavior is created, but we
   must still take the step of placing it in the Score.

10. Make certain that frame 145 is selected in the Script channel of
    the Score, then choose Brief Pause from the Sprite Script pop-up
    menu at the top of the Score. This will place the Brief Pause
    behavior into the Score. The Brief Pause behavior will delay the
    playback head an additional 5 seconds so that we don't exit the
    Wink area of the Score too quickly.

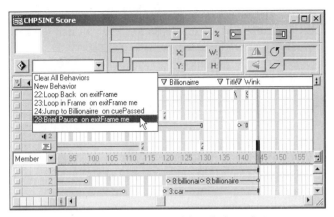

**FIGURE 5.31** *Brief Pause being selected from the Sprite Script pop-up menu at the top of the Score.*

11. **Rewind and play the movie. The digital video file and wink animations play. When the playback head reaches the last frame of the presentation, the playback head delays for 5 seconds before looping back to the beginning of the Title area of the Score.**

12. **Stop the movie.**

Our next step is to substitute the Title.mov digital video sprite object with the Title.pct image in the last frames of the presentation so far.

## ADDING THE TITLE.PCT IMAGE TO THE SCORE

Earlier in this chapter we mentioned that digital video files are not affected by transitions in the Transition channel. In this session we will substitute the last few frames of the Title.mov file with the Title.pct image. This will allow the transition that we will add to the Score in the next chapter to dissolve the title image when we jump to the next scene of the Billionaire's Shop.

1. **Drag Cast member 27 (the Title.pct image) to frame 143 of channel 10 in the Score. This is where we will have the Title.pct image appear in the presentation.**

2. **Position the Title.pct image sprite on Stage in the same location as the Title.mov digital video file on the Stage. If you are working with the Windows version of Director, the image will appear behind the digital video sprite. This will also occur on the Macintosh if the Direct To Stage setting is selected in the Cast member properties for the video file. The file will be positioned**

correctly if the left and upper edges of the sprite are flush with the left and upper edges of the Stage. You can use the same coordinates that we used for the Title.mov sprite to position this image perfectly, by setting an X coordinate of 180 and a Y coordinate of 35.

The Title.pct image will appear behind the digital video sprite on the Stage even though the image is in a higher numbered sprite channel. This is due to unmodifiable settings on Windows that optimize playback of video files. This effect will also occur if the Direct To Stage setting is selected in the Cast member properties for the video file. Use the settings indicated in step 2 above to ensure appropriate positioning.

The image sprite object is also visible on the Stage. The top of the Score is visible on the Stage with **180** typed into the X: window and **35** typed into the Y: window. Arrows identify these settings at the top of the Score.

**FIGURE 5.32** *The Title.pct image file dragged to channel 10 of frame 143 of the Score.*

3.   Drag the endpoint for the Title.pct sprite object in channel 10 from frame 171 back to frame 145. Now the Title.pct image ends in the same frame as the other objects in the Score.

4.   Drag the endpoint for the sprite object in channel 8 (the digital video sprite) from frame 145 to frame 142. This will have the Title.pct image replace the Title.mov image in both the Score and on the Stage at frame 143. There will be virtually no visual difference to the user, and we will now be able to dissolve from this scene in chapter 6.

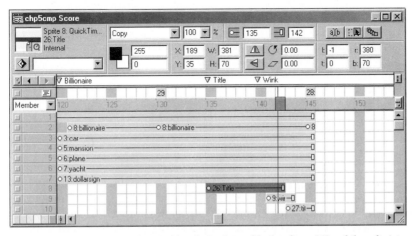

**FIGURE 5.33** *The Score with sprite 8's endpoint dragged back to frame 142 and the endpoint for the sprite in channel 10 dragged to frame 145, so that it is located in frames 143 through 145.*

5.   Play and then stop the movie.

The movie plays as before. Now the last few frames contain the Title.pct image instead of the Title.mov image. Use this time to make sure that the positioning of the Title.pct image is identical to the positioning of the Title.mov file in the earlier frames. Our next step is to link the Title and Wink areas of the Score to the rest of the opening animation.

## LINKING THE BILLIONAIRE ANIMATION TO THE TITLE AND WINK ANIMATIONS

We will place a new behavior at the end of the Billionaire animations that will send the playback head to the beginning of the Title animation. Currently there is a behavior there that causes the playback head to loop back to the beginning of the Score. We will create a new behavior that will cause the playback head to jump to the marker labeled Title.

1.   Highlight frame 130 of the script channel. This is the last frame of the Billionaire animation.

2.   Choose New Behavior from the Script pop-up menu at the top of the Score. This will directly open the Script window with the default event handler on exitFrame. The Script pop-up menu will also allow you access to the other scripts that have been added to the Score so far.

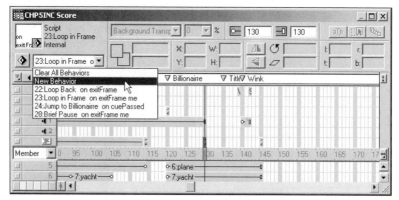

**FIGURE 5.34** *New Behavior selected from the Script pop-up menu.*

3.   Type the following script in the Script window. You will only need to add the script that is presented in bold in figure 5.35.

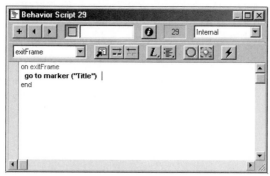

**FIGURE 5.35** *The Script window.*

```
on exitFrame
  go to marker ("Title")
end
```

4.  Close the Script window. Scripts that are entered in this direct manner do not need the additional step of being selected from the Sprite Script pop-up menu.

5.  Choose Control>Selected Frames Only. This will deselect the Selected Frames Only option for playback. The green line on the frame bar indicates that this option that is turned on should disappear. Now we can view the entire opening animation.

6.  Rewind and play the movie. The entire opening animation plays: first the Icons of Wealth, then the Billionaire animation, followed by the digital video Title animation, ending with the wink. The playback head then waits 5 seconds, and loops to the beginning of the Score by default because there is nothing further along in the Score to play. On some computers, it might seem that the sound effect behind the Billionaire's animation doesn't finish playing before the playback head jumps over to the Title area of the Score. We can prevent this by using a tempo setting in the tempo channel of the Score. We have already created the tempo setting that we need for the end of the Wink animation, so we will copy that setting and reuse it in frame 130.

7.  Highlight frame 142 of the tempo channel of the Score. This is where we added the tempo setting that waits for the Wink sound effect to finish playing before letting the playback head continue. Because the setting here holds the playback head in place until the sound in channel 1 has finished playing, the same tempo setting will work for the Billionaire animation because the Billionaire's sound effect is also located in sound channel 1.

8.  Choose Edit>Copy Sprites. This will copy the tempo setting. Now we will paste it into frame 130.

9.  Highlight frame 130 of the tempo channel and choose Edit>Paste Sprites. This will place the tempo setting in frame 130. Now we will play the movie again to see if we have corrected the problem (see figure 5.36).

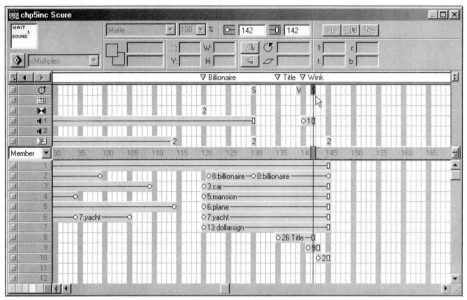

**FIGURE 5.36** *The Tempo channel sprite located in frame 142 of the Score.*

10. **Rewind and play the movie. The movie plays as it did before, but now the playback head waits for the sound effect behind the Billionaire's animation to finish playing before jumping over to the Title area of the Score.**

11. **Stop the movie.**

Now we are ready to start doing some more detailed work with the behavior inspector and Lingo in chapter 6.

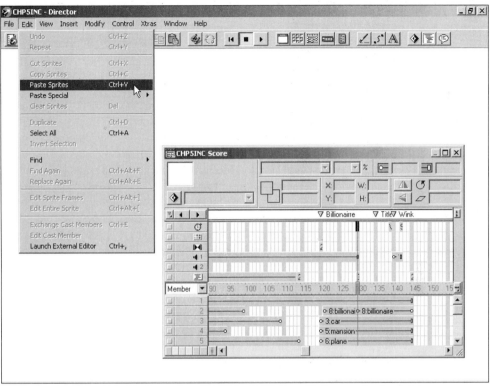

**FIGURE 5.37** *Frame 130 of the Tempo channel highlighted. Edit>Paste Sprites menu item is selected.*

## SUMMARY

Digital video files are images and sound combined into a single file that can be played in a single frame or across multiple frames in Director's Score. These files are created with applications, such as Adobe Premiere, that allow the import of video from videotape and other video sources such as camcorders. Premiere also allows the import of images created with other applications, such as Adobe Photoshop and Strata StudioPro, to allow them to be edited together with the video. Audio can also be added to these files to produce a soundtrack for music, sound effects, and voiceovers. Once created in a digital video editing program, these files can then be output as QuickTime or Microsoft Video for Windows, or the newer Directshow, files; these files will be recognized and played in other applications, including Director.

Digital video files require the presence of special system software extensions that might already be installed in your computer's system software. QuickTime files require the installation of QuickTime for Macintosh or Windows. Other video formats such as Microsoft Video for Windows must be installed. The video file that is used in The Billionaire's Shop is a single QuickTime file that can be played on either platform. The most current QuickTime system extensions are available from Apple's Web site: http://www.apple.com. Video for Windows or Directshow can be downloaded from Microsoft.com. Video for Windows is not needed for The Billionaire's Shop.

Director can be used to create digital video files by choosing File>Export; we can then choose the option to output Director's frames as the frames in a digital video file. Director for Windows will output Microsoft Video for Windows files, and Director for Macintosh will output QuickTime files. Director for Macintosh can play, but not create, QuickTime movies. Digital video files that are created with Director will retain the images and sound in each frame, but they will lose any interactivity and transitions that are created using the transition channel in the Score.

Digital video files can be imported into Director, where they can be used just as any other Cast member. The only difference is that the original digital video file must be included on the hard drive, along with the Director file that uses the file. Digital video files remain external to the Director file because they tend to be large and require access to the software that is installed in your computer's system. Be certain that any Director files that use digital video files also include the original digital video media. It is helpful to first organize your digital video files into a single directory and then import them into Director; this allows for the easy transport of the digital video files together.

The tempo channel can be used to delay the playback head until a cue point is reached in a sound or in the sound track of a digital video file. All video and sound files that are located in the same frame will be available from a pop-up menu in the Tempo Settings dialog box. Any cue points in the selected file will be available from another pop-up menu in the Tempo Settings dialog box. If there are no cue points in the digital video or sound file, the Tempo Settings dialog box will give you the option to wait until the end of the file before allowing the playback head to proceed through the Score.

Scripts can be entered directly into the script channel of the Score by double-clicking in the frame of the script channel that the new script will occupy. This will bypass the behavior inspector and allow the script to be entered directly into the Script window. Scripts entered this way are still accessible and can be modified through the behavior inspector.

## QUESTIONS

1. Why is it necessary to distribute the original Digital movie files along with the Director movies that they are used in?

2. What are two digital video file formats? Which one is cross-platform (able to be used on both the Macintosh and Windows operating systems)?

3. Why are digital video files maintained externally in Director movies?

4. Why was it necessary to substitute the Title.mov sprite object with a sprite object created with the Title.pct file?

5. What is the tempo setting that we can use to cause the playback head to wait until a digital video sprite has finished playing before continuing?

## EXERCISES

1. Create a movie and import a digital video file. You can use the digital video file that we used in this chapter. Add the digital video file to the first 20 frames of channel 1 in the Score. Add a script to frame 10 that will cause the playback head to loop in place. (Use the script "go to the frame.") When you play the movie, you will see that the digital video file will play on the Stage and the playback head will stop in frame 10. There are an additional 10 frames that the video sprite occupies that are not seen at this point.

2. In the movie you created in exercise 1, create an animation from frame 11 to frame 20. The animation should be a text Cast member—any word or phrase you choose, such as your name. Have the text Cast member animate from one of the sides of the Stage to a point near the digital video sprite. When you have created the new animation, delete the script that is located in frame 10 of the Score. Now when you play this movie, the playback head will pass frame 10 and play through frames 11 to 20. The digital video file might not finish its playback before the new animation has completed moving across the Stage.

3. Again, in the movie that we have been working with in the past two exercises, add a tempo setting to frame 10 of the tempo channel that will cause the playback head to wait until the digital video sprite in channel 1 has finished playing. Now when you play this movie, the digital video sprite will finish playback in frame 10 before continuing into frame 11, where it will play the new animation. Because the digital video sprite will have finished before playing into frame 11, the digital video sprite will not continue animating past frame 10, it will remain in its last frame through the end of the Score. Tweak tempo and property settings in the movie to achieve the final result you would like.

# CHAPTER 6

# DRAG-AND-DROP BEHAVIORS AND USING EXTERNAL CASTS

# 6 Drag-and-Drop Behaviors and Using External Casts

**In this chapter, you will learn how to:**

- Link external Cast Libraries to a Director movie
- Use drag-and-drop behaviors
- Send the playback head to a new frame with a Lingo script
- Place a sprite at a precise location
- Use the name of Cast members to improve the efficiency of scripts
- Make three state buttons

Two of Director's most significant features are scriptless authoring and the use of multiple Casts. Scriptless authoring provides us with access to Director's powerful Lingo scripting language by allowing us to simply choose combinations of options using the behavior inspector, even with no knowledge of how the Lingo scripting language is structured. Another possibility is the use of drag-and-drop behaviors, which are preprogrammed behaviors that can simply be added to a Director movie. A library of drag-and-drop behaviors is included with Director. Various other libraries are available for purchase from third-party developers.

Multiple Cast files allow us to create libraries of media that can be used to organize the media in a Director movie and can also be shared with different movies. In chapter 1 we discussed that Cast files can be external as well as internal. Using external Cast files provides a convenient way to transfer multiple media elements, or different file types, together in a single file. In this chapter we will link The Billionaire's Shop to three new external Cast files that contain images and drag-and-drop behaviors that we will use to create some of the interactive parts of The Shop. Let's take a look at the completed version of this chapter's lesson.

## VIEWING THE COMPLETED FILE

1.   **If it is not already open, launch Director.**

2.   **Choose File>Open.**

3.   **Locate and select the file named Chp6cmp.dir, which is located on the CD-ROM in the directory Lessons/Chaptr6/Part2/Complete/Chp6cmp.dir.**

     This chapter's lesson is split into two parts, so we will view the complete version of the second part. This version contains all of the additions that are made in this chapter.

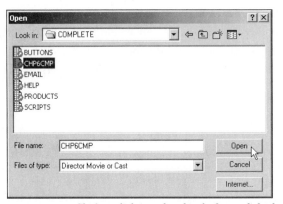

**FIGURE 6.01** *Chp6cmp.dir being selected in the Open... dialog box.*

4.   **Click Open.**

5.   **Play the movie.**

     This movie begins with the same opening animation that we created in earlier chapters. At the end of the animation, the playback head delays a few seconds, then dissolves to the main screen of The Billionaire's Shop. There are five buttons on this screen that become highlighted when the mouse pointer is passed or rolled over them. They will also appear depressed when they are clicked. The only buttons that will currently result in an action are the Quit and Help buttons. Clicking on the Quit button will result in a jump to a screen where we are asked, "Are you sure you want to quit?" with two other buttons: Yes and No. Clicking the Yes button will cause Director to quit; clicking the No button will return us to the main screen of The Billionaire's Shop (see figure 6.03). The Help button activates the Help feature of The Billionaire's Shop and will cause Help Balloons to appear over several of the screen elements in the main screen when the mouse pointer is passed over them. Clicking the Help button a second time will deactivate this feature (see figure 6.04). In this session we will add all of these new button images, and we will use preprogrammed drag-and-drop behaviors to program the buttons.

6.   **Stop the movie.**

Now we will prepare the files that we will use in this lesson.

**FIGURE 6.02** *The main screen of The Billionaire's Shop.*

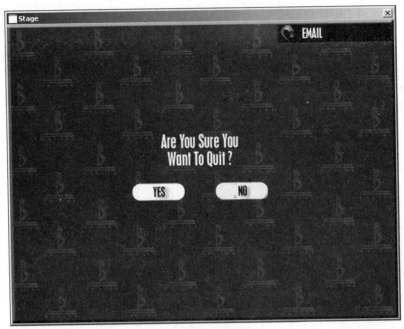

**FIGURE 6.03** *The Quit screen of The Billionaire's Shop.*

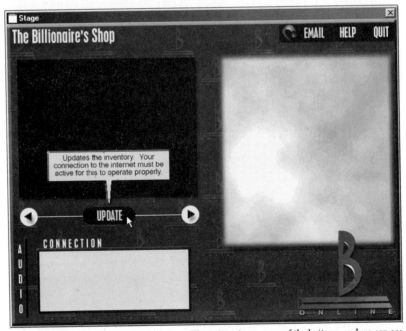

**FIGURE 6.04** *The activated Help feature. The pointer is over one of the buttons, and we can see a Help Balloon.*

## PREPARING FILES FOR THIS LESSON

If you are working with the commercial version of Director and would like to continue working with the file that you created in an earlier chapter, you will need to copy three new files to the directory that contains the file that you worked with. If you are using the Trial version of Director, you can continue from the section titled Opening the Partly Completed File.

1.   Locate and open the Lessons folder on your CD-ROM.

2.   Open the folder named Chaptr6.

3.   Locate and copy the files named buttons.cst, scripts.cst, and help.cst to the Billshop directory on your hard drive. These are the external Cast files that contain all of the buttons and scripts that we will use in this movie, as well as the background images for the main interface and Quit screens for The Billionaire's Shop.

> **NOTE**
>
> If you are working with the commercial version of Director but would still like to work with the partly completed file for this lesson, then copy the file named Chp6inc.DIR along with the three external Cast files. You can locate Chp6inc.dir in the following directory on the Billshop CD: Lessons/Chaptr6/Part1/Starter/.

## OPENING THE PARTLY COMPLETED FILE

1.   Choose File>Open. The Open... dialog box will appear.

2.   Open the file named Chp6inc.DIR located in the directory: Lessons/Chaptr6/Part1/Starter on the CD-ROM.

If you are working with a commercial version of Director, you can continue working with the file that you created and saved in the earlier lessons. This is the first half of the lesson in this chapter. You can view the completed version of this part by viewing the files located in the directory Lessons/Chaptr6/Part1/Complete on the CD-ROM. Our next step is to link the new external Cast files to The Billionaire's Shop.

> **NOTE**
>
> Remember to save your work frequently because the end result of each lesson is the beginning of the next lesson. We have also supplied you with the partly completed version of each lesson on the CD-ROM so that you can work with the working copy of Director that is on the CD-ROM.

## LINKING THE NEW CAST FILES TO
## THE BILLIONAIRE'S SHOP

1.  Choose Modify>Movie>Casts.... The Movie Casts dialog box appears, with a single Cast file listed: Internal. This is the default Cast window within every Director file. You can create any number of additional Cast files by choosing File>New>Cast. To import any media into that new Cast window, make the selected Cast window active, then choose import or use one of Director's other tools to generate a Cast member. You can also connect a Director file to an external Cast file by using the Link... button.

2.  Click the Button labeled Link.... A browser window will appear; it will allow you to locate the file that you would like to link to the current movie.

3.  Locate and select the file name buttons.cst, which you just copied to your hard drive. If you are working with the Trial version of Director, you can work with the files directly from the CD-ROM. Copying the files onto the hard drive will allow you to save changes to the Cast files if you are working with the commercial or academic version of Director.

4.  Click the button labeled Open. This Cast file is now included in the Director movie.

5.  Click the Button labeled Link... again. We are going to add the Help.cst file.

6.  Locate and select the file named help.cst, which you just copied to your hard drive.

7.  Click the button labeled Open. This Cast file is now included in the Director movie. Finally, we are going to add the external Cast file that contains the drag-and-drop behaviors we are going to use in this lesson.

8.  Click the button labeled Link... again. We are going to add the Scripts.cst file.

9.  Locate and select the file name scripts.cst, which you just copied to your hard drive.

10. Click the button labeled Open. This Cast file is now included in the Director movie.

11. Click the button labeled OK.

Now the button images and the scripts to activate them are available. The Scripts.cst Cast also contains behaviors that we will use in upcoming lessons.

## VIEWING THE NEW CAST WINDOWS

Multiple Cast windows located in the same Director file can be viewed separately by using the Choose Cast menu button at the upper left corner of the Cast window. You can view multiple Cast windows simultaneously by choosing Windows>Cast>(Cast window name). We will view the Buttons Cast by using the Window menu method.

1.  **Choose Window>Cast>Buttons. The Buttons Cast window will open. If the Internal Cast window is not open, you can choose Window>Cast>Internal to open that window as well. This Cast file contains the background and button images we will use in this lesson, along with several of the images we will use in upcoming chapters.**

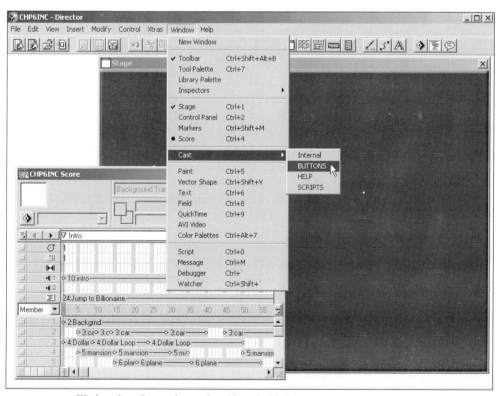

**FIGURE 6.05** *Window>Cast>Buttons being selected from the Window menu.*

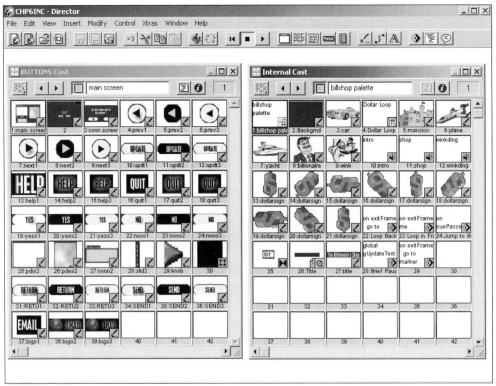

**FIGURE 6.06** *The Internal and Buttons Cast windows open side by side.*

There are three images for each button: a highlighted version, a normal state, and a depressed state. They are differentiated both in appearance as well as by name because the names of each of the three button states ends with a different number. The behaviors that we will place on these images use the names of the images to make the buttons work. We can double-click on any of the image Cast members here to view the images up close.

2.    **Double-click on Cast member 1 of the Buttons Cast. This will launch the Paint window and display the main screen image at full size. Use the Previous Cast Member and Next Cast Member buttons to view the Cast members in sequence. If you click far enough to view the buttons, you will see that each set of three buttons has a four-letter name that ends in a number from 1 to 3. These numbers are how the drag-and-drop behavior that we will use to activate these buttons can distinguish between the different states of the buttons: 1 = up, 2 = rollover, and 3 = down. The rollover state is the appearance of the button when the pointer is passed across it.**

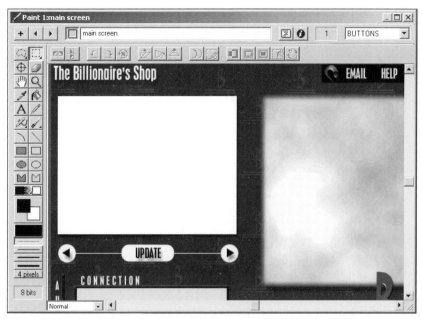

**FIGURE 6.07** *The main screen background open in the Paint window.*

3.    Close the Paint window. Now we will view the other Cast files.

4.    Choose Window>Cast>Help. This Cast window contains images
      we will use to create the Help feature for The Billionaire's Shop.
      Let's look at these Cast members at full size.

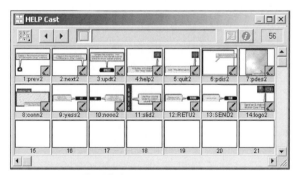

**FIGURE 6.08** *The Help Cast.*

5.    Double-click on Cast member 1 in the Help Cast window. Once
      again the Paint window will open and display the help image for
      the Prev2 button. Notice that each of these images uses the
      mouse rollover state (the number 2 at the end of the name) for
      the button it represents, along with the Help Balloon that

explains what that button does. Each image also has a name that
is identical to the rollover state of the button it represents.
When we program and activate the Help feature, each button
will use the rollover state from the Help Cast instead of the Buttons Cast. Clicking the Help button once will activate the feature, clicking it again will deactivate it.

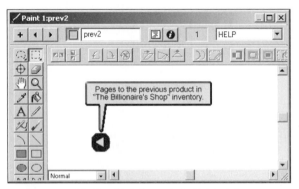

**FIGURE 6.09** *The Prev2 help button in the Paint window.*

6.  Close the Paint window. Now we will look at the Scripts Cast.

7.  Choose Window>Cast>Scripts. This Cast window contains the
    pre-programmed behaviors that we can apply to the buttons in
    The Billionaire's Shop. There are other scripts in this window
    that will be used later. We will also create scripts later that we
    will save in this Cast file.

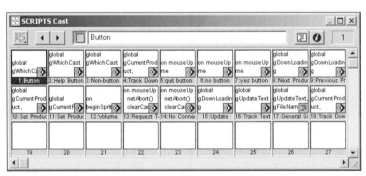

**FIGURE 6.10** *The Scripts Cast.*

## VIEWING BOTH THE NAME AND NUMBER OF THE CAST MEMBERS

In the Label area beneath each Cast member, you should be able to see the Cast member's name and number, separated by a colon, like this 1:Main Background. If you do not, then follow these directions. Setting this feature will make it easier for you to identify which Cast members are being referenced in these lessons.

1.  **Choose File>Preferences>Cast.... The Cast Window Preferences for the Buttons dialog box appears.**

2.  **Choose Number:Name from the pop-up menu beside the word Label:**

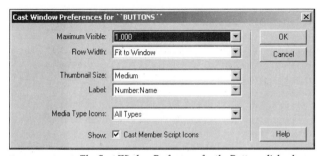

**FIGURE 6.11** *The Cast Window Preferences for the Buttons dialog box.*

3.  **Click the button labeled OK. You can change the way the Cast members are labeled in the other Cast files by opening the Cast file and setting this feature for each Cast in the Cast Window Preferences For... dialog box.**

4.  **Repeat steps 1 to 3 above for the Internal, Help, and Scripts Cast windows.**

Now we will set up the main screen of The Billionaire's Shop.

## SETTING UP THE BILLIONAIRE'S SHOP SCREEN

The main screen for The Billionaire's Shop is composed of two basic elements: the background, and the buttons to be placed on it. Cast Member 1 in the Buttons Cast is the main-screen background. This image includes the positions for placement of the buttons. This way we can use the background as a guide. In this session we will create the area of the Score that will contain the main screen of The Billionaire's Shop. We will also place the buttons on the background.

## ADDING THE SHOP MARKER

Adding a marker to the Score will help to identify where the main screen is located and can later be used as the destination for a Script that will bring users here.

1.  **Click in the marker channel at frame 150. A new marker will appear at frame 150.**

2.  **Name the marker Shop.**

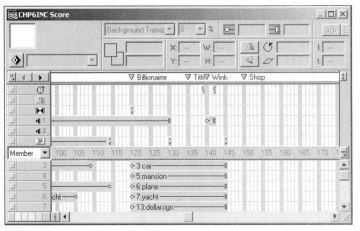

**FIGURE 6.12** *A marker at frame 150 named Shop.*

## PLACING THE SHOP BACKGROUND AND BUTTONS

1.  **Click the cell in frame 150 of channel 1 in the Score. This will ensure that the Cast members that we drag out to the Stage or Score will begin in frame 150.**

2.  **Drag Cast member 1 from the Buttons Cast window to frame 150 of channel 1 and set the ink effect to Background Transparent. Dragging the main-screen background Cast member directly to the Score will center the sprite object that is created on the Stage.**

3.  **Click directly on frame 150 of channel 2 in the Score. Now we will place one of the buttons that we will program for this screen. This will ensure that the sprites we place on the Stage will begin in frame 150.**

4.  Drag Cast member 4 (prev1) over the area that contains the left-pointing arrow image on the main screen background and set the ink effect to Matte. Place the image in precisely the same position. You can use the arrow keys to move the button image on the Stage one pixel at a time.

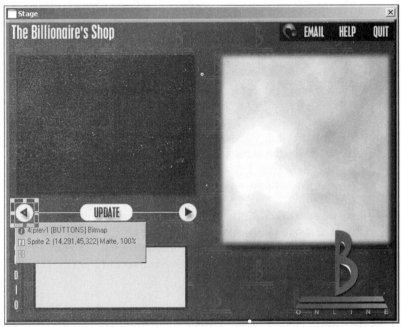

**FIGURE 6.13** *The left arrow dragged to the Stage.*

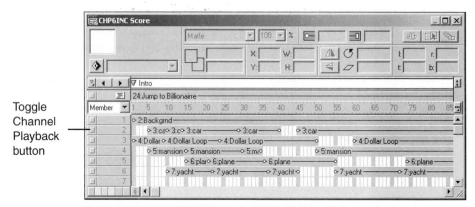

Toggle
Channel
Playback
button

**FIGURE 6.14** *The Score with an arrow identifying one of the Toggle Channel Playback buttons.*

5.    Drag Cast member 7 (next1) over the area that contains an iden-
      tical image on the main screen background image and set the
      ink effect to Matte. These are the two buttons that will later be
      programmed to browse the products in The Billionaire's Shop.

6.    Drag Cast member 10 (updt1) over the area that contains an
      identical image on the main-screen background image and set
      the ink effect to Matte. In a later lesson we will program this
      button to connect The Billionaire's Shop to the Internet for
      updates to the inventory.

7.    Drag Cast member 13 (help1) over the area that contains the
      Help button image on the main-screen background image and set
      the ink effect to Matte. We will program this button to activate
      an online help tool that will provide information about the fea-
      tures of the main screen in The Billionaire's Shop as you roll the
      mouse pointer over the buttons and other interface features.

8.    Drag Cast member 16 (quit1) over the area of the main-screen
      background image that contains the Quit button image and set
      the ink effect to Matte.

         We will program this button to exit The Billionaire's Shop. Our next
      step is to bring the endpoints of the new sprite back to frame 155.

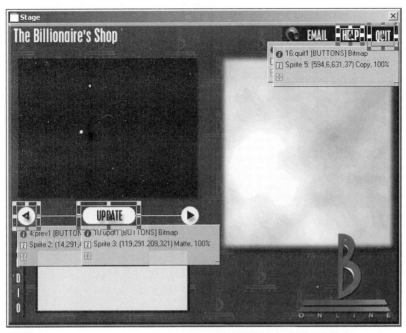

**FIGURE 6.15** *The Right, Left, Update, Help, and Quit buttons dragged to the Stage.*

## REPOSITIONING THE ENDPOINTS OF THE SHOP AREA SPRITES AND SETTING THEIR INK EFFECTS SIMULTANEOUSLY

We only need a few frames for the sprite objects in the Shop area of the Score, so we will use the Extend Sprite feature to bring the endpoints for all of the sprites back simultaneously. We will also want to set the Ink effect of the button sprites to Matte, which will render background pixels around the edges of the sprites transparent, but will leave pixels of that color visible that appear within the image.

1. Drag-select the sprite objects in the Shop area of the Score. These are the sprite objects that are located in channels 1 to 6 in frames 150 to 178.

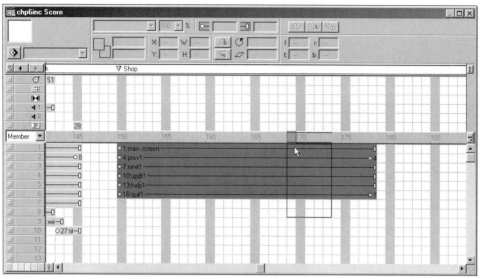

**FIGURE 6.16** *The sprite objects located in channels 1 to 6 of frames 150 to 178. A selection is currently being dragged across the Score.*

2.  Click in the frame bar at frame 155. Make certain you click directly on the frame bar so that the selected sprites remain selected. If you click elsewhere in the channels of the Score, you will remove the highlight applied to the selected sprites.

3.  Activate the Extend Sprite option. You can activate this feature by choosing Modify>Extend Sprite. When you have done this, the endpoints for all of the selected sprites will move to frame 155.

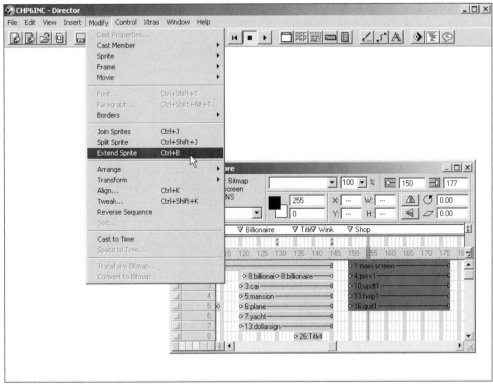

**FIGURE 6.17** *The playback head moved to frame 155. Modify>Extend Sprite option selected*

## CONTROLLING THE POSITION OF THE PLAYBACK HEAD

In this session we will use the Selected Frames Only setting to restrict the playback head to the Shop area of the Score. We will also add the Looping behavior we created in chapter 5 to the last frame of the Shop area of the Score.

1.  Select the main-screen background directly on the Stage. This will highlight the entire main-screen background sprite object in the Score. This sprite spans the length of the Shop area of the Score and can be used to define the Selected Frames Only setting.

2.  Choose Control>Selected Frames Only. Now the playback head will only play through the Shop area of the Score.

3.  Click in the cell at frame 155 of the Script channel.

4.    **Choose the behavior named Loop in Frame (on exitFrame me is displayed beside it) from the Sprite Script pop-up menu at the top of the Score.**

This will keep the playback head in frame 155, using the behavior we created earlier. Next, we will add the Button behavior, which will activate the buttons we have added to this screen.

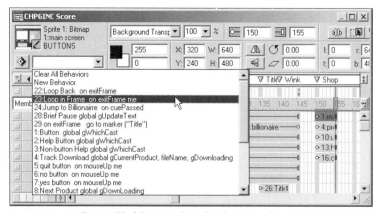

**FIGURE 6.18** *Frame 155 of the script channel in the Score selected. The Loop in Frame behavior is selected from the Sprite Script pop-up menu at the top of the Score.*

**NOTE**   When a behavior or other type of script is created, it automatically generates a Cast member. This script Cast member can be used in multiple locations throughout a Director movie. Editing a script Cast member at any time will alter the script in every place it is used. Therefore, if you find there is no existing script that can be used to accomplish something you would like to add to a movie, you should create a new script instead of editing the old one.

## USING A DRAG-AND-DROP BEHAVIOR

Cast member 1 of the Scripts Cast is the preprogrammed behavior that we can apply to a button. We can learn how to properly use this behavior by viewing it in the behavior inspector.

1.    **Open the Scripts Cast window. You can do this by choosing Scripts from the Choose Cast menu in the upper left corner of the Cast window. You can also select Window>Cast>Script.**

2.  Double-click Cast member 1 of the Scripts Cast. This is the But-
    ton behavior we will be using. Double-clicking on this Cast mem-
    ber will launch the behavior inspector, where we can view more
    detailed information about this behavior.

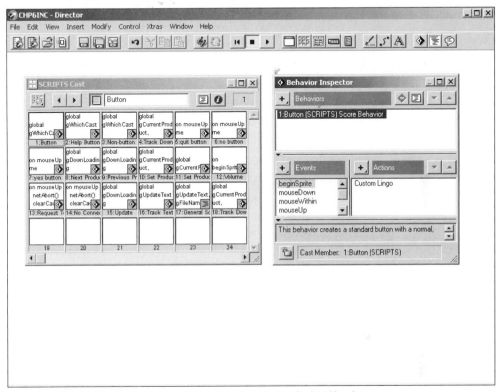

**FIGURE 6.19** *The Scripts Cast window with the behavior inspector displayed beside it.*

3.  If the Behavior Description display area at the bottom of the
    behavior inspector is not visible, then click the second arrow
    along the left side of its window. The following information is
    displayed as a description of the Button behavior. This behavior
    creates a standard button with a normal, highlighted, and
    depressed state. Follow these steps to use it:

    1.  Create three images for each button: a highlighted ver-
        sion, a normal version, and a depressed version.

    2.  Name each Cast member an identical four-letter name,
        ending with 1, 2, or 3 for the normal, highlighted, and
        depressed states, respectively.

3.  **Place the normal-state Cast member for the button on the Stage.**

4.  **Drag this behavior onto the sprite object on the Stage.**

For example, to create a button named Quit, create three Cast members:

Quit1: the button's normal, unclicked state.

Quit2: the button's highlighted version, which will activate when the button is rolled over.

Quit3: the button's depressed state when clicked.

This behavior is also equipped with an optional Help feature that is activated when this behavior is combined with the Help behavior that is also included in the Scripts Cast of The Billionaire's Shop.

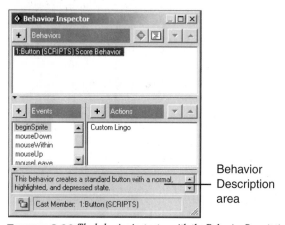

**FIGURE 6.20** *The behavior inspector with the Behavior Description area visible.*

We already have most of the steps accomplished that we need to use this behavior. Each button has three states: up, highlighted, and down. Each button also has a four-letter name that ends with a 1, 2, or 3 for the three different states. We have also already placed the normal state of the buttons on the Stage. The only step left to use this behavior is to place it on the buttons on the Stage.

5.  **Close the behavior inspector.**

Now we will place the Button behavior on the button sprites on the Stage.

## PLACING THE BUTTON BEHAVIOR ON THE BUTTONS OF THE BILLIONAIRE'S SHOP

1.  Make certain the playback head is in frame 150. We will need to see the button sprites on the Stage in order to drag the Button behavior onto them.

2.  Drag Cast member 1 of the Scripts Cast (Button) directly over the Quit button on the Stage. When the Button behavior is dragged onto the Quit button, the sprite overlay for the Quit button will become visible. Notice that the word Button appears on the third line beside the green diamond that represents the behavior inspector. This means the Button behavior has been applied to the Quit button.

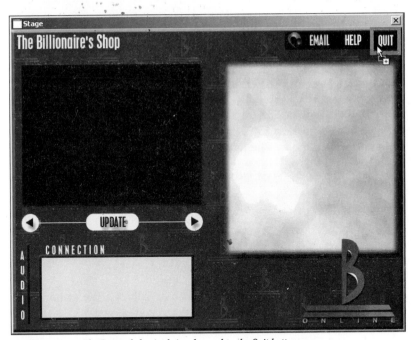

**FIGURE 6.21** *The Button behavior being dragged to the Quit button.*

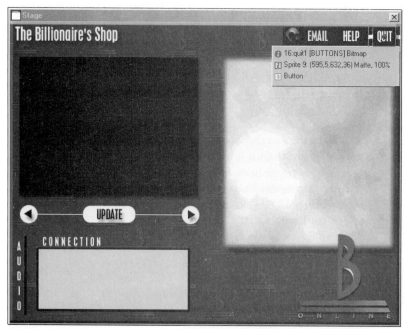

**FIGURE 6.22** *The Quit button's sprite overlay with the Button behavior applied.*

3. **Play the movie. The Quit button will highlight if you roll the mouse pointer over it. It will also appear depressed when the button is clicked. The button behavior is working.**

4. **Stop the movie. Now we will place the Button behavior over the other buttons.**

5. **Drag the Button behavior from the Scripts Cast to the remaining four buttons on the Stage—the left-arrow button, the right-arrow button, the Update button, and the Help button. This will give all of the buttons on the Stage the same properties.**

6. **Play the movie. Now all of the buttons will look the same way the Quit button does when clicked and rolled over.**

7. **Stop the movie.**

## ADDING THE QUIT SCREEN

Our next step is to begin programming the buttons on the main screen interface. That is, we will provide for an action in addition to having the buttons change appearance. We will begin with the Quit button. Our first step is to build the Quit screen, which will become the Quit button's destination.

1. Move the playback head to frame 160. This is where we will locate the Quit screen.

2. Place a marker in frame 160 and label it Quit. We will use this as the destination for the Quit button.

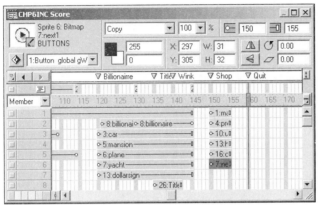

**FIGURE 6.23** *A marker placed in frame 160 labeled Quit.*

3. Drag Cast member 2 of the Buttons Cast (the Quit Screen background) to frame 160 of channel 1. This is the screen we will program to be the Quit button's destination when clicked. The user will be presented with the phrase, "Are you sure you want to quit?" and two button choices, Yes and No. The images of the Yes and No buttons that are already incorporated into the background are for placement reference for the actual buttons.

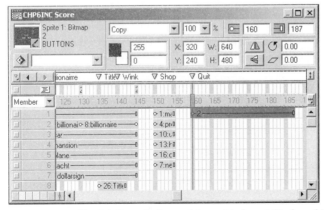

**FIGURE 6.24** *The Quit Screen background dragged to frame 160, channel 1.*

4.  Drag Cast member 19 of the Button Cast (the Yes button) to frame 160 of channel 2 and set the ink effect to Matte. Position the Yes button image so that it is superimposed over the image of the Yes button on the Quit Screen background. Use the arrow keys on the keyboard to move the image one pixel at a time.

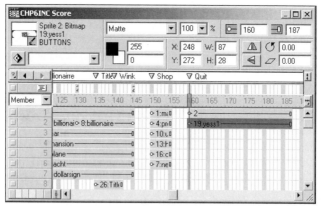

**FIGURE 6.25** *Cast member 19 of the Button Cast dragged to frame 160 of channel 2.*

5.  Drag Cast member 22 of the Buttons Cast (the No button) to frame 160 of channel 3 and set the ink effect to Matte. Position the No button image so that it is superimposed over the image of the No button on the Quit Screen background. Use the arrow keys on the keyboard to move the image one pixel at a time.

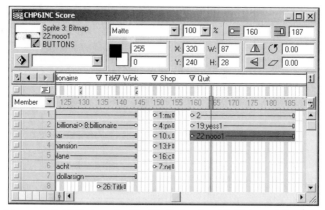

**FIGURE 6.26** *Cast member 22 of the Button Cast (the No button) dragged to frame 160 of channel 3.*

Our next step is to reposition the endpoints of the sprite object back to frame 165.

## REPOSITIONING THE ENDPOINTS FOR THE SPRITE OBJECTS IN THE QUIT AREA OF THE SCORE

Currently all of the endpoints of the sprite objects in the Quit area of the Score extend to frame 188. In this session we will reposition the endpoints for all of these sprites in frame 165.

1.  **Drag-select the sprite objects in channels 1 to 3 of the Quit area on the Score. We will use the Extend Sprite control to reposition the endpoints.**

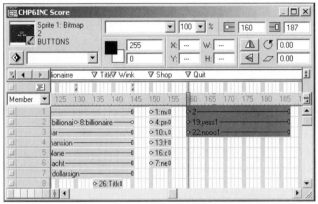

**FIGURE 6.27** *The sprite objects in the Quit area of the Score being drag-selected.*

2.  **Place the playback head in frame 165. Make certain you move only the playback head and do not deselect the highlighted sprite objects.**

3.  **Choose Modify>Extend Sprite. This will move the endpoints for the sprite objects to frame 165.**

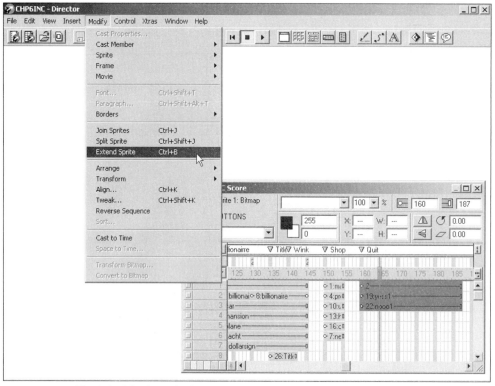

**FIGURE 6.28** *The playback head moved to frame 165. Modify>Extend Sprite is selected.*

## PLACING THE LOOP IN FRAME BEHAVIOR INTO THE QUIT AREA OF THE SCORE

When we program the Quit button to jump to the Quit area of the Score, we will want the playback head to remain in the last frame until the view has made another selection. We will make certain that the playback head remains in the last frame by adding the Loop in Frame behavior to frame 165.

1.   **Highlight frame 165 of the script channel. This is the last frame in The Billionaire's Shop Score.**

2.   **Choose the behavior named Loop in Frame from the Sprite Script pop-up menu at the top of the Score.**

Now the playback head will remain in frame 165 when we program the Quit button to jump to the Quit area of the Score. Our next step is to program the buttons associated with Quit.

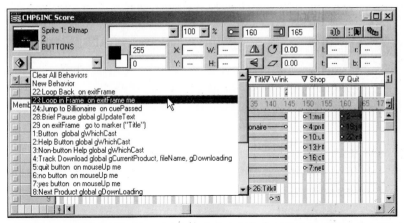

**FIGURE 6.29** *Frame 165 of the script channel selected. The Loop in Frame behavior is selected from the Sprite Script pop-up menu at the top of the Score.*

## PLACING THE BUTTON BEHAVIOR ON THE QUIT SCREEN BUTTONS

The Button behavior that we used for the Shop area of the Score is designed to work with any buttons that meet the Cast member naming convention criteria. Both the Yes and No buttons of the Quit screen have three Cast members with four-letter names that end in 1, 2, or 3, so we can use the Button behavior here.

1.  **Open the Scripts Cast. The Button behavior is Cast member 1 in the Scripts Cast.**

2.  **Drag Cast member 1 of the Scripts Cast (the Button behavior) directly on to the Yes button on the Stage. When you release the mouse button with the behavior, the sprite overlay for the Yes button will appear and show that the Button behavior has been placed.**

3.  **Drag Cast member 1 of the Scripts Cast (the Button behavior) directly on to the No button on the Stage.**

The buttons on the Quit screen are now both programmed. We will test them in a moment. First we will need to extend the Selected Frames Only setting so that the playback head will be permitted into these frames.

**FIGURE 6.30** *The Button behavior dragged to the No button on the Stage. The sprite overlay for the Yes button is visible with the Button behavior listed.*

## EXTENDING THE SELECTED FRAMES ONLY SETTING

Currently the Selected Frames Only setting is programmed to play through the Shop area of the Score. We are at a point in the development of The Billionaire's Shop where we would like to test the buttons on the Quit screen as well as program the Quit button on the Shop screen to branch to the Quit screen. In this session we will include the Quit area of the Score in the restricted playback area.

1.    If it is not currently open, open the Score.

2.    Click directly on the center of the sprite object in channel 1 of the Shop area in the Score. This will highlight the main screen background, which spans the Shop area of the Score. Make certain you click on the center of the sprite object so that you highlight the entire sprite object. If you click on a cell that contains a key frame, then you will only highlight that frame.

3.    Hold the Shift key down and click directly on the sprite object in channel 1 of the Quit area in the Score. Holding the Shift key while clicking on another sprite will extend the selected area of the Score to include that sprite. Now the selected area of the Score includes the Shop and Quit areas of the Score.

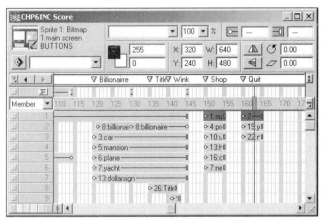

**FIGURE 6.31** *The sprite objects in channel 1 of both the Shop and Quit areas of the Score selected.*

4. **If it is not currently open, open the Control Panel. You can do this by choosing Window>Control Panel.**

5. **Click the Selected Frames Only button to reset this feature. The first time you click the button, it will actually turn the Selected Frames Only feature off. This is necessary to redefine the area that is included in the restricted playback area.**

**FIGURE 6.32** *The Selected Frames Only button in the process of being selected.*

6. **Click the Selected Frames Only button again. This will turn the Selected Frames Only feature back on, with the currently selected area of the Score defining what is included in playback.**

We can see that the green line along the frame bar in the Score now extends to the Quit area of the Score. Now we will be able to preview the Quit screen along with the Shop screen.

Our next step is to program the Quit button.

**FIGURE 6.33** *The Selected Frames Only feature reset to include the Shop and Quit areas of the Score.*

## PROGRAMMING THE QUIT BUTTON

All of the buttons we have added to The Billionaire's Shop share the Button behavior; this gives them all the same general properties for mouse interaction. Now we can begin adding behaviors that will give each button a specific purpose. We will start with the Quit button.

1.  Move the playback head to the Shop area of the Score. You can click anywhere in the Score between frames 150 and 155 to move the playback head to the Shop area. We need access to the Quit button on the Stage.

2.  If it is not currently open, open the Scripts Cast window. Any new Cast members, scripts or otherwise, are added to the currently active Cast window. By making the Scripts Cast window active, we are letting Director know that we would like to locate our new script in this Cast window. We have already created several scripts that were included in the internal Cast window, but now that we have a Scripts Cast, we will place any new scripts that we create here. This will make locating our scripts easier when we need them.

3.  Click directly on the Quit button on the Stage. The sprite overlay for the Quit button will appear. At the bottom of the sprite overlay is the line that indicates which behaviors have been applied to that sprite. Currently the only behavior on the Quit button is the Button behavior. Sprite objects can carry more than one behavior, so we can add another here to tell the playback head to jump over to the Quit area of the Score when the Quit button is clicked.

4.  Click the behavior inspector button in the lower left corner of the Quit button sprite overlay. This will open the behavior inspector just as if we had clicked the button at the top of the Score or chosen Window>Inspectors>Behavior.

5.  Choose Behaviors>New Behavior... from the Behavior pop-up menu at the top of the behavior inspector. The Name Behavior dialog box will appear.

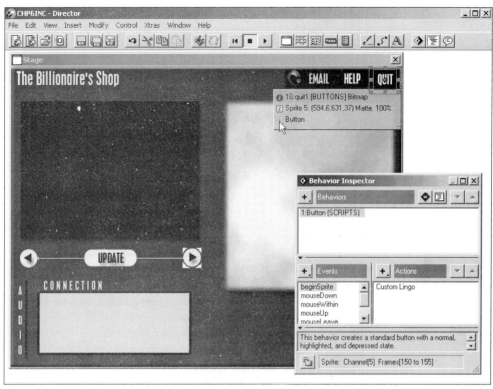

**FIGURE 6.34** *The pointer over the behavior inspector button on the Quit button's sprite overlay.*

6. Name the new behavior Quit Button. Note that as soon as the new behavior is named, it is added to the behaviors listed on the bottom line of the Quit button's sprite overlay.

7. Choose Events>Mouse Up from the Events pop-up menu in the behavior inspector. If the Events and Actions areas of the behavior inspector are not currently visible, click on the first arrow along the left side of the behavior inspector.

8. Choose Actions>Navigation>Go to Marker.... The Specify Marker dialog box will appear.

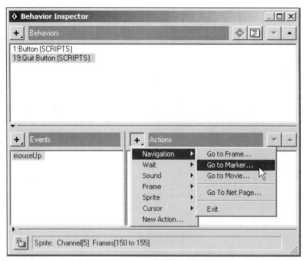

**FIGURE 6.35** *Actions>Navigation>Go to Marker... selected in the behavior inspector.*

9.  **Choose Quit from the Go to Marker: menu in the Specify Marker dialog box. The word Quit here indicates the label attached to the marker we placed at the Quit area of the Score. Choosing Quit here will apply the necessary programming to have the Quit button branch properly.**

**FIGURE 6.36** *The Specify Marker dialog box with Quit selected.*

10. **Click the OK button in the Specify Marker dialog box. Now we can test the new behavior.**

11. **Play the movie, then stop it.**

As you move the pointer over the Quit button, you will see the programming applied by the Button behavior immediately as the button highlights. When you click and release the button, it branches to the Quit area of the Score. This is caused by the Quit Button behavior. The ability to apply more than one behavior to a sprite object is remarkably powerful because it allows a single button to perform multiple tasks. It also allows us to add programming to a presentation without needing to reprogram the scripts that are already there.

At the Quit screen you will see evidence of the Button behavior as the Yes and No buttons become highlighted and perform the other reactions to mouse activity. Now we will add the programming that will give the user the option to confirm the decision to quit The Billionaire's Shop or to continue shopping there.

## PROGRAMMING THE YES AND NO BUTTONS

Generally it is a good idea to give the viewer the option of confirming the choice to quit out of an application. This way if the Quit button is accidentally activated, the viewer can abort the selection and continue working. Also, without a confirmation screen, you may think you've crashed the program if you accidentally click the Quit button. It isn't entirely necessary, but a confirmation screen is an intelligent courtesy.

1.  Locate and open the file named Chp6inc.DIR in the directory Lessons/Chaptr6/Part2/Starter on the CD-ROM. If you are working with the commercial or academic versions of Director, you can continue to work with the file that you have been developing on your hard drive. This is the second half of the lesson in this chapter. You can view the completed version of this part by viewing the files located in Lessons/Chaptr6/Part2/Complete on the CD-ROM.

2.  Move the playback head to the Quit area of the Score. You can click anywhere in the Score between frames 160 to 165 to move the playback head to the Quit area.

3.  If it is not currently open, open the Scripts Cast window. This will ensure that the new behaviors we create will be added to the Scripts Cast window.

4.  Click directly on the No button on the Stage. We will have the No button return the user to the Shop area of the Score.

5.  Click the Behavior Inspector button in the lower left corner of the No button sprite overlay. As we learned earlier, clicking this button will open the behavior inspector just as if we had clicked the button at the top of the Score or chosen Window>Inspectors>Behavior.

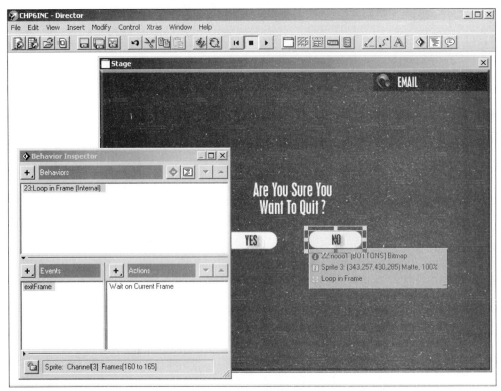

**FIGURE 6.37** *The sprite overlay for the No button displayed on the screen. The behavior inspector is displayed on the screen.*

6.    Choose Behaviors>New Behavior... from the Behavior pop-up menu at the top of the behavior inspector. The Name Behavior dialog box will appear.

7.    Name the new behavior No Button. The new behavior will be added to the behaviors listed on the bottom line of the Quit button's sprite overlay.

8.    Choose Events>Mouse Up from the Events pop-up menu in the behavior inspector. We will have this script activated when the viewer releases the mouse button.

9.    Choose Actions>Navigation>Go to Marker.... The Specify Marker dialog box will appear.

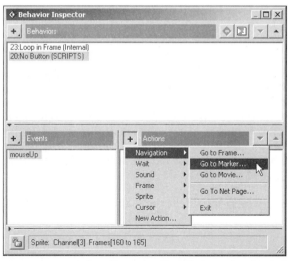

**FIGURE 6.38** *Actions>Navigation>Go to Marker... selected in the behavior inspector for the No Button behavior.*

10. **Choose Shop from the Go to Marker: menu in the Specify Marker dialog box. This will instruct the playback head to return to the Shop area of the Score when the No button is clicked.**

**FIGURE 6.39** *The Specify Marker dialog box with Shop selected.*

11. **Click the OK button in the Specify Marker dialog box and close the behavior inspector. This closes the Specify Marker dialog box, and we can see that the new behavior has been added to the list of behaviors on this button in the behavior inspector. Let's test what we have programmed so far.**

12. **Return the playback head to the Shop area of the Score. We will begin our test by clicking on the Quit button while the movie is playing.**

13. **Play the movie, then stop it. When you click on the Quit button, you will branch over to the Quit area of the Score. Click on the No button, and you will return to the Shop area of the Score. Our next step is to program the Yes button.**

14. Move the playback head to the Quit area of the Score. We want access to the Yes button on the Stage.

15. Click the Yes button on the Stage. We will program this button to confirm the choice to quit. The command we will use will stop the movie while we are still working in Director. When we create a projector, the same command will behave as if Quit was selected from the File menu. This will allow us to test the button without needing to re-launch Director every time the button is used.

16. Click the behavior inspector button at the bottom of the sprite overlay for the Yes button.

17. Choose Behaviors>New Behavior... and name the new behavior Yes Button.

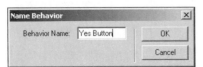

**FIGURE 6.40** *The Name Behavior dialog box with Yes Button typed into it.*

18. Choose Events>Mouse Up.

19. Choose Actions>Navigation>Exit. This uses the Exit command, which stops the presentation as if the Stop button had been clicked.

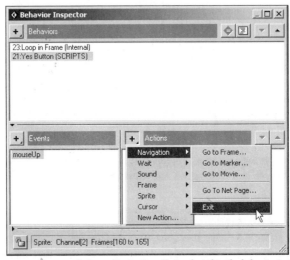

**FIGURE 6.41** *Actions>Navigation>Exit selected in the behavior inspector for the Yes Button behavior.*

20. Return the playback head to the Shop area of the Score. Let's test our work so far.

21. Play the movie. Click the Quit button to branch to the Quit area of the Score. The No button returns us to the Shop area. Click the Quit button again, but this time click the Yes button. The movie stops playing and we can continue working. We have completed programming the Quit button and the Quit screen.

## ACTIVATING THE HELP FEATURE

Now we will activate the Help feature of The Billionaire's Shop. In the completed version of this chapter's lesson, we were able to click the Help button on the Shop screen to activate a Help feature. The Help feature produces a Help Balloon over each screen element when the pointer is rolled over them. This is produced by a second behavior added to the Help button, in addition to the Button behavior. This additional behavior instructs the Button behavior to use the rollover state of each button that is located in the Help Cast instead of the Button Cast. Clicking the Help button again will instruct the Button behavior to use the original rollover state for each button. From this we learn that information can be passed between behaviors. In this case, because we are working with drag-and-drop behaviors, we do not need to be concerned about the Lingo that was used to create the behavior, we need only follow the instructions that will allow the behavior we are using to work. In this session we will add the Help feature to The Billionaire's Shop.

1. Open the Scripts Cast window. This is where the Help behavior is located.

2. Move the playback head to the Shop area of the Score. We will drag the Help behavior onto the Help button on this screen.

3. Drag Cast member 2 of the Scripts Cast (the Help behavior) directly onto the Help button on the Stage. The sprite overlay for the Help button will appear. The Help behavior will be listed along with the Button behavior at the bottom of the sprite overlay. Let's take a look at the description for how to properly use this behavior.

4. Close the Cast window. This is to conserve the working area, but is not a necessary step.

5. Click the Behavior Inspector button on the sprite overlay for the Help button on the Stage. This will produce the behavior inspector, where we will see the Button and Help behaviors listed.

6.   **Select the Help button in the top window of the behavior inspector. The description for how to use this behavior will appear in the bottom display area of the behavior inspector. If this area is not currently visible, you can make it visible by clicking the second arrow along the left side of the behavior inspector.**

**FIGURE 6.42** *The Help behavior description area.*

The description for the Help behavior is the following:

> This behavior will activate a Help feature designed into the images that are used for buttons that use the Button behavior. Follow the instructions for using the Button behavior as listed in that behavior, then place this behavior onto the button that is to serve as the Help button.

> The following files are necessary for the Help behavior to operate properly:

> • A Cast window named Help that contains all help images.

> • One Cast member for each button that uses the Button behavior.

> The image should appear identical to the rollover state for the button it represents and should have the same registration point. The Help window Cast member should also have an identical name (i.e., quit2). The Help Balloon associated with each image in the Help Cast can be added to each image as long as it does not interfere with the registration point.

This behavior can be used for onscreen image elements that do not use the Button behavior by creating a Help Cast member for the onscreen image that is located in the Help Cast; then you must apply the Non-Button Help behavior on the images that you would like to have produce a Help Balloon when the Help feature is activated.

Warning: Each Cast member that uses the Button or Non-Button Help behaviors must have a Help Cast member in the Help Cast if this behavior is to be used. If a Help Cast member is not present for a button or other onscreen element, this will result in an error message when that image is rolled over when the Help feature is activated.

Registration is the center point of a Cast member. It is used by Director as a common positioning point for all Cast members and sprites. **NOTE**

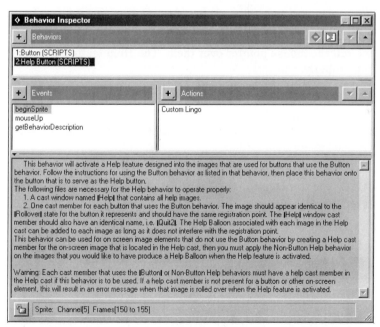

**FIGURE 6.43** *The behavior inspector displaying the description of the Help behavior.*

7.     **Close the behavior inspector.**

We have all the media that we will need to use the Help behavior in The Billionaire's Shop. We have a Cast file named Help that contains roll-over states for each button and other screen elements. In a few steps we will add to the state the non-button screen elements that we would like to also have produce a Help Balloon. First, let's test the Help feature.

## TESTING THE NEW HELP FEATURE

We have added the Help behavior to the Help button on the main screen. Let's test it to make certain that it works properly.

1.    **Move the playback head to the Shop area of the Score. This is where we want to start our playback for this test.**

2.    **Play the movie. Just as before, the buttons will highlight when they are passed over, and the Quit button will work properly.**

3.    **Click the Help button. This will activate the Help feature. Now, when we roll the mouse pointer over the buttons on the screen, we see a Help Balloon that describes the purpose of that button.**

4.    **Click the Help button again. This will deactivate the Help feature, and we will see the normal highlight for each button when we roll the mouse pointer over them. The Help feature is working properly.**

5.    **Stop the movie.**

Our next step is to add the non-button screen elements that we would like to include in the Help feature.

## ADDING THE NON-BUTTON SCREEN ELEMENTS TO THE MAIN SHOP SCREEN

In the completed version of this lesson, we were able to roll the mouse pointer over the product display, product description, and connection status areas of the screen to produce Help Balloons when the Help feature was activated. In this session we will add this aspect of the Help feature to The Billionaire's Shop.

1.    **Make certain that the playback head is in the Shop area of the Score. This is where we want to add the new screen elements.**

2.    **Open the Buttons Cast window. This Cast window contains the new media that we will want to include here. This Cast window contains the various states of each of the buttons; it also con-**

tains sections of the area of the main screen that we would like to have display a Help Balloon when they are rolled over. We must use a separate image to produce this effect because we must somehow distinguish when the pointer rolls over something new on the Stage. The only way to accomplish this is by having different sprites on the Stage. We can use sprites that are identical to parts of the main screen background so that there is no visual difference to the user.

3.   Drag Cast member 25 of the Buttons Cast (the product display) to frame 150 of channel 7 (see figure 6.45). This is the area of the screen where we will display the products in The Billionaire's Shop in upcoming lessons.

4.   Position the new sprite object on the Stage so that it is superimposed over the area of the main screen background that it resembles and set its ink effect to Background Transparent (see figure 6.44). Use the arrow keys to move the sprite one pixel at a time. Make certain that the sprite is superimposed seamlessly against the background.

5.   Drag Cast member 26 of the Buttons Cast (the product description) to frame 150 of channel 8 (see figure 6.44). This is the area of the screen where we will display the product description in The Billionaire's Shop in upcoming lessons.

6.   Position the new sprite object on the Stage so that it is superimposed over the area of the main screen background that it resembles and set its ink effect to Background Transparent (see figure 6.44). As with the product display sprite, make certain that it is superimposed seamlessly against the background.

7.   Drag Cast member 27 of the Buttons Cast (the connection status) to frame 150 of channel 9. This is the area of the screen where we will display the Internet connection status in The Billionaire's Shop in upcoming lessons.

8.   Position the new sprite object on the Stage so that it is superimposed over the area of the main screen background that it resembles and set its Ink effect to Matte. Make certain that the new sprite is superimposed seamlessly against the background.

**FIGURE 6.44** *Cast members 25–27 of the Buttons Cast dragged to the Stage.*

9.    Drag-select the three new sprite objects in the Score. The three new sprite objects are located in channels 7 through 9 of frame 150 through 178.

10.   Place the playback head in frame 155 of the Score. Make certain that you move only the playback head and do not accidentally deselect the sprite objects.

11.   Choose Modify>Extend Sprite. This will move the endpoints for all three sprite objects from frame 178 through frame 155.

12.   Select the sprites in channels 7 through 9 between frames 150 through 155 in the Score (see figure 6.45). We will rearrange the sprites in the Score in a manner that will allow them all to display their Help Balloons properly. Rearranging the order of these sprites will prevent their Help versions from interfering with the display of sprites appearing behind them when the Help feature is active.

13.   Choose Modify>Arrange>Move backward. This will shuffle these sprites up one channel in the Score.

14. **Repeat step 13 above 4 more times. This will position these sprites appropriately in channels 2, 3, and 4.**

15. **Open the Scripts Cast window. Now we will place the Non-Button Help behavior on all of the new sprite objects on the Stage.**

16. **Drag Cast member 3 of the Scripts Cast (the Non-Button Help behavior) directly onto the three new screen elements: the product display, product description, and connection status sprites. As you drag the behavior to each sprite object, the sprite overlay will appear and a display will indicate that the new behavior has been applied.**

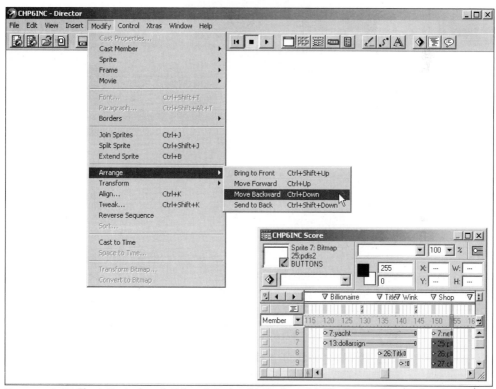

**FIGURE 6.45** *The sprites in channels 7 through 9 selected in the Score. Modify>Arrange>Move Backward selected.*

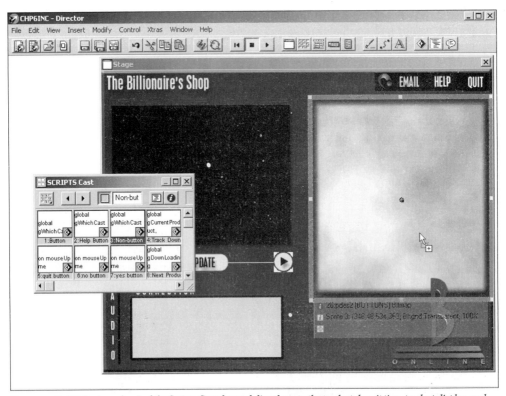

**FIGURE 6.46** *Cast member 3 of the Scripts Cast dragged directly onto the product description, product display, and connection status sprites on the Stage.*

**17.   Close the Cast window.**

We will not need any new Cast members. We can now test the new additions to the Help feature.

## TESTING THE NEW HELP ADDITIONS

Now that we have added the new screen elements to the Shop area of the Score, and we have also applied the new Non-Button Help behavior to each of these elements, we should see a Help Balloon beside each new element when the Help feature is activated. We will test this now.

**1.   Move the playback head to the Shop area of the Score. We will start our playback in the main Shop screen.**

**2.   Play the movie. The buttons will all perform as they have before. We will now activate the Help feature to see what is different.**

3.   Click the Help button. In addition to each button producing a Help Balloon, the new screen elements will produce a Help Balloon when they are rolled over.

4.   Click the Help button again. This will deactivate the Help feature.

5.   Stop the movie.

Now that we have programmed the Quit button and screen as well as having added the Help feature to The Billionaire's Shop, we can add some finishing touches to the Shop and Quit areas of the Score and test the entire project so far, including the opening animations.

## ADDING FINISHING TOUCHES TO THIS LESSON AND LINKING THE OPENING ANIMATION TO THE SHOP AREA OF THE SCORE

Currently we must place the playback head in the Shop area of the Score in order to see that screen. We want the playback head to branch to the Shop area when it reaches the end of the opening animation. In addition to this, we want transitions to appear when the playback head enters the Shop and Quit areas of the presentation. In this session we will add these new elements to The Billionaire's Shop.

1.   Open the Internal Cast file. This Cast file contains the transition Cast member that we added to the Score in an earlier chapter's lesson. We will reuse this Cast member here.

2.   Drag Cast member 25 (the transition) directly to frame 150 of the transition channel. This will apply this transition when the playback head enters the Shop area of the Score.

3.   Drag Cast member 25 (the transition) from the Internal Cast again, this time directly to frame 160 of the transition channel. Now the transition will also appear when the playback head enters the Quit area of the Score.

4.   Choose Control>Selected Frames Only. This will deactivate the Selected Frames Only feature so that we can also view the opening animation during playback.

5.   Double-click in frame 145 of the script channel. This will open the Script window for the Brief Pause behavior in the last frame of the opening animation.

6.   Make an addition to the script for the Brief Pause behavior.

```
on exitFrame
   delay 300
   go to marker ("Shop")
end
```

7. **Close the Script window. Now we can test the new additions.**

8. **Rewind and play the movie. The playback head now branches to the Shop area of the Score when it reaches the end of the opening animation. We also see a transition as the playback head enters the Shop area. If we click the Quit button, we will see another transition as the playback head enters the Quit area of the Score. The new additions are all working properly.**

9. **Stop the movie.**

We have finished building the interactive elements of the main Shop and Quit screens. Most of the buttons are programmed, with the exception of the Product Arrow buttons and the Update button; we must also add the volume slider. In the next chapter, we will add products to The Billionaire's Shop and we will program the arrow buttons to allow us to page through them.

## SUMMARY

By linking external Casts to a Director movie, we can easily manage and transfer media among multiple Director movies. In The Billionaire's Shop we used different Casts to store scripts, buttons, animation elements, and Help image Cast members.

Drag-and-Drop behaviors make it easier to add interactivity to a Director movie by allowing us to use scripts that have already been written to achieve commonly sought results. Drag-and-Drop behaviors result in Lingo scripts, which allow them to be modified by any Director author. No knowledge of Lingo or scripting is required to use them in their prepackaged form. Libraries of preprogrammed behaviors are shipped with Director and are available from a variety of third-party developers.

Multiple behaviors can be applied to the same sprites. We can use pre-programmed behaviors in addition to behaviors that we create. In The Billionaire's Shop we used a preprogrammed Drag-and-Drop behavior to program the common activity of all of the buttons. We then created a second behavior for the Quit button that instructed the playback head to jump over to a frame that we labeled Quit. All behaviors that are applied to a sprite are listed in the behavior inspector as well as on the sprite overlay for each sprite.

We learned several methods for the precision placement of sprites on the Stage. One method is to design the images of non-moving sprites directly into the backgrounds that they will be placed against as a reference for placement. We also learned that we can use the arrow keys on the keyboard to move sprites a single frame at a time. Finally, we learned that the buttons on the far left of each channel can be used to temporarily render the sprite in that channel invisible; this allows us to see precisely where the sprite is positioned relative to the background that it has been placed against. The windows at the top of the Score can be used to set the position of sprites according to numerical coordinates on the Stage.

The Button behavior used the names of the button image Cast members to determine the highlight, up, and down stages of the button on the Stage. Using naming conventions allows us to set patterns in our scripts to reduce the amount of programming that is required for each behavior. Used properly, naming conventions can greatly reduce the amount of time required to create a presentation.

## QUESTIONS

1. How can multiple Cast files be used to organize media?

2. What is an advantage to using external Cast files?

3. What is the procedure for linking external Cast files to a Director movie?

4. Although we used multiple Cast files for The Billionaire's Shop, could we have used a single Cast file?

5. How can we access the Lingo script for a behavior?

## EXERCISES

1. In a separate movie file, create a three-state (rollover, up, and down) button that uses the Button Behaviors. Add this button to the first 5 frames of your new movie. You can access the scripts by opening the external Scripts Cast that is used in The Billionaire's Shop. When you are finished, add a new Cast file to your movie, name it Help, and create a Help Balloon version of your new button. Be certain to name all of the button graphics after the naming convention of four characters followed by a 1, 2, or 3. Use the Loop in Frame behavior from the Scripts Cast to keep the playback head in the same frames as the buttons. You can place the Loop in Frame behavior in frame 5 of the Score.

2.  Create a second three-state button with a Help Balloon version in the Help Cast. This button will serve as the Help activation button, so you might want to name it Help. Use the Button and Help behaviors from the Scripts Cast to program this button.

3.  Add a second scene to your new movie that uses another new three-state button that you will create and program using the Button behavior. This button will serve as your Return button. Use the Loop in Frame behavior to keep the playback head in the same frame as the Return button. You can use frames 10 to 15 for your new scene. Label the new scene with a marker in the Score. Add a label to frame 1 as well. You can name the markers in any way you choose.

4.  When your new scene is completed, use the behavior inspector to add a new behavior to the first button that you created in frames 1 to 5. Program this behavior to jump to the second scene in frame 10. Use the behavior inspector to also add a behavior to your Return button that will program this button to jump back to the first scene.

# CHAPTER 7

# USING LINGO

# 7 Using Lingo

In this chapter, you will learn how to:

- Structure Lingo scripts and some uses
- Use an event handler
- Use a global variable
- Control the elements of a Director presentation with Lingo
- Use an if...then statement
- Concatenate text strings
- Use a naming convention to support a script
- Use the dot operator

In chapter 6 we added interactivity to The Billionaire's Shop by using pre-programmed behaviors. We also created simple scripts for the buttons in the shop that controlled the positioning of the playback head, such as sending the playback head to the area of the Score labeled Quit. Lingo, the scripting language that we used to create these scripts, is a complete programming language that can be used to control virtually every part of Director's interface. In this chapter we will use Lingo to add products to The Billionaire's Shop.

Lingo basically makes you a god in the universe that you create in Director. You can use the animation tools to create the "Heavens, the Earth, and all their hosts" in your presentation. Then you can use Lingo to program how the different parts of your universe interact: What happens when two bodies in space collide; how do things grow; what can be moved; what is immovable; how does time pass; what color is the sun at various stages of the day? Lingo is a remarkable, and expansive, tool because its uses are virtually limitless.

In chapter 2 we raised the point that understanding the relationships between the different parts of Director's interface was the key to being effective with Director, even in the most detailed presentations. This extends to the use of Lingo because essentially Lingo scripts are used to accomplish such things as moving a sprite to a new position or changing the Cast member used to display a sprite.

The power in using Lingo is the ability to give control over the presentation to the viewer. This is what will make your presentation interactive. Besides providing the viewer with control, Lingo can be used to control system elements, such as the volume of a sound. Lingo can be used to perform actions that are not directly controlled by the viewer, such as automatically updating a Hybrid Internet application when the presentation is launched.

## THE STRUCTURE OF LINGO

Lingo activity in Director is divided into two basic categories, the event that triggers a script and the activity that the script performs. For example, the viewer might click a button that causes the script associated with that button to activate. A script can also be placed in a location that will trigger it as the playback head passes it in the Score. The events that trigger scripts are called *event handlers*. We have already worked with many of them, such as *mouseUp* and *exitFrame*. Event handlers always begin with "on." We can also write our own custom handlers, called *user-defined handlers*, which we will work with in later lessons. We will come across others as we write the scripts that are used in The Billionaire's Shop.

After an event triggers a script, the commands in that script will perform their function. For example, in this chapter we will program two buttons to allow us to page through the products in The Billionaire's Shop. The event that will trigger the script is mouseUp. The action the script will perform will change the Cast member used to display the products sprite on the Stage. The basic structure for the script that modifies the elements of a Director presentation is a single line: Set the (element within Director) to (a new value). You will find that any action you program into a script will take some form of this basic line of script. For example, one of the scripts that we will use to change the Cast member used to display the product is `set the memberNum of sprite 1 to 3`. An understanding of this basic structure will allow you to program anything with Lingo. We will go through a step-by-step analysis of the scripts that we will create in this chapter so that you will have a thorough understanding as we progress.

Creating detail in a script involves something called *logical constructs*. This is grammar in a script that allows you to control if or when different parts of a script should occur. The three basic logical constructs are if...then statements, case statements, and repeat loops. We will work with if...then statements in this chapter, repeat loops in chapter 8, and case statements in chapters 9 and 10.

Lingo scripts can be placed on images, placed in frames, or stored as individual Cast members. Scripts that are placed on images are activated when the image is clicked on as a sprite; these are called sprite scripts and Cast scripts. Scripts that are placed in a frame are located in the script channel of the Score and are called frame scripts. Scripts that are stored as independent Cast members are called movie scripts and serve as a community chest of scripts that can be used anywhere.

In chapter 6 we worked with behaviors and the behavior inspector. This is how we will continue to author our scripts, because it is convenient and easy. The majority of the scripts we will create in the rest of this book will be entered in the Score. Scripts in these locations are behaviors, like the Button behavior and other behaviors that we created in chapter 6. We will name our scripts, and they will be available through the behavior inspector, just as the scripts in chapter 6 were.

At any rate, as with most subjects in Director, there is no better way to learn than to do.

There are many instances in which Director must choose between scripts **NOTE**
that are attempting to be executed at the same time. For example, there
might be a script in a frame that is identical to a script that is on a button. If
the button is clicked, then Director must determine if it should execute the
script from the button or the script from the frame. In all instances Director
follows the same order of priority, as is demonstrated in figure 7.01.

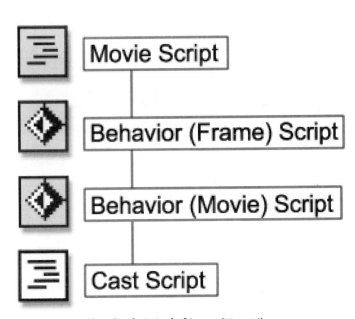

**FIGURE 7.01** *The order of priority for Lingo script execution.*

## ADDING PRODUCTS TO THE BILLIONAIRE'S SHOP

Now that we have created most of The Billionaire's Shop, we can start to add the products. The products will be added to the display window in the upper left corner of the Shop screen. We will also program the left and right arrow buttons beneath the display area to page through the products so we can see them all.

To program the arrow buttons, we will need to write a Lingo script that will change the appearance of the product image in the display area to the next product that is available. The script we create will be a behavior, just like the scripts that we placed over the buttons, but the effect we want is too detailed for the behavior inspector.

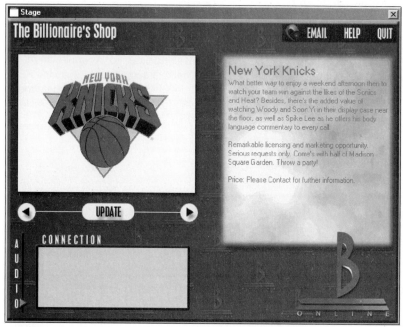

**FIGURE 7.02** *The Billionaire's Shop Main Interface with a product displayed in the display area.*

## VIEWING THE COMPLETED FILE

1.    **If it is not already open, launch Director and choose File>Open.**

2.    **Locate and select the file named Chp7cmp.dir, which is on the Billshop CD in the directory Lessons/Chaptr7/Complete/ Chp7cmp.dir.**

3. **Click Open, and play the movie.**

   You can see that a product is currently visible in the display area on the Shop screen. If you click the left- and right-arrow buttons, you will see that that product in the display window will change along with the description of the product in the description display window on the right. In this chapter we will add this new programming to The Billionaire's Shop.

## PREPARING THE FILES FOR THIS LESSON

You will need to add one file to the folder that contains the file you have been working with, the Products.cst Cast file. You can locate this file on the Billshop CD at Lessons/Chaptr7/Starter. The Products.cst file contains the images for the products that we will display in The Billionaire's Shop. Remember to save your work frequently.

## ADDING THE PRODUCTS CAST TO THE BILLIONAIRE'S SHOP

1. **Choose Modify>Movie>Casts.... The Movie Casts dialog box appears.**

2. **Click the button labeled Link.... The dialog box will appear that will allow you to browse through your directories for a Cast file to link to this movie.**

3. **Locate the file named Products.cst, which should be located in the same directory as the file you are currently working with. In the section titled, "Preparing Files for this Lesson," you either copied the Products.cst file to the directory that contains the files you are working with, or you are using the incomplete version of the chapter 7 file on the CD-ROM.**

4. **Select Products.cst and click Open.**

   The Products.cst file will be added to the list of Cast files in the Movie Cast dialog box.

5. **Click OK.**

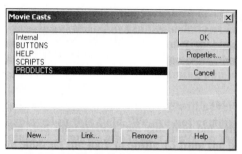

**FIGURE 7.03** *The Products.cst Cast file added to the Movie Casts dialog box.*

## PLACING A PRODUCT IN THE BILLIONAIRE'S SHOP

1.  Choose Window>Cast>Products. The Products Cast window will open. The products are located in Cast positions 1 through 5. Positions 7 through 11 are the descriptions of the products that will be displayed on the right. Cast member 12 is a Field Cast member that contains information that we will later use when The Billionaire's Shop is connected to the Internet. Cast member 6 is just a place holder that we will use in a script to indicate where the products Cast members end and the description Cast members begin. You can double click on any of the product-image Cast members to view them in greater detail in the Paint window.

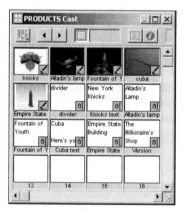

**FIGURE 7.04** *The open products Cast.*

2.  Make certain that the playback head is at frame 150 in the Score. This is the Shop area of the Score.

3.    Drag Cast member 1, the Knicks logo, directly to frame 150 of
      channel 10 in the Score. Then select the sprite on the Stage and
      position it over the upper left-side window. The sprite object
      that we have created on the Stage is too large to appear within
      the Products Display window. We can correct this by moving the
      sprite into a lower-numbered sprite channel in the Score chan-
      nel. Before we correct this problem, we will place the endpoint
      for the products sprite into frame 155 using a new method, the
      sprite inspector.

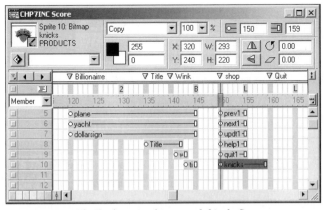

**FIGURE 7.05** *The Knicks sprite object extended in the Score.*

4.    Choose Windows>Inspectors>Sprite. The sprite inspector offers
      details about sprites that are selected in the Score. It is very
      useful for modifying sprites without needing the presence of the
      Score. Now that you are familiar with how the Score works and
      how to edit sprites, we can use this window to become even
      more efficient.

5.    Highlight the number inside the text-entry window for the
      sprite's end, found to the right of the following logo.

6.    Type 155 in the end field, then press the Return (Macintosh) /
      Enter (Windows) key on your keyboard.

      The endpoint of the Knicks logo sprite object will move to frame
      155. The sprite inspector allows us to modify sprite features in
      fewer steps.

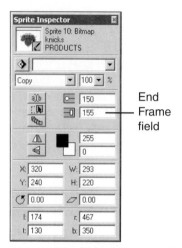

End
Frame
field

**FIGURE 7.06** *The sprite inspector with the Knicks logo sprite-object information displayed.*

## MOVING THE PRODUCTS SPRITE INTO A LOWER-NUMBERED CHANNEL

Next we will place the products sprite into channel 1 so that it appears within the products display area of the background. Currently the products sprite is in channel 10, so it is superimposed over the background in channel 1. The dimensions of the products sprite are larger than the dimensions of the products display area designed into the background sprite object, so we will need to place the products sprite object into a channel that is lower than the channel that the background sprite object is located in. This will place the products sprite behind the background so that it will be displayed within the products display area.

1.  **Select the products sprite in channel 10 of the Shop area of the Score. We will use a command that will move the products display sprite directly to channel 1.**

2.  **Choose Modify>Arrange>Send to Back.**

    This will send the products display sprite directly to channel 1. All of the other sprites will be shuffled one channel forward in the Score so they will now appear in channels 2 through 10.

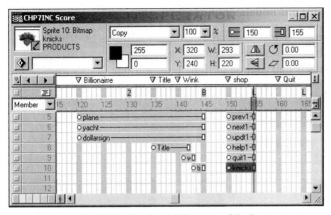

**FIGURE 7.07** *Sprite 10 selected in the Shop area of the Score.*

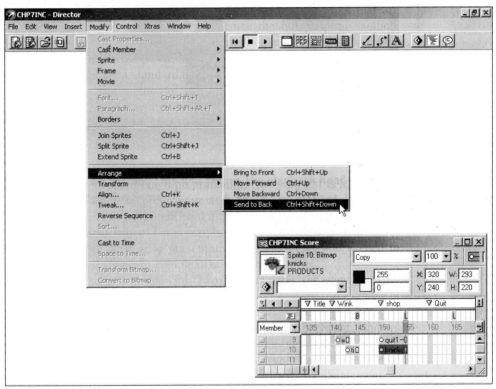

**FIGURE 7.08** *Modify>Arrange>Send to Back selected from the Modify menu.*

## PROGRAMMING THE NEXT PRODUCT ARROW BUTTON

In the completed version of this lesson we were able to click on the arrow buttons on the Stage and page through all of the products in The Billion-aire's Shop. This is accomplished with a second behavior over the arrow buttons that switches the Cast member used to display the products sprite object with the next product in the Products Cast. In this session we will write the scripts for the behavior that will allow us to page through the products.

1.  **Open the Scripts Cast. We want any new scripts that we create to be added to the Scripts Cast window. You can drag it aside or make it as small as possible so that it doesn't take up much of your working area. Next we want to make sure that we have restricted the playback to the Shop and Quit areas of the Score; this way we can avoid replaying the Intro animation while we are still building the Shop area. If there is a green line already spanning this region on the frame number bar, then you do not need to complete steps 2 through 5.**

2.  **Select the sprite object at channel 1 of the Shop area of the Score. This is the products display sprite background.**

3.  **Hold down the Shift key on your keyboard and select the sprite object at channel 1 of the Quit area of the Score. This will high-light the area spanning both the Shop area and the Quit area in the Score.**

4.  **Choose Control>Selected Frames Only. You should now see a green line spanning the Shop and Quit areas of the Score along the frame bar. If you do not, then this feature might have already been turned on, and you just switched it off. In that case, just choose Control>Selected Frames Only again. Our next step is to return the playback head to the Shop area of the Score so that we can access the sprites on that screen.**

5.  **Move the playback head to the Shop area of the Score. Now we will program a behavior for the next product-arrow button.**

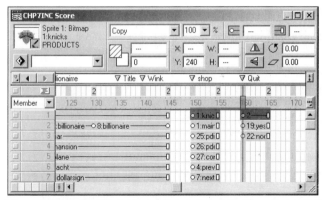

**FIGURE 7.09** *The Selected Frames Only feature applied from Shop to Quit.*

6. Close the Score. Make sure the sprite inspector is still open. We will be able to access everything we want through other windows now, so we can free up some work space by removing the Score.

7. Click on the next product-arrow button on the Stage. Information about the next product-arrow sprite object will be displayed in the sprite inspector. We will access the behavior inspector from the sprite inspector to create the new behavior.

8. Click the Behavior Inspector button on the sprite inspector. This will open the Behavior Inspector window just as if it had been chosen from the Windows menu or the top of the Score. Displayed in the behavior inspector is the only behavior that is currently applied to the next product button, the Button behavior. We will now add a new behavior to the next product button.

9. Choose New Behavior... from the Behaviors pop-up menu at the upper left of the behavior inspector. The Name Behavior dialog box will appear.

10. Name the new behavior Next Product. This is the arrow that we will program to page forward to the next available product.

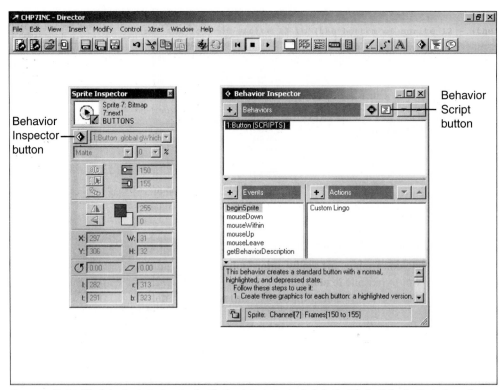

**FIGURE 7.10** *The behavior inspector open beside the sprite inspector. Labels identify the Behavior Inspector and Behavior Script buttons.*

**FIGURE 7.11** *The Name Behavior dialog box with Next Product entered.*

11. Choose Mouse Up from the Events pop-up menu in the behavior inspector. This will cause the script that we are about to write to be triggered when the Next arrow button is clicked. The action that we want to have occur is a custom action, so we will need to enter this script directly into the Script window.

12. Click the Script window button at the top of the behavior inspector. The Script window will appear with the mouseUp handler that we entered using the behavior inspector. Now we will write the scripts that will cause the product to change when this button is clicked. First let's examine what we want to accomplish.

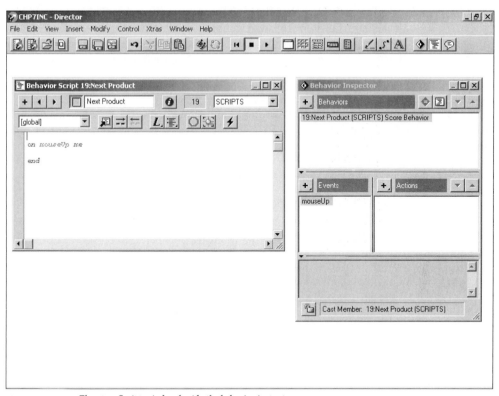

**FIGURE 7.12** *The open Script window beside the behavior inspector.*

## USING LINGO COMMANDS

We want the product in the display area to change to the next product in the Products Cast. If we were to do this without Lingo, we would simply replace the sprite that displays the current product with a sprite that uses the Next Product Cast member. Lingo has several commands that allow you to manipulate the objects on the Stage. One of these commands allows you to change the Cast member used to display a Sprite. So, the script that we want to write will tell Director to exchange the Cast member that is being used to create the products sprite to the next Cast member in the Products Cast.

When you issue a command in Lingo that is intended to change something, the command usually begins with the word *set*. Just think of *set* as being synonymous with *change*. The next thing that Lingo will expect after the word *set* is the item that you would like to change; for example if you could change traffic lights at will, the command in Lingo might look like:

**set the color of the traffic light...**

The last thing that Lingo will expect is the value that you would like to change the item to; for example, set the color of the traffic light to green. To shorten the length of scripts, Lingo compounds words so our imaginary command would probably look more like this:

**set the trafficColor = "green"**

Now, let's apply this information to what we want to accomplish in The Billionaire's Shop. First, we want to change something:

**Set...**

Next we want to change the Cast member of the products sprite. We can identify the products sprite by the channel that it occupies, which is channel 1:

**set the memberNum of sprite 1...**

The *memberNum* is a compound way of saying "the number of the Cast member used to create a sprite;" in this case sprite 1. Currently the Cast member used to create sprite 1 is Cast member 1 of the Products Cast window, the Knicks logo. Next we want to change the Cast member used to display sprite 1 to the next Cast member in the Products Cast window, Aladdin's lamp, which is Cast member 2 of the Products Cast window:

**set the memberNum of sprite 1 = 2**

Let's enter this script and see what we get.

**13.   Type the following script in the Script window:**

```
on mouseUp me
  set the memberNum of sprite 1 = 2
end
```

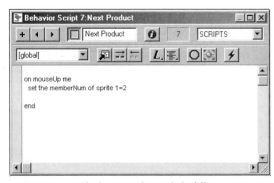

**FIGURE 7.13** *The Script window with the following script entered.*

14. **Press the Recompile All Scripts button at the top of the Script window. The Recompile All Scripts button is labeled with a light-ning-bolt image. This button tells Director to add the script change you just made to the movie that we are currently working with.**

15. **Close the Script window.**

You don't need to use the Recompile All Scripts button every time you create a script, but if you make too many changes without recompiling, Director will present you with a dialog box requesting that you do so. Aside from making Director aware of all of the changes you have made, it also helps to conserve memory, which will enhance Director's performance while you are working.

16. **Play the movie.**

Click the Next Product arrow button. The displayed product changes from the Knicks logo to Aladdin's lamp. If you click this button again, there is no further change. The script that we created will only change the product once, from Cast member 1 to Cast member 2. If this button is to perform as we want, it will need to be able to continue changing to the next product in the Products Cast.

17. **Stop the movie.**

## ENHANCING THE NEXT PRODUCT BEHAVIOR

1. **Select the Next Product arrow button on the Stage and return to the behavior inspector.**

2. **Select the Next Product behavior in the Behaviors display area in the upper area of the behavior inspector.**

3. **Click the Cast Member Script button at the top of the behavior inspector. This returns us to the next product behavior script.**

Currently our script reads as follows:

```
on mouseUp
  set the memberNum of sprite 1 = 2
end
```

This would be fine if we only wanted to change the product once, but we don't. We want the product to change to the next Cast member in the Products Cast window. We need it to look something more like this.

```
on mouseUp
  set the memberNum of sprite 1 = "the next cast member in the
  cast"
end
```

This isn't the actual Lingo script, but it describes what we want to accomplish. Thinking out scripts this way is called *pseudo code,* writing out a script in descriptive terms without necessarily using terms from a programming language.

Closer to how Lingo will work here is the following:

```
on mouseUp
  set the memberNum of sprite 1 from the cast member being used
  to the next cast member in the cast
end
```

What this does is instruct Director to first check which Cast member is being used before switching; this way it knows which Cast member is next. For example, if we have switched from the Knicks to Aladdin's lamp, then we have switched from Cast member 1 to Cast member 2. The next time we click the button, we want to switch from Aladdin's lamp to Fountain of Youth, which is a change from Cast member 2 to Cast member 3. This is how this looks in the actual Lingo script.

```
on mouseUp
  set the memberNum of sprite 1 = the memberNum of sprite 1 + 1
end
```

Let's add this to the Next Product behavior script.

4. **Make the following changes to the mouseUp handler in the Script window (changes will always appear below the figure in bold, for easy visual identification).**

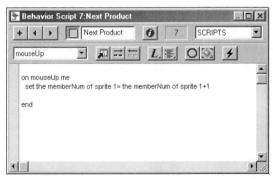

**FIGURE 7.14** *The Script window for the Next Product behavior open, with the following script in it.*

```
on mouseUp
   set the memberNum of sprite 1 = the memberNum of sprite 1 + 1
end
```

Using "the memberNum of sprite 1" after the equal sign instructs Director to find out which Cast member is currently being used. If it is the Knicks logo, then the value is Cast member 1; therefore, the script is performing the following:

```
on mouseUp
   set the memberNum of sprite 1 = the memberNum of sprite 1 + 1
end
```

or

```
on mouseUp
   set the memberNum of sprite 1 = (the current cast member) + 1
end
```

Once we have switched to Aladdin's lamp, the memberNum of sprite 1 will equal 2. In this case this script will add 1 to 2 and switch the Cast member to Fountain of Youth, Cast member 3.

5. **Close the Script window. Let's test the new change.**

6. **Play the movie.**

The displayed product now changes each time the Next Product arrow button is clicked. However, if you click the button five times, you will have passed the last available product in the Products Cast because there are currently only five products. This causes the products sprite to change to the Divider Cast member, and on to the Description Cast member. We need to set a limit in the Next Product behavior script that tells Lingo to stop changing the product if the last one has been reached.

**FIGURE 7.15** *The product browsing area of the shop, with the cursor over the Next Product arrow button.*

## SETTING A LIMIT USING AN IF...THEN STATEMENT

The Next Product will allow us to page forward through the available products, but it does not stop when it reaches the last available product in the Products Cast. We can let the Next Product behavior script know that it has reached the last available product by using an *if...then statement,* a conditional statement that requires that a logical test be passed before executing the then statement.

Let's look at how an if...then statement would be applied to the traffic light example we used earlier:

> **If the traffic light is red then**
> **set the traffic light to green**
> **end if**

According to this script, the light will not be turned to green *unless* it is red. For the Next Product behavior script, we are interested in knowing if we have reached the last product yet. This is determined by the position number of the last Cast member in the Products Cast; in this case it is member 7.

This is what the script would look like in pseudo code:

```
If cast member position of sprite 1 is before cast position 5 then
   set the memberNum of sprite 1 to the memberNum of sprite 1 + 1
end if
```

This ensures that the only way that the script will continue to the next Cast member is if we have not yet reached the maximum Cast position. Notice that an if...then statement requires an end if statement at the end of the scripts that you want to include in the conditional statement.

Here is the actual Lingo script:

```
If the memberNum of sprite 1 < 5 then
   set the memberNum of sprite 1 to the memberNum of sprite 1 + 1
end if
```

Now, let's add these changes to the Next Product behavior script.

> **NOTE** The less than (<) and greater than (>) symbols can be added to the script by typing Shift+,(comma) and Shift+.(period), respectively.

1.   **Select the Next Product arrow button on the Stage and return to the behavior inspector.**

2.   **Select the Next Product behavior in the Behaviors display area in the upper area of the behavior inspector.**

3.   **Click the Cast Member Script button at the top of the behavior inspector. This returns us to the Next Product behavior script.**

   Currently our script reads as follows:

```
on mouseUp
   set the memberNum of sprite 1 = the memberNum of sprite 1 + 1
end
```

4.   **Make the following changes to the mouseUp handler in the Script window.**

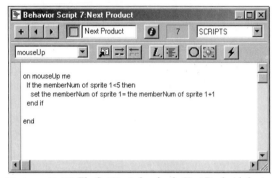

**FIGURE 7.16** *The Script window for the Next Product behavior open with the following script in it.*

```
on mouseUp
  If the memberNum of sprite 1 < 5 then
    set the memberNum of sprite 1 = the memberNum of sprite 1+1
  end if
end
```

5.   **Close the Script window.**

6.   **Play the movie.**

When you click the Next Product arrow button it will change the product in the display area. If you click it five times, it will stop changing the products sprite because it has reached the limit that we set with the if...then statement. The only remaining issue to consider is the possibility that there might be more or fewer than five products in a future update of The Billionaire's Shop when it is connected to the Internet. We can accommodate this possibility by making one final and simple modification to the Next Product behavior script.

## USING THE DIVIDER MEMBER TO DETECT THE NUMBER OF MEMBERS IN A CAST FILE

When The Billionaire's Shop is completed, it will be able to connect to the Internet to update its inventory. Updates to the inventory will contain more or fewer products than the local inventory that we have added so far. It will be important for The Billionaire's Shop to detect how many Cast members are in the Cast that is used for the inventory because that will allow the behavior script that is currently applied to the Next Product arrow button to work properly. We will make this modification to the Next Product behavior script.

1.  **Select the Next Product arrow button on the Stage and return to the behavior inspector.**

2.  **Select the Next Product behavior in the Behaviors display area in the upper area of the behavior inspector.**

3.  **Click the Cast Member Script button at the top of the behavior inspector. This returns us to the Next Product behavior script.**

    Currently our script reads as follows:

    ```
    on mouseUp
      if the memberNum of sprite 1 < 5 then
        set the memberNum of sprite 1 = the memberNum of sprite 1+1
      end if
    end
    ```

4.  **Make the following changes to the mouseUp handler in the Script window.**

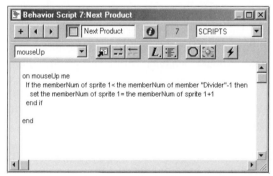

**FIGURE 7.17** *The Script window for the Next Product behavior open with the following script in it.*

```
on mouseUp me
  If the memberNum of sprite 1 < the memberNum of member "Divider" - 1 then
    set the memberNum of sprite 1 = the memberNum of sprite 1 + 1
  end if
end
```

> When referring to cast members by name in scripts, the member name must appear inside quotation marks.   **NOTE**

The Divider Cast member is positioned immediately after the last available product in The Billionaire's Shop. Now this script will know how many products are in the inventory, no matter how many there are. If there are 27 products, then Divider will be in position 28; by subtracting 1 from this position, we can calculate where the last product is located. Future updates to the inventory will require the presence of a member named Divider immediately following the last product.

5.  **Close the Script window.**

6.  **Play the movie.**

    If you click the Next Product arrow button, it will behave just as it did before our most recent modification to the script. The difference will be apparent when the inventory is updated through the Internet with a number of products that are different from the number in the current inventory. Next we will program the Previous Product button.

## PROGRAMMING THE PREVIOUS PRODUCT BUTTON

The script that we will write for the Previous Product button will be similar to the script that we wrote for the Next Product button. The significant difference will be that the Previous Product button will move backward through the products instead of forward. Because the scripts will be similar, let's copy the Next Product behavior script and paste it into a new behavior script window to save some time.

1.  **Select the Next Product arrow button on the Stage and return to the behavior inspector.**

2.  **Select the Next Product behavior in the Behaviors display area in the upper area of the behavior inspector.**

3.  **Click the Cast Member Script button at the top of the behavior inspector.**

4.  **Highlight the entire mouseUp handler.**

5.  **Choose Edit>Copy Text.**

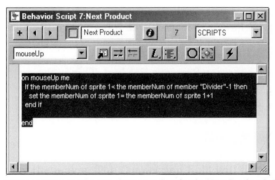

**FIGURE 7.18** *The open Script window for the Next Product behavior with the entire MouseUp script highlighted.*

6. **Click on the Previous Product arrow button on the Stage. Information about the Previous Product arrow sprite object will be displayed in the sprite inspector. The behavior inspector will list the behaviors that are currently applied to this sprite object. Currently there is only one, the Button behavior.**

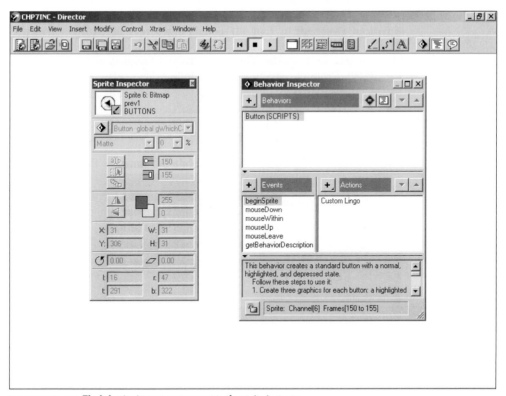

**FIGURE 7.19** *The behavior inspector open next to the sprite inspector.*

7.    Choose New Behavior... from the Behaviors pop-up menu at the top left of the behavior inspector. The Name Behavior dialog box will appear.

8.    Name the new behavior Previous Product. This is the arrow that we will program to page backward to the next product back in the Products Cast.

**FIGURE 7.20** *The Name Behavior dialog box with Previous Product entered.*

9.    Click OK. Because we already copied the Next Product button to save time, we can go directly to the Script window to paste the script. Then we will make the changes needed to have the script work for the Previous button.

10.   Click the Script Window button at the top of the behavior inspector. This will open the Script window with nothing currently typed in it. We will paste the Next Product behavior script here.

11.   Choose Edit>Paste. The Next Product script is added to the Previous Product behavior script window. The script for this button is very similar to the Next Product behavior. The main difference is that this script should move backward through the products in the Products Cast window instead of forward. Now we can make modifications that will have this script work for the Previous Product arrow button.

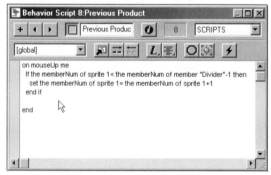

**FIGURE 7.21** *The Previous Product behavior script window with the following script pasted into it.*

```
on mouseUp
  if the memberNum of sprite 1 < the memberNum of member Divider - 1 then
    set the memberNum of sprite 1 = the memberNum of sprite 1 + 1
  end if
end
```

**12. Make the following changes to the script in the Previous Product behavior script window.**

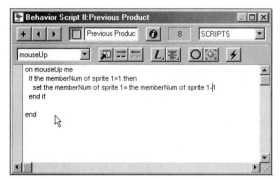

**FIGURE 7.22** *The Previous Product behavior script window with the following changes made to the script. Changes are in bold below.*

```
on mouseUp
  if the memberNum of sprite 1 > 1 then
    set the memberNum of sprite 1 = the memberNum of sprite 1-1
  end if
end
```

The two changes that needed to be made concerned the limit that is set in the if...then statement, and the direction that we move through the Cast members in the Products Cast window. First let's examine the change to the if...then statement:

```
If the memberNum of sprite 1 > 1 then
```

Remember that we want to page backward through the Cast members in the Cast. We cannot allow the script to try to change the Cast member of sprite 1 to a number lower than 1, because there is no such member in the Cast window. This script is designed to make certain that we have not yet reached member 1 before executing the script that changes the Cast member used to display sprite 1.

Now let's look at the next change:

```
set the memberNum of sprite 1=the memberNum of sprite 1-1
```

This script instructs Lingo to switch the Cast member used to display sprite 1 to the Cast member directly behind it in the Cast. The

Previous Product arrow button is now programmed. Let's play the movie and test it.

**13.    Close the Script window and play the movie; then stop it.**

When you click the Next Product button, you move forward through the products; when you click the Previous Product button, you move back through the products. Remember that when you start the movie, you are already displaying the first Cast member in the Products Cast window, so the Previous Product button will not work until you use the Next Product button.

## ADDING PRODUCT DESCRIPTIONS TO THE BILLIONAIRE'S SHOP

Now that we have added products to The Billionaire's Shop, we can add the descriptions of the products, which are also located in the Products Cast window. The technique we will use is similar to how we added the products, but the description sprite object will be in a different channel. We will also have our scripts determine which description should be displayed by using the name of the currently displayed product. For example, if we are displaying the Knicks product (member 1) then we should be displaying the member named Knicks Text (member 7). The scripts we will write will attach the word Text to the end of the current product's name then use this new name to determine which description should be displayed.

**1.    Open the Score and place the playback head in frame 150. We want to make certain that the playback head is in the first frame of the Shop area of the Score.**

**2.    Open the Products Cast window.**

**3.    Drag Cast member 7 (the Knicks text member) to the description display area on the right side of the background in the Shop area of the Stage. The sprite object that is created will automatically be placed in the next available sprite position, channel 11.**

**4.    While the product description sprite is still selected in the Stage, go to the sprite inspector and type the number 155 into the text entry area labeled "End," then press the Return key (Macintosh)/ Enter key (Windows). This will shorten the product description sprite object so that it only spans the Shop area of the Score.**

5. Verify that the product description sprite object is in channel 11 in frames 150 through 155, and set the sprite's ink effect to Background Transparent. Now we will shuffle the product description sprite back into a channel in the Score that will work appropriately for the rest of the movie.

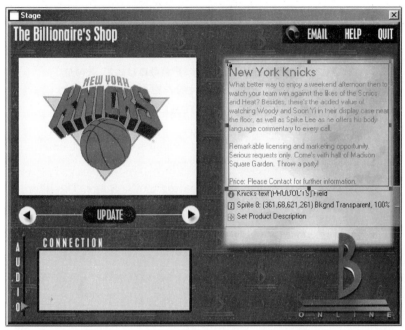

**FIGURE 7.23** *The Shop screen with the Knicks text member dragged to the Product Description display area.*

**FIGURE 7.24** *The sprite inspector with the product description sprite (Knicks text) selected and the end frame number set to 155.*

6.  While sprite 11 is still selected in the Score, select Modify>Arrange>Move Backward. This will move the product description sprite back one channel.

7.  Repeat step 6 above two more times.

This will move the product description sprite into channel 8, placing it behind the Update, Help, and Quit buttons. This will allow the Help Balloon versions of these images to appear in front of the product description sprite.

## PROGRAMMING THE NEXT PRODUCT AND PREVIOUS PRODUCT ARROW BUTTONS TO CHANGE THE PRODUCT DESCRIPTION

The Next Product arrow button already changes the displayed product. It will only take a single line of script to change the product description sprite (channel 8).

1.  Select the Next Product arrow button on the Stage. The information about the Next Product arrow sprite will appear in the sprite and behavior inspectors.

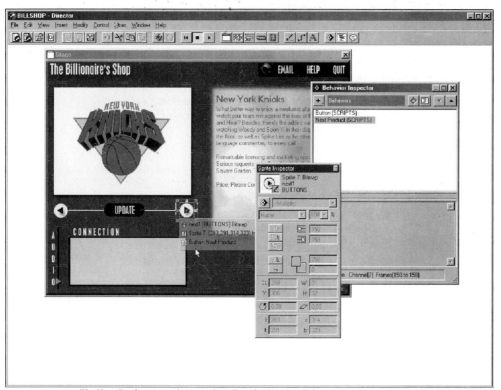

**FIGURE 7.25** *The Next Product arrow button selected on the Stage and the sprite inspector window open.*

2. Select the Next Product behavior in the behavior inspector, then click the Script Window button at the top of the behavior inspector. By first selecting the Next Product behavior, we can directly access the script used for this behavior when we click the Script Window button.

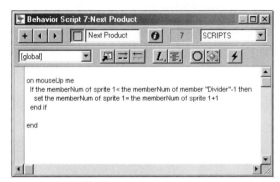

**FIGURE 7.26** *The Next Product behavior script is open in the Script window with the following script displayed.*

```
on mouseUp
   if the memberNum of sprite 1 < the memberNum of member Divider - 1 then
      set the memberNum of sprite 1 = the memberNum of sprite 1 + 1
   end if
end
```

3. Make the following addition to the Next Product behavior script.

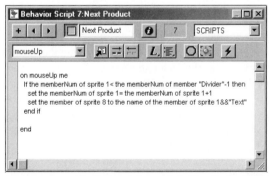

**FIGURE 7.27** *The Script window with the Next Product behavior script.*

```
on mouseUp
   if the memberNum of sprite 1 < the memberNum of member "Divider" - 1 then
      set the memberNum of sprite 1 = the memberNum of sprite 1 + 1
      set the member of sprite 8 to the name of the member of sprite 1&&"Text"
   end if
end
```

This script will change the product description sprite on the Stage. We already know what "set the member of sprite 8..." means. Let's look at what the rest of this script does:

```
to the name of the member of sprite 1&&"Text"
```

The word "to" is equivalent to using the equal (=) sign in a script. This script could be written as:

```
set the member of sprite 8 = the name of the member of sprite 1&&"Text"
```

Let's look at the next part of the script:

```
to the name of the member of sprite 1&&"Text"
```

This part of the script returns the name of the Cast member used to display the products sprite. It accomplishes this in two steps. First, it requests the Cast position of the Cast member used to display the products sprite: "...the member of sprite 1...." Next, the script requests the name of the member at that position: "the name of the member of sprite 1." This will return that Cast member's name. For example, if we are currently viewing the Knicks product, then this part of the script will return the name Knicks.

Now, let's examine the last part of the new script:

```
to the name of the member of sprite 1&&"Text"
```

Based upon how we have named the Cast members in the Products Cast window, if we know the name of the Cast member used to display the products sprite, then we can retrieve the name of the appropriate product description sprite. We can accomplish this by adding the word "text" to the end of the products sprite Cast member's name. For example, the product description Cast member for Aladdin's lamp is Aladdin's lamp text. This is what the last part of the script accomplishes with && "Text."

The phrase "the name of the member of sprite 1" gives us a Cast member name; let's say Aladdin's lamp. The ampersand (&) *concatenates*, which means it combines separate words or phrases into a single word or phrase. A single ampersand connects two words with no spaces. For example, "Some"&"Where" becomes "SomeWhere." Two ampersands together (&&) connect two words with a space between them. For example, "Some"&&"Where" becomes "Some Where." In the case of our script, if we are currently viewing Aladdin's lamp, then "the name of the member of sprite 1&& 'Text'" gives us "Aladdin's lamp text."

Let's test the script.

4.  **Close the Script window.**

5.  **Play the movie. When you click the Next product button, you will see that the product description sprite changes along with the Next Product button. Now let's add the script to the Previous Product button.**

6.  **Stop the movie.**

7.  **Select the Previous Product arrow button on the Stage. This will display information about the Previous Product button in the sprite and behavior inspectors.**

8.  **Highlight the Previous Product behavior in the behavior inspector and click the Script Window button at the top of the behavior inspector.**

    ```
    on mouseUp
      if the memberNum of sprite 1 > 1 then
        set the memberNum of sprite 1 = the memberNum of sprite 1-1
      end if
    end
    ```

9.  **Make the following addition to the Previous Product behavior script.**

    ```
    on mouseUp
      if the memberNum of sprite 1 > 1 then
        set the memberNum of sprite 1 = the memberNum of sprite 1 - 1
        set the member of sprite 8 to the name of the member of sprite 1&&"Text"
      end if
    end
    ```

10. **Close the Script window and Play the movie. When you click the Next Product and Previous Product arrow buttons, they change both the displayed product and the product description.**

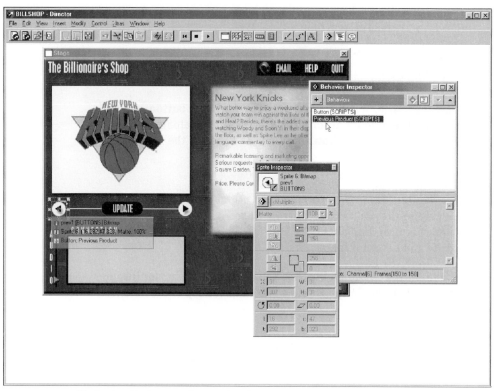

**FIGURE 7.28** *The Previous Product arrow button selected on the Stage. The behavior and sprite inspectors display information about the sprite.*

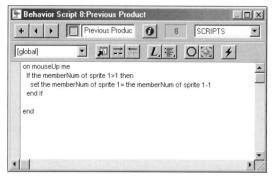

**FIGURE 7.29** *The Previous Product behavior is highlighted in the behavior inspector. The Previous Product behavior script is open in the Script window.*

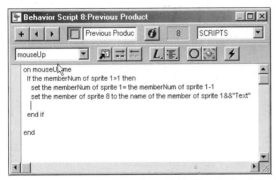

**FIGURE 7.30** *The Script window with the Next Product behavior script.*

11. Click the Next Product arrow button a few times. We are going to perform an experiment that requires that we display a product somewhere beyond the first product.

12. Click the Quit button. This will send the playback head to the Quit area of the Score.

13. Click the No button. This will return the playback head to the Shop area of the Score. Notice that the product that is currently displayed has reverted to Knicks. This happens because we have not programmed The Billionaire's Shop to remember the last product that was displayed. We can accomplish this by placing a new behavior, this time directly on the products sprite, that will remember the Cast position of the Cast member last used to display the products sprite object. This way The Billionaire's Shop will know which product to display if the Quit button is pressed, and we then hit Return.

14. Stop the movie.

## USING A GLOBAL VARIABLE TO REMEMBER WHICH PRODUCT WAS LAST DISPLAYED

The fact that the products sprite object reverts back to the original first product is not an error in programming, but an error in design. Generally, a viewer will expect that if they can make choices in a movie, those choices will remain present if they go elsewhere in the movie and then return. We can store information about items in Lingo scripts using a *global variable*, an author-defined variable that can store a value and pass it between scripts. We name this variable so we can access it.

1.  Make certain that the Scripts Cast window is open. Click on the Scripts Cast to make it active. This will ensure that the new behavior we create will be added to the Scripts Cast window.

2.  Select the products sprite object on the Stage and return to the Score and verify that the sprite in channel 1 of the Shop area has been selected.

    This will display information about the currently displayed products sprite. It isn't important which product is displayed. We are only concerned with applying a new behavior to the channel that the Product occupies, channel 1.

TIP   If you have difficulty selecting the products display sprite on the Stage, then click directly on the sprite in channel 1 in the Shop area of the Score.

3.  Choose Behaviors>New Behavior... from the behavior inspector.

4.  Name the new behavior Set Product.

5.  Click OK.

6.  Choose Events>Exit Frame from the behavior inspector. We will be entering a custom script, so at this point we will need to directly enter the script in the Script window.

7.  Click the Script Window button at the top of the behavior inspector. This will reopen the Script window with the Set Product behavior script displayed in it. Currently there is only an empty *exitFrame* handler.

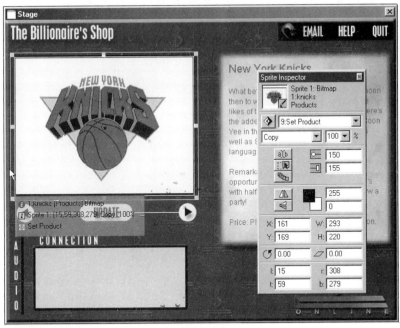

**FIGURE 7.31** *The products sprite selected on the Stage.*

**FIGURE 7.32** *The Name Behavior dialog box with Set Product entered.*

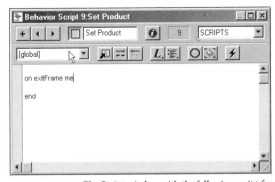

**FIGURE 7.33** *The Script window with the following script from the Set Product behavior script in it.*

```
on exitFrame
end
```

8.   **Make the following addition to the *exitFrame* handler.**

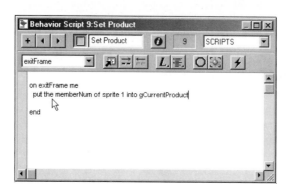

**FIGURE 7.34** *The Script window with the following Set Product behavior script in it.*

```
on exitFrame
  put the memberNum of sprite 1 into gCurrentProduct
end
```

This will put the value of "the memberNum of sprite 1" into the variable named *gCurrentProduct* every time the playback head loops in this frame. At this point *gCurrentProduct* will save this value, but it will not save the value beyond this script's execution. We need this value to be saved so that we know which products Cast member to use if we leave the Shop area of the Score and return again later. To accomplish this, we will need to make another addition to this script to make *gCurrentProduct* a global variable.

**NOTE**   *gCurrentProduct* is a word that we made up specifically for this purpose. This is one of the requirements for using a variable; the other is that the word can have no spaces in it.

9.   **Make the following addition to the *exitFrame* handler.**

```
global gCurrentProduct
on exitFrame
  put the memberNum of sprite 1 into gCurrentProduct
end
```

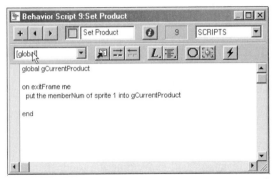

**FIGURE 7.35** *The Script window with the following Set Product behavior script in it.*

Adding the word "global" to the top of a script window, then typing the words that are used to name the globals, is called *declaring the globals*. This lets Director know which words should be used to carry values. Now that we have created a way to keep track of which Cast member is being used for the products sprite, we can add a way to use *gCurrentProduct* to actually change the products sprite if we use the Quit button to leave and return to the Shop area of the Score.

10. **Make the addition to the *exitFrame* handler as shown in figure 7.36. Because the product display sprite was selected when we created this new behavior, the Set Product behavior is automatically applied to the sprite. Now we will make additions to the script that will make certain that the product display sprite always displays the current product.**

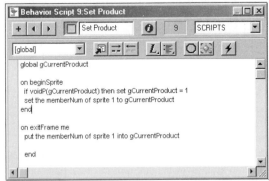

**FIGURE 7.36** *The Script window with the following addition to the Set Product behavior script.*

```
global gCurrentProduct
on beginSprite
  if voidP(gCurrentProduct) then set gCurrentProduct = 1
  set the memberNum of sprite 1 to gCurrentProduct
end
on exitFrame me
  put the memberNum of sprite 1 into gCurrentProduct
end
```

*BeginSprite* is activated when the sprite that it is applied to appears on the Screen. This means that every time the products sprite object appears, the beginSprite handler in the Set Product behavior will occur. The command that we have attached to the *beginSprite* handler will change the member used to display the product's sprite to the value that has been stored in *gCurrentProduct*.

For example, if Aladdin's lamp is currently the displayed product, then the memberNum of the products sprite (sprite 1) is member 2 of the Products Cast file.

```
on beginSprite
  if voidP(gCurrentProduct) then set gCurrentProduct = 1
  set the memberNum of sprite 1 to gCurrentProduct
end
```

When the movie first begins playing, *gCurrentProduct* will not have a value. This line checks to see if there is anything within *gCurrent-Product*; if not, then *gCurrentProduct* will be set to a value of 1. This line is also programmed using a one-line if...then statement, which does not require an *end if* at the end of the statement. One-line if...then statements must have only a single line of code; multiple lines require that each line be separate and will require an end if at the bottom of the script.

```
on beginSprite
  if voidP(gCurrentProduct) then set gCurrentProduct = 1
  set the memberNum of sprite 1 to gCurrentProduct
end
```

This takes the value of "the memberNum of sprite 1" and places it in the global variable named *gCurrentProduct*. The part of the script that reads "the memberNum of sprite 1" will change if different products are displayed. This script will update with the changes because it is activated every time that the playback head loops in the Shop area of the Score due to the exitFrame handler.

11. Close the Script window. The Set Product behavior will control the product image displayed in channel 1. Before we test this script, we will create a second behavior for the product description sprite in channel 8 so that it is controlled simultaneously.

12. Select the sprite in channel 8 in the Shop area of the Score, then return to the behavior inspector. We will create a new behavior, which we will name Set Product Description.

13. Choose Behaviors>New Behavior... from the behavior inspector.

14. Name the new behavior Set Product Description, then click OK.

**FIGURE 7.37** *The Name Behavior dialog box, with Set Product Description entered.*

15. Click the Script Window button at the top of the behavior inspector. We will type the script for this behavior directly into the window without using any of the other options in the behavior inspector.

16. Enter the script from figure 7.38 in the Script window for the Set Product Description behavior. This script will now control the product description that appears in channel 8 based upon the product that is currently displayed in channel 1.

The behavior in channel 1 will be activated first, because scripts that are on sprites are activated in sequence from the lowest channel number to the highest. This will ensure that the sprite in channel 1 has been set before channel 8 attempts to display the corresponding description. **NOTE**

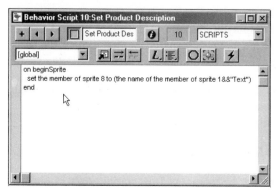

**FIGURE 7.38** *The Script window with the following Set Product Description behavior script.*

```
on beginSprite
    set the member of sprite 8 to (the name of the member of sprite 1&&"Text")
end
```

Let's take a look at the script for the Set Product Description behavior. When the product display sprite changes, the product description sprite must be changed as well. This line uses the same script that we used in the Next Product and Previous Product behaviors to change the product description sprite along with the Product Display sprite when it appears on the Stage.

Along with the exitFrame handler, these scripts will now keep track of the last product that was displayed, first by using the exitFrame handler to store the Cast member number of the currently displayed sprite in *gCurrentSprite*. The beginSprite handler in the Set Product behavior uses the value in *gCurrentSprite* to change the Cast members used to display the products sprite. Then the beginSprite handler in the Set Product Description behavior uses the name of the currently displayed product to control the product description displayed in channel 8.

17.  **Close the Script window.**

18.  **Play the movie. Be certain to use the paging buttons to click through a few products. This way we will really be testing the new script that we have added.**

19.  **Click the Quit button.**

20.  **Click the No button. We can see now that our script is remembering which product was displayed last and is displaying it on the Stage now.**

21.  **Stop the movie.**

## ABOUT THE DOT OPERATOR

Lingo is an ever-evolving scripting language that continually adds new ways to write scripts. One new technique is the use of the *dot operator*, which allows us to shorten the length of scripts that use properties. The dot operator is a period (.) that is inserted between words to indicate a relationship between the words instead of using more descriptive text.

Using the dot operator, the following script:

```
Set the memberNum of sprite 2 to 8
```

becomes:

```
memberNum.sprite(2) = 8
```

Basically the dot operator replaces much of the grammar in a script. While this certainly helps to simplify our scripts, it is far more helpful to write out the full script while we are learning. Currently scripts that are created using the behavior inspector, and the syntax of scripts that are described in Macromedia's literature, all use the full scripting method. This means that, although the dot operator is helpful, saves scripting time, and will ultimately make movies smaller because there is less script text in the file, it is not yet a standard in Lingo scripting. We will be concentrating on the full script method of writing our scripts for The Billionaire's Shop, but keep the dot operator on your list of things to learn about. It's an extremely useful programming tool.

## SUMMARY

There are many levels to Lingo programming. The simplest is a drag-and-drop behavior, which is preprogrammed; the more detailed levels use scripting methods such as conditional if...then statements. An understanding of the basic structure of Lingo scripts and the relationship between different elements in a Director presentation are the foundation needed to program Lingo for simple or complex Director movies.

Each Lingo script is divided into two different parts: the event that triggers the script and the activity performed by the script itself. An example of an event handler is mouseUp, which is activated when the mouse button is clicked and released over a sprite that contains the script. Event handlers always begin with the word "on" and terminate with the word "end."

You can control the way in which the scripts in your movie are executed by using *logical constructs*. In this chapter we used an if...then statement.

Global variables allow information to be passed from one script to another. These variables allow you to create a sense of continuity in a presentation, because global variables can do the job of remembering what has happened so far in the movie. Global variables must always be identified as global at the top of the Script window; otherwise Director will treat them as local variables, which hold their values only temporarily and cannot pass their values between scripts.

Many of the elements of a Director presentation can be controlled through scripts. The basic line of script that is used for this purpose is `set the (element within Director) to (a new value)`. To use this line of script effectively, you need to know the Lingo term for the item you would like to modify, and the possible values for that item. One example from this chapter was the property memberNum, which was used to change the Cast member used to display the products sprite on the Stage. To work with memberNum, we used the following script: `set the memberNum of sprite 1 to the memberNum of sprite 1 + 1`. Studying the variety of properties that are available to you in the Lingo part of Director's Help application will help you expand your knowledge and effectiveness with Lingo. Other sources of useful information are the Lingo Dictionary and the Learning Lingo manuals that are shipped with the commercial version of Director.

## QUESTIONS

1. What is a global variable?

2. What is an event handler? Give two examples of event handlers and where they are used in a Director presentation.

3. What is a property? Give four examples of properties.

4. What is the sprite property that is used to determine the name of the Cast member used to display a sprite?

5. What does it mean to concatenate a text string?

6. What is the script that would make the variable *testVariable* equal to the integer value 25?

## EXERCISES

1.  Using the Message window, write a script that uses the member-Num property to change the products sprite from its current Cast member to another Cast member in The Billionaire Shop inventory. Remember that you must use the *updateStage* command to have your script execute on the Stage. You do not need to play the movie for this exercise.

2.  Once again in the Message window, write a script that changes the products sprite from its current Cast member to another Cast member. This time, use the name of member property. Again, remember that you must use the *updateStage* command to have your script execute on the Stage, and you do not need to play the movie for this exercise to work.

3.  Now, modify the script you created in exercise 2 so that it will change the description sprite to the description for the new products sprite Cast member. Use the ampersand (&) to append the word text to the end of the Cast member's name. Remember that you will need to use two ampersands to insert a space between words. As was the case in the last two exercises, you do not need to play the movie for this exercise, and you will need to use *updateStage*.

4.  Use the interactive part of the storyboards you created in chapter 1, along with the flowchart you created, to add the buttons to your three animations. You have now successfully planned and created your first Director file from concept.

# CHAPTER 8

# CONTROLLING SOUND VOLUME AND MORE LINGO

# 8 Controlling Sound Volume and More Lingo

In this chapter, you will learn how to:

- Manipulate audio sprite properties
- Restrict the position of a sprite on a stage
- Control the volume of a sound
- Restrict a sprite to the area defined by another sprite
- Use the position of a sprite to change the volume of a sound
- Create a new behavior from scratch
- Use calculations to create detail in a script
- Create a beginSprite handler
- Use the Lingo command *puppetSound*

In chapter 7 we learned that the appearance of a sprite can be changed by changing the Cast member used to display the sprite. We used the *member-Num* of a Cast member to help accomplish this. The memberNum is a Lingo *property*, which is a characteristic of an object in a Director movie that in most instances can be controlled with Lingo scripts. Lingo has numerous properties. In this lesson, we will work with three properties of a sprite object to create a volume control slider that will allow us to change the volume of a background sound that we will add to The Billionaire's Shop. The properties we will be working with are the *locH* of sprite, which is used to control the horizontal location of a sprite on the Stage. This is how we will create a slider button that can be clicked and dragged up and down along a slider to raise and lower the volume setting. We will also be working with the *constraint* of sprite, which is used to restrict the movement of a sprite to the area covered by another sprite. This will be important to use because we want to be able to move the slider button, but we do not want the slider button to be moveable past the edges of the slider background. The third property, *volume of sound*, will be used to control the volume level of the background music that we will add to The Billionaire's Shop in this lesson.

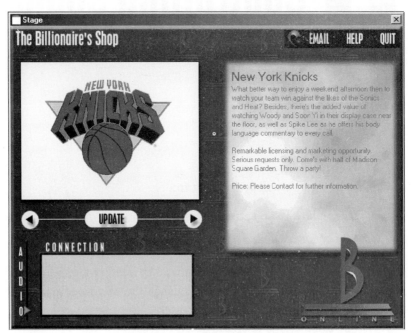

**FIGURE 8.01** *The Billionaire's Shop Main Interface with the volume controller in the lower left.*

## VIEWING THE COMPLETED FILE

1. **Launch Director and choose File>Open.**

2. **Locate and select the file named Chp8cmp.dir, which is located on the CD-ROM in the directory ...Lessons/Chaptr8/Complete/ Chp8cmp.dir.**

3. **Click Open.**

4. **Play the movie.**

This file contains all that we have created to this point. When we reach the main interface of The Billionaire's Shop, there is a new sound playing in the background at a lower volume than the sound that was playing behind the Intro animation. If you click the knob on the volume controller, you can drag it up and down to change the volume. Notice that you cannot drag the knob past the top or bottom of the slider.

## PREPARING THE FILES FOR THIS LESSON

For this lesson you can work with the file named Chp8inc.dir, which is on the Billshop CD in the directory ...Lessons/Chaptr8/Starter/.

## ADDING THE VOLUME CONTROL SLIDER

The background of the main image already contains the image of the slider for your reference in placing the actual image. The slider image is located in position 28 in the button Cast.

1.  Open the Score.

2.  Position the playback head at frame 150 of the Score. This is the Shop area of the Score.

3.  Open the buttons Cast file. You can open the buttons Cast file by choosing Windows>Cast>buttons.

4.  Drag Cast member 28 (slid2) to the Stage and position it directly over the image of the slider on the Shop background and set the ink effect to Background Transparent. This will place the slider background in channel 12. You can drag the slider background to approximately the correct position at this point. We will use other settings to place it in the precise position.

5.  Drag Cast member 29 (slider knob) to the Stage and position it over the slider background on the Stage. Set its ink effect to Background Transparent. This will place the slider knob in channel 13. You can drag the slider background to approximately the correct position at this point. We will use other settings to place it in the precise position.

6.  Close the Score and the Cast window. You can close any other windows that are open as well. We can make all of the modifications we need from the sprite inspector.

7.  Choose Window>Inspectors>Sprite.

8.  Select sprite 12, the slider background, on the Stage. The sprite inspector will present information about the slider background. We will use the settings in the sprite inspector to precisely position this sprite.

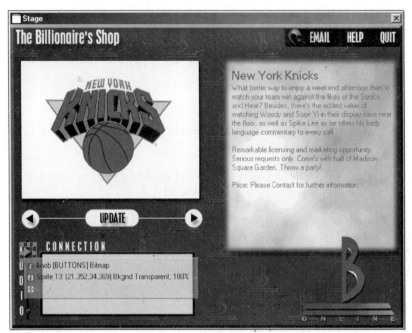

**FIGURE 8.02** *The slider background already on the Stage and the slider knob dragged from position 28 of the buttons Cast window to the Shop background on the Stage.*

9.  Type 155 into the text entry area labeled End: in the sprite inspector. This will ensure that this sprite only spans the Shop area of the Score (frames 150–155).

10. Press the Return(Macintosh)/Enter(Windows) key. This will enter the new change.

11. Type 19 into the text entry area labeled X: in the sprite inspector. This is called the *Reg Point Horizontal window* (Reg is short for Registration). The *registration point* of a sprite is the reference that Director uses to determine where the sprite is located on the stage. The registration point is located at the center of the image by default. *Reg point horizontal* refers to the distance in pixels to the registration point of the sprite from the left edge of the Stage. The setting that we have entered will place the center of the slider background 19 pixels from the left side of the Stage, which is the exact distance from the left side of the Stage to the image of the slider background that is designed into the Shop background.

12. Press the Return(Macintosh)/Enter(Windows) key. This will enter the new change.

13.　Type 401 into the text entry area labeled Y: in the sprite inspector. This is called the *Reg Point Vertical window*. The location of a sprite on the Stage requires two coordinates: horizontal and vertical. The vertical coordinate is determined by the distance from the top edge of the Stage to the registration point. This setting will place the center of the slider background 401 pixels away from the top of the Stage.

14.　Press the Return(Macintosh)/Enter(Windows) key. This will enter the new change. You will see now that the slider background is exactly over the image of the volume slider that was incorporated into the Shop background image.

The X and Y settings on the sprite inspector can be used to precisely position a sprite on the Stage. The X setting is the horizontal positioning in pixels from the left side of the Stage; the Y setting is the vertical positioning in pixels from the top of the Stage.

> **NOTE**
> In addition to controlling the position of a sprite on the Stage, the settings on the sprite inspector can be used to resize a selected sprite as follows: W and H will resize the width and height of the sprite, respectively; l, r, t, and b will move the left, right, top, and bottom of the bounding rectangle around the selected sprite. The last four settings will move only one edge of the sprite. Experiment with them to test their effect. See figure 8.03 for the locations of these settings on the sprite inspector.

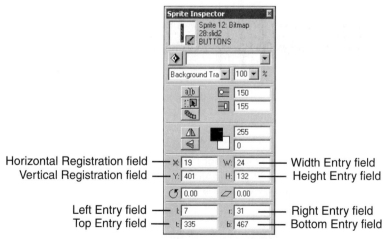

**FIGURE 8.03** *The sprite inspector with the slider background selected. Arrows identify the vertical registration, horizontal registration, width, height, left, right, top, and bottom entry windows.*

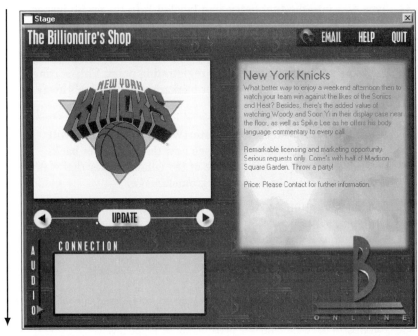

X direction - horizontal distance in pixels from the left side of the stage

**FIGURE 8.04** *The Shop background with an arrow indicating the direction of the X and Y settings.*

15.   Select sprite 13, the slider knob, on the Stage. The sprite inspector will display information about the slider knob. We will use the settings in the sprite inspector to precisely position this sprite and change its duration in the Score.

16.   Make the following entries in the sprite inspector for the slider knob sprite:

      End: 155

      X:    26

      Y:    452

This will reduce the number of frames that the slider knob spans so that it will be located only in the Shop area of the Score. These settings will also center the slider knob toward the bottom of the slider background.

17.   Press the Return(Macintosh)/Enter(Windows) key. This will enter the new changes for the slider knob.

## PROGRAMMING THE SLIDER'S MOVEMENT

In order to have the slider operate the way it does in the completed version, we need to write a script that will change the location of the slider knob when it is clicked and dragged. There are two properties that can be used to change the location of a sprite: LocH for the horizontal position and LocV for the vertical position. We only need the slider knob to move along a vertical path, so in this lesson we will use the LocV property of a sprite's registration point.

1.   **Choose Window>Cast>Scripts. We want the new scripts that we write to be entered in the Scripts Cast window.**

2.   **Select the slider knob on the Stage. The sprite overlay for the slider knob should appear and display information about the sprite.**

3.   **Click the Behavior Inspector button on the sprite overlay for the slider knob. The Behavior Inspector button is the button at the lower left corner of the sprite overlay.**

**FIGURE 8.05** *The selected slider knob on the Stage. The sprite overlay for the slider knob is visible. The cursor identifies the Behavior Inspector button on the sprite overlay.*

4.  **Choose Behaviors>New Behavior.... We are going to begin creating the volume control behavior now.**

5.  **Name the behavior Volume.**

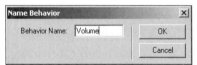

**FIGURE 8.06** *The Name Behavior dialog box with Volume entered in it.*

6.  **Choose Events>MouseDown. We want the volume controller to be activated when the slider knob is clicked.**

7.  **Click the Script Window button at the top of the behavior inspector. The volume control behavior will require custom scripts that are not available from the selections under the Actions menu, so we will enter the scripts directly through the script window.**

## USING A REPEAT LOOP AND updateStage

If we describe how we would like the volume slider to work it would be something like this:

> When the slider knob is clicked and dragged, the position of the slider knob will follow the mouse pointer. The dragging movement will continue as long as the user is holding the mouse button down on the knob. The volume will increase when the knob is dragged upward and decrease when the knob is moved downward.

First we will program the dragging movement of the slider knob as described in the sentence:

> When the slider knob is clicked and dragged, the position of the slider knob will follow the mouse pointer.

1.  **Enter the following script in the Script entry window for the volume behavior.**

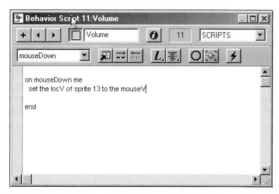

**FIGURE 8.07** *Type the following script in the Volume Behavior Script window.*

```
on mouseDown me
  set the locV of sprite 13 to the mouseV
end
```

Let's examine what this script will do:

```
Set the locV of sprite 13 to the mouseV
```

This part of the script will change the locV of the sprite located in channel 13 (the slider knob) to something called the mouseV, which we will examine in a moment. ThelocV of a sprite is its vertical location on the Stage. Loc stands for location and V for vertical.

Let's look at the rest of the Script:

```
Set the locV of sprite 13 to the mouseV
```

The action we want the slider knob to take when it is clicked is to follow the direction in which the mouse pointer is dragged. Fortunately, Lingo is equipped with a property that tracks the vertical position of the mouse pointer on the Stage, the *mouseV*. By setting the locV of a sprite to be equal to the mouseV, we are saying that we want the sprite to follow the vertical positioning of the mouse wherever it goes. We want this to be a continuous action, as described in the statement:

> The dragging movement will continue as long as the user is holding the mouse button down on the knob.

Having an action occur consistently within a script is accomplished with a *repeat loop*. For example, we can use a repeat loop to have the volume knob follow the mouse pointer as it is dragged, by entering the following script:

2.  **Add the following repeat loop to the script in the Volume Behavior Script window.**

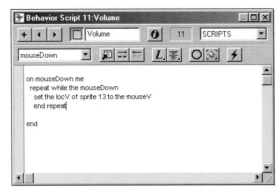

**FIGURE 8.08** *Type the following script in the Volume Behavior Script window.*

```
on mouseDown me
  repeat while the mouseDown
    set the locV of sprite 13 to the mouseV
  end repeat
end
```

Repeat loops are a versatile way to repeatedly perform an action while something is occurring. For example, in this case we are saying that we want the slider knob to follow the mouse as long as the mouse button is held down. This will repeat until the mouse button is released.

When something visible on the Stage is changed through a script, it often requires an addition to the script that will allow the change to be displayed on the Stage. This is frequently the case with repeat loops, because the change is continuous until the mouse button is released. Every time the command set the locV of sprite 13 to the mouseV occurs, we want to see the new position immediately. The way that we can ensure that we see it immediately is by using a command called *updateStage*.

*UpdateStage* tells Director to redraw the Stage immediately. Normally this updating occurs when the playback head passes between frames or loops into a frame as it does with go to the frame. When a repeat loop is occurring, the playback head does not have an opportunity to redraw the Stage, so we must tell Director to force the Stage to redraw. This is the job of the *updateStage* command.

3.  **Make the following addition to the mouseDown handler in the Volume Behavior Script window.**

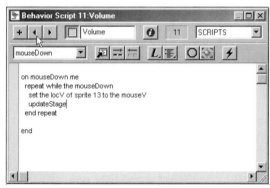

**FIGURE 8.09** *Type the following script in the Volume Behavior Script window.*

```
on mouseDown me
  repeat while the mouseDown
    set the locV of sprite 13 to the mouseV
    updateStage
    end repeat
end
```

We can now test what we have programmed for the volume slider so far.

4.    **Make certain that the playback head is in frame 150, then close the script window and play the movie. You can now click on the slider knob and drag it up and down. Notice that the slider knob is restricted to a vertical path, so it will follow the mouse pointer's position without moving from side to side, but it can be dragged past the top and bottom of the slider background. In the next few steps we will restrict the slider knob so that it can only be dragged as far as the top and bottom of the slider background.**

5.    **Stop the movie.**

## SETTING THE CONSTRAINT OF A SPRITE

We want to restrict the range of motion of the slider knob to the height of the slider background. Lingo is equipped with another sprite property called the constraint, which will allow you to use the area covered by one sprite on the Stage as the bounding area for another sprite on the Stage. If we were to describe this in non-Lingo terms, it would look like this:

> Do not allow the slider knob to pass the top or bottom of the slider background.

Closer to how Lingo will actually handle this is:

> Restrict the range of motion of the slider knob to
> the area that is covered by the slider background.

Let's add this to the Volume Behavior script.

1.  **Select the slider knob on the Stage. The sprite and behavior
    inspectors should display information about the slider knob so
    that we can edit the Volume Behavior script.**

2.  **Select the Volume behavior in the behavior inspector and click
    the Script button at the top of the behavior inspector. This will
    open the script window and display the mouseDown handler in
    the Volume Behavior script. Figure 8.09 is what is currently dis-
    played, and the script is repeated below.**

    ```
    on mouseDown me
      repeat while the mouseDown
        set the locV of sprite 13 to the mouseV
        updateStage
      end repeat
    end
    ```

    Now we will add the script that will restrict the range of motion of
    the slider knob. This restriction must be applied to the knob before it
    is clicked on, so we can't add it to the mouseDown handler; we will
    need to create another one. There is a handler that can be used to
    apply changes and make other settings as soon as a sprite becomes
    present in the Score called beginSprite. We can use a beginSprite
    handler to apply the restricted movement of the knob before the user
    has an opportunity to click on it.

3.  **Add the following handler and script to the Volume Behavior
    script.**

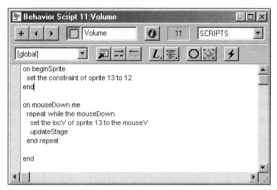

**FIGURE 8.10** *Type the following script in the Volume Behavior Script window.*

```
on beginSprite
  set the constraint of sprite 13 to 12
end


on mouseDown me
  repeat while the mouseDown
    set the locV of sprite 13 to the mouseV
    updateStage
  end repeat
end
```

Let's examine what this script adds to the Volume Behavior script.

```
on beginSprite
  set the constraint of sprite 13 to 12
end
```

This part of the script is the handler that will activate when the slider knob sprite appears in the Score. This way the script that restricts the knob's movement will occur before the user has an opportunity to click on it.

```
on beginSprite me
  set the constraint of sprite 13 to 12
end
```

The *constraint* is the sprite property of a sprite that indicates an area that we would like to restrict a sprite's movement to. In this case we are restricting the movement of the sprite located in channel 13 (the slider knob).

```
on beginSprite me
  set the constraint of sprite 13 to 12
end
```

To restrict the movement of a sprite using the constraint sprite property, you must use another sprite as a reference. The area that is covered by the sprite used as a reference defines the area of restriction. The sprite located in channel 9 is the slider background, so by setting the constraint of sprite 13 to 12 we are saying, restrict the movement of the slider knob to the area covered by the slider background. Let's test our new script.

4.    **Close the script window and play the movie. Now you will find that when you click the slider knob, it will not pass beyond the top or bottom of the slider background. Setting the constraint of the sprite has worked.**

5.    **Stop the movie.**

## ADDING A BACKGROUND SOUND TO THE BILLIONAIRE'S SHOP

In chapter 2 we imported several sounds and images that will be used in later lessons. In this lesson, we will place the sound in the Shop area of the Score and add a script to the Volume behavior that will allow us to control the volume of the sound with the slider that we added to The Billionaire's Shop earlier in this chapter.

1.    **Choose Window>Cast>Internal. This is the internal Cast file where we imported the images and sounds from chapter 2.**

2.    **Select Cast member 11 in the Internal Cast window.**

3.    **Click the *i* button at the top of the Cast window. This is the Cast Member Info button that will give detailed information about the selected Cast member. This window will allow a sound Cast member to be previewed.**

4.    **Click the button labeled Play. The Shop sound will play. It lasts a few seconds then stops. We will want the sound to play continuously while the user is shopping so we can extend the sound by setting it to loop. This will cause the sound to replay.**

5.    **Click the loop option checkbox in the Sound Cast Member Properties dialog box. This will set the sound to play repeatedly.**

6. Click the Play button in the Sound Cast Member Properties dialog box again. Now the sound will cycle repeatedly. The button that was labeled Play now reads Stop.

7. Click the button labeled Stop that was previously labeled Play in the Sound Cast Member Properties dialog box. Now that we have made this setting, we can add the sound to The Billionaire's Shop.

8. Click the button labeled OK.

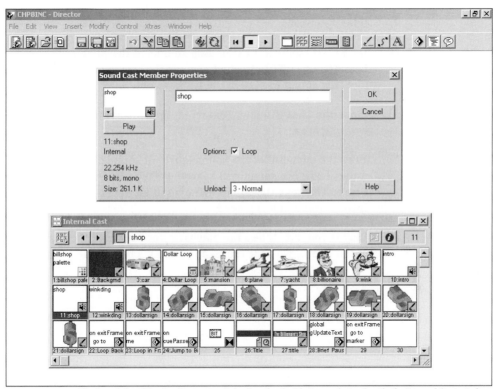

**FIGURE 8.11** *The Sound Cast Member Properties dialog box for the Shop sound open beside the Internal Cast window.*

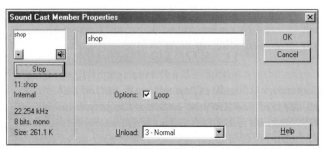

**FIGURE 8.12** *The Sound Cast Member Properties dialog box for the Shop sound with the sound preview button displaying Stop.*

9.  Open the Score.

10. Drag Cast member 11 (the loop sound) to the Shop area of the Score (frame 150) of sound channel 2. This is where we would like this sound to play in the background.

11. Close the Cast window. This will help conserve space in your working area.

12. Drag the endpoint of the sound sprite in sound channel 2 over to frame 165. The sound will span the Shop and Quit areas of the Score. This way the sound will play in all of the areas after the Intro animation has played.

13. Play the movie. When the playback head reaches the Shop area of the Score, we hear the Shop sound playing in the background.

14. Stop the movie.

Now we will go through the steps of controlling the volume of the sound.

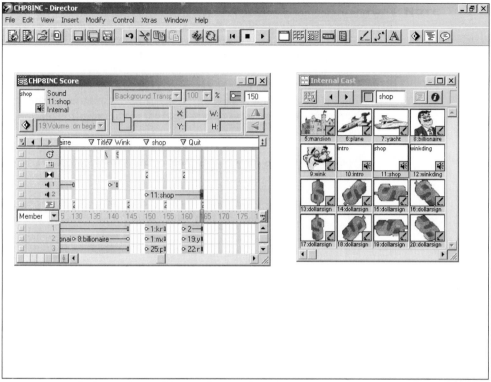

**FIGURE 8.13** *The Score and Internal Cast windows open beside each other.*

## CONTROLLING THE VOLUME OF THE BACKGROUND SOUND

At this point any sounds we play through Director will play at the current sound settings in your computer's control panels. Lingo can be used to control this volume. You can control the volume of the sound playback of your computer overall, or you can control the volume of each sound channel independently. We want to control the volume of the sound playing in sound channel 2 independently.

All sprites, image or otherwise, have several properties that can be controlled through Lingo. For example, we have worked with the *memberNum,* which we know is the Cast member property used to display a sprite. One of the properties available for a sound is *the volume of sound.* You can set the volume of a sound to a number value from 0 to 255: 0 = mute and 255 = maximum. This will not change the volume setting of your computer, only the volume of the designated sound channel. We will use the volume of sound property to control the volume of the background sound in sound channel 2.

1.  Rewind and play the movie. When the playback head reaches the Shop area of the Score, we hear the Shop sound in the background. Now we will experiment with changing the volume of sound property while the movie is playing.

2.  Choose Window>Message. Do not stop the movie. The message window can be used to test Lingo scripts without adding them to the movie. However, the message window will only permit you to test a single line of Lingo script at a time.

3.  Type the Lingo statement in figure 8.14 in the message window.

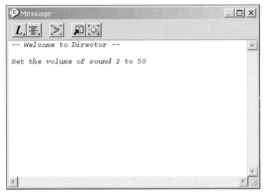

**FIGURE 8.14** *Type the following script in the Message window.*

```
Set the volume of sound 2 to 50
```

4.  Press the Return(Macintosh)/Enter(Windows) key on your keyboard. This will activate the script in the message window and lower the volume of the sound. Let's see how a different setting will change the sound.

5.  Add the Lingo statement in figure 8.15 in the message window.

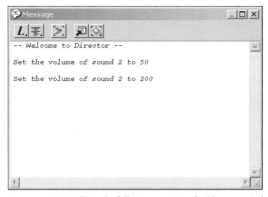

**FIGURE 8.15** *Type the following script in the Message window.*

```
Set the volume of sound 2 to 50
Set the volume of sound 2 to 200
```

6.   Press the Return(Macintosh)/Enter(Windows) key on your keyboard. This will increase the volume of sound 2 to a setting of 200. Now we will set the volume of sound 2 to the level where we would like it to begin before the user has the opportunity to change it with the volume slider.

7.   Add the Lingo statement in figure 8.16 in the message window.

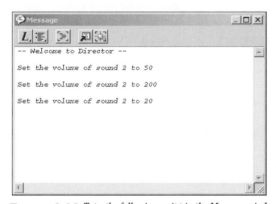

**FIGURE 8.16** *Type the following script in the Message window.*

```
Set the volume of sound 2 to 50
Set the volume of sound 2 to 200
Set the volume of sound 2 to 20
```

8.   Press the Return(Macintosh)/Enter(Windows) key on your keyboard.

9.    **Stop the movie and close the Message window.**

Now we will add the Volume Control script to the Volume Behavior script.

## ADDING THE VOLUME CONTROL SCRIPT TO THE VOLUME BEHAVIOR

The command for controlling the volume of the background sound playing in channel 2 is *set the volume of sound 2 to new setting*. We know that the value that we need to put in place of *new setting* is a number between 0 and 255. The way we would like to control which number is used is by dragging the slider knob on the volume slider that we added to the Shop screen earlier in this chapter. In this session we will create the relationship between the position of the knob along the slider and the volume level.

1.    **Click on the slider knob on the Stage. The sprite overlay for this sprite will appear, displaying information about the knob.**

2.    **Click on the Behavior Inspector button on the sprite overlay for the slider knob. This will open the behavior inspector and display the volume behavior that we started creating earlier.**

3.    **Select the volume behavior in the behavior inspector and click the Script window button at the top of the Behavior Inspector window. This will open the script window and display the current script for the volume behavior. Figure 8.10 shows the current window and the script is repeated below.**

```
on beginSprite
  set the constraint of sprite 13 to 12
end


on mouseDown me
  repeat while the mouseDown
    set the locV of sprite 13 to the mouseV
    updateStage
  end repeat
end
```

4.    **Add the following script in figure 8.17 to the Volume Behavior script. We will add the script that will allow the volume to be controlled, then we will evaluate the script piece by piece.**

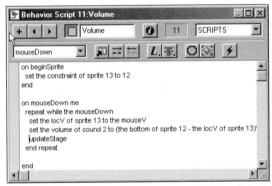

**FIGURE 8.17** *Type the following script in the Volume Behavior Script window.*

```
on beginSprite
  set the constraint of sprite 13 to 12
end

on mouseDown me
  repeat while the mouseDown
    set the locV of sprite 13 to the mouseV
    set the volume of sound 2 to (the bottom of sprite 12 - the locV of sprite 13) * 2
    updateStage
  end repeat
end
```

This script will change the volume setting for the sound in sound channel 2 relative to the position of the slider knob on the volume slider.

5.   **Play the movie. When you reach the Shop area of The Billionaire's Shop, you can click and drag the slider knob to interactively change the volume of the background sound.**

6.   **Stop the movie.**

## EXAMINING THE NEW SCRIPT

The script that we added to the volume behavior uses the position of the slider knob to change the volume setting. It's common to "manufacture" relationships between different parts of a Director presentation to yield results. In this case we have used the positioning of the slider knob relative to the bottom of the slider background to generate a number between 0 and 255. This number can then be used to generate a new volume setting. Here's how:

```
set the volume of sound 2 to (the bottom of sprite 12 - the locV
of sprite 13) * 2
```

This part of the script indicates that we are going to change the volume setting for the sound placed in sound channel 2. The values that we can use for this setting must be numbers between 0 and 255; the latter part of this script will result in a number within this range.

```
set the volume of sound 2 to (the bottom of sprite 12 - the locV
of sprite 13) * 2
```

"The bottom of sprite 12" is the distance in pixels from the top of the Stage to the bottom of the specified sprite. We can determine what this value is by selecting sprite 12 on the Stage and looking at the sprite inspector:

1.  **Click on the slider background (sprite 12) on the Stage.**

2.  **Open the sprite inspector.**

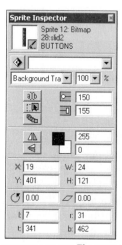

**FIGURE 8.18** *The sprite inspector displaying information about the slider background.*

We are interested in the number displayed in the window labeled "b". This is the current setting for the bottom of this sprite, which is 462; this is the number of pixels from the top of the Stage to the bottom of the slider background. If we were to use this exact value in the script, it would look like this:

```
set the volume of sound 2 to (462 - the locV of sprite 13) * 2
```

Let's look at how this number works with the rest of the script:

```
set the volume of sound 2 to (462 - the locV of sprite 13) * 2
```

This part of the script subtracts the value of the locV of sprite 13 from 462, which we will temporarily use in place of the bottom of sprite 12. The locV of sprite 13 is the distance from the top of the Stage to the center of the slider knob on the Stage. Because we have programmed the slider knob so that it can be moved, the locV of sprite 13 can change. Because we have constrained the range of motion of the slider knob to the distance from the top to the bottom of the slider background, the locV of sprite 13 can only be a number between 341 and 462.

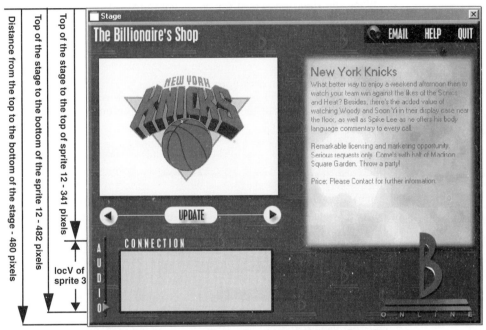

**FIGURE 8.19** *Screen grab of the Shop screen, showing the manufactured sprite relationship.*

In figure 8.19, the top of the arrow is labeled 0, and the bottom is labeled 480. The center of the arrow is labeled "the distance from the top to the bottom of the Stage."

Another arrow extends from the top of the Stage to the bottom of the slider background. The top of the arrow is labeled 0, and the bottom is labeled 462. The center of the arrow is labeled the bottom of sprite 12.

A third arrow extends from the top to the bottom of the Background Slider. The top of the arrow is labeled 341, and the bottom is labeled 462. The center of the arrow is labeled the locV of sprite 13.

The bottom of sprite 12 is the number of pixels from the top of the Stage to the bottom of sprite 12. In this case, it is 462 pixels.

The locV of sprite 13 is the distance from the top of the Stage to the center of sprite 13. Because we have programmed this sprite to be constrained to the area of the Background Slider, the highest the locV of sprite 13 can be is 462 at the bottom of the slider and 341 at the top of the slider.

Now that we have identified the relationships between the positions of the slider sprites, we can add the range of numbers that can possibly take the place of the locV of sprite 13:

```
set the volume of sound 2 to (462 - (341 to 462)) * 2
```

Given this information, we can find out what can possibly turn up when we subtract the locV of sprite 13 from the bottom of sprite 12.

When the slider knob is at the bottom of the slider background sprite, we get:

```
set the volume of sound 2 to (0) * 2
```

or

```
set the volume of sound 2 to (462 -462) * 2
```

When the slider knob is at the top of the slider background sprite, we get:

```
set the volume of sound 2 to (121) * 2
```

or

```
set the volume of sound 2 to (462 -341) * 2
```

Now that we know the range of numbers we can get from the bottom of sprite 12 - the locV of sprite 13, we can see how these numbers will work with the rest of the script:

```
set the volume of sound 2 to (the bottom of sprite 12 - the locV
of sprite 13) * 2
```

Remember that we need a number between 0 and 255 for the volume setting. The bottom of sprite 12 - the locV of sprite 13 will only give us a number between 0 and 121. An asterisk (*) in Lingo means multiply, so * 2 means multiply by two. In this case we are multiplying the difference produced by the bottom of sprite 12 - the locV of sprite 13 by 2. This results in the following:

```
set the volume of sound 2 to (0 to 121) * 2
```

or

```
set the volume of sound 2 to (0 to 242)
```

We have successfully created a relationship between two sprites on the Stage that can be used as a setting for the volume of the sound in channel 2. The higher number, 242, is not quite the maximum setting of 255, but there is little difference between a volume setting of 242 and 255. This is just one example of the limitless possibilities for creative relationships that produce results through Lingo. Let's continue building the volume control slider.

## SETTING AN INITIAL VOLUME SETTING FOR THE BACKGROUND SOUND

The volume of a sound defaults to the maximum setting of 255 unless there is a script that changes the volume. We want the sound in the introduction animation to be loud, but we do not want the sound in the background of the Shop area of the Score to start at a high-volume setting. We will add the initial setting for the sound that plays in the background of The Billionaire's Shop.

In chapter 6, we added a script to the end of the introduction animation that branches the playback head to the Shop area of the Score. We will add a script to this handler that will set the volume of sound 2 to a low background setting.

1.   Select frame 145 of the script channel in the Score.

2.   Open the behavior inspector.

3.   Select the Brief Pause behavior and click the Script window button at the top of the behavior inspector. Figure 8.20 displays the script for the Brief Pause behavior.

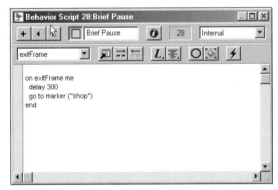

**FIGURE 8.20** *The script for the Brief Pause behavior displayed in the Script window.*

```
on exitFrame me
  delay 300
  go to marker ("Shop")
end
```

4.   Make the following addition to the script in the Brief Pause behavior.

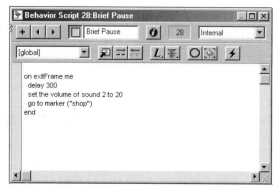

**FIGURE 8.21** *The following addition made to the script in the Brief Pause behavior.*

```
on exitFrame me
  delay 300
  set the volume of sound 2 to 20
  go to marker ("Shop")
end
```

This new script will cause the sound in channel 2 to play at a setting of 20. We placed the script before the line `go to marker (Shop)` because we would like the script to be activated before we go to the Shop area of the Score. This way the sound setting will already be set before we go to a frame where there is a sound to play in channel 2.

**5.    Close the Script window, then rewind and play the movie.**

When we go to the Shop area of the Score, after the introduction animation, the sound in the background is playing at a low setting of 20. This way the sound is evident, but not a point of focus.

The initial location that we used for the placement of the slider knob was 452 pixels from the top of the Stage, which is 10 pixels higher than the bottom of sprite 12. According to the script that we created to control the sound volume, this would result in a sound setting of 20: `set the volume of sound 2 to (the bottom of sprite 12 (462) - the locV of sprite 13 (452)) * 2`. The original placement of the slider knob is exactly where the knob should be for a volume setting of 20. Naturally, this was not a coincidence and is why we went through such detail in making certain that the slider knob and slider background were in precise positions on the Stage.

**6.    Drag the volume slider knob to a higher setting. You can drag the knob to any point toward the top, so long as it is above the current setting.**

7.  **Click the Quit button. The sound is also in the Quit area of the Score, so we still hear it playing at the setting we made with the volume slider.**

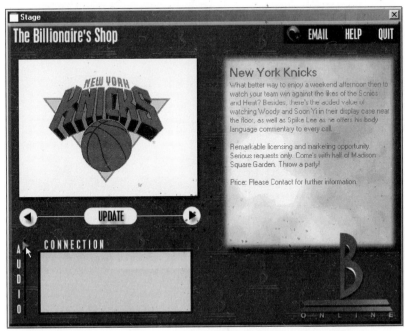

**FIGURE 8.22** *The volume slider in the process of being dragged to a higher setting.*

8.  **Click the No button. This will return the playback head to the Shop area of the Score.**

Notice that the volume setting is the same, but the volume slider has returned to its original position. This is because the script that changes the position of the sprite when it is clicked and dragged only changes the knob's position temporarily. When we jump to another location in the Score, where the slider knob sprite isn't present, Director discards the temporary change in position and reverts to whatever was originally placed in the Score. We will need to add another script to the volume slider to have it remember its last position and remain consistent with the volume setting.

9.  **Stop the movie.**

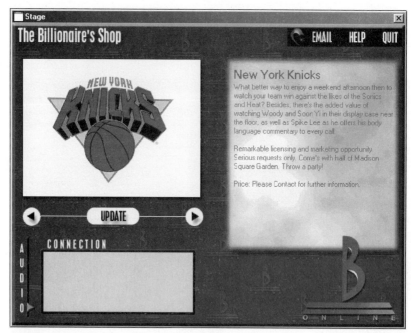

**FIGURE 8.23** *The volume slider reverted to its original position after jumping to and from another location in the Score.*

## PROGRAMMING THE VOLUME SLIDER TO REMEMBER THE LAST VOLUME SETTING

The change in the position that is produced by clicking and dragging the volume slider is temporary. If you jump to the Quit screen and then return to the Shop area of the Score, the volume slider reverts to its original position. In this session we will add a script that will use the current volume setting to determine where the slider knob should be positioned on the volume slider. The script will then place the knob in the appropriate position.

1.    Select the slider knob on the Stage.

2.    Open the behavior inspector.

3.    Select the volume behavior in the behavior inspector.

4.    Click the Script window button at the top of the behavior inspector.

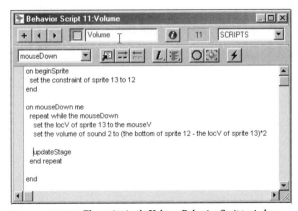

**FIGURE 8.24** *The script in the Volume Behavior Script window.*

```
on beginSprite
  set the constraint of sprite 13 to 12
end
on mouseDown me
  repeat while the mouseDown
    set the locV of sprite 13 to the mouseV
    set the volume of sound 2 to (the bottom of sprite 12 - the locV of sprite 13) * 2
    updateStage
  end repeat
end
```

5. **Make the following addition to the beginSprite handler in the Volume Behavior Script window.**

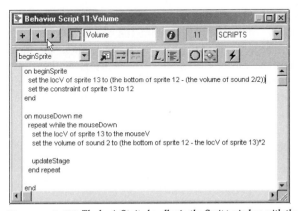

**FIGURE 8.25** *The beginSprite handler in the Script window with the changes in place.*

```
on beginSprite
  set the locV of sprite 13 to (the bottom of sprite 12 - (the
  volume of sound 2 / 2))
  set the constraint of sprite 13 to 12
end


on mouseDown me
  repeat while the mouseDown
    set the locV of sprite 13 to the mouseV
    set the volume of sound 2 to (the bottom of sprite 12 - the
    locV of sprite 13) * 2
    updateStage
  end repeat
end
```

The line that we added to the beginSprite handler uses the current volume setting to determine where the slider knob should be located on the slider. Let's look at the parts of the Lingo line in figure 8.25 to determine how this is accomplished.

```
set the locV of sprite 13 to (the bottom of sprite 12 - (the
volume of sound 2 / 2))
```

This, we know, is the part of the script that indicates that we are going to make a change to the locV, or vertical position, of the sprite on the Stage. The value of the new setting will be determined by whatever results from the scripts within the parentheses.

```
set the locV of sprite 13 to (the bottom of sprite 12 - (the
volume of sound 2 / 2))
```

The beginning of what will determine the new position for the slider knob is the bottom of sprite 12, which we know is the distance in pixels from the top of the Stage to the bottom of the slider background. The value of the bottom of sprite 12 is 462 and does not change. Let's continue with the value 462 substituted for the bottom of sprite 12 to make the script in this example seem less cryptic.

```
set the locV of sprite 13 to (462 - (the volume of sound 2/2))
```

Here we are subtracting the result of what is in the second set of parentheses from 462. Let's break down what is in the second set of parentheses.

```
set the locV of sprite 13 to (462 - (the volume of sound 2/2))
```

The volume of sprite 2 returns the numerical value of the current volume setting, which will be a number from 0 to 242. Let's pick a random number with this range: 164.

```
set the locV of sprite 13 to (462 - (164 / 2))
```

This will give the slider knob a *locV* position of 380. A backslash (/) in Lingo represents division, so /2 means that we are taking the result of the volume of sound 2 (164 in our example) and dividing it by 2. Remember that we created the volume setting in the first place by subtracting the locV of sprite 13 (the slider knob) from the bottom of sprite 12 (the slider background). This gave us a number between 0 and 121, and by multiplying this number by 2 we derived a number that could be used for the volume's setting. In this script we are simply reversing the process: The volume setting is divided by two, and this number is subtracted from the bottom of sprite 12 (462), which gives us the correct position for the slider knob on the volume control slider. Placing this script in the beginSprite handler ensures that this positioning of the slider knob occurs before the slider knob becomes visible on the Stage.

6.   **Close the Script window.**

7.   **Play the movie. When the playback head reaches the Shop area of the Score, the volume of sound 2 is set to 20 and the volume slider is in its initial position.**

8.   **Change the volume setting. Drag it toward the top so that it is in an obvious new position.**

9.   **Click the Quit button. When we jump to the Quit area of the Score, the volume slider is no longer visible or present.**

10.  **Click the No button. The volume slider's position has remained consistent with the volume setting. Our new script has worked.**

11.  **Stop the movie.**

## ACTIVATING THE HELP FEATURE FOR THE VOLUME SLIDER

Next we will activate the Help feature for the volume slider. In chapter 6 we added a Help feature to the buttons and other features of The Billionaire's Shop, including non-button features such as the product display area. The Help feature can also be added to the volume slider so that a Help Balloon is produced upon mouse rollover when the Help feature is activated. In the final section of this chapter we will add the Non-Button Help behavior to the slider background sprite in channel 12.

1.  **Open the Scripts Cast window. This contains the Non-Button Help behavior.**

2.  **Move the playback head to the Shop area of the Score. This will make the volume slider visible on the Stage.**

3.  **Drag Cast member 3 from the Scripts Cast directly to sprite 12 in the Shop area of the Score. This is the slider background sprite. We can also drag the behavior directly onto the slider background sprite on the Stage. Now we can test the new help feature.**

4.  **Play the movie. If you play the movie while the playback head is in the Shop area of the Score, you will avoid waiting through the opening animation.**

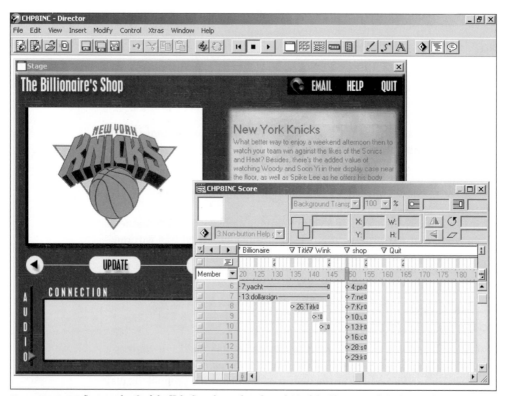

**FIGURE 8.26** *Cast member 3 of the Help Cast dragged to channel 12 of the Shop area of the Score. The volume slider is visible on the Stage.*

5.   Click the Help button on the Stage. This will activate the Help
     feature.

6.   Roll the mouse pointer over the slider background on the Stage.
     This will produce a Help Balloon for the volume slider. This is
     because the volume slider sprite is being switched to a Help Bal-
     loon version Cast member from the Help Cast window.

7.   Stop the movie.

Next, we will look at the Lingo command *puppetSound*.

## USING PUPPET SOUNDS

You might have noticed that we placed the loop sound in sound channel 2,
even though sound channel 1 is available. This is to demonstrate that the
two channels in Director's Score can operate independently. This is primarily useful if you want to play two sounds simultaneously, such as music
and a voiceover that describe what the viewer is seeing. There are other
instances in which you might want to play a sound that cannot be served
through the score. These would be sounds that you would want to occur
randomly, such as a button click, or a sound effect in a game. Sounds in
the Score will only play when the playback head passes through the
frames that that sound occupies. You can control sounds for random playback using a Lingo command called *puppetSound*.

   To add a puppet sound to a movie, you need to import the sound that
you would like to use, then add the scripts that will activate the sound
when you would like it to occur. The script that plays a puppet sound looks
like this: `puppetSound sound name`. *Sound Name* represents the name of
the sound Cast member in the Cast. When this command is executed, it
will play the sound using channel 1 of the Score. This means that any
sound that is playing in channel 1 will not be heard when the *puppetSound*
command is executed. In fact, no other sound, other than puppet sounds,
will play in channel 1 until another command is executed: *puppetSound 0*.
Placing a zero after the command *puppetSound* indicates that you would
like to return control over channel 1 to the Score.

   Although puppet sounds will play in channel 1 by default, it is possible
to have them play in other sound channels that are available in Director, but
not visible in the Score. You can access these channels by typing a channel
number after the puppetSound command. This number can be anything
from 1 to 8; numbers greater than 2 will play the sound in the sound channels that are not accessible in the Score. The script to accomplish this
would look like this: `puppetSound 3, sound name`. Using the *puppet-
Sound* command in this way will play the sound in sound channel 3; because
channel three will not contain the sounds that you will place in the sound

channels of the Score, it isn't necessary for you to execute the *puppetSound 0* command. Using this feature of Lingo will add dimension to your presentation by attaching sounds to the things that the viewer does in your presentation. Next, we will add a puppet sound to The Billionaire's Shop.

**NOTE**  The sound channels in the Score are different from the sprite channels, which are numbered from 1 to 1000.

## ADDING A PUPPET SOUND TO THE BILLIONAIRE'S SHOP

As described in the previous section, puppet sounds can be used to add sounds to your presentation that are attached to specific actions, such as button clicks. This will make the interactive elements of your presentation more engaging to the viewer. In this section we will add a puppet sound to the button behavior that we have placed on all of the buttons so that a sound will play each time a button is clicked.

1.   **Open the internal Cast window. We are going to import the sound file that we will use as a sound effect for the buttons. We want to include the sound in the same Cast library as the other media elements that are used for The Billionaire's Shop interface. Opening the internal Cast window will ensure that any files we import now will appear in the internal Cast library. We can open the internal Cast library by selecting Window>Cast>Internal.**

2.   **Choose File>Import... This will open the Import dialog box.**

3.   **Locate and select the file named Button.aif on the Billshop CD in the directory ...Lessons/Chaptr8/Starter/. When you have located and selected the file, click the button labeled Import in the Import dialog box. This will import the Button.aif sound file in the internal Cast library. The .aif file extension should be removed from the Cast member name for the sound file when it is imported; if it is not, then select the new sound Cast member and remove the .aif extension from the Cast member's name. Next we will play the sound file to have an idea of how our buttons will soon sound when they are clicked.**

4.   **Locate the button sound file Cast member in the internal Cast library and select it. While it is selected, click the Cast Member Properties button (labeled with a lowercase *i*) at the top right corner of the Cast window.**

5.  Click the Play button in the Cast Member Info dialog box. When you have finished listening to the sound file, click the button labeled OK to close the dialog box. This is the sound that we will attach to each of the buttons in The Billionaire's Shop interface. Now we will make the addition to the Button Behavior script that will cause the button sound to play when any of the buttons are clicked.

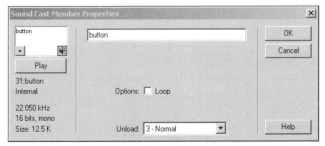

**FIGURE 8.27** *The Sound Cast Member Properties dialog box for the button sound file.*

We can preview the button sound file by selecting it in the Cast and clicking the Cast Member Properties button (labeled with a lower case i) at the top of the Cast window. When the dialog box is open, click the Play button to hear the sound.

The Import dialog box will permit the preview of many media types as they are selected for import into Director. The button sound file can also be previewed in this dialog box in addition to the Cast Member Info dialog box.     **NOTE**

6.  Open the Scripts Cast window. We are going to add a line to the Button behavior that we used to program the buttons in The Billionaire's Shop. Unlike the way in which we have played sound so far in The Billionaire's Shop, the puppet sound that we will add to the buttons will play when a script is executed. You can access the Scripts Cast window by selecting Window>Cast>Scripts.

7.  Select Cast member 1 in the Scripts Cast window, then click the Cast Member Script button at the top right in the Cast window (labeled with a script icon). Cast member 1 is the button behavior. Clicking the Cast Member Script button will open the Script window so that we will have access to the Lingo behind the button behavior. Scroll down until you locate the mouseUp handler, as seen in figure 8.28.

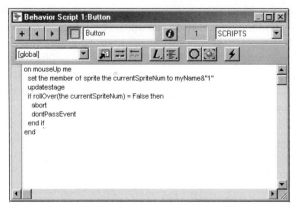

**FIGURE 8.28** *Scrolled down to show the Button Behavior script open in the Script window.*

```
on mouseUp me
  set the member of sprite the currentSpriteNum to myName&"1"
  updateStage
  if rollOver(the currentSpriteNum) = False then
    abort
    dontPassEvent
  end if
end
```

8.    **Add the following line of code to the mouseUp handler in the Button behavior script.**

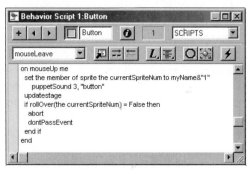

**FIGURE 8.29** *The new code for the Button behavior script.*

```
on mouseUp me
  set the member of sprite the currentSpriteNum to myName&"1"
  puppetSound 3, "button"
  updateStage
  if rollOver(the currentSpriteNum) = False then
    abort
    dontPassEvent
  end if
end
```

This script will play the Cast member named Button when any of the buttons are clicked while The Billionaire's Shop is playing. The number 3 in the script indicates that the sound will be played in sound channel 3. This will mean that we do not need to use the *puppetSound 0* command as discussed earlier.

**WARNING**

**The *puppetSound* command will look for the first Cast member in The Billionaire's Shop that has the name "Button," or any other name that we might have used with the *puppetSound* command. In The Billionaire's Shop there are two Cast members named "Button"—the sound that we just imported, and the behavior that is used to control the buttons. The sound file is located in the internal Cast library, which is the first Cast library in our movie. This will permit the *puppetSound* command to activate the correct Cast member, because it will encounter the button sound before it encounters the Button behavior, which is located in the fourth Cast (scripts) in our movie. If the positioning of these two Cast members were reversed, then we would need to use a different name for the sound Cast member and use that new name in the *puppetSound* command; otherwise, *puppetSound* would attempt to play the behavior Cast member and nothing would result, not even an error message.**

9.  Close the script window.

10. Rewind and play the movie.

11. Click any of the buttons in The Billionaire's Shop interface. Now we will hear the button sound when any of the buttons are clicked and the Mouse button is released. Of course all of the buttons will play the same sound file because they all share the same script. If we want to have different buttons play different

**sounds, then we will need to create multiple behaviors that each play a different sound using the *puppetSound* command.**

**12.  Stop the movie and save your work.**

This completes our work in this chapter. In the next chapter we will connect The Billionaire's Shop to the Internet!

## SUMMARY

The primary objective of this lesson was to add a volume control slider to The Billionaire's Shop. We accomplished this by adding two new images to the Stage, a sound to the Score, and a script that used the position of one of the two new sprites to change the volume of the new sound. As was first pointed out in chapter 2, we can use the relationships between different elements of a Director presentation to produce results using Lingo.

The script that we used to generate the volume controller was a behavior that we created from scratch. The behavior was activated when the volume controller became visible on the Stage. It allowed the volume to be changed when the sprite to which the behavior was applied was clicked and dragged along a sprite volume slider.

In this lesson we used the coordinate property, locV, to move the volume controller up and down. We used the volume of sound property to change the volume of the background sound. We also used the constraint of sprite property to restrict the volume controller's movement to the volume slider.

Scripts can be applied to a sprite and activated as soon as that sprite becomes visible on the Stage using the beginSprite event handler. This is particularly helpful for applying settings to multiple sprites, such as the starting position on the Stage for an interactive game. In this chapter we used the beginSprite event handler to place the volume controller at a position that was appropriate for the current volume setting whenever the playback head returned to the Shop area of the Score.

Puppet sounds are audio files that are controlled through Lingo commands. This allows us to attach sound playback to specific events, such as mouse clicks. The commands that we use to activate puppet sounds are *puppetSound sound name* to play a sound file and *puppetSound 0* to return control of sound channels to the Score. We can also play puppet sounds in sound channels outside of the two visible sound channels in the Score by indicating the sound channel that we would like the puppet sound to play in. The command to perform this would look something like this: *puppetSound 3, sound name,* with the number 3 representing the channel that the sound should play in. You can use any number from 1 to 8 in this type of puppet sound use.

## QUESTIONS

1. Are sprites the only elements in a Director movie that have properties? Explain.

2. Why was it necessary to have two sprites for the volume controller?

3. Could we have created a volume controller that moved from left to right?

4. When would we create a behavior with the behavior inspector, and when would we create one directly in the script window?

5. Why is the height of the volume slider background precisely 121 pixels?

6. Why was it necessary to introduce the beginSprite event handler to the volume behavior?

## EXERCISES

1. Create a new movie and place a sound in sound channel 1. You can import the music from The Billionaire's Shop of any other sound file that you might have. Set the sound to "loop" in the Cast Member Properties dialog box. Also, add a script to frame 5 that will keep the playback head in that frame (go to the frame). Use the message window to set the volume of the sound playing in sound channel 1 to various settings.

2. Create a new movie and place a sound in sound channel 1. You can import the music from The Billionaire's Shop or any other sound file that you might have. Set the sound to "loop" in the Cast member properties dialog box. Also, add a script to frame 5 that will keep the playback head in that frame (go to the frame). Use the message window to set the volume of the sound playing in sound channel 1 to various settings.

3. Add three simple buttons to the movie you created in exercise one. They do not need to be as detailed as the buttons we have created for The Billionaire's Shop, they can be simple graphics created in the Paint window. Add a sprite script to each button that will set the volume of the music to a specific setting (such as no volume (mute), middle volume, and high volume).

4. In the same movie, add a sound to sound channel 2 in the Score. This should be a different sound. It will work best if the two different sounds are of different types, such as a voiceover recording and a music file. Again, you can use any sound files that you have available. When you have done this, create a second set of buttons identical to the buttons that you created in exercise two;

these buttons should control the volume settings of the second sound. When the movie is playing, you should be able to control the volume of both sounds independently. Also, import a sound effect audio file that can be used as a button sound and edit the script for the buttons so that they play the new sound effect when a button is pressed.

# CHAPTER 9

# RETRIEVING TEXT FROM THE INTERNET WITH DIRECTOR

# 9 Retrieving Text from the Internet with Director

**In this chapter, you will learn how to:**

- Display information in a text field
- Use Lingo to request information from the Internet
- Use Lingo to detect an error in an Internet download
- Use Lingo to detect the completion of an Internet download
- Store retrieved information in a variable
- Display retrieved information in a text field
- Create Alert displays, which will provide the user with information about the status of network events in The Billionaire's Shop
- Use the *NetDone()* and *netTextResult()* commands

So far The Billionaire's Shop has a nearly complete interface and will allow us to browse through a number of products. However, there is no way to determine if something new has been added to the shop, if a product has been sold, or if something has changed in price. Generally this type of up-to-the-minute information has been reserved for the Internet because new information can be updated in one location and viewed by anyone who has access to the Internet.

Director is capable of retrieving information from a network such as the Internet in much the same way that a browser retrieves the information that is used to display a Web page. Once the information has been retrieved, conventional Lingo commands can be used to incorporate the new files into a presentation. This network downloading capability is the root of Director's Hybrid feature set. It allows a developer to create a standard multimedia presentation with typically large file formats, such as video and audio, and enhance them with smaller, regularly changing data located somewhere on a network.

Director's Hybrid capability is divided into three basic categories: the commands to retrieve and download data; the functions that check the status of the download for completion, errors, and other such considerations;

and display of retrieved data. Any file format can be downloaded. There are two categories of file format: text files and all other file formats (such as images, sounds, animation, and video). Text files are simply files that can be created with a word-processing application and can be used to perform such functions as updating the articles in a CD-ROM newsletter. Also within the category of text files are network executables, such as CGI scripts, which are used to channel email messages and other network queries such as online product ordering. The wide category of all other file formats is truly only useful to Director if the file downloaded can be used in Director, so this category generally includes images, audio, and other media. In this chapter we will work with the command that allows the download of text files: *getNetText()*. This is also the command that can be used to activate online executables, which we will do when we add an email feature to The Billionaire's Shop in chapter 11. The text file that we will download will contain information about updates to the inventory of the shop. In chapter 10 we will work with the command to download other file formats: *downloadNetThing()*. Also in chapter 10 we will work with the Lingo scripts that track the status of a network download and display the data that has been downloaded.

**NOTE**    When you work with Hybrid scripts, it is important to recognize that Director's performance can be affected by the speed of your network connection, traffic on the network, and other influences that change the performance of network operations. If you believe you are experiencing difficulties with Hybrid scripts that are not a result of scripting errors, you can use a standard network browser, such as Netscape Navigator or Microsoft Internet Explorer, to visit the Motion Over Time site at **www.motionovertime.com**. If your browser seems slow in establishing a connection, then the scripts that Director uses to communicate with files on the Internet will also be slow. This is the nature of the Internet and cannot be modified or optimized through Director. Your best option is to log off and try again later.

## VIEWING THE COMPLETED EXAMPLE FILE

In this chapter we will concentrate on the *getNetText()* command, which is used to download a text file from the Internet. In the completed version of The Billionaire's Shop, we will use the text we retrieve with *getNetText()* to determine if the inventory in the shop needs to be updated. If no update is required, then the text is simply discarded and no further downloads are attempted.

This means that we are using *getNetText()* in a way that is never directly apparent to the users. Users simply launch The Billionaire's Shop, and the *getNetText()* command works invisibly in the background. The *get-*

*NetText()* command is an extremely useful addition to Director, so in this session we will work on a file that illustrates precisely what this new command accomplishes. First let's take a look at the completed sample file.

1. **Establish a connection to the Internet. Use the software that you normally use to connect to the Internet. Most services, such as America Online and CompuServe, provide access to the Internet simply by going online using their software. If you use another Internet service provider (ISP), then use the software they provided.**

**NOTE** It is not necessary to launch a browser, such as Microsoft Internet Explorer or Netscape Navigator, to use the Lingo commands that retrieve information from the Internet. You only need to use the software that is required to establish your Internet dial-up connection.

**WARNING** Director cannot currently detect the status of your Internet connection. As a result, it is important to be certain that your Internet connection is active before attempting to use Lingo commands that request information from the Internet, such as *getNetText()* and *downLoadNetThing*.

2. **If it is not already open, launch Director.**

3. **Choose File>Open.**

4. **Locate and select the file named Textcmp.dir on the Billshop CD in the directory ...Lessons/Chaptr9/Text/Complete/Textcmp.dir.**

5. **Click Open.**

6. **Play the movie. This movie uses *getNetText()* to retrieve a text file from the Internet. Notice that the Status window displays information about what is currently occurring with the requested file. When the file is completely transferred, it is presented in the Results window.**

7. **Stop the movie.**

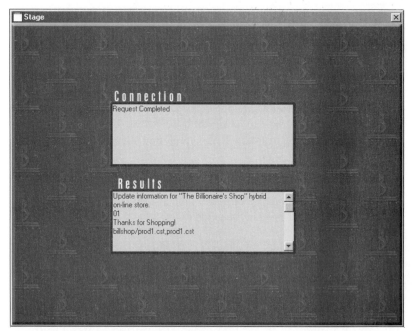

**FIGURE 9.01** *The completed getNetText() example movie, with the text results from the retrieved text displayed in the Results window.*

## USING THE WATCHER WINDOW

There will be many times in the remaining lessons in which we will request information from the Internet. The time that it takes for these requests to be answered varies according to the amount of traffic that is currently on the Internet and the quality of your connection. Sometimes these network requests can take longer than usual, but it might not be because anything is wrong. To help us know if something is taking longer than usual or isn't working for some reason, we can use the Watcher window. The Watcher allows us to display variables from Lingo so that we can see when they change and how they change. This can be very helpful in debugging complex code, but in this case it is helpful to see if a network request using a Hybrid script is working or not.

There are two important commands that we will be using in this lesson: *netDone()* and *netTextResult()*. *NetDone()* is used to determine if a network request is completed. If we can see that the value of *netDone()* is 0, then we know that anything we have requested is still in progress. If *netDone()* is equal to 1 and we haven't seen the results that we expected, then we know that something has gone wrong. This can save us some time in knowing that we should be looking for a problem, perhaps in our script, instead of thinking that our connection to the Internet is the only reason why the script isn't working.

The *netTextResult()* command will show us the results of a network request using the *getNetText()* command. In the example lesson that we used earlier, *getNetText()* was used to retrieve the text that was later displayed in the text window on the screen. The command that receives the text and decodes it into a format that is understood by a text field is *netTextResult()*. When a network request for text is in progress, *netTextResult()* is equal to empty quotation marks " ". When a network request is successful, then *netTextResult()* is equal to the text that was requested. If we can see *netTextResult()* while a network request is in progress, then we have another way of checking for the success of that request while we are working in Director.

So to review, before a network request is sent, *netDone()* should be equal to 1 because there is nothing in progress, and *netTextResult()* will have a value of empty quotation marks " ". These are the default values for these two commands. During a network request, *netDone()* should have a value of 0, and *netTextResult()* should continue to have a value of empty quotation marks. If the network request was for text and was successful, (as opposed to another file type, which will be covered in chapter 10), then *netDone()* should be equal to 1 and *netTextResult()* should contain the text that was requested.

In this short session, we will set up the Watcher window to display *netDone()* and *netTextResult()* at all times so that we can track their activity while we work.

1.   **Select Window>Watcher. This will open the Watcher window.**

2.   **In the text field at the upper left of the Watcher window, type netDone(). This is the command we will use to display the status of network requests using Lingo.**

**FIGURE 9.02** *The netDone() command typed into the field at the upper left of the Watcher window.*

3.   **Click the Add button. This will move the *netDone()* command to the display area below. You will see that the current value for *netDone()* is 1.**

4.  In the text field at the upper left of the Watcher window, type netTextResult(). This is the command we will use to display the information that is retrieved from the Internet using the *getNet-Text()* command.

5.  Click the Add button. Now the *netTextResult()* command will be added to the display area below. You will see that the current value for *netTextResult()* is empty quotation marks " ", also described as an empty string. If you get a value other than an empty string, please refer to the following note for steps to correct this.

**NOTE**   You might find that, after running the complete version of this movie, *netTextResult()* returns text instead of an empty string. We can clear *netTextResult()* by using the *netAbort()* command, which we will go into in greater detail later in this lesson. For now, do the following:

- Open the Message window (Window>Message).

- Type *netAbort()* in the Message window.

- Press Return(Macintosh)/Enter(Windows).

After these steps, the value for *NetTextResult()* in the Watcher window should return to an empty string.

**FIGURE 9.03** *netTextResult() typed into the field at the upper left of the Watcher Window.*

6.  Rewind and play the Textcmp.dir movie again. When we run the Textcmp.dir movie now, we can watch the activity within the *netDone()* and *netTextResult()* commands.

7.  Stop the movie.

In the next lesson we will build the Textcmp.dir movie from the beginning.

> **NOTE**
>
> The information that is typed into the Watcher window is temporary and will not be saved with the movie. The information will remain there as long as you are running Director and will persist if you open movies in succession, but it will not be there if you quit Director and return later. One technique you can use to avoid the need to retype all of the information is to type the terms you would like to track into a separate field Cast member that only resides in the Cast and is not necessarily used in the movie. You can then copy and paste each item into the Watcher window one at a time.

## PREPARING THE FILES FOR THIS LESSON

Save a copy of the file named Textinc.dir to your hard drive. You can locate Textinc.dir on the Billshop CD in the directory ...Lessons/Chaptr9/Text/ Starter/. There are no other files that are necessary for this chapter. Remember to save frequently.

> **NOTE**
>
> Hybrid scripting methods in Director require a great deal of writing scripts before you can test their capabilities. This means that you will be typing Lingo code for some time before you have an opportunity to see what your new scripts do. Unlike the earlier chapters in this book, these chapters require much more preparation. So, be patient, move slowly, and pay careful attention that you type scripts precisely as they appear on these pages. You may even need to review the material in this chapter several times to fully this lesson. Hybrid scripting is exciting and new and still evolving as the needs for "pushing around" information change. Macromedia watches closely for these needs and implements them into future versions of Director. This type of scripting opens up a lot of possibilities, so move forward attentively, and enjoy!

## ADDING TEXT DISPLAY FIELDS TO THE INTERFACE

Any text-based information in a Director file can be displayed in field Cast members. This is particularly useful for providing a user with information, such as their score in a game. Field Cast members can also be used for user input, such as responding to questions in an interactive test. The text that is displayed in a field Cast member is similar to text that is displayed in a word processor in that the text requires the presence of an installed system font in order to be displayed properly. If the font is not present, the computer will substitute a default system font, such as Courier.

> **NOTE**
>
> A live connection to the Internet is not required for this part of the lesson.

1.   If it is not already open, launch Director.

2.   Open the file named Textinc.dir.

3.   If it is not already open, open the Score. Notice that there is already a sprite located in channel 1, frames 1 through 5. This is the image that we will use as the background for the sample file.

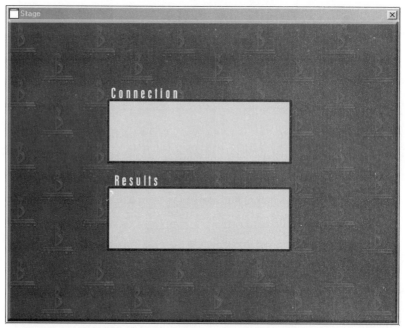

**FIGURE 9.04** *The background image for the getNetText() example file.*

4.   Make certain that the playback head is in frame 1 of the Score. This will ensure that all of the sprites that we will add to the Stage will appear in frame 1.

5.   Choose Window>Tool palette. The Tool palette can be used to create simple shapes, buttons, and text. The button labeled Field can be used to create data display fields in your movies.

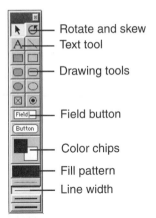

Rotate and skew

Text tool

Drawing tools

Field button

Color chips

Fill pattern

Line width

**FIGURE 9.05** *The Tool palette. Arrows identify the Field button, the color chips, and the line buttons. Another arrow identifies the Text tool.*

6.      **Click the button labeled Field in the Tool palette. While this button is selected, the mouse will become a crosshair when it is moved over the Stage.**

> **WARNING**
>
> **Be sure that you use the field Cast member type as opposed to the text Cast member type. Both Cast member types can be used to display text information, but the text Cast member is generally used only for artistic display and not data display. This is because Cast members created with the text tool are automatically anti-aliased and are converted into bitmapped images when the movie is made into a projector so that the text is no longer dependent upon the presence of a particular font to display properly. Field Cast members are always dependent upon the presence of the font that was used to create the text in the field, even when they are in a projector. As a result, field Cast members should only be used when the text they contain is intended to change, such as in this example. In all other instances it is best to use text Cast members.**

7.      **Click and drag the crosshair from the upper left corner to the upper right corner in the display area labeled Connection in the background image. We will use this field to display the download status of the text that we will retrieve with *getNetText()*. The field will be tall enough to display a single line of text. We will adjust its height in the next few steps.**

8. **Once again, click the button labeled Field in the Tool palette. We are going to create the display field for the Results area of the interface.**

9. **Click and drag the crosshair from the upper left corner to the upper right corner of the display area labeled Results in the background image.**

   We will use this field to display the actual text file that we retrieve using *getNetText()*.

10. **Do not close the Tool palette .**

    We will be using some of the features of this palette later in this lesson. Now we will modify the fields that we have created so that they cover the entire display areas on the background image.

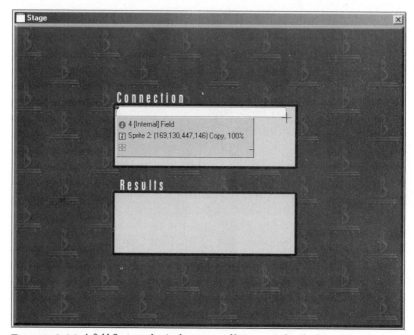

**FIGURE 9.06** *A field Cast member in the process of being created in the Connection area on the Stage.*

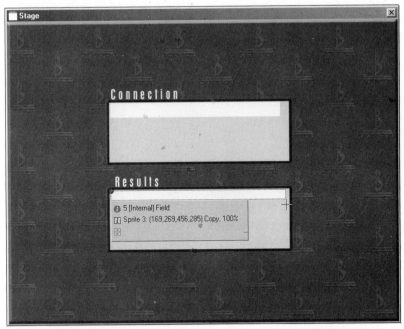

**FIGURE 9.07** *A field Cast member in the process of being created in the Results area on the Stage.*

11. Click directly on the sprite located in channel 2 of the Score. This is the field we created in the Connection area on the background image. When it is selected, the sprite overlay will appear.

12. Click the blue *i* button on the sprite overlay for the selected field. This will open the Field Cast Member Properties dialog box.

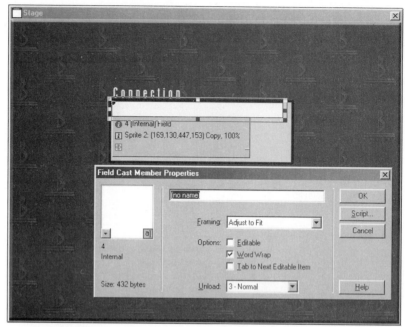

**FIGURE 9.08** *The selected Connection field on the Stage with the open Field Cast Member Properties dialog box.*

13.  **Name the field Connection. The Cast member name field currently reads (no name). You can replace this text with the name Connection. Naming the field Cast member will make it possible to refer to the field by name in Lingo scripts.**

**NOTE**   It is common to use field Cast members that do not contain any text until a movie is running and scripts display information in the field. We must give the empty field Cast member a name, because Director will not retain an empty field Cast member without one.

14.  **Choose Fixed from the Framing pop-up menu in the Field Cast Member Properties dialog box. This option in this menu will determine how text is displayed in the field. Adjust to Fit will change the size of the field based upon the amount of text that is placed in the field. Scrolling will create a standard scrolling text display window with scrolling arrows on the right side of the window. Fixed will display only the text that will fit in the window's display area. Any remaining text is entered in the field but will not be visible to the user. Limit to Field Size will eliminate any text beyond precisely what will fit in the field's display area.**

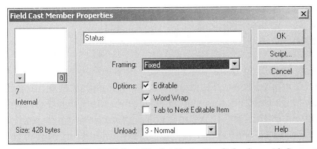

**FIGURE 9.09** *The Field Cast Member Properties dialog box with Connection in the name field and Fixed selected from the Framing pop-up menu.*

15. **Click the button labeled OK. This will close the Field Cast Member Properties dialog box. Now we'll set the Cast member properties for the field in the Results area of the background.**

16. **Click directly on the sprite located in channel 3 of the Score. This is the field that we created in the Results area on the background image. When it is selected, the sprite overlay will appear.**

17. **Click the blue *i* button on the sprite overlay for the selected field. This will open the Field Cast Member Properties dialog box.**

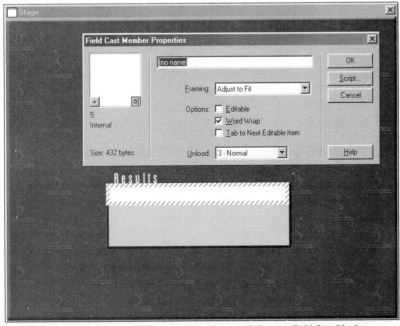

**FIGURE 9.10** *The selected Results field on the Stage with the open Field Cast Member Properties dialog box.*

18. Name the field Results. The Cast member name field currently reads (no name). You can replace this text with the name Results.

19. Choose Scrolling from the Framing pop-up menu in the Field Cast Member Properties dialog box. We chose Fixed for the Connection field because there will never be more than two lines displayed in this field. We are not certain how much text will be returned when we use *getNetText()*, so the best option is to use a scrolling field, which can contain as much text as needed.

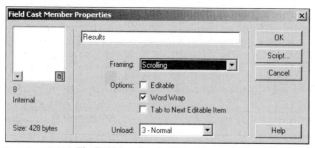

**FIGURE 9.11** *The Field Cast Member Properties dialog box with Results in the name field and Scrolling selected from the Framing pop-up menu.*

20. Click the button labeled OK. This will close the Field Cast Member Properties dialog box. Now we will resize the Connection and Results fields so that they cover the defined display areas.

21. Select and resize the Connection field on the Stage so that it covers the Connection area on the background image. You can resize the Connection field by clicking and dragging the control points on the selected sprite.

22. Select and resize the Results field on the Stage so that it covers the Results area on the background image. After the Connection and Results fields are resized, we will choose the settings for the text that will be displayed in them.

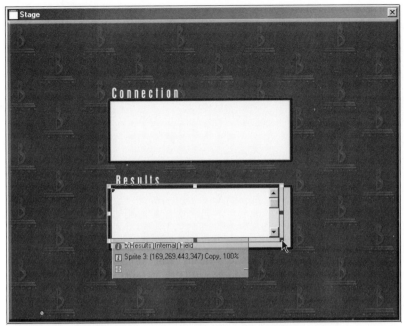

**FIGURE 9.12** *The Connection and Results fields in the process of being resized.*

23. **Choose Window>Inspectors>Text. This will open the text inspector, which we can use to modify the text displayed in the Connection and Results fields.**

**FIGURE 9.13** *The text inspector.*

24. **Double-click on the Connection field on the Stage. Double-clicking on a field will put it in editing mode, which will allow you to enter and modify text. The text inspector will show the current settings for this field. These settings can vary, depending upon the fonts installed in your computer's system software.**

25. **Type Waiting for Status into the Connection field, then highlight the new text.**

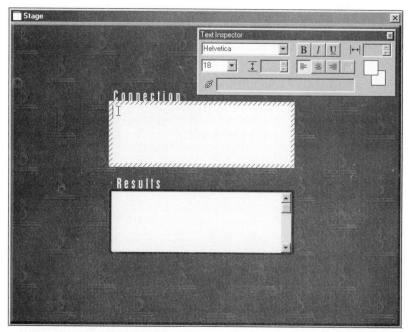

**FIGURE 9.14** *The Connection field in editing mode. The text inspector is open beside it.*

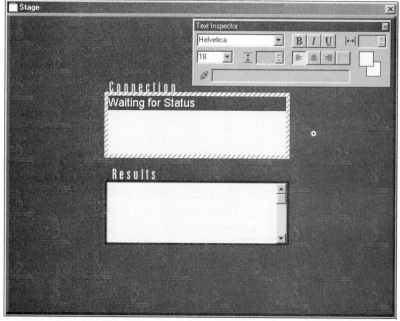

**FIGURE 9.15** *Waiting for Status typed into the Connection.*

26. Choose any font from the Font menu in the text inspector and set the text to display at 18 points. It is not important to choose a specific font. Use any standard alphabet character font that is installed in your system.

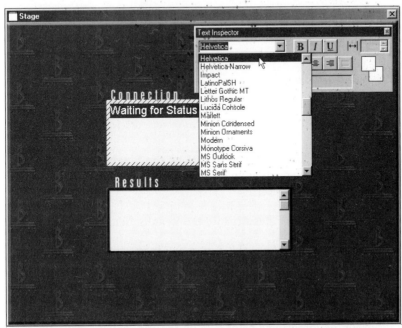

**FIGURE 9.16** *The Connection field in editing mode, with Helvetica selected from the Font menu on the text inspector.*

27. While the text is still highlighted, choose the color black, or another dark color, after clicking on the foreground color chip on the Tool palette to get a palette. You will notice that the text will disappear when it is deselected. This is because the ink effect applied to the text field is Copy. This will cause the text to be displayed against a white background and, therefore, to be invisible. We will change the ink effect for this sprite so that the background will no longer be visible and the text will be displayed against the black of the background image. You can locate white at the upper left corner of the Color palette that is produced when you click on the foreground color chip.

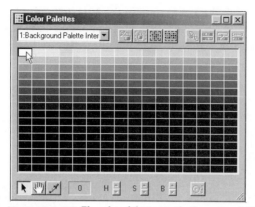

**FIGURE 9.17** *The color of the text in the Connection field set to white.*

28.  Double-click on the Results field on the Stage. We are going to repeat the same steps to make the text settings for the Results field.

29.  Type Waiting for Results into the Results field on the Stage.

30.  Choose any font from the Font menu in the text inspector. You can choose a different font from the one you selected for the Connection field.

31.  Just as we did with the Connection field, choose the color white from the foreground color chip on the Tool palette while the text is still highlighted. This text will become visible when we change the ink effect for both text fields.

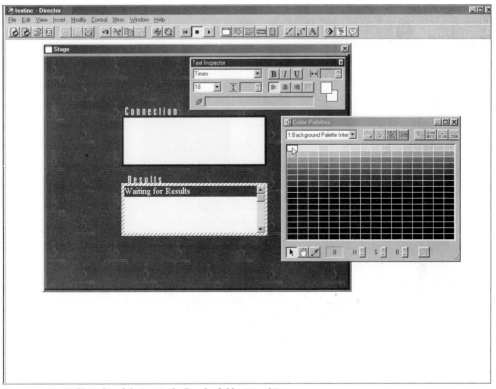

**FIGURE 9.18** *The color of the text in the Results field set to white.*

32. Close the text inspector. Now we will bring the endpoints for the two new fields to frame 5 so that they end in the same frame as the background sprite. We will also change their ink effect to background transparent, which will reveal the text.

33. If it is not currently open, open the Score.

34. Drag-select the sprite objects in channels 2 and 3 in the Score. These are the two text fields. We will use Extend Sprite to bring them back to frame 5.

35. Move the playback head to frame 5.

36. Choose Modify>Extend Sprite.

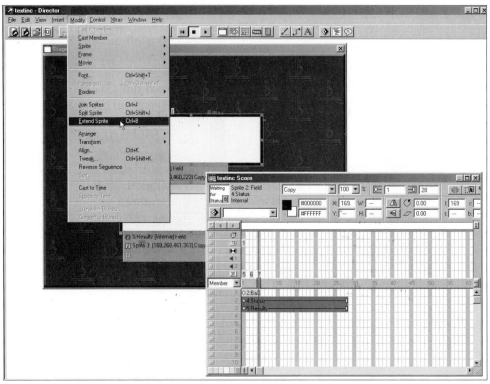

**FIGURE 9.19** *The sprites in channels 2 and 3 selected with the playback head in frame 5 and Modify>Extend Sprite selected.*

37.   **While sprites 2 and 3 are still selected, choose Background Transparent from the ink menu at the top of the Score. You will see that the text will now be displayed as white against green on the Stage.**

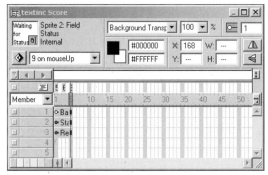

**FIGURE 9.20** *Sprites 2 and 3 selected, with Background Transparent selected from the Ink pop-up menu.*

## ADDING THE getNetText() COMMAND TO THE SAMPLE FILE

There are three steps in the procedure for using NetLingo commands in your script. NetLingo commands are the Lingo terms that are used to communicate with and download files from the Internet, such as *getNetText()*.

1.   **The information is requested from the Internet.**

2.   **The download status of the requested information is checked.**

3.   **The completely downloaded information is used in the Director file.**

The process is very similar to downloading information from the Internet using a conventional browser, such as Netscape Navigator. Now we will add the *getNetText()* command in a manner that will automatically retrieve the information from the Internet as soon as the movie starts playing:

1.   **Close all open windows except the Score. We will be able to make all of the adjustments we want from the Score.**

2.   **Double-click in frame 1 of the script channel. Double-clicking in the script channel will directly access the Script window. This will save the step of opening and entering scripts through the behavior inspector. Notice that the *me* argument is not automatically added. This is because it is only automatically added to scripts that are entered through the behavior inspector.**

3.   **Add the following script to the exitFrame handler in the Script window.**

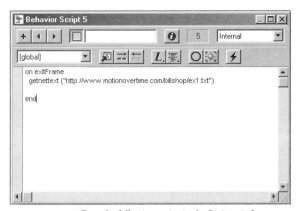

**FIGURE 9.21** *Type the following script in the Script window.*

```
on exitFram e
 getNetText ("http://www.motionovertime.com/billshop/ex1.txt")
end
```

The *getNetText()* command will search and retrieve the text file that
is indicated by the network URL (Universal Resource Locator) that
is typed beside the command. In this case we are looking for a text
file named *ex1.txt* that is located at the Internet location **http://
www.motionovertime.com/billshop/**. After making the request for
the text file from the Internet, we must use other network Lingo
commands to actually use the retrieved information.

4.  **Close the Script window. Now we will add the scripts that will
    display the information in the text fields from the ex1.txt text
    file.**

5.  **Double-click frame 3 of the script channel. This will open the
    Script window for frame 3.**

6.  **Add the following script to the exitFrame handler.**

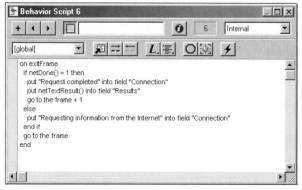

**FIGURE 9.22** *Enter the script in the Script window.*

```
on exitFrame
  if netDone() = 1 then
    put "Request completed" into field "Connection"
    put netTextResult() into field "Results"
    go to the frame + 1
  else
    put "Requesting information from the Internet" into
    field "Connection"
  end if
  go to the frame
end
```

The *netDone()* command checks to see if the last network request has completed. It will return a value of 0 (the programming equivalent of False) if there is a network request that is in progress. If there is no network activity or if a network operation is completed, *netDone()* returns a value of 1, which is the programming equivalent of True.

The parentheses that follow the word *netDone* can be used to check the status of several network operations simultaneously. You can place a network request into a variable as follows:

```
put getNetText ("http://www.test.com/sampletext.txt") into
AVARIABLE
```

Then you can check on the completion status of the request by using:

```
netDone(AVARIABLE)
```

If no variable is indicated within the parentheses, then *netDone()* will check the status of the last network request by default. Because we are only making a single network request in this movie, there is no need to place anything in the parentheses.

Let's continue the examination:

```
on exitFrame
  if netDone() = 1 then
    put "Request completed" into field "Connection"
    put netTextResult() into field "Results"
    go to the frame + 1
  else
    put "Requesting information from the Internet" into
    field "Connection"
  end if
  go to the frame
end
```

This else statement will be activated if the network operation that we started with *getNetText()* is not completed. The status report: "Requesting information from the Internet" will be displayed in the field we added to the movie earlier named Connection.

```
on exitFrame
  if netDone() = 1 then
    put "Request completed" into field "Connection"
    put netTextResult() into field "Results"
    go to the frame + 1
  else
    put "Requesting information from the Internet" into
    field "Connection"
  end if
  go to the frame
end
```

Placing the go to the frame script outside of the if . . . then statement will ensure that this script will be activated, whether *netDone()* detects a completed operation or not. This way the script will repeatedly check to see if the requested information was retrieved.

```
on exitFrame
  if netDone() = 1 then
    put "Request completed" into field "Connection"
    put netTextResult() into field "Results"
    go to the frame + 1
  else
    put "Requesting information from the Internet" into
    field "Connection"
  end if
  go to the frame
end
```

When *netDone()* detects that the *getNetText()* command has completed retrieving the requested text, this script will put the status report "Request completed" into the field we named Connection.

```
on exitFrame
  if netDone() = 1 then
    put "Request completed" into field "Connection"
    put netTextResult() into field "Results"
    go to the frame + 1
  else
    put "Requesting information from the Internet" into
    field "Connection"
  end if
  go to the frame
end
```

The *netTextResult()* command will read the text that is requested by *getNetText()*. Using this command in this script will place the results of the requested text file into the field we created earlier and named Results.

```
on exitFrame
  if netDone() = 1 then
    put "Request completed" into field "Connection"
    put netTextResult() into field "Results"
    go to the frame + 1
  else
    put "Requesting information from the Internet" into
    field "Connection"
  end if
  go to the frame
end
```

When the information we requested with *getNetText()* has successfully been downloaded, this script will send the playback head to the next frame in the Score. In the next few steps we will add a script to frame 5 that will cause the playback head to loop in that frame. We want to send the playback head to another frame because this script will have accomplished its job and will no longer be needed.

7.     **Close the Script window. Let's add the script to frame 5 that will cause the playback head to loop in that frame.**

8.     **Double-click in frame 5 of the script channel.**

9.     **Add the following script to the exitFrame handler in the Script window.**

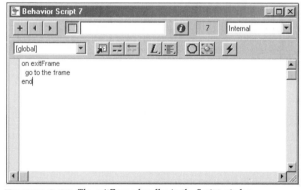

**FIGURE 9.23** *The exitFrame handler in the Script window.*

```
on exitFrame
  go to the frame
end
```

**10.    Close the Script window.**

Let's test the movie so far.

## TESTING THE GETNETTEXT() AND NETTEXTRESULT() SCRIPTS

In order to test the scripts in this movie, you will need to have a live connection to the Internet. Use the software you would normally use to connect to the Internet, then return to this movie and play it. It will automatically retrieve the text information we requested in the script.

1.    **Establish a live connection to the Internet. Do not quit Director to do this. Minimize Director on the PC or use the Finder in the Macintosh to allow you to locate and activate your Internet communication software. Keep your Internet connection active for the rest of this lesson.**

2.    **Return to Director, make certain the Stage is active, and play *textinc.dir*.**

The scripts will activate automatically. First the Connection field will display "Requesting information from the Internet," then it will display "Request completed" along with the text from *ex1.txt* in the Results field. We have successfully downloaded the text file from the Internet. There are still other things to take into consideration, especially because Internet connections can be interrupted, or heavy traffic on the Internet can cause long delays in sending downloading information. In the next few steps we will add commands that will help manage both of these potential problems.

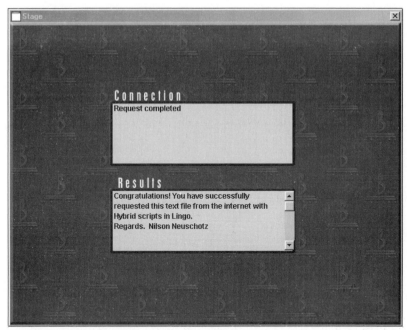

**FIGURE 9.24** *The getNetText() sample movie, with "Request completed" displayed in the Connection field and the text from ex1.txt in the Results field.*

## USING NETERROR()

Many things can interfere with the transmission of information across a network or the Internet, such as an interrupted connection or a damaged or non-existent file. Director can detect these errors and will return an error message in the form of a number. If all goes well with a network operation, *netError()* returns the word "OK." In this session we will use the *netError()* script to detect errors and return an error message.

1.  **Double-click in frame 3 of the script channel. This is the script that we have entered to read and display the text information that we requested from the Internet.**

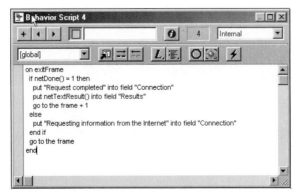

**FIGURE 9.25** *The Script window with the script entered in frame 3 of the script channel.*

```
on exitFrame
  if netDone() = 1 then
    put "Request completed" into field "Connection"
    put netTextResult() into field "Results"
    go to the frame + 1
  else
    put "Requesting information from the Internet" into
    field "Connection"
  end if
  go to the frame
end
```

**2.    Make the following additions to the script in channel 3.**

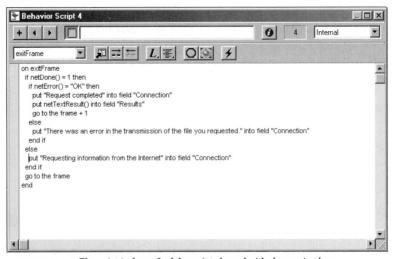

**FIGURE 9.26** *The script in frame 3 of the script channel with changes in place.*

```
on exitFrame
  if netDone() = 1 then
    if netError() = "OK" then
      put "Request completed" into field "Connection"
      put netTextResult() into field "Results"
      go to the frame + 1
    else
      put "There was an error in the transmission of the file
      you requested." into field "Connection"
    end if
  else
    put "Requesting information from the Internet" into field
    "Connection"
  end if
  go to the frame
end
```

Now this script will first check for the completion of the network operation using *netDone()*, then it will check to see if the file that was requested was successfully transferred using *netError()*. If the transfer was successful (if *netError()* = "OK"), the retrieved information will be displayed in the Results field. If the information was not successfully transferred, the "else" statement will be activated and the statement "There was an error in the transmission of the file you requested" will be displayed in the Connection field. We can test the *netError()* command by requesting a file that we know does not exist with the *getNetText()* command.

3. **Close the Script window. Now we will change the file that we request with the *getNetText()* command in frame 1 of the script channel. This will allow us to test the *netError()* command.**

4. **Double-click in frame 1 of the script channel. This will open the script that contains the *getNetText()* command.**

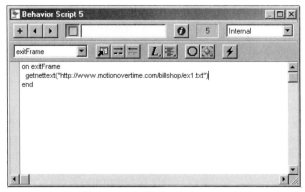

**FIGURE 9.27** *The script in the Script window.*

```
on exitFrame
  getNetText ("http://www.motionovertime.com/billshop/
  ex1.txt")
end
```

5.    **Make the following additions and modifications to the script in frame 1 of the script channel.**

**FIGURE 9.28** *The script in the frame of the script channel with changes in place.*

```
on exitFrame
  put EMPTY into field "Connection"
  put EMPTY into field "Results"
  getNetText ("http://www.motionovertime.com/billshop/DUMMY.txt")
end
```

The script *put EMPTY into field (field Cast member name)* will remove any information that is currently displayed in the identified field. This will clear the way for the new information that is to be displayed in those fields. Changing the file identified at the end of the URL in the *getNetText()* command will cause Director to retrieve a file by that name. The Dummy.txt file does not actually exist, so when *getNetText()* requests it the *netError()* command will be forced to activate. This way we can test *netError()*'s usefulness.

6. **Close the Script window. Now we will play the movie to test the *netError()* script.**

7. **If your Internet connection is not currently active, activate it now. Remember that all network Lingo commands require a live connection to a network to operate properly.**

8. **Play the movie. The Connection field will indicate that it is "Requesting information from the Internet," then it will display "There was an error in the transmission of the file you requested" in the Connection field. This is because the file never existed on the Internet, and *netError()* returned an error number instead of OK. If we request a valid file from the Internet, *netError()* will return "OK" and the information will be read and presented in the field named Results.**

9. **Stop the movie.**

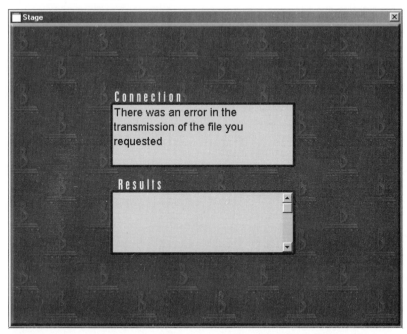

**FIGURE 9.29** *The sample movie with error message displayed in the connection field.*

Now we will program a timer that will abort a request for information from the Internet if it has taken too long.

## USING NETABORT() AND ADDING A TIMER TO THE GETNETTEXT() SAMPLE MOVIE

Activity on the Internet can sometimes cause extended delays in the transfer of information along a network or the Internet, but long delays can also mean that something has gone wrong. It is usually a good idea to include a timer in any scripts that request Internet information that will stop the request if it has taken too long. This will prevent *hang-up*, or long periods of inactivity in a program without explanation. If you are familiar with the information you are requesting, you can usually determine a reasonable period of time for a download to occur. For example, downloading a 10 page text file should take no more than 8 or 9 seconds; if you are waiting longer than that, it is probably a sign that something is wrong. In this session we will add a timer to the script that contains the *getNetText()* command that will abort after 9 seconds, which is more than enough time for the few lines of text that we are actually downloading.

1.   **Double-click frame 1 of the script channel. This is the script that contains the *getNetText()* command (see figure 9.28).**

2.   **Make the following addition to the script in frame 1 of the script channel.**

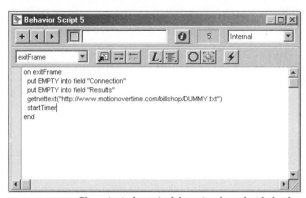

**FIGURE 9.30** *The script in frame 1 of the script channel with the changes in place.*

```
on exitFrame

  put EMPTY into field "Connection"

  put EMPTY into field "Results"

  getNetText ("http://www.motionovertime.com/billshop/
  DUMMY.txt")

  startTimer

end
```

Director automatically keeps track of how long it is in use from the moment the application is launched. It counts the time in units of *ticks*, which are 1/60th of a second. Using the script, startTimer resets the timer to a value of 0 so that you can use it to time other events in a presentation. In this case we will time how long it takes the *getNetText()* command to retrieve information from the Internet.

3. **Close the Script window. Now we will add the scripts that will time the *getNetText()* command.**

4. **Double-click in frame 3 of the script channel.**

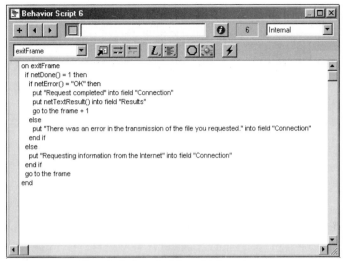

**FIGURE 9.31** *The script in frame 3 of the script channel.*

```
on exitFrame
  if netDone() = 1 then
    if netError() = "OK" then
      put "Request completed" into field "Connection"
      put netTextResult() into field "Results"
      go to the frame + 1
    else
      put "There was an error in the transmission of the file
      you requested." into field "Connection"
    end if
  else
    put "Requesting information from the Internet" into field
    "Connection"
  end if
  go to the frame
end
```

5. **Make the following addition to the script in frame 3 of the script channel.**

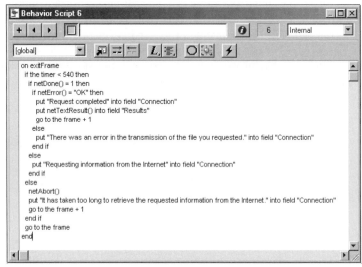

**FIGURE 9.32** *The script in frame 3 of the script channel with the changes in place.*

```
on exitFrame
  if the timer < 540 then
    if netDone() = 1 then
      if netError() = "OK" then
        put "Request completed" into field "Connection"
        put netTextResult() into field "Results"
        go to the frame + 1
      else
        put "There was an error in the transmission of the file
        you requested." into field "Connection"
      end if
    else
      put "Requesting information from the Internet" into field
      "Connection"
    end if
  else
    netAbort()
    put "It has taken too long to retrieve the requested
    information from the Internet" into field "Connection"
    go to the frame + 1
  end if
  go to the frame
end
```

After issuing the command *startTimer* in frame 1 of the script channel, we reset Director's internal clock to 0. It then immediately starts counting up in ticks. By using the command *if the timer < 540,* we are saying that as long as the timer has not counted off 540 ticks (540 / 60 ticks = 9 seconds) we can continue to check to see if the network request is completed with the next line, which contains *netDone()*. If *netDone()* does not complete its job in 540 ticks, then the if...then statement will be passed on to the else statement, which will cancel the last network request with *netAbort()* to stop the *getNetText()* command from continuing its request. The next line will put the message "It has taken too long to retrieve the requested information from the Internet" into the field named "Connection." And finally, the script `go to the frame + 1` will send the playback head into the next frame so that the if...then statement that contains the network Lingo scripts will not be executed needlessly.

This is how we will enter this script in the final version of this lesson, but in order to test the script, we will need to create a situation in which the *getNetText()* command takes more than 9 seconds to retrieve information from the Internet. Now, remember that there are many factors that can contribute to delays in the transfer of information across a network. Because it is virtually impossible to predict when these delays will occur, we will simply reduce the period of time allowed for *getNetText()* to complete its request to a duration that we know is too short.

6. **Make the following adjustment to the script in frame 3 of the script channel.**

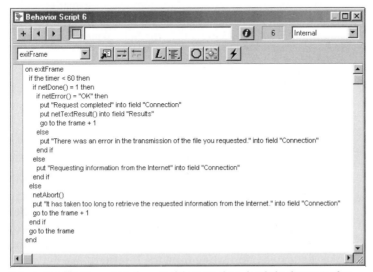

**FIGURE 9.33** *The script in frame 3 of the script channel with the changes in place.*

```
on exitFrame
  if the timer < 60 then
    if netDone() = 1 then
      if netError() = "OK" then
        put "Request completed" into field "Connection"
        put netTextResult() into field "Results"
        go to the frame + 1
      else
        put "There was an error in the transmission of the file
        you requested." into field "Connection"
      end if
    else
      put "Requesting information from the Internet" into field
      "Connection"
    end if
  else
    netAbort()
    put "It has taken too long to retrieve the requested
    information from the Internet." into field "Connection"
    go to the frame + 1
  end if
  go to the frame
end
```

By reducing the duration of the timer to 60 ticks (1 second), we are not providing the *getNetText()* command enough time to complete the request. As a result, the *else* statement will be executed and will display the statement "It has taken too long to retrieve the requested information from the Internet" in the field named "Connection."

Let's test the new script.

**7.   Close the Script window.**

**NOTE**    Remember that your Internet connection must be active for the *getNetText()* command to work.

**8.    Play the movie.** The *getNetText()* command is executed and we are briefly presented with the statement "Requesting Information from the Internet" in the "Connection" field. This is quickly replaced with the statement "It has taken too long to retrieve the requested information from the Internet." We did not change the file that we requested from the Dummy.txt file, but this will not make a difference because 1 second is an unrealistic duration for most Internet requests.

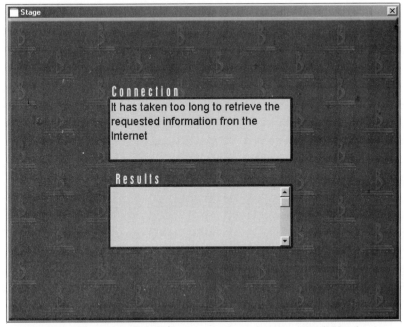

**FIGURE 9.34** *The movie with the "It has taken too long..." error message displayed.*

**NOTE**

If you find that 1 second is too long for this test on your machine, reduce the number in the second line of the script in frame 3 of the script channel:

*if the timer < (lower number) then.*

This will only happen if you are using a particularly fast Internet connection or if you have already successfully downloaded a file that is in your computer's memory. In the case of your having already downloaded a file, Director will use the file that is already in the computer instead of reaching back out to the Internet. This greatly reduces the amount of time needed to retrieve the requested data. There will be more on this in chapter 10.

9.  Stop the movie. Now that we have tested each part of the script so far, we will modify the scripts to request the actual information that will be requested in The Billionaire's Shop.

10. Double-click frame 1 of the script channel. This will open the script located in frame 1 of the script channel.

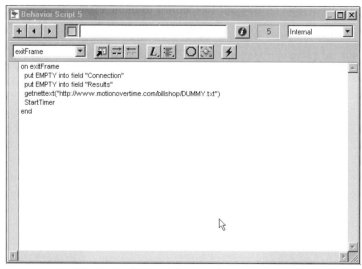

**FIGURE 9.35** *The script in frame 1 of the script channel.*

```
on exitFrame
  put EMPTY into field "Connection"
  put EMPTY into field "Results"
  getNetText("http://www.motionovertime.com/billshop/
  DUMMY.txt")
  StartTimer
end
```

### 11. Make the following modification to the script in frame 1 of the script channel.

```
on exitFrame
  put EMPTY into field "Connection"
  put EMPTY into field "Results"
  getNetText ("http://www.motionovertime.com/billshop/
  Billshop.txt")
  StartTimer
end
```

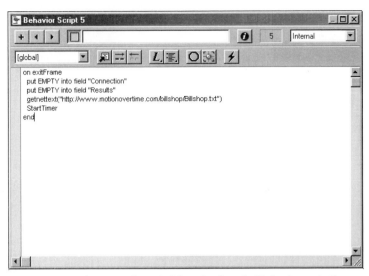

**FIGURE 9.36** *The script in frame 1 of the script channel with the changes in place.*

The Billshop file contains the information that The Billionaire's Shop will use to update itself. We will add scripts in chapter 10 that will compare the contents of this file with the current contents in The Billionaire's Shop and then download any new files that are indicated.

12. **Close the Script window. Our next step is to change the timer setting in the script in frame 3 back to 9 seconds.**

13. **Double-click frame 3 of the script channel.**

This will open the script that contains the timer. Currently the timer setting is 60 ticks, or 1 second. We will adjust the timer so that it will wait 9 seconds.

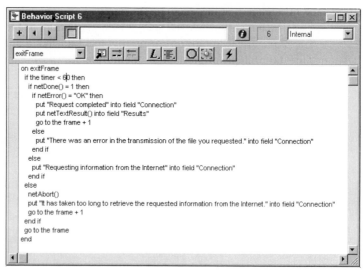

**FIGURE 9.37** *The script in frame 3 of the script channel.*

```
on exitFrame
  if the timer < 60 then
    if netDone() = 1 then
      if netError() = "OK" then
        put "Request completed" into field "Connection"
        put netTextResult() into field "Results"
        go to the frame + 1
      else
        put "There was an error in the transmission of the file
        you requested." into field "Connection"
      end if
    else
      put "Requesting information from the Internet" into field
      "Connection"
    end if
  else
    netAbort()
    put "It has taken too long to retrieve the requested
    information from the Internet." into field "Connection"
    go to the frame + 1
  end if
  go to the frame
end
```

14. **Make the following adjustment to the timer setting in the script for frame 3 of the script channel. We will change the timer setting to 540 seconds so that *getNetText()* will have up to 9 seconds to retrieve the requested text file.**

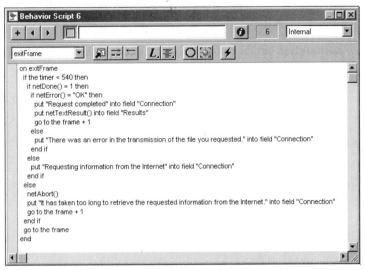

**FIGURE 9.38** *The script in frame 3 of the script channel with the changes in place.*

```
on exitFrame
  if the timer < 540 then
    if netDone() = 1 then
      if netError() = "OK" then
        put "Request completed" into field "Connection"
        put netTextResult() into field "Results"
        go to the frame + 1
      else
        put "There was an error in the transmission of the file
        you requested." into field "Connection"
      end if
    else
      put "Requesting information from the Internet" into field
      "Connection"
    end if
  else
    netAbort()
    put "It has taken too long to retrieve the requested
    information from the Internet." into field "Connection"
    go to the frame + 1
  end if
  go to the frame
end
```

15. **Close the Script window. Now we can test this file and retrieve the file that will actually be retrieved by The Billionaire's Shop.**

16. **Play the movie. The information in the Connection window occurs as it had in the earlier parts of this lesson. When the text file Billshop.txt is successfully downloaded, it is presented in the Results window.**

    The first line of this file is a number, which determines which version of The Billionaire's Shop is currently posted on the MotionOver-Time.com Web site. We will use this number in a script in chapter 11 that will determine if The Billionaire's Shop needs to be updated.

    The next line of text from the Billshop.txt file is the name of the file that should be downloaded to update The Billionaire's Shop. The first line will always be the same name as the products Cast file name on the hard drive: *Products.cst*. This is because the products Cast file determines which products are available in the Shop. Other updates to the shop might include more than one file to download, which will expand The Billionaire's Shop even further!

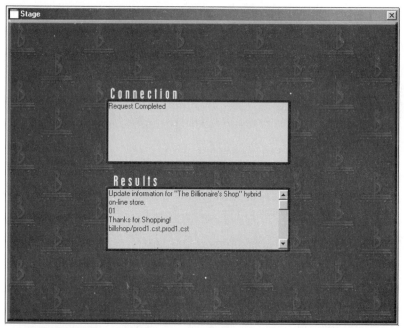

**FIGURE 9.39** *Screen grab of the Stage with the information from Billshop.txt displayed in the Results field.*

17. **Stop the movie.**

Now we will add a StopMovie handler, which we will use to reset the Results and Connection display areas.

## RESETTING THE DISPLAY AREAS

When we stop the movie from playing, we can see that the text from the previous playback is still visible. We will add a script to this movie that will empty those fields so that they are free to display new data; then we can use them to test different scripts.

1.   **Open the Script window. We can do this by opening the script for an existing behavior, or we can choose Window>Script.**

2.   **Click the + sign button at the upper left corner of the Script window. This will bring us to the next available Cast member, so that we can add our StopMovie handler to its own Cast position.**

**FIGURE 9.40** *Open the Script window and click the + sign button in the upper left corner.*

3.   **Type the following script in the Script window: The command *EMPTY* will remove any text that is displayed in the Connection and Results text fields. This script will empty both fields each time the movie is stopped.**

```
on stopMovie
   put EMPTY into field "Connection"
   put EMPTY into field "Results"
end
```

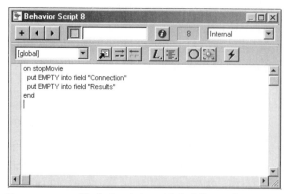

FIGURE 9.41 *The Script window with the following StopMovie handler typed into it.*

## ADDING THE GETNETTEXT() COMMAND TO THE BILLIONAIRE'S SHOP

### VIEWING THE COMPLETED FILE

1.    Confirm that your connection to the Internet is still active.

2.    Choose File>Open.

3.    Locate and select the file named Chp9cmp.dir on the Billshop CD in the directory ...Lessons/Chaptr9/Complete/Chp9cmp.dir.

4.    Click Open.

5.    Choose Window>Message. The contents of the text file that will be retrieved by *getNetText()* in this movie will be displayed in the Message window. In chapter 11 we will use the retrieved text to update The Billionaire's Shop.

6.    Close all other windows.

7.    Play the movie. The first screen that dissolves in is an image that asks, "Are you currently connected to the Internet?" It shows two button options: Yes and No. Beneath the two buttons is the statement "Click No if you do not want to update The Billionaire's Shop." You will have the option to update it later if you have an active Internet connection.

8.    Click Yes. The presentation continues as it had in the earlier lessons. When we reach the end of the animation, the contents of the retrieved text file are presented in the Message window. In this session we will add this screen and the script that will

retrieve the update information for The Billionaire's Shop from the Internet.

9.  Stop the movie.

Now we will add the new elements.

## PREPARING THE FILES FOR THIS LESSON

You can continue with the file that you created in chapter 8. All of the new images for this presentation are already included in the Buttons Cast. If you would like to start with the partly completed version of this file that came with the CD-ROM, you can copy it to your hard drive from the ...Lessons/Chaptr9/starter/ directory. Copy all of the files in this directory except the folder named Complete. Remember to save your work frequently.

## REMINDING THE USER TO CONNECT TO THE INTERNET

The first thing we saw in the new file was a screen asking if we are connected to the Internet. This is important because Director cannot detect an active Internet connection unless it attempts to download something from the Internet. If the file is successfully downloaded, then Director knows that there is an active Internet connection. Unfortunately, attempting to download information from the Internet without an active connection can yield unpredictable results, depending upon the Internet software that you are using. Results can be anything from a system freeze to nothing at all. Therefore, it is a good idea to remind your users that they must establish their Internet connection before they run your Hybrid Internet application.

In this session we will add the reminder screen.

> **Attempting to use network Lingo scripts when there is no active connection to a network or the Internet might cause your computer to crash.**    **WARNING**

1.  Choose File>Open.

2.  Locate and open the file named Chp9inc.dir or open the file that you have created working from chapters 2 through 8. Refer to the section titled "Preparing the Files for this Lesson" earlier in this chapter for more information about where to find the appropriate files for this lesson.

3.  Open the Score.

4.   Drag to select all of the sprites in the Score from frames 1 to 114, channels 2 to 6. Make certain not to select the background sprite in channel 1. We are going to drag this part of the intro animation three frames to the right to make room for the new opening screen.

**NOTE**   You can use the Zoom menu to increase the number of frames that are visible in the Score. This will make it easier to select all of the sprites from frames 1 to 114 without needing to scroll.

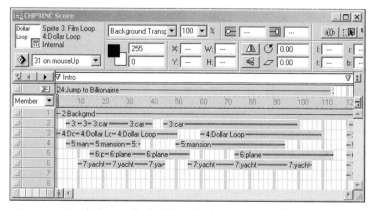

**FIGURE 9.42** *The Score with all of the sprites in channels 2 to 6 from frames 1 to 114 selected. The sprite in channel 1 is not selected.*

5.   Drag the selected sprites four frames to the right. This will place the entry point of the first sprite that appears in the intro animation at frame 5 and the endpoint of the last sprite to leave the animation in frame 118. Now we will drag the other elements of the intro animation to their new locations.

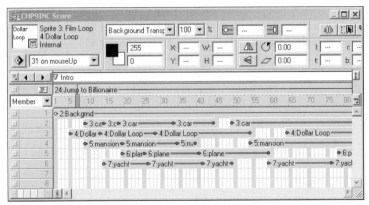

**FIGURE 9.43** *The Score with all of the sprites in channels 2 to 6 from frame 1 to 114 selected and being dragged four frames to the right.*

6.    Select and drag the entry point of the sound in sound channel 1 five frames to the right. This sound extends to the end of the intro animation, so it is not necessary to drag the entire sprite object. We will be adding a transition to the first frame of the intro area of the Score. Placing the entry point of the sound one frame further will ensure that the transition will complete before the sound begins. Now that we have made this modification, we need to change the Loop Back behavior to return to the frame immediately after the intro frame; otherwise the sound will restart with each loop back in the intro area of the Score.

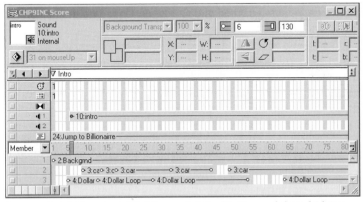

**FIGURE 9.44** *The entry point of the sound sprite object in sound channel 1 being dragged to frame 6.*

7.    Double-click in frame 114 of the script channel of the Score. This will open the Script window for the Loop Back behavior.

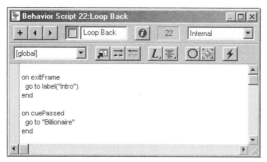

**FIGURE 9.45** *The Script window for the Loop Back behavior.*

8.  **Make the following modifications to the script for the Loop Back behavior.**

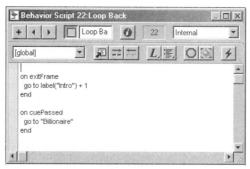

**FIGURE 9.46** *The Loop Back behavior with changes in place.*

```
on exitFrame
   go to label("Intro") + 1
end
```

9.  **Drag the script located in frame 114 of the script channel to frame 118 of the script channel. This is the script that we programmed in the section titled "Adding the Cue Point Behavior" to the script in the last frame of the Icons of Wealth animation in chapter 4. This script causes the playback head to loop back to the marker labeled intro until the cue point in the sound is reached.**

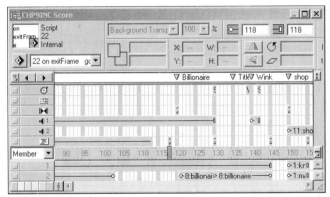

**FIGURE 9.47** *The script in frame 114 of the script channel being dragged to frame 118 of the script channel.*

10. **Drag the script object located in frame 1 to 113 of the script channel four frames to the right, so that it appears in frames 5 to 117. This will place this script in the same frames as the sprites that we moved in the earlier steps.**

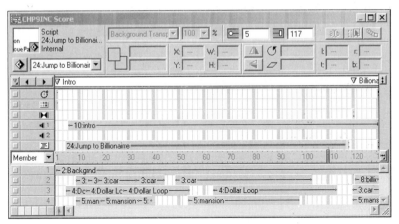

**FIGURE 9.48** *The script object in frames 1 to 113 dragged four frames to the right so that it appears in frames 5 to 117.*

11. **Drag the marker labeled Intro from frame 1 to frame 5. It's important to move the marker with the animation because the script in frame 118 refers to this label.**

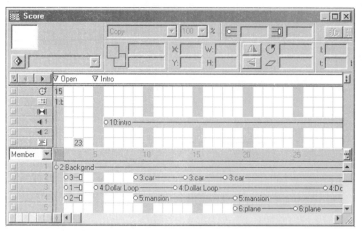

**FIGURE 9.49** *The Intro marker being dragged to frame 5.*

12. Place a marker into frame 1 and name it Open. This will identify where the new screen is located.

13. Open the Buttons Cast. This Cast window contains the images that we need for the new screen.

14. Make sure the playback head is in frame 2 of the Score. We will want all of the new screen elements to appear in the second frame of the presentation. This way we can use a transition to dissolve the new elements onto the Stage.

15. Drag Cast member 3 (Conn Screen) to frame 2 of channel 2.

16. Drag Cast member 19 (Yess1 button) to frame 2 of channel 3.

17. Drag Cast member 22 (Nooo1 button) to frame 2 of channel 4.

18. Make certain that the endpoints of the sprite objects in channels 2 through 4 are in frame 3.

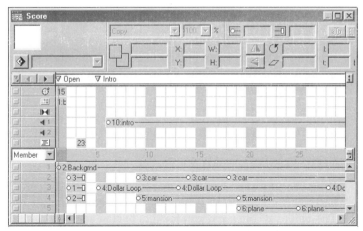

**FIGURE 9.50** *The new sprite objects in channels 2 through 4 of the Score with their endpoints in frame 3.*

19. Position the three new sprites on the Stage as they appear in figure 9.51. The positioning of the sprites can be approximate. It will not affect how they will work in the finished program.

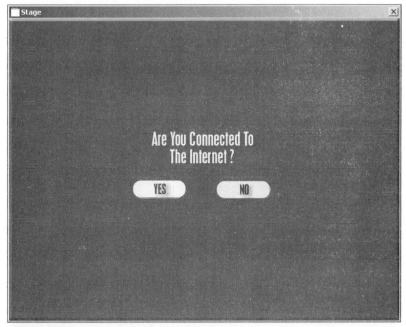

**FIGURE 9.51** *The Internet Connection Alert screen.*

## PROGRAMMING THE NEW SCREEN

1.  Open the Internal Cast. We are going to add the Loop in Frame behavior to frame 3 and place the Button behavior that we used in the section titled "Using a Drag and Drop Behavior" in chapter 6 on the Yes and No buttons.

2.  Drag Cast member 23 (the Loop in Frame behavior) to frame 3 of the script channel. This will apply the behavior to frame 3.

3.  Open the Scripts Cast window.

4.  Drag Cast member 1 of the Scripts Cast directly over the Yes button. The Yes button is located in channel 3, frames 2 and 3. The names of the members for this button conform to the naming convention for the button behavior: four characters (Yess) followed by a 1, 2, or 3.

5.  Drag Cast member 1 of the Scripts Cast directly over the No button. The No button is located in channel 4, frames 2 and 3. Like the Yes button, the No button has a four-character name (Nooo) followed by a 1, 2, or 3. Now that both buttons are programmed with the button behavior, we can add the scripts that will activate the *getNetText()* command.

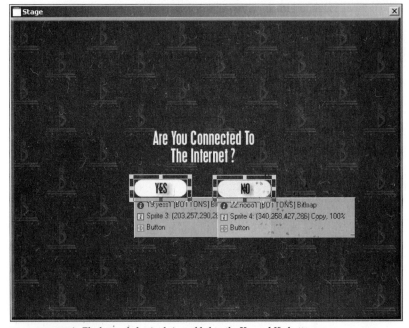

**FIGURE 9.52** *The button behavior being added to the Yes and No buttons.*

6. Select the Yes button on the Stage. The sprite overlay for the Yes button will appear.

7. Click the Behavior Inspector button on the sprite overlay for the Yes button. The behavior inspector will open. Now we can add the script that will use *getNetText()*.

8. Choose Behaviors>New Behavior.... This will open the Name Behavior dialog box.

9. Name the new behavior Request Text.

10. Click the button labeled OK. This will close the Name Behavior dialog box.

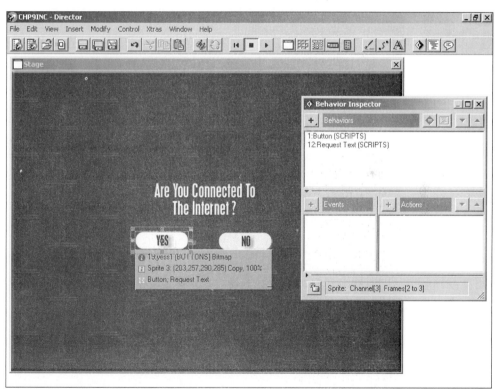

**FIGURE 9.53** *The Yes button selected on the Stage. The behavior inspector is open, with the button behavior and a behavior named Request Text listed.*

11.  **Click the Script Window button at the top of the behavior inspector.**

This will open the Script window, where you will see the on mouseUp me handler.

## PROGRAMMING THE NEW BUTTONS AND USING THE CLEARCACHE AND NETABORT() COMMANDS

Any information that is retrieved from the Internet is temporarily stored in an area of memory called the *cache*. This allows Director to quickly access information requested from the Internet if it is later requested again within the same movie. This way Director doesn't need to download some-thing that is repeatedly requested each time it is needed. When an item is requested from the Internet by a script, Director will first look in the cache for it; if it isn't there, Director will reach out to the requested file at the network or Internet location.

The *clearCache* command empties anything that is currently stored in the cache, which means that any new requests for information from the Internet or other network will be forced to be downloaded. This is a way of ensuring that the movie is only using the most recent, updated copy of the requested file. Because the text file that we are using in The Billionaire's Shop contains information about updates to the shop, we want to be cer-tain that we are always using the most recent version of the file. To make sure of this, we will use the *clearCache* command just before we request the inventory text file for The Billionaire's Shop. The *netAbort()* command will stop any current network operations to ensure that we don't cause too many things to occur simultaneously, which might slow down the speed of data transfer and potentially cause the application to crash.

1.  **Add the following script to the mouseUp handler in the Script window for the request text behavior.**

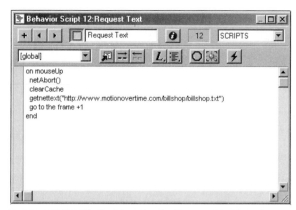

**FIGURE 9.54** *The Script window for the request text behavior.*

```
on mouseUp
    netAbort()
    clearCache
    getNetText ("http://www.motionovertime.com/billshop/billshop.txt")
    go to the frame + 1
end
```

2.  Close the Script window. Next we'll program the No button.

3.  Select the No button on the Stage. The sprite overlay for that button will appear, and the behavior inspector will switch to display the script (the Button behavior) that is currently applied to the No button.

4.  Choose Behaviors>New Behavior... from the behavior inspector. The No button will simply send the playback head to the next frame without requesting information from the Internet. It will also not make any changes to The Billionaire's Shop.

5.  Name the new behavior No Connection.

6.  Click the button labeled OK.

7.  Click the Script Window button on the behavior inspector.

8.  Add the following script to the Script window for the no connection behavior.

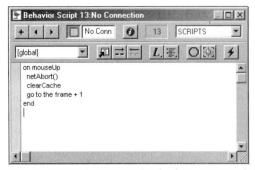

**FIGURE 9.55** *The Script window for the no connection behavior.*

```
on mouseUp
   netAbort()
   clearCache
   go to the frame + 1
end
```

The No button will simply send the playback head to the next frame. Because it does not use the *getNetText()* command, it does not risk any conflict with a missing Internet connection. This will also allow a user to choose not to update The Billionaire's Shop even with a live Internet connection. Later we will program the Update button on the main interface screen to bring any new information into The Billionaire's Shop while the user is in the shop.

9.   **Close the Script window. Our next step is to add a transition to frames 2 and 4 to dissolve the elements of the new screen onto the Stage when The Billionaire's Shop is launched, and off the Stage when the user has clicked the Yes or No button.**

10.  **Close the behavior inspector.**

## ADDING A TRANSITION TO THE NEW SCREEN

1.   **Open the Internal Cast. Remember that when a transition is created it will create a Cast member. By bringing up the Internal Cast, we are making certain that the new transition Cast member will appear in this Cast window.**

2.   **Double-click frame 2 of the transition channel in the Score. This will open the Frame Properties:Transition dialog box.**

3.   **Choose any transition type. We recommend Center Out, Square. The transition that you choose is not important. Use this as an**

opportunity to experiment. The Center Out, Square transition is the second option under the Wipe category.

4. Set the duration of the transition to .50. This represents half a second. This will keep the time it takes for the new transition to execute down to half of a second.

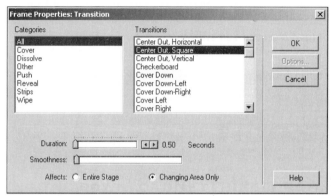

**FIGURE 9.56** *The open Transition dialog box.*

5. Click the button labeled OK. This will close the Frame Properties:Transition dialog box.

6. Select the new transition in frame 2 of the transition channel. We are going to use the same transition in frame 5 of the transition channel.

7. Copy the transition in frame 2 of the transition channel.

8. Paste the transition into frame 5 of the transition channel.

Now this transition will appear when we enter the intro animation part of the Score.

## ADDING THE NETTEXTRESULT() SCRIPT TO THE BILLIONAIRE'S SHOP

When the *getNetText()* command is issued, it will start a background download of the requested information, which means that the information will download without interfering with other Director operations. This means that the opening animation for The Billionaire's Shop will play while the requested text information downloads invisibly in the background. This will give sufficient time for the download to occur. We will place the *net-*

*TextResult()* script in a frame script at the end of the animation to check for the contents of the requested text file.

1.  **Double-click in frame 145 of the script channel. This is the script for the Brief Pause behavior, which branches the playback head to the Shop area of the Score when the introductory animations are completed. We will not need this behavior elsewhere in the movie, so we will change it to perform the additional task of tracking the completion of the text requested by the *getNetText()* command on the Yes button.**

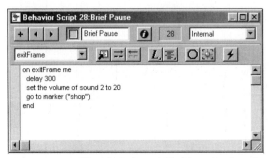

**FIGURE 9.57** *The script in frame 145 of the script channel.*

```
on exitFrame me
  delay 300
  set the volume of sound 2 to 20
  go to marker ("shop")
end
```

2.  **Make the following modification to the script in frame 145 of the script channel.**

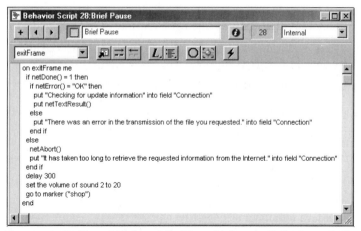

**FIGURE 9.58** *The script in frame 145 of the script channel with the changes in place.*

```
on exitFrame
  if netDone() = 1 then
    if netError() = "OK" then
      put "Checking for update information" into field
      "Connection"
      put netTextResult()
    else
      put "There was an error in the transmission of the file
      you requested." into field "Connection"
    end if
  else
    netAbort()
    put "It has taken too long to retrieve the requested
    information from the Internet" into field "Connection"
  end if
  delay 300
  set the volume of sound 2 to 20
  go to marker ("shop")
end
```

3.   **Do not close the Script window. We will be adding more to this script in the next few steps.**

The first thing you might notice in our new additions is that we did not use a timer for this script. This is because the *getNetText()* command should be completed while the introductory animation is running. If the requested text has not been successfully loaded in the time it takes the playback head to play through frames 3 to 140, then something has probably gone wrong and the *getNetText()* command should be aborted. Later in this chapter we will program the

Update button to use the *getNetText()* command. This will give the user the opportunity to attempt an update later.

Let's go through the script section by section. Part of the following is in bold to identify the item being discussed.

```
on exitFrame
  if netDone() = 1 then
    if netError() = "OK" then
      put "Checking for update information" into field
      "Connection"
      put netTextResult()
    else
      put "There was an error in the transmission of the file
      you requested." into field "Connection"
    end if
  else
    netAbort()
    put "It has taken too long to retrieve the requested
    information from the Internet" into field "Connection"
  end if
  delay 300
  set the volume of sound 2 to 20
  go to marker ("shop")
end
```

The first line of the script, *if netDone() = 1*, will determine if the *get-NetText()* command has successfully completed. If everything has gone well, then the script will be passed on to the next part of the script *netError()*. If the *getNetText()* request has not completed, then it will be aborted and "It has taken too long to retrieve the requested information from the Internet" will be displayed in a field that we will add to The Billionaire's Shop later in this lesson.

```
on exitFrame
  if netDone() = 1 then
    if netError() = "OK" then
      put "Checking for update information" into field
      "Connection"
      put netTextResult()
    else
      put "There was an error in the transmission of the file
      you requested." into field "Connection"
    end if
  else
    netAbort()
```

```
        put "It has taken too long to retrieve the requested
        information from the Internet" into field "Connection"
    end if
    delay 300
    set the volume of sound 2 to 20
    go to marker "shop"
end
```

After the *netDone()* command has completed its request, we can use *netError()* to determine if the requested file is intact. If there is anything wrong with the file, or if the file was not actually downloaded, then the statement "There was an error in the transmission of the file you requested" will be displayed in the field that we will create later in this lesson and name Connection. If *netError()* returns *OK*, then the requested text file was successfully downloaded and the next line will display "Checking for update information" in the Connection field, then the next line, put *netTextResult()* will be executed. Because we have not determined a destination for *netTextResult()* to place the requested text file, it will be displayed in the Message window automatically. In chapter 10 we will use the requested text file to determine if The Billionaire's Shop is ready to be updated.

The last lines of the script are the original Brief Pause behavior scripts, which will delay the playback head 5 seconds, set the volume of the background sound to 20, then send the playback head to the Shop area of the Score.

> The *netDone()* command only checks for activity between Director and a network or the Internet. A value of 1 does not mean that a request was successful, only that there is currently no network activity.     **NOTE**

## ENHANCING THE NETTEXTRESULT() AND NETERROR() COMMAND

The description of the script in frame 145 of the script channel will operate properly if the Yes button is clicked because the Yes button contains the *getNetText()* request. However, the No button does not contain a *getNetText()* request, so the script in frame 145 will not behave in exactly the same manner.

The first line, *if netDone() = 1*, will operate the same way, but remember, *netDone()* will return a value of 1 just because there is no network activity in Director. We will need to rely on *netError()* and *netTextResult()* to let us know that no request for information has been made.

The *netTextResult()* command will return the results of a successful network request, and the *netError()* command will return a value of OK if a network operation has been started and completed successfully. The *net-TextResult()* command will return an empty line of text (also called an empty string) if no data was returned by a network request. The *netError()* command will return an error number if a network operation is unsuccessful. However, if there was never a network request, as with the No button, then *netTextResult()* and *netError()* will both return an empty string (see table 9.01). This looks like open and closed quotes with nothing between them (""). We will need to include this possibility in the script in frame 145 to accommodate the No button; otherwise Director will always display that something has gone wrong.

**TABLE 9.01** *Table of results from three primary network request status commands.*

| Command | Successful Result | Unsuccessful |
|---|---|---|
| NetTextResult() | Returns requested text or media | Returns an empty string ("") |
| Requested using a command such as *getNetText()*. | | |
| NetError() | OK | Returns an error number |
| NetDone() | 1 (Binary Yes) | 0 (Binary No) |

**NOTE** These are the results you can expect from network status commands. Please note that some of the error messages returned by *NetError()* are documented in the Help and Lingo Dictionary within Director. Others can be found at Macromedia's Web site in their tech notes for Director, **(www.macromedia.com)**.

1.  **Make the following modification to the script in frame 145 of the script channel.**

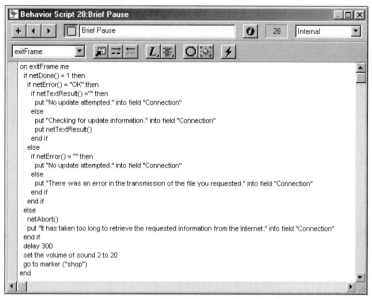

**FIGURE 9.59** *The script in frame 145 of the script channel, with the changes in place.*

```
on exitFrame
  if netDone() = 1 then
    if netError() = "OK" then
      if netTextResult() = "" then
        put "No update attempted." into field "Connection"
      else
        put "Checking for update information" into field
        "Connection"
        put netTextResult()
      end if
    else
      if netError() = "" then
        put "No update attempted" into field "Connection"
      else
        put "There was an error in the transmission of the file
        you requested." into field "Connection"
      end if
    end if
  else
    netAbort()
    put "It has taken too long to retrieve the requested
    information from the Internet" into field "Connection"
  end if
  delay 300
  set the volume of sound 2 to 20
  go to marker ("shop")
end
```

Now, if *netTextResult()* contains no text (something has gone wrong or no request was attempted), this script will catch the problem and display a status on the screen. This script will also not attempt to read information if none is present because this can potentially cause errors in The Billionaire's Shop. In addition to this, if *netError()* does not equal OK (which also means that something has gone wrong, or no request has been made), the second new group of scripts will first check what exactly *netError()* has returned. If it returns an empty string (""), this will mean that no network request was made and "No update was attempted" will be displayed in the Connection field. Any other value will be an error number; this means that a network request was made and something went wrong.

2.   **Close the Script window.**

We're just a few more steps from testing our new scripts!

## ADDING THE CONNECTION FIELD TO THE BILLIONAIRE'S SHOP

As the script that contains *netTextResult()* executes, it will send information to a field named Connection. In this session we will add this field to The Billionaire's Shop.

1.   **Open the Internal Cast window. When we create the Connection field, we will automatically add a new Cast member to the movie. Opening the Internal Cast helps ensure that the new Cast member is displayed in the Connection field.**

2.   **Make certain that the playback head is in frame 150 of the Score. This is the Shop area of the Score.**

3.   **Choose Window>Tool Palette. We will use the field member tool to create the Connection field.**

4.   **Click the button labeled Field in the Tool palette. While this button is selected, the mouse will become a crosshair when it is moved over the Stage.**

5.   **Click and drag the crosshair from the upper left corner to the upper right corner of the display area labeled Connection. We will use this field to display the download status of the text that we will retrieve using *getNetText()*.**

**FIGURE 9.60** *The Tool palette.*

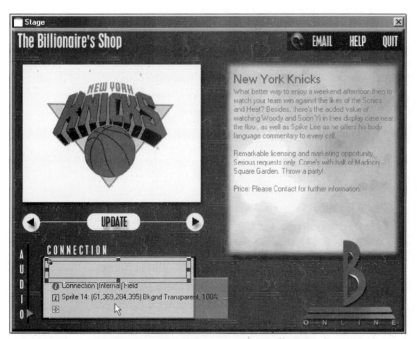

**FIGURE 9.61** *A field Cast member in the process of being created in the Connection area on the Stage.*

6.   Click directly on the new Connection field on the Stage. We are going to make the settings that will allow us to adjust the size of the new Connection field. The field might be in Text Entry mode, which will not permit access to the sprite overlay. In this case, deselect, then reselect the sprite, and the sprite overlay will appear.

7.   Click the blue *i* button on the sprite overlay for the selected field. This will open the Field Cast Member Properties dialog box.

8.   Name the field Connection. The Cast member name field currently reads (no name). You can replace this text with the name Connection.

9.   Choose Fixed from the Framing pop-up menu in the Field Cast Member Properties dialog box. This option will allow us to resize the Connection field.

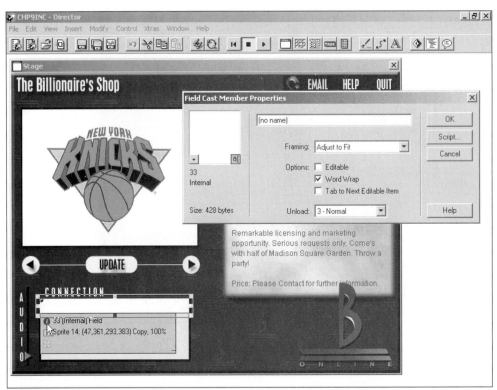

**FIGURE 9.62** *The selected Connection field on the Stage, with the open Field Cast Member Properties dialog box.*

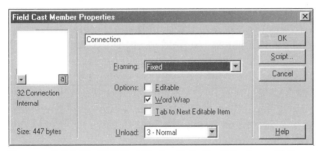

**FIGURE 9.63** *The Field Cast Member Properties dialog box, with Connection in the name field and Fixed selected from the Framing pop-up menu.*

10. **Click the button labeled OK. This will close the Field Cast Member Properties dialog box.**

11. **Resize the Connection field so that it covers the area beneath the word Connection on the background image. This will ensure that the text that can be displayed in this field appears in the appropriate location on the Stage.**

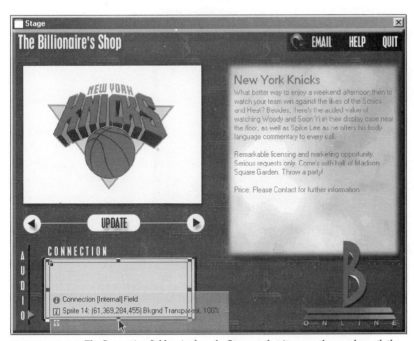

**FIGURE 9.64** *The Connection field resized on the Stage so that it covers the area beneath the word Connection on the background image.*

12. Double-click in the Connection field and type Waiting. You will be able to enter text into the field if you double-click on it on the Stage. This will cause the field to enter text entry mode. From previous sessions the text color might be set to white so you might not see the word that you are typing because it is against a white background. Now we will change the color of the text and set the ink effect of the field to background transparent, which will permit us to see the text that we have typed against the green background.

13. Highlight the word Waiting in the Connection text field.

14. Choose black from the foreground color chip on the Tool palette. The text will appear to vanish against the white background of the text field. It will become visible again when we change the ink effect of the text field.

**FIGURE 9.65** *The text in the Connection field highlighted. Black is selected from the foreground color chip on the Tool palette.*

15.   If it is not already open, open the Score.

16.   Drag the endpoint for the Connection field (sprite 14) back to frame 155. The endpoint for the sprite object that was created for the Connection field extends well beyond where we want it to appear in the Score. We are going to drag it back so that it is only in the Shop area of the Score.

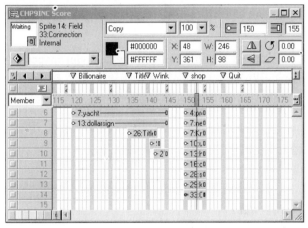

**FIGURE 9.66** *The open Score, with the endpoint for sprite 14 in the process of being dragged back to frame 155.*

17.   Select the entire Connection field sprite object, then choose background transparent from the Ink pop-up menu. Now that we have added the new Connection field, we can add a line to the request text behavior on the Yes button in the first screen of the score.

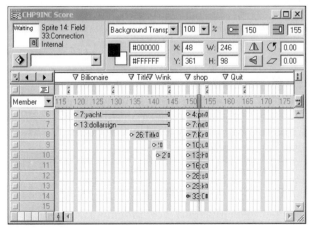

**FIGURE 9.67** *The Connection field sprite selected in channel 14 of the Score. Background transparent is selected from the Ink pop-up menu at the top of the Score.*

18. Move the playback head to frame 3 of the Score. This is where the first screen of the movie is located.

19. Click on the Yes button on the Stage. The sprite overlay for the Yes button will appear over the Yes button.

20. Click the green Behavior Inspector button in the sprite overlay for the Yes button. This will open the behavior inspector, which will display the behaviors that are currently applied to the Yes button.

21. Select the request text behavior in the behavior inspector and click the Script Window button at the top of the Behavior Inspector window. This will open the Script window for the Request Text behavior.

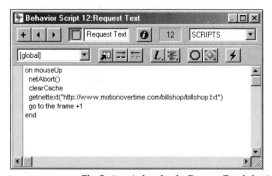

**FIGURE 9.68** *The Script window for the Request Text behavior.*

```
on mouseUp
  netAbort()
  clearCache
  getNetText("http://www.motionovertime.com/billshop/billshop.txt")
  go to the frame + 1
end
```

22. Add the following script to the Request Text behavior: This new line will display the word Waiting in the Connection text field just before the text data is requested by the *getNetText()* command. This will immediately display a status for the user when the movie begins playing.

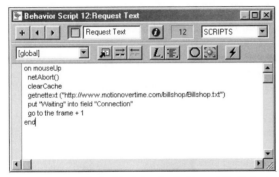

**FIGURE 9.69** *The Script window for the Request Text behavior with changes in place.*

```
on mouseUp
  netAbort()
  clearCache
  getNetText (http://www.motionovertime.com//billshop/billshop.txt)
  put "Waiting" into field "Connection"
  go to the frame + 1
end
```

## TESTING THE NETWORK LINGO THAT HAS BEEN ADDED TO THE BILLIONAIRE'S SHOP

We have added all of the scripts that will automatically request the text Billshop.txt file from the Internet. Let's test to make certain the new scripts work.

1.  **If you are not already connected to the Internet, establish your connection.**

2.  **If it is not already open, open the Message window. Currently the script that contains the** *netTextResult()* **command sends the contents of the requested text file to the Message window. In chapter 11 we will use the results of** *netTextResult()* **to update The Billionaire's Shop.**

3.  **Close all open windows except the Message window. This will allow us to view all activity on the Stage except the area covered by the Message window.**

4.  **Rewind and play the movie. The movie plays, and we are presented with the first screen.**

5.  **Click the Yes button. This will activate the** *getNetText()* **command. The opening animation will play while the requested text**

is downloading. When the playback head reaches the last frame of the animation, the *netTextResult()* command will execute and the playback head will go to the Shop area of the Score. If all goes well, the statement "Checking for update information" will be displayed in the Connection field and the contents of the Billshop.txt file will be displayed in the Message window.

NOTE    If you do not see the results described in step 5 above, check your Internet connection, then rewind and play Director.

6.    Stop the movie.

**FIGURE 9.70** *Shop area of the Score, with "Checking for update information" in the Connection field and the contents of the billshop.txt file displayed in the Message window.*

## PROGRAMMING THE UPDATE BUTTON

So far we have added scripts that will automatically request the text file that will determine if The Billionaire's Shop is ready for an update. Now we will add the scripts that will allow the user to choose to update The Billionaire's Shop by clicking the Update button while they are in the Shop.

1.  **Open the Scripts Cast window. This way all of our new scripts will be included in the same Cast window as the scripts that we used in earlier lessons.**

2.  **Open the Score and move the playback head to the Shop area. This is where the Update button is located.**

3.  **Click the Update button on the Stage. The sprite overlay for the Update button will appear.**

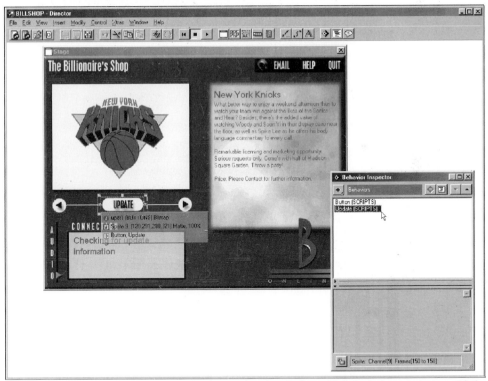

**FIGURE 9.71** *The Shop area, with the Update button selected on the Stage. The behavior inspector is open, with the Update behavior selected.*

4. **Click the Behavior Inspector button on the sprite overlay for the Update button. This will display the scripts that are currently applied to the Update button. At this point the only behavior on the Update button is the Button behavior.**

5. **Create a new behavior for the Update button and name it Update. This is where we will place the *getNetText()* script for the Update button.**

6. **Select the new Update behavior in the behavior inspector and click the Script Window button. This will open the Script window. Now we will add the new script.**

7. **Add the following script to the Script window for the Update behavior.**

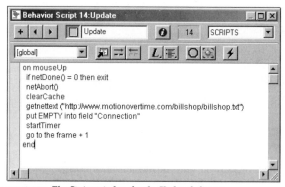

**FIGURE 9.72** *The Script window for the Update behavior.*

```
on mouseUp
  if netDone() = 0 then exit
  netAbort()
  clearCache
  getNetText ("http://www.motionovertime.com/billshop/
  billshop.txt")
  put EMPTY into field "Connection"
  startTimer
  go to the frame + 1
end
```

This script will allow the user to check for new updates in The Billionaire's Shop at any time while they are browsing through the Shop. If this button is pressed while a download is in progress, it will cause the current download to abort and begin a new one. Let's go through the script.

If *netDone() = 0 then exit* will ensure that if a download is already in progress a new one will not begin. The *netAbort()* command will make certain that any other requests that are still in memory and not effected by the *netDone()* command will be stopped. This way there is no chance of causing an error due to excessive simultaneous requests.

The *clearCache* command will empty Director's cache, so that we are always working from the latest file from the Internet location.

The *getNetText (http://www.motionovertime.com/billshop/billshop.txt)* command line will request the file named Billshop.txt from the Motion Over Time Web site.

The *put "Waiting" into field "Connection"* command line will place the word Waiting into the Connection field.

The *startTimer* command will reset Director's internal clock, so that we can later time how long it takes for the information to be downloaded. If it takes too long, we will abort the request and alert the user of the problem in the Connection window.

The *go to the frame + 1* command line will send the playback head to the next frame in the Score, where we will place the script that will contain the *netTextResult()* command. Currently there is nothing in the next frame of the Score except the background sprite, which extends across to the Quit area of the Score. We will create this frame and add the *netTextResult()* script next.

8. **Close the Script window.**

9. **Close the behavior inspector.**

## ADDING THE NETTEXTRESULT() COMMAND FOR THE UPDATE BUTTON

We are going to place the *netTextResult()* script that will work with the Update button in frame 148 of the Score. Our first steps will be to create the content of this new screen, so that we do not send the user to an empty area of the Score.

1. **If it is not already open, open the Score.**

2. **Move the playback head to frame 155 of the Score.**

This is the last frame of the Shop area of the Score. We are going to drag the endpoints of all of the sprites one frame to the right, so that they extend into frame 156.

3. **Select and drag the endpoints for all of the sprite objects in frame 155 to frame 156. This includes all of the sprites from channels 1 to 14 in the Shop area of the Score.**

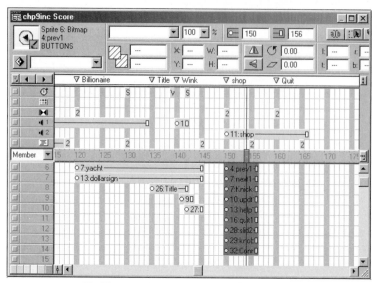

**FIGURE 9.73** *The Shop area of the Score. The endpoints for all of the sprites in frame 155 have been dragged to frame 156.*

4. **Open the Scripts Cast window, then double-click in frame 156 of the script channel in the Score.**

   This is where we will locate the new *netTextResult()* script. Opening the scripts Cast window will ensure that the new script will be placed in that window.

5. **Add the following script to frame 156 of the Score.**

```
on exitFrame
  if the timer < 3600 then
    if netDone() = 1 then
      if netError() = "OK" then
        put "Checking for update information." into field
        "Connection"
        put netTextResult()
      else
        netAbort()
        put "There was an error in the transmission of the file
        you requested. Your Internet connection may have
        failed." into field "Connection"
      end if
```

```
      go to the frame - 1
    else
      put "Requesting information from the Internet." into field
      "Connection"
    end if
  else
    netAbort()
    put "It has taken too long to retrieve the requested
    information from the Internet" into field "Connection"
    go to the frame - 1
  end if
  go to the frame
end
```

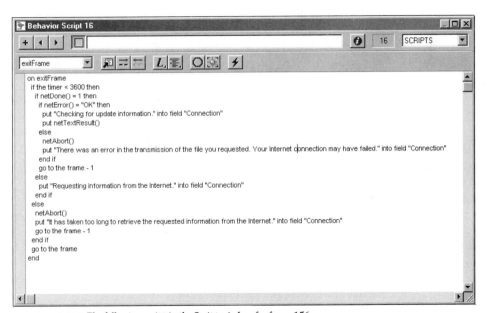

**FIGURE 9.74** *The following script in the Script window for frame 156.*

This script will display information in the Connection field, based upon what is occurring with the text file that is requested from the Internet when the Update button is clicked. It's similar to other scripts we have written that use the *netTextResult()*, with some differences. Let's examine the script:

The *if the timer < 3600 then* command line will place a 1-minute time limit on the *getNetText()* request. If it takes longer than this, the request will be stopped with *netAbort()* and the message "It has taken too long to retrieve the requested information from the Internet" will be displayed in the Connection field.

The *if netDone() = 1 then* command line will determine if the network request made by *getNetText()* has been completed. If it has not been completed, the message "Requesting information from the Internet" will be displayed in the Connection field.

The *getNetText ("http://www.motionovertime.com/billshop/billshop.txt")* command line will request the file named Billshop.txt from the Motion Over Time Web site.

The *if netError() = "OK" then* command line will determine that the text file requested by *getNetText()* has been successfully downloaded. If it has, then the message "Checking for update information" will be displayed in the Connection field, and the contents of the requested text file will be displayed in the Message window by *netTextResult()*. If the file requested by *getNetText()* is not successfully downloaded, the request will be stopped by *netAbort()*, and the message "There was an error in the transmission of the file you requested. Your Internet connection might have failed" will be displayed in the Connection field. In either case, the playback head will then be returned to frame 155 by "go to the frame - 1."

The "go to the frame" command line will keep the playback head in frame 155 until the 1 minute timer runs out or the script `go to the frame - 1` is activated elsewhere in the script.

The Update button is now programmed. Let's test it!

6. **Name the script Track Text and close the Script window. We should now have a new Script in Cast position 16 of the Scripts.cst.**

7. **Close all windows except the Message window. If the Message window is not currently open, open it now. This is where the contents of the Billshop.txt file will be displayed.**

8. **Clear the text in the Message window. You can do this by highlighting and deleting the text in the Message window just as if you were working with a word-processing program.**

9. **Make certain that your Internet connection is active.**

10. **Rewind and play the movie.**

11. **Click the No button in the first screen. This will send the playback head into The Billionaire's Shop without requesting any information from the Internet. Information indicating this will be displayed in the Connection field, then the playback head will branch to the Shop area of the Score. The message "No update attempted" will be displayed in the Connection field on the Stage.**

12. **Click the Update button. This time all of the same information will be displayed in the Connection field, then the contents of the text file that are requested by *getNetText()* are displayed in the Message window. The scripts worked!**

13. **Stop the movie.**

In the next chapter we will program The Billionaire's Shop to use the information from the Billshop.txt file to update the shop.

## SUMMARY

By using new Hybrid Internet Lingo we can use frequently updated information from the Internet to enhance presentations that are delivered by CD-ROM and other non-network delivery methods. In The Billionaire's Shop, we are using these Lingo commands to retrieve a text file that contains information about the updates available for the inventory in the Shop. This technique permits us to reduce the amount of work necessary to create and redistribute new data in presentations.

To use Hybrid Internet Lingo commands, you must first establish a connection to the Internet using the same software that you would use for this purpose outside of Director, such as America Online or another Internet service provider. Director cannot detect the presence of an active Internet connection, but Lingo includes a command that will detect an error in the transmission of data that is requested from the Internet. One of the events that will cause an error to be detected is if the information never arrives. This can be attributable to a request for information that is not at the targeted location, or a corruption in the data or a bad connection to the Internet. The lack of a connection will simply be translated as an error in transmission.

Director will respond differently to errors that involve downloading of data, depending on the configuration of the software that is used to connect to the Internet. In most cases Director will simply pause momentarily and then continue as normal. You can then use Lingo to determine if the requested event was successful. Checking for the presence of the requested data in a variable is enough to check for success. If the data is there, the download was successful.

As information is retrieved from the Internet, it can be used immediately. It is recommended to first place the data into a variable, then use the variable wherever you would like access to the retrieved information. Not only does this simplify scripts, but it also allows us to initiate other Internet downloads while the data from previous requests is already being used in our scripts.

Most applications that download information from the Internet provide a Connection display for both the connections as well as for any downloads that are occurring. We can add this feature to Director movies by using the capability to display information in text fields. We can display any errors that occur during transmission or the completion status of a requested download. Displaying information in a text field is accomplished in much the same way information is placed into a variable; the only difference is that the name of the text field is used in place of the name of a variable.

## QUESTIONS

1.  Why was it necessary to add an opening screen to The Billionaire's Shop that allows the user to indicate the presence of a connection to the Internet?

2.  In this lesson we used Hybrid Internet Lingo to retrieve text data and display it. Once downloaded, this text can be used just as any other text created in Director. Describe three other uses for data that is retrieved from the Internet.

3.  What does the command *netDone()* detect?

4.  What does the command *netError()* detect?

5.  Why is it necessary to use the command *netTextResult()*?

6.  Why was it important to add a timer and the command *netAbort()* to the script that uses *getNetText()*?

## EXERCISES

1.  Using the Message window, use *getNetText()* to download the file named billshop.bmp from the Web site. Remember that the URL for this bitmap is **http://www.motionovertime.com/billshop/billshop.txt**. Remember that you must have an open connection to the Internet to successfully use *getNetText()*. When *getNetText()* is finished, use *netTextResult()* to display the retrieved text in the Message window.

2.  Using the same script that you used in exercise 1, use *getNetText()* to retrieve billshop.txt again. This time, use a script in the Message window that will display *netTextResult()* in a text field.

3.  Create a movie that contains a frame script in the first frame that will use *getNetText()* to retrieve billshop.txt. In the second frame, add a script that will check for the success of *getNetText()* using the *netDone()* command from our lessons in this chapter. When *netDone()* indicates that the download is complete, display the information from *netTextResult()* in a field on the Stage. The same script that checks for *netDone()* should keep the playback head in frame 2 when *getNetText()* is finished. Use "go to the frame" to keep the playback head in frame 2.

# CHAPTER 10

# DOWNLOADING FILES FROM THE INTERNET

# 10 Downloading Files from the Internet

**In this chapter, you will learn how to:**

- Use the *downloadNetThing()* command to retrieve files from the Internet
- Switch the file used for an external Cast file using Lingo
- Use the *importFileInto* command to add new media to a Director file using Lingo
- Use the results produced by the *GetNetText()* command to support the use of the *downloadNetThing()* command
- Examine a text file line by line using Lingo
- Use the *PreloadNetThing* command

There are two basic methods for retrieving files from the Internet: *getNetText()*, which we used in chapter 9 and is used to retrieve only text, and *downloadNetThing()*, which we will use in this chapter. This command can be used to download any media type from a network. The differences between the two, besides the fact that one is only capable of working with text files, is that *getNetText()* retrieves data that can be used immediately, such as being displayed in a text window. The *getNetText()* command also does not generate any new media on the viewer's hard drive. The data is retrieved and exists only in temporary memory. Once the application is exited, the data is purged.

The *downloadNetThing()* command creates a file on the hard drive. This file must then somehow be incorporated into the application, such as by importing the file or by linking to the file as an external Cast member or Cast file. The *downloadNetThing()* command will also take more time to complete because there is typically more data in images and sounds than in text files. You can think of the two options as the difference between watching TV and receiving a delivery. With TV you need only turn on the set to receive and process the data that it sends. With a delivery, you need to open the package, then use the contents accordingly. Also, with TV, there's no trace of the data that the TV transmitted when the set is turned off. With a package you have the contents and the container. Storage of some sort is necessary, or you need to take the additional step of discarding the package or some part of it. The TV is an excellent option if all we want is the delivery of information. The package is required if we want a tangible item that can be stored and manipulated.

In this chapter we will use the getNetText() scripts that we added to The Billionaire's Shop to determine if there is a new download available for the shop. We only require the quick transmission of information for this. However, if a download is needed, then we will use *downloadNetThing()* to request the new inventory, which we will then incorporate into the shop. First we will work with a sample file that will allow us to experiment with the *downloadNetThing()* command before we make changes to The Billionaire's Shop.

An important factor of working with files that are downloaded from the Internet is understanding that there are many things that can affect download times. Traffic on the Internet is an example of what might cause downloads to take a long time, but there are other possibilities, such as a malfunctioning server or a file that has been deleted from a server. To accommodate these unforeseeable problems, we must add timers to our scripts that will limit the duration that a script will attempt to download a file. If the download attempt exceeds the allotted time limit, then we will add items to our script that will alert the user to the unsuccessful attempt and then abort the download. This will prevent unnecessarily extended waiting periods and will be an indication that the user should log off and try again later.

Another important point that we will cover in this chapter is checking whether a download is necessary at all. We have devised a system for maintaining versions of the inventory for The Billionaire's Shop, and we will write scripts that will check this system before attempting a download. This will prevent any unnecessary downloads when the most current information for The Billionaire's Shop is already present on the user's hard drive.

## VIEWING THE COMPLETED EXAMPLE FILE

The *downloadNetThing()* command is similar to the *getNetText()* in that they both request data from the Internet. Other commands, such as *netDone()* and *netError()*, are used to determine the progress of the download. As mentioned earlier, the main difference between the two commands is that *downloadNetThing()* can download any file type and *getNetText()* is only used for text. In this session we will work with a file that uses *downloadNetThing()* to retrieve an image from our Web site.

We will also add scripts to determine how much time will be allowed for a download. If the time permitted elapses, then the download will abort and a message will be returned that reports that the download was unsuccessful. Other scripts we will add in this session will check for the successful completion of a download and errors in the transmission of files over the Internet.

1.  **Locate the folder named Chaptr10 in the Lessons folder on the CD-ROM.**

    This folder contains the complete and incomplete versions of the sample file that, along with the files from the previous lessons, continues the development of The Billionaire's Shop. Because we will be downloading files from the Internet, we will need to place the Director files for this lesson on the hard drive. This is because the downloaded file will not be able to be saved to the CD-ROM.

2.  **Drag a copy of the folder named Chaptr10 to your hard drive.**

    The *downloadNetThing()* command will attempt to write a file to the hard drive that The Billionaire's Shop's movie is running on in Director. We are unable to write new information to the CD-ROM, so we must work from a standard hard drive.

3.  **Establish a connection to the Internet. Use the software that you normally use to connect to the Internet.**

4.  **If it is not already open, launch Director.**

5.  **Choose File>Open.**

6.  **Locate and open the file named Downcmp.dir, which is located in the directory that we just created: ...Chaptr10/Chp10Smp/Complete.**

    The Score in this movie only contains two areas; one labeled Activate allows us to click a button to download a new image, which will replace the image that is currently displayed at the center of the background on the stage. The other, labeled, Download, removes the download button from the stage and contains the script that tracks the download of the new image. A text field on the background will give the download status of the requested image.

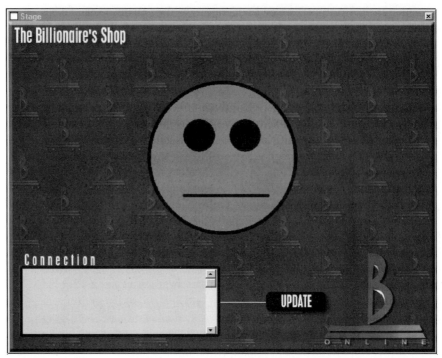

**FIGURE 10.01** *The completed downloadNetThing() example movie with the image that is to be replaced by a downloaded file displayed on the Stage.*

7.   **Play the movie.**

If we click the button labeled Update on the Stage, the *download-NetThing()* command will be issued. We will see information displayed in the text field about the download status. When the download is completed, the image at the center of the Stage is replaced with a montage image of the five products that are currently available in The Billionaire's Shop.

8.   **Stop the movie.**

Now we will work with the incomplete version of this file and add the *downloadNetThing()* command.

**FIGURE 10.02** *The completed downloadNetThing() example movie after the downloadNetThing() command has been executed. The products montage image is displayed on the stage.*

This chapter requires a great deal of script writing before testing. Director is usually excellent about identifying errors in scripts, but it is still very important that you write your scripts precisely as they appear on these pages. A single mistake can cause your scripts not to work. Be patient if it doesn't happen the first time. One of the greatest challenges of programming is debugging. Type slowly and triple-check your work. **NOTE**

As you probably discovered in chapter 9, hybrid scripting methods require quite a bit of script writing before you can test their capabilities. This chapter contains very simiilar scripts, so you will find that your experience here will be the same. As recommended earlier, be patient, move slowly, and pay careful attention that you type scrripts precisely as they appear in this chapter. You may find it helpful to review the material in this chapter again when you are done. Hybrid scripting is exciting and new and still evolving as the needs for "pushing around" information change. Macromedia watches closely for these needs and implements them into future versions of Director. This type of scripting opens up a lot of possibilities, so move forward attentively, and enjoy! **NOTE**

## BUILDING THE EXAMPLE FILE

We have viewed the complete version of the example movie. Now we will add the Lingo that downloads the new image to the incomplete version.

1. **Locate and open the file named Downinc.dir in the directory Chaptr10/Chp10Smp/STARTER/.**

    This file is in the same directory as the completed version of this file. We can see that this file is almost identical to the completed version. The only difference is the absence of the Lingo commands that retrieve and use the images that are imported from the Internet.

2. **Open the Internal Cast.**

    Cast member 1 is the image that will be replaced by the image that we will download using *downloadNetThing()*. The Cast member is actually linked to an image that is outside of the Director movie. If we select this Cast member and click the Cast Member Properties Info button at the top of the Cast window, we will see the directory where this image is located. We will replace this Cast member with the new downloaded Cast member by changing the file that this Cast member is linked to.

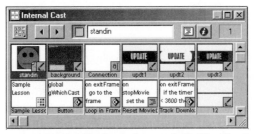

**FIGURE 10.03** *The Cast in the example file. We will replace Cast member 1 with the new file that we will download from the Internet.*

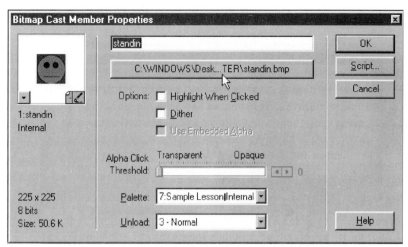

**FIGURE 10.04** *The Cast Member Info dialog box for Cast member 1. The cursor identifies the path.*

## ADDING THE DOWNLOADNETTHING() COMMAND

We will design the example movie to activate the *downloadNetThing()* command when the Update button is clicked on the Stage. We have already placed the Button behavior on the Update button, so we will now create another behavior to include the *downloadNetThing()* command.

1. Place the playback head in the first part of the Activate area of the Score. This will make the Update button visible on the Stage.

2. Select the Update button on the Stage.

3. Open the behavior inspector.

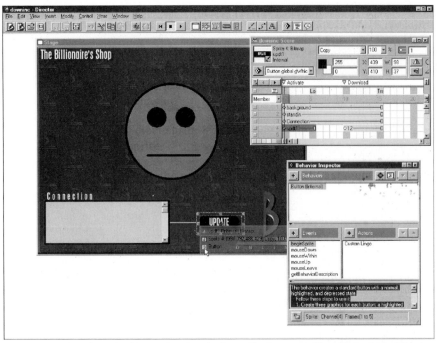

**FIGURE 10.05** *The Update button selected on the Stage. The Score is visible, with the playback head in the Activate area of the Score.*

4.    **Create a new behavior on the Update button and name it Download.**

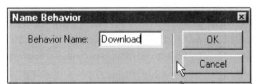

**FIGURE 10.06** *The Name Behavior window with Download in the entry window.*

5.    **Click the Script Window button at the top of the behavior inspector and add the following script:**

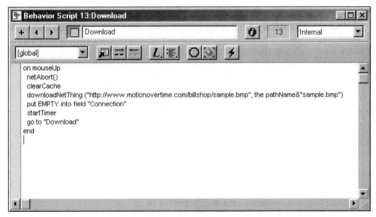

**FIGURE 10.07** *The script for the Download behavior.*

```
on mouseUp
  netAbort()
  clearCache
  downloadNetThing ("http://www.motionovertime.com/billshop/
  sample.bmp", the pathName&"sample.bmp")
  put EMPTY into field "Connection"
  startTimer
  go to "Download"
end
```

The scripts in this handler are similar to the script we added to The Billionaire's Shop in chapter 9. In chapter 9 we used the *getNetText()* command, which only required one parameter, the path to the file that was requested. The command looked like this in chapter 9:

```
getNetText(http://www.motionovertime.com/billshop/Billshop.txt)
```

The *downloadNetThing()* command requires two parameters, the path to the requested file and the location where we would like the file placed on our hard drive. The first parameter in the script that we added here is http://www.motionovertime.com/billshop/sample.bmp, the same location where the Billshop.txt file is located on the Internet. The second parameter is the pathName&"sample.bmp" The pathname is the path to wherever the current Director movie is located on the hard drive. To complete the command, we must also indicate a name for the new file that will be created when it is downloaded from the Internet.

The way that Director downloads files from the Internet is similar to how a standard browser downloads the images and text for a Web site. First the files are requested, then they are downloaded to the browser's cache, where they are accessed directly by the browser.

Before the files are downloaded from the Internet, they are present on their host server with the names that they were given by the Web site's designer. When they are downloaded to the browser's cache, they are given generic names that are tracked by the local browser. This is how Director's *downloadNetThing()* command works when it allows us to specify which file we want to download and allows us to rename the file on the local hard drive.

**6.    Close the script window.**

Now we will add the script that will track the download of the sample.bmp file, then replace Cast member 1 with the new image.

## ADDING THE SCRIPT TO TRACK THE DOWNLOAD OF THE SAMPLE.BMP FILE

The script in frame 15 of the script channel contains most of the script that will track the download of the new image. We will add the script that will incorporate the new image into the Director presentation.

**1.    Double-click in frame 15 of the script channel of the Score.**

This will open the script window and display the script as it is currently written. Notice that this script is almost identical to the script that was used to track the transfer of the text file in chapter 9. The only significant difference is the amount of time the scripts will wait for the download to complete. The script set a time limit of 5 minutes (18,000 ticks = 5 minutes) for the download of the image. It checks to see if the network operation was completed. It also checks that the operation was actually successful in its completion and not stopped due to an error. Each of these tests has a message to display in the Connection field if it is not successful. However, when this script reaches its conclusion, it will return the playback head to the Activate area of the Score. Now we will add the scripts that will integrate the new image when it is successfully downloaded.

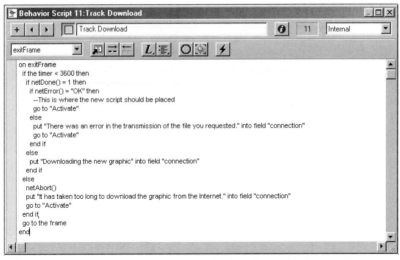

**FIGURE 10.08** *The script in frame 15 of the script channel open in the Script window.*

```
on exitFrame
  if the timer < 3600 then
    if netDone() = 1 then
      if netError() = OK then
        --This is where the new script should be placed
        go to "Activate"
      else
        put "There was an error in the transmission of the file you
        requested." into field "Connection"
        go to "Activate"
      end if
    else
      put "Downloading the new image" into field "Connection"
    end if
  else
    netAbort()
    put "It has taken too long to download the image from the
    Internet." into field "Connection"
    go to "Activate"
  end if
  go to the frame
end
```

2. **Add the following to the script in frame 15 of the script channel.**

We do not need to use a network Lingo command to incorporate media that is downloaded from the Internet because once the files are downloaded, they are on the hard drive and can be worked with using ordinary Lingo. In this example, we are simply switching the file that is used for Cast member 1 to the new image. We can make this change because Cast member 1 is a linked Cast member. When the switch is made, any sprites that were created with Cast member 1 will change to the appearance of the new image.

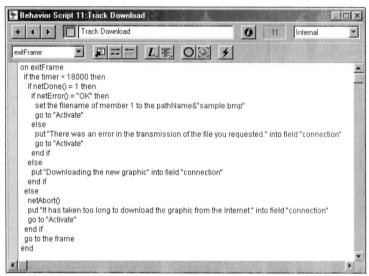

```
Behavior Script 11:Track Download                                    _ □ ×
 +  ◄  ►  □  │Track Download                    │  ❶ │ 11 │ │Internal     ▼
│exitFrame      ▼│ 🔲 ⇄ ╤  L E  O🔲  ⚡
  on exitFrame
    if the timer < 18000 then
     if netDone() = 1 then
      if netError() = "OK" then
       set the filename of member 1 to the pathName&"sample.bmp"
       go to "Activate"
      else
       put "There was an error in the transmission of the file you requested." into field "connection"
       go to "Activate"
      end if
     else
      put "Downloading the new graphic" into field "connection"
     end if
    else
     netAbort()
     put "It has taken too long to download the graphic from the Internet." into field "connection"
     go to "Activate"
    end if
    go to the frame
   end
```

**FIGURE 10.09** *The following additions to the script in frame 15 of the script channel. Changes are in place.*

```
on exitFrame
  if the timer < 18000 then
    if netDone() = 1 then
      if netError() = "OK" then
        set the filename of member 1 to the pathName&
        "sample.bmp"
        go to "Activate"
      else
        put "There was an error in the transmission of the file
        you requested." into field "Connection"
        go to "Activate"
      end if
    else
      put "Downloading the new image" into field "Connection"
    end if
  else
    netAbort()
    put "It has taken too long to download the image from the
    Internet". into field "Connection"
    go to "Activate"
  end if
  go to the frame
end
```

### 3. Close the Script window.

Now we will test the new scripts.

### 4. Establish a connection to the Internet if you are not already connected. If you've been reading while you work, you might have been kicked off. It happens.

### 5. Rewind and play the movie.

Click the Update button. Information tracking the download of the new image is displayed on your screen. When the image is downloaded, the script will replace the image on the Stage with the new image.

> If the download is not successful for any reason, click the Update button again. If the problem persists, make certain your scripts are correct and your connection to the Internet is live.

**NOTE**

> The time required to download the requested image will vary based upon the amount of activity on the Internet. You can program this movie to wait a longer period of time by increasing the number of ticks this movie will wait from 18000 to a larger number. Five minutes should be long enough for most files that have been prepared for use over the Internet.

**NOTE**

### 6. Stop the movie.

You will see that the image on the Stage reverts to the original image. (You may need to rewind the movie to force the screen to refresh.) This is because we have already included a script that uses *set the filename of member...* to revert to the original image again when the movie is stopped. If this script were not included, the new Cast member would be viewed by the application as a new change in Director and would remain a part of the movie.

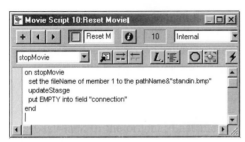

**FIGURE 10.10** *The stopMovie handler contains the updateStage command—a script that reverts the image in the position 1 to the original image. This is to allow us to reuse this movie for other tests.*

```
on stopMovie
  set the fileName of member 1 to the pathName&"standin.bmp"
  updateStage
  put EMPTY into field "Connection"
end
```

**NOTE**   If the movie is played again and Update is clicked, it will once again
download the sample.bmp image. The new download will replace the old
file without warning. You might be used to seeing a message such as
"There is an older file named *sample.bmp* in this location. Do you want to
replace this file?" This will not occur with *downloadNetThing()*. We can use
this to our advantage by having updates to a movie that reference the same
file name, but simply change the file's contents. This is ultimately how The
Billionaire's Shop will be updated. We will replace the external Products.cst
Cast file with a new Cast file that contains the new products.

## USING THE IMPORTFILEINTO COMMAND

In this lesson we used the Lingo script `set the filename of member...`
to integrate a new image into a Director file. There is another method for
incorporating new media using the command *importFileInto*. It works just
as if we had selected Import from the file menu, except that there is no
dialog box with a browser to select files to be imported. This must all be
determined as part of the script itself. Here is an example of how a script
would appear that imports an image into Cast position 12 of a Director
movie:

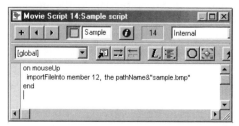

**FIGURE 10.11** *A sample script that uses importFileInto.*

```
on mouseUp
  importFileInto member 12, the pathName&"sample.bmp"
end
```

The first parameter in this handler is the member position where we
would like to locate the new Cast member. The second parameter is the
file that we would like to import. Once the command is completed, there
will be a new Cast member that is not linked to an external source, just as
if we had imported the file using the menu command. Once the file is in the

Cast, we can use commands such as *set the memberNum of sprite 3 to 12* to incorporate the new Cast member into the movie.

If we are working with multiple Cast libraries, we can specify which Cast we would like to add the new member to by extending the first parameter as follows:

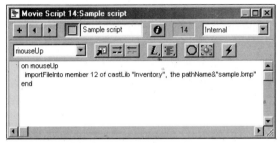

**FIGURE 10.12** *The sample script with an extended first parameter.*

```
on mouseUp
    importFileInto member 12 of castLib "Inventory", the
    pathName&"sample.bmp"
end
```

> If we use *importFileInto* and do not specify a Cast library in a movie that uses multiple Casts, then the new Cast member will be created in the first Internal Cast library that is already present when a new Director movie is created. If a Cast member already occupies the desired location in a Cast file, the new Cast member will overwrite the old Cast member.   **NOTE**

## PLAYING THE COMPLETED VERSION OF THIS LESSON

Earlier in this chapter we duplicated the entire directory that contains all of the files for this chapter. The *downloadNetThing()* command in this lesson will write a file to your hard drive, so we will work with the files in the duplicate directory.

1.   **Make certain that you are still connected to the Internet.**

2.   **Choose File> Open.**

3.   **Locate and open the file named "Chp10Cmp.dir" in the directory Chaptr10/Complete/.**

4.   **Rewind and play the movie.**

This file is the almost complete version of The Billionaire's Shop. We will watch carefully for the changes that will be added in this lesson. When the presentation reaches the end of the opening animation, the Connection field displays information about the download status of an update for The Billionaire's Shop. When the download is completed, we are given this information in the Connection window and can now browse through the new products in The Billionaire's Shop using the right- and left-arrow buttons.

In this session we will add the scripts that will use the Billshop.txt file that we download with the *getNetText()* command to determine if there is a new update for the shop, then we will add the scripts that will download the new inventory. After we have added these new scripts, we will be able to use the Update button programmed in chapter 9.

5.   **Stop the movie.**

Now we will add these new features to The Billionaire's Shop.

## PREPARING FILES FOR THIS LESSON

If you are working with the partly completed version of this lesson, follow the instructions above. If you would like to continue working with the file you have created from earlier chapters, then locate and open that file.

1.   **Choose File> Open.**

2.   **Locate and open the file named "Chp10inc.dir" in the directory Chaptr10/STARTER/.**

**NOTE**   The *downloadNetThing()* command can be used to add files to any hard drive on your computer in any directory through a connection to the Internet. A required step for the *downloadNetThing()* command is to define the path to the target location on the hard drive. This capability allows us to run a Director movie from a CD-ROM that can update itself by downloading files to a local hard drive, then referencing the new media from that location. For simplicity purposes in this lesson we used the *pathName* command, which targets the precise location of the movie that is currently running. This is the only reason why we *must* copy the files that we are working with to the hard drive before we can use them.

## USING A GLOBAL VARIABLE TO STORE THE RESULTS OF THE DOWNLOADED BILLSHOP.TXT FILE

In chapter 9 we used the *getNetText()* command to retrieve a text file that contains information about the update status of The Billionaire's Shop. The first part of this text file is a number that is the version number of the latest update, which we will compare with the version number that is located in the products Cast file in the field Cast member named Version. If the number in the downloaded file is larger than the number in the Cast file, then an update is available. We will begin with the existing script that currently retrieves the text file from the Internet and add the scripts that will compare the version number from the text file with the version number in the field Cast member. Our first step is to store the content of the Billshop.txt file in a global variable that we can use in other scripts.

1. **Open the script in frame 145 of the script channel.**

   This is the script at the end of the opening animation that tracks the download of the Billshop.txt file and displays the results in the Message window.

```
on exitFrame me
  if netDone() = 1 then
    if netError() = "OK" then
      if netTextResult() = "" then
        put "No update Attempted." into field "connection"
      else
        put "Checking for update information" into field "connection"
        put netTextResult()
      end if
    else
      if netError() = "" then
        put "No update attempted" into field "connection"
      else
        put "there was an error in the transmission of the file you requested." into field "connection"
      end if
    end if
  else
    netAbort()
    put "It has taken too long to retriueve the requested information from the internet" into field "connection"
  end if
  delay 300
  set the volume of sound 2 to 20
  go to marker ("shop")
end
```

**FIGURE 10.13** *The Script in frame 145 of the script channel.*

```
on exitFrame
  if netDone() = 1 then
    if netError() = "OK" then
      if netTextResult() = "" then
        put "No Update Attempted." into field "Connection"
      else
        put "Checking for update information" into field
        "Connection"
        put netTextResult()
      end if
    else
      if netError() = "" then
        put "No update attempted" into field "Connection"
      else
        put "There was an error in the transmission of the file
        you requested." into field "Connection"
      end if
    end if
  else
    netAbort()
    put "It has taken too long to retrieve the requested
    information from the Internet" into field "Connection"
  end if
  delay 300
  set the volume of sound 2 to 20
  go to marker ("Shop")
end
```

2. **Make the following modification to the script in frame 145 of the script channel.**

By adding the user-defined global variable that we have named updateText, we can store the content of the Billshop.txt file in a location where it can be retrieved later. Do not close the Script window when you are done.

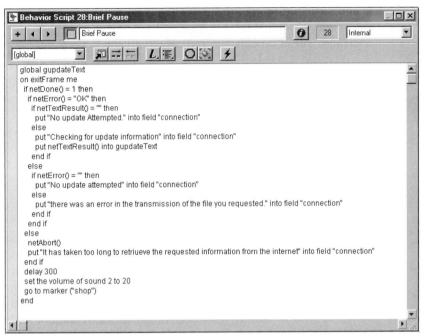

**FIGURE 10.14** *The script in frame 145 of the script channel with the changes in place.*

```
global gupdateText
on exitFrame
  if netDone() = 1 then
    if netError() = "OK" then
      if netTextResult() = "" then
        put "No Update Attempted." into field "Connection"
      else
        put "Checking for update information" into field
        "Connection"
        put netTextResult() into gupdateText
      end if
    else
      if netError() = "" then
        put "No update attempted" into field "Connection"
      else
        put "There was an error in the transmission of the file
        you requested." into field "Connection"
      end if
    end if
  else
    netAbort()
```

```
    put "It has taken too long to retrieve the requested
    information from the Internet" into field "Connection"
end if
delay 300
set the volume of sound 2 to 20
go to marker ("Shop")
end
```

## CREATING A USER-DEFINED HANDLER TO COMPARE VERSIONS OF THE BILLIONAIRE'S SHOP AND ADDING THE DOWNLOADNETTHING() COMMAND

It will take several steps to compare the version number in the Billshop.txt file and the version number that is in the Version field Cast member, which would greatly increase the number of lines in the exit-Frame handler in frame 145. Rather than complicate this script any further, we will create another handler, which will contain only the comparison scripts.

We can accomplish this by creating a user-defined handler, a script that has a custom name and can be referred to by its name in other scripts. It's a bit like delegating responsibilities to different people. For example, if Joe orders all of the office supplies, then we know that we can call Joe's extension for anything related to that category of responsibility. By having one person at one extension with one specific responsibility, we have created a way in which everyone in the company can achieve the same goal without needing to have separate solutions to office supplies independently. In this case we will create a script named *checkForUpdate* which will have the sole purpose of comparing version numbers in The Billionaire's Shop. This script can then be used anywhere we would like to perform version comparisons.

Custom handlers can be located in any script window in a Director Cast and can be accessed using any other script, simply by using the name of the handler in the summoning script. We will take these steps in the following session.

1. **Make the following modification to the script in frame 145 of the script channel.**

   This script should still be open on your screen. If not, then reopen the script in frame 145 of the script channel. By adding the custom handler, checkForUpdate, to the Script window, we can access the scripts that will compare the versions of The Billionaire's Shop in different windows. By using the name of the new custom handler in other scripts, as we do in the exitFrame handler, we activate the checkForUpdate handler.

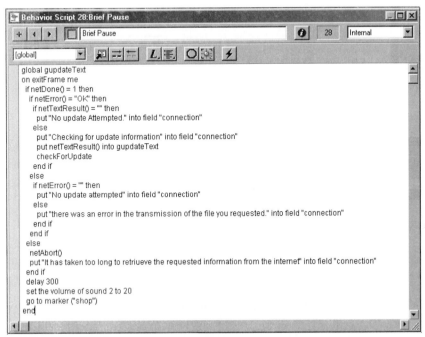

```
global gupdateText
on exitFrame me
  if netDone() = 1 then
    if netError() = "OK" then
      if netTextResult() = "" then
        put "No update Attempted." into field "connection"
      else
        put "Checking for update information" into field "connection"
        put netTextResult() into gupdateText
        checkForUpdate
      end if
    else
      if netError() = "" then
        put "No update attempted" into field "connection"
      else
        put "there was an error in the transmission of the file you requested." into field "connection"
      end if
    end if
  else
    netAbort()
    put "It has taken too long to retrieve the requested information from the internet" into field "connection"
  end if
  delay 300
  set the volume of sound 2 to 20
  go to marker ("shop")
end
```

**FIGURE 10.15** *The script in frame 145 of the script channel with changes in place.*

```
global gupdateText
on exitFrame
  if netDone() = 1 then
    if netError() = "OK" then
      if netTextResult() = "" then
        put "No Update Attempted." into field "Connection"
      else
        put "Checking for update information" into field
        "Connection"
        put netTextResult() into gupdateText
        checkForUpdate
      end if
    else
      if netError() = "" then
        put "No update attempted" into field "Connection"
      else
        put "There was an error in the transmission of the file
        you requested." into field "Connection"
```

```
    end if
  end if
else
  netAbort()
  put "It has taken too long to retrieve the requested
  information from the Internet" into field "Connection"
end if
delay 300
set the volume of sound 2 to 20
go to marker ("Shop")
end
```

In the exitFrame handler we will activate a handler named checkForUpdate when the Billshop.txt text file is downloaded. We will create the checkForUpdate handler in a different window. If there is a download necessary, the checkForUpdate handler will send the playback head to a frame that we will create and name Download. If no download is needed, we will send the playback head to the Shop area of the Score. The checkForUpdate handler uses a few new commands that we have not yet used. We will go through it line by line.

2.   **In the Script window, verify that the Cast is the Scripts Cast by looking at the upper right box. If it isn't, use the drop-down menu to switch to the Scripts Cast.**

     This will ensure that the new script we are about to create is located in the Scripts Cast.

3.   **Click the + button at the top of the Script window.**

     This will advance to the next available Cast member in the Script Cast window. Make sure that the current Cast showing is the Scripts Cast.

4.   **Click the *i* button in the upper right corner of the Script window.**

     This will open the Cast Member Info window for this Script window. It is currently categorized as a Behavior script under the Type pull-down menu. This is because we were in a Behavior script when we clicked the + button. We must change this script to a Movie script because Behavior scripts can only be used on sprites and in the script channel of the Score. Movie scripts are general locations for scripts that allow them to be referenced by scripts that are located on buttons, in the script channel, or in any other location in a Director movie. We will be referencing the scripts that we will create in this window from other locations within The Billionaire's Shop, so we will need to convert this into a Movie script.

**5. Select movie from the Type pull-down menu.**

This script is now converted.

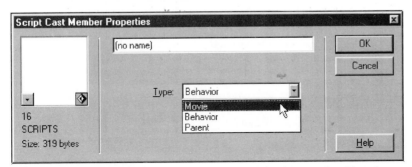

**FIGURE 10.16** *The Script Cast Member Properties window with movie selected from the Type menu.*

**6. Click the OK button to close the dialog box.**

Now we can write our new scripts.

**7. Type the following script in the open Script window (Cast member 16) and name the Script window General Scripts.**

This is the checkForUpdate handler, which will be activated by the exitFrame handler in frame 145. Placing it in a Movie script window will allow it to be accessed by other scripts. Later in this lesson, we will modify the scripts to add the Update button, which will also use the checkForUpdate handler.

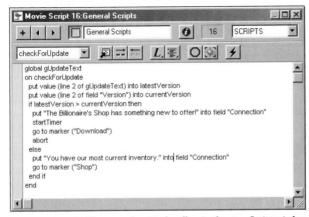

**FIGURE 10.17** *The general scripts handlers in the open Script window.*

```
global gUpdateText
on checkForUpdate
  put value(line 2 of gUpdateText) into latestVersion
  put value(line 2 of field "Version") into currentVersion
  if latestVersion > currentVersion then
    put "The Billionaire's Shop has something new to offer!"
    into field "Connection"
    startTimer
    go to  marker ("Download")
    abort
  else
    put "You have our most current inventory." into field
    "Connection"
    go to marker ("Shop")
  end if
end
```

Let's examine this script:

```
put value(line 2 of gUpdateText) into latestVersion
```

The first new item is the command *value*, which is used to convert numbers that are displayed in bodies of text into numbers that can be used in Lingo calculations. For example, if the number 543 were displayed in the first line in a text field named Current Score, we could extract the number by using the script, *line 1 of field "Current Score;"* however, this number would only be text; it is just as useful as extracting the word Hello from a text field. In fact, if we tried to use *line 1 of field "Current Score"* in a calculation, we would get an error message because a number cannot be added to a word. To use this character number, we must convert it into its numeric representation by using the term *value*. This would appear as follows: *value(line 1 of field "Current Score")*.

The text that we are converting into an integer is line 2 of the text in the global variable *gupdateText*. This is the same variable that we used to store the text that was retrieved from the Internet in the Billshop.txt file using *getNetText()*. The format of the text is maintained in text stored in a variable, so items on different lines on the screen will be recognized as items on separate lines in the variable. The second line of the Billshop.txt file contains the version number.

Now that we have extracted the latest version number and converted it into an integer, we must set it in a calculation that compares it to the current version of The Billionaire's Shop currently on your hard drive. To simplify this process, we are storing only this number in a local variable named *latestVersion*. A local variable is a variable that temporarily can store a value within the handler that uses it.

```
put value(line 2 of field "Version") into currentVersion
```

We used the same technique to extract the value of the current version of The Billionaire's Shop on the hard drive by placing *value(line 2 of field "Version")* into another local variable that we named *currentVersion*. With this done, we can compare the two values with the first line of the following if...then statement:

```
if latestVersion > currentVersion then
```

If the latest version number is greater than the current version number, we will execute the following scripts to initiate a download of the new inventory:

```
    put "The Billionaire's Shop has something new to offer!" into
    field "Connection"
    startTimer
    go to marker ("Download")
    abort
end if
```

The first line alerts the viewer to the fact that there is new inventory for The Billionaire's Shop. The second line starts the timer we will use to track the download of the new inventory file. The third line sends the playback head to a marker labeled *Download*, which we will create later. That will be the location of the scripts that will download the new inventory. Finally, all of the scripts necessary in this Script window will have been used, so we can use the *abort* command to leave these scripts immediately and move on to new ones. The importance of using the *abort* command is that it prevents scripts that are located in the same handler, or other connected handlers, from being activated. For example, the exitFrame handler that is used to activate the checkForUpdate handler contains a script that will cause the playback head to loop in this frame, `go to the frame`. In the checkForUpdate handler, we will want to use the script `go to frame ("Download")` and not the script `go to the frame` that appears later in the exitFrame handler. The *abort* command ensures that this is what will occur by not permitting the later scripts to activate at all.

```
else
    put "You have our most current inventory." into field
    "Connection"
    go to marker ("Shop")
end if
```

If the latest version number is not greater than the current version, no update is necessary; so we need only alert the user of The Billionaire's Shop to this fact by displaying information in the Connection field. We can then let the command *go to marker ("Shop")* in the exit-Frame handler send the playback head into The Billionaire's Shop, where we can browse the current inventory.

Now that we have added the scripts that determine if a download is necessary, we can add the *downloadNetThing()* command to the checkForUpdate handler to bring the new inventory down from the network.

**8.    Do not close the Script window.**

We will be adding to the checkForUpdate handler in the next section.

## ADDING THE DOWNLOADNETTHING() COMMAND

Once the checkForUpdate handler has successfully determined that a download is necessary, we can execute the *downloadNetThing()* command. This will begin the download process that we will track with the script we will add later in this lesson.

**1.    Make the following modifications to the checkForUpdate handler.**

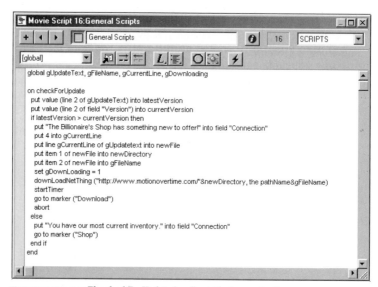

**FIGURE 10.18** *The checkForUpdate handler with changes in place.*

```
global gUpdateText, gFileName, gCurrentLine, gDownloading

on checkForUpdate
  put value(line 2 of gUpdateText) into latestVersion
  put value(line 2 of field "Version") into currentVersion
  if latestVersion > currentVersion then
    put "The Billionaire's Shop has something new to offer!"
    into field "Connection"
    put 4 into gCurrentLine
    put line gCurrentLine of gUpdatetext into newFile
    put item 1 of newFile into newDirectory
    put item 2 of newFile into gFileName
    set gDownLoading = 1
    downLoadNetThing ("http://www.motionovertime.com/"
    &newDirectory, the pathName&gFileName)
    startTimer
    go to marker "Download"
    abort
  else
    put "You have our most current inventory." into field
    "Connection"
    go to marker ("Shop")
  end if
end
```

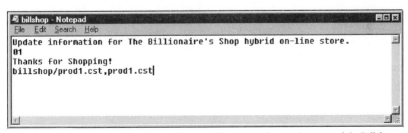

**FIGURE 10.19** *The contents of the billshop.txt file. This is the actual content of the Billshop text file and is not a script in the script window.*

```
Update information for The Billionaire's Shop hybrid on-line store.
01
Thanks for Shopping!
billshop/prod1.cst,prod1.cst
```

The name of the new inventory file is located in line four of the Billshop.txt file. Later in this lesson we will incorporate scripts that will allow The Billionaire's Shop to download multiple files. To prepare for this, we will use the global variable gCurrentLine to keep track of the line that contains the name of the file to be downloaded next. At this point we only want to download a single file, so the usefulness of gCurrentLine won't show up until later.

The second of the new lines that we have added to this script places the name and location of the new file in a local variable named newFile. The text in newFile is actually split into two parts: the directory to the file that we would like to download, and the name of the file that we would like to download. This is organized as a line of text that is separated with a comma—billshop/prod1.cst, prod1.cst. We have organized the information this way because the *downloadNetThing()* command requires the location of the text file on the network (part 1 of the text) and the name that we would like to label the downloaded file with on the hard drive (part 2 of the text). The name of the file is actually included in the directory location, but separating the text this way will make it easier to isolate the file name using Lingo, as will be demonstrated with this script. We will be using the name of the file in a script in another location, so we will use a global variable called gFileName, which will allow us to pass it on to other scripts in the movie.

The third new line of the checkForUpdate handler extracts the first part of the text in the newFile variable and places it into another variable named newDirectory. The fourth new line of checkForUpdate extracts the second part of newFile and places it into FileName.

The next line sets a global variable named gDownloading equal to 1. This variable will be used to let other scripts that we will write later know that a download is occurring. Finally, the two variables, newFile and new-Directory, will be used as the two arguments that are required by *downloadNetThing()*; the first is the name of the requested file and its location on the Internet, the second is the location and name that we would like for the file placed on the hard drive. In this case we are retrieving a file from www.motionovertime.com, naming it after the name that is located in the Billshop.txt file, and placing it in the same directory as The Billionaire's Shop. Our next step is to create the Download screen, where we will add the script that will track the download of the new inventory file.

## SETTING UP THE DOWNLOAD SCREEN

The images on the download screen will be identical to the Shop area of the Score; the only difference is that we will add a Frame script to the script channel that will track the download of the inventory files from the Internet. Currently the Shop area of the Score ends in frame 156. We will extend this to frame 158 and add a marker, which we will label Download.

1. **Extend the endpoints for all of the sprites in frame 156 to frame 158.**

   We can accomplish this by clicking and dragging each endpoint individually, or we can select all of the sprite objects in frame 156, place the playback head in frame 158, and choose Modify>Extend Sprite.

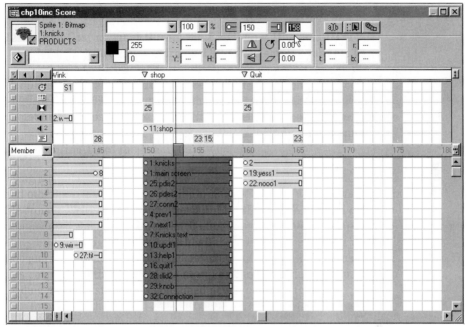

**FIGURE 10.20** *The endpoints in the Shop area of the Score dragged from frame 155 to 158.*

2. **Place a new marker in frame 158 of the Score and label it Download.**

   This will be the destination of the script we created earlier that determines if a download is necessary. Now we will place the script that will track the download of the new inventory. You will see that this marker will overlap the Quit marker. Our next step will be to use the Insert Frame command to move the Quit area of the Score to the right.

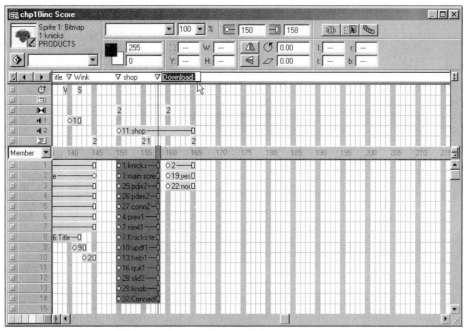

**FIGURE 10.21** *A new marker placed in frame 158 of the Score.*

3.   **Place the playback head in frame 159 of the Score.**

4.   **Choose Insert>Frames... from the Insert menu.**

     This will produce the Insert Frames dialog box, which will allow you
     to indicate how many new frames to add to the Score.

5.   **Type 5 into the entry field in the Insert Frame dialog box for the
     number of new frames to add to the Score.**

6.   **Click the button labeled OK.**

     The new frames will be added to the Score, and all of the information
     following this frame will be pushed forward.

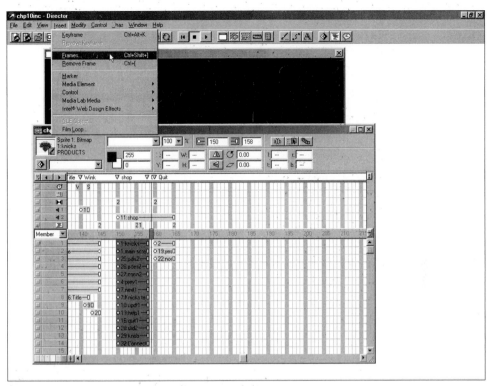

**FIGURE 10.22** *The Insert>Frames... option selected from the menus.*

## WRITING THE SCRIPT TO TRACK THE DOWNLOAD OF THE NEW INVENTORY

The download times for information from the Internet vary based upon activity on the Internet, the speed of the user's connection to the Internet, and the size of the files that are requested. To accommodate this, we will add a script that will track the download of the new inventory for a maximum of 5 minutes. The script will stop downloading if the file is successfully transferred or if the 5 minutes pass.

1.  Open the Scripts Cast, then double-click on frame 158 of the script channel in the Score. This is where we will create the exitFrame handler that will track the download.

2.  Add the following to the Script window for frame 158 in the script channel and name the script Track Download (Cast member 17).

**FIGURE 10.23** *The script in the Script window for frame 158.*

```
global gCurrentProduct, gFilename, gDownloading

on exitFrame
  if the timer < 18000 then
    if netDone() = 1 then
      if netError() = "OK" then
            set the filename of castLib "Products" = the
            pathName&gFileName
            put "The Billionaire's Shop inventory has been updated.
            Happy shopping!" into field "Connection"
      else
        netAbort()
        if netError() = "" then
          put "No update attempted." into field "Connection"
        else
          put "There was an error in the transmission of the file you
          requested." into field "Connection"
        end if
      end if
```

```
        set gCurrentProduct = 1
        set gDownLoading = 0
        set the member of sprite 1 to member (1, "products")
        set the member of sprite 8 to the name of the member of sprite
        1&&"Text"
        go to marker ("Shop")
      else
        put "Updating the inventory for The Billionaire's Shop." into
        field "Connection"
      end if
    else
      netAbort()
      put "It has taken too long to retrieve the requested information
      from the Internet." into field "Connection"
      set gCurrentProduct = 1
      set gDownLoading = 0
      set the member of sprite 1 to member (1, "products")
      set the member of sprite 8 to the name of the member of sprite
      1&&"Text"
      go to marker ("Shop")
    end if
    go to  the frame
  end
```

This script will track the download of the new inventory file with the same commands that we used earlier to track the retrieval of the Billshop.txt file. When the file is downloaded, we will use the property the fileName of CastLib to change the external file that is used to create the products Cast file by directing the Cast to link to the new file on the hard drive. This will add the updated inventory to The Billionaire's Shop. This script will then display the first product in the Products Cast. Before we test this script, we will add the scripts that will complete the programming of the Update button. We will also modify the beginSprite handlers on the product display and product description sprites so that they display temporary images while the download is occurring.

## COMPLETING THE UPDATE BUTTON

To program the Update button, we actually only need to add scripts to the exitFrame handler in frame 156 of the Score. This is the script that tracks the download of the Billshop.txt file when the Update button is pressed. We will add the scripts that will check to see if an update is necessary and then send the playback head to the Download area of the Score.

1.  **Double-click in frame 156 of the script channel in the Score.**
    *Track Text* **is the script that tracks the download of the**
    **Billshop.txt file.**

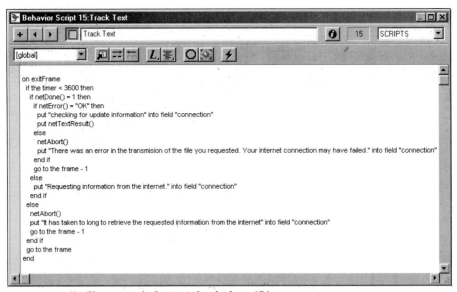

**FIGURE 10.24** *The script in the Script window for frame 156.*

```
on exitFrame
    if the timer < 3600 then
        if netDone() = 1 then
            if netError() = "OK" then
                put "Checking for update information" into field
                "Connection"
                put netTextResult()
            else
                netAbort()
                put "There was an error in the transmission of the file
                you requested. Your Internet connection may have
                failed." into field "Connection"
            end if
            go to the frame - 1
        else
            put "Requesting information from the Internet." into field
            "Connection"
        end if
    else
        netAbort()
        put "It has taken too long to retrieve the requested
        information from the Internet" into field "Connection"
        go to the frame - 1
    end if
    go to the frame
end
```

2. **Make the following modification to the script in frame 156 of the Score. Do not close the Script window when you are done. These scripts will determine if a download is necessary and will then send the playback head to the Download frame.**

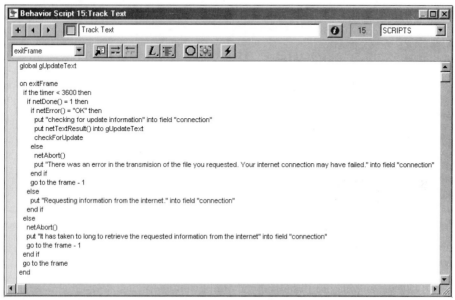

**FIGURE 10.25** *The script in the Script window for frame 156 with changes in place.*

```
global gUpdateText

on exitFrame
  if the timer < 3600 then
    if netDone() = 1 then
      if netError() = "OK" then
        put "Checking for update information" into field
        "Connection"
        put netTextResult() into gUpdateText
        checkForUpdate
      else
        netAbort()
        put "There was an error in the transmission of the file
        you requested. Your Internet connection may have
        failed." into field "Connection"
      end if
      go to the frame - 1
    else
```

```
      put "Requesting information from the Internet." into field
      "Connection"
    end if
  else
    netAbort()
    put "It has taken too long to retrieve the requested
    information from the Internet" into field "Connection"
    go to the frame - 1
  end if
  go to the frame
end
```

These new lines will check if an update is necessary and send the playback head to the appropriate frame. Let's look at the new lines one at a time.

```
put netTextResult() into updateText
```

This line uses the updateText global variable to store the text that is retrieved in the Billshop.txt file. We can then use this text to determine if a download is necessary.

```
checkForUpdate
```

This will activate the script that we created earlier in the Movie script located at Cast position 17 in the Scripts Cast. It will compare the version number in the Billshop.txt file with the version number that is in the current products Cast file and will send the playback head to the Download frame if a download is necessary.

```
go to marker (Shop)
```

If no download is necessary, we will leave the checkForUpdate handler without changing frames. The next line here will be activated and the playback head will be sent to the Shop area of the Score. With these new lines, we have added the scripts that will allow the Update button to check for any new additions to The Billionaire's Shop.

**3.    Close the Script window.**

In a moment we will test these scripts, but first let's modify the Set Product and Set Product Description behaviors.

## DISPLAYING A TEMPORARY IMAGE WHILE THE INVENTORY UPDATES

When the inventory for The Billionaire's Shop is updating, it will be useful to display a temporary image that will let the user know when the download is occurring. When the download has completed, the scripts that we have written will swap the temporary image with the first image in the new products Cast.

1. Select sprite 1 in the Shop area of the Score. This is the product display sprite.

2. Open the Internal Cast file. This Cast file contains the temporary images that we brought into this file in chapter 2.

3. Select Cast member 999 in the Internal Cast file. This is the standby image.

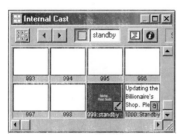

FIGURE 10.26 *Sprite 1 selected in the Score. Cast member 999 selected in the Internal Cast window.*

4. Choose Edit>Exchange Cast Members. This will switch the Knicks image Cast member that is currently displayed in channel 1 with the standby image. Now we will edit the script for the Set Product behavior.

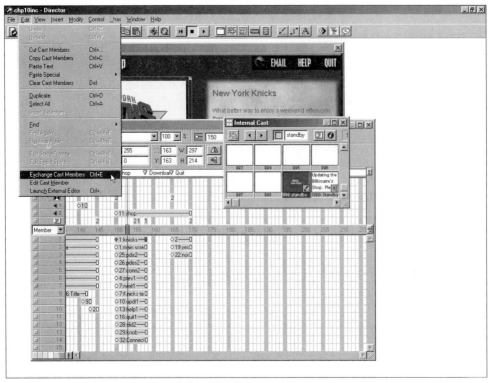

**FIGURE 10.27** *Edit>Exchange Cast Members selected.*

5.    While sprite 1 is still selected in the Score, open the behavior
      inspector.

6.    Select the Set Product behavior in the behavior inspector. Then
      click the Script Window button at the top of the behavior inspec-
      tor. This will display the script for the Set Product behavior.

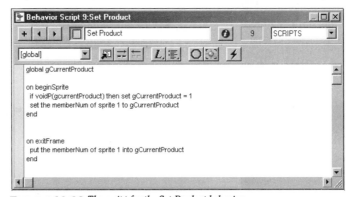

**FIGURE 10.28** *The script for the Set Product behavior.*

```
global gCurrentProduct

on beginsprite
  if voidP(gcurrentProduct) then set gCurrentProduct = 1
  set the member of sprite 1 to gCurrentProduct
end

on exitFrame
  put the memberNum of sprite 1 into gCurrentProduct
end
```

7.  **Make the following adjustments to the script for the Set Product behavior. These changes will use the gDownloading global variable that we introduced earlier in the checkForUpdate handler to determine if the Standby image should be displayed when the playback head enters this area of the Score. If a download is initiated, then the gDownloading variable is set to 1, which will cause the Standby image to be displayed.**

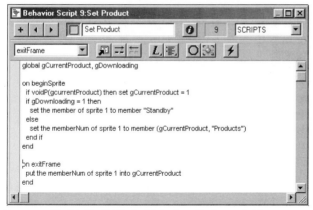

**FIGURE 10.29** *The Set Product behavior with changes in place.*

```
global gCurrentProduct, gDownloading

on beginsprite
  if voidP(gcurrentProduct) then set gCurrentProduct = 1
  if gDownloading = 1 then
    set the member of sprite 1 to member "Standby"
  else
    set the member of sprite 1 to member (gCurrentProduct,
    "Products")
  end if
end
```

```
on exitFrame
  put the memberNum of sprite 1 into gCurrentProduct
end
```

8.   Close the Script window. Next we will make similar adjustments to the product description sprite and Set Product Description behavior.

9.   Select sprite 8 in the Score. This is the product description sprite.

10.  Open the Internal Cast and select Cast member 1000. This is the standby text Cast member, which we created in chapter 2.

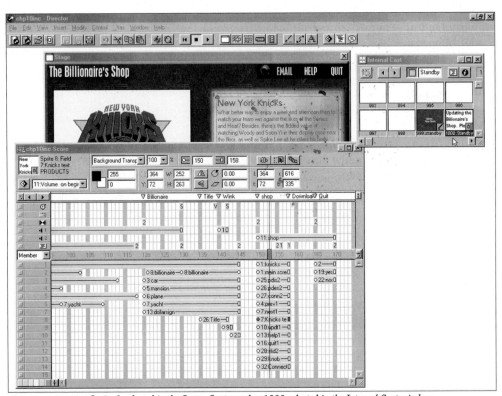

**FIGURE 10.30** *Sprite 8 selected in the Score. Cast member 1000 selected in the Internal Cast window.*

11. **Choose Edit>Exchange Cast Members. This will swap the Cast member displayed in channel 8 (Knicks text) with the standby text Cast member.**

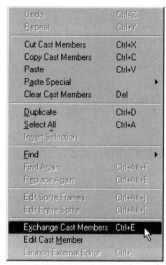

**FIGURE 10.31** *Edit>Exchange Cast Members selected.*

12. **While the sprite is still selected in channel 8, open the behavior inspector. If Set Product Description behavior is not displayed in the behavior inspector, press the + button to see the list of behaviors.**

13. **Select the Set Product Description behavior and click the Script Window button at the top of the behavior inspector. This will open and display the script for the Set Product Description behavior.**

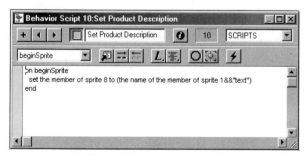

**FIGURE 10.32** *The script for the Set Product Description behavior.*

```
on beginsprite

  set the member of sprite 8 to (the name of the member of
  sprite 1&&"Text")

end
```

14. **Make the following modifications to the script for the Set Product Description behavior. These modifications will use the value in the gDownloading global variable to determine if the Standby Text image should be displayed. This will be determined by the activation of a download. Note that the gCurrentProduct global variable is not used in this behavior, because it is not referenced anywhere in the new script.**

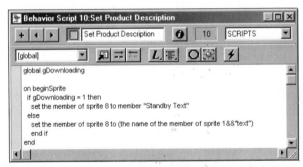

**FIGURE 10.33** *The Set Product description behavior with changes in place.*

```
global  gDownloading

on beginsprite

  if gDownloading = 1 then

    set the member of sprite 8 to member "Standby Text"

  else

    set the member of sprite 8 to (the name of the member of
    sprite 1&&"Text")

  end if

end
```

## ADDING startMovie AND stopMovie HANDLERS TO THE BILLIONAIRE'S SHOP

When we run this movie, it will update itself to the new inventory file. Remember that you must have an active connection to the Internet for the updating scripts to work. When this has been done once, the update scripts will not attempt another update until something new is added to The Billionaire's Shop. Although this is how we would like the scripts to work when we are finished, it will be helpful if the update scripts download something every time they are activated. We will add a stopMovie handler to the movie with Scripts that will revert the Products Cast to the original file each time the movie is stopped. This will cause The Billionaire's Shop to detect that a download is necessary every time the movie is played. When we are finished, we will remove these scripts so that The Billionaire's Shop will only detect an update when there actually is one available on the Internet.

We will also add a startMovie handler to the movie that will give the global variables that we are working with a starting value. This is especially important at this point because we are likely to start and stop the movie multiple times as we test it. The global variables in our scripts will have different values in them, depending upon when the movie is stopped. Adding a Script that gives these critical global variables a starting value, or *initializes* them, will ensure that we are always starting from the same starting point.

The stopMovie and startMovie handlers are event handlers that can exist only once in each movie. They must also be located in a Director Script, so we will place them in the same Script window as the checkForUpdate handler.

1.  Locate the checkForUpdate handler in the Scripts Cast window. The checkForUpdate handler is in Cast position 16, the General Scripts Cast member in the Scripts Cast window.

2.  Add the following scripts to the Script window that contains the checkForUpdate handler.

**FIGURE 10.34** *The General Scripts Cast window with changes in place.*

```
global gUpdateText, gFileName, gCurrentLine, gDownloading,
gCurrentProduct

on startMovie
  put netTextResult() into gUpdateText
  set gCurrentProduct = 1
  set gDownloading = 0
end

on stopMovie
  netAbort()
clearCache
  if the runMode = "Author" then
    set the fileName of castLib "Products" to "Products.cst"
  else
    set the fileName of castLib "Products" to "Products.cxt"
  end if
```

```
    put EMPTY into field "Connection"
    set gCurrentProduct = 1
end

on checkForUpdate
  put value(line 2 of gUpdateText) into latestVersion
  put value(line 2 of field "Version") into currentVersion
  if latestVersion > currentVersion then
    put "The Billionaire's Shop has something new to offer!"
    into field "Connection"
    put 4 into gCurrentLine
    put line gCurrentLine of gUpdatetext into newFile
    put item 1 of newFile into newDirectory
    put item 2 of newFile into gFileName
    set gDownLoading = 1
    downLoadNetThing ("http//www.motionovertime.com/
    "&newDirectory, the pathName&gFileName)
    startTimer
    go to  marker ("Download")
    abort
  else
    put "You have our most current inventory." into field
    "Connection"
    go to marker ("Shop")
  end if
end
```

**3.   Close the Script window.**

A startMovie handler is activated each time a movie begins playing; a stopMovie handler is activated each time a movie stops playing. Here the startMovie handler will give the gUpdateText, gCurrent-Product, and gFileName global variables a starting value. These are the variables that can confuse this movie if it is stopped and restarted in mid-playback. The stopMovie handler will use the *netAbort()* and *clearCache* commands to make certain that there are no lingering network operations or inventory files from previous updates in memory, then it will use the *clearGlobals* command to clear any globals that are currently in memory, this will solve the problem we pointed out in chapter 9 of Help Balloons appearing in the Connection Reminder screen if the movie is stopped and rewound. Next, *stopMovie* will set the file name used for the products Cast back to the original Cast file that we added in chapter 6. The *runMode* command that is used in the if...then statement is used to determine if Director is playing through a projector or through the Director application. We are adding this command because in chapter 11 we will be working with projectors and other Director movie file formats (such as Shockwave movies) that can only be played by a projector or through a browser. Shockwave movies cannot be played through the Director application. The other file type that we will be working with in chapter 11 is protected files, which cannot be opened in Director once they are converted. This prevents them from being changed by other Director users. The last 2 lines of the stopMovie handler will clear the Connection display field to reset it for the next run through and then reset the gCurrentProduct variable so that the next time we play the movie, the product that is displayed in The Billionaire's Shop will be the first in the inventory.

In a moment we will test these new scripts, but first we will make four final adjustments to the movie. We will add a single line to the Next Product and Previous Product behaviors, so that they cannot be used to change the product display and product description sprites while the movie's inventory is updating. We will also change the command that is used to activate the Quit button so that it *will* work properly while an update is occurring.

4.  **Make certain that the playback head is in the Shop area of the Score, then select the Previous Product arrow button on the Stage. We will change the behavior on this button first.**

5.  **Open the behavior inspector and select the Previous Product behavior, then click the Script Window button at the top of the behavior inspector. When the behavior inspector is opened while the Previous Product arrow button sprite is selected, we will be able to see a list of the behaviors that are applied to this sprite; this will consist of the Button and Previous Product behaviors. When the Previous Product behavior is selected and the Script window is opened, the Button behavior displayed in the behavior inspector will disappear as a selection. This will also be true for any other behaviors that we might add to this sprite later.**

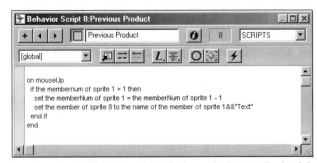

**FIGURE 10.35** *The Script window displaying the Previous Product behavior.*

```
on mouseUp me
  if the memberNum of sprite 1 > 1 then
    set the memberNum of sprite 1 = the memberNum of sprite 1 - 1
    set the member of sprite 8 to the name of the member of sprite
    1 && "Text"
  end if
end
```

6. **Make the following additions to the script for the Previous Product behavior. This adjustment will prevent this script from activating while an update is occurring.**

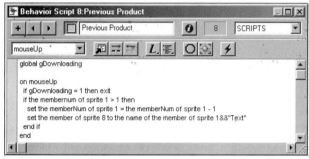

**FIGURE 10.36** *The Script for the Previous Product behavior with the changes in place.*

```
global gDownloading

on mouseUp
  if gDownloading = 1 then exit
  if the memberNum of sprite 1 > 1 then
    set the memberNum of sprite 1 = the memberNum of sprite 1 - 1
    set the member of sprite 8 to the name of the member of sprite
    1 && "Text"
  end if
end
```

7. **Close the Script window. Now we will make the same adjustment to the script for the Next Product behavior.**

8. **Select the Next Product arrow button on the Stage, then return to the behavior inspector. The Next Product behavior will be displayed in the behavior inspector.**

9. **Select the Next Product behavior in the behavior inspector, then click the Script Window button at the top of the behavior inspector. This is where we will add the final adjustment before we test our new scripts.**

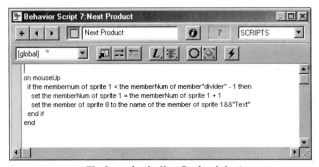

**FIGURE 10.37** *The Script for the Next Product behavior.*

```
on mouseUp me
  if the memberNum of sprite 1 < the memberNum of member
  "divider" - 1 then
    set the memberNum of sprite 1 = the memberNum of sprite 1+1
    set the member of sprite 8 to the name of the member of
    sprite 1&&"Text"
  end if
end
```

10.  **Make the following additions to the script for the Next Product behavior. This will prevent the Next Product behavior from being activated during an update. Now we will modify the Quit button.**

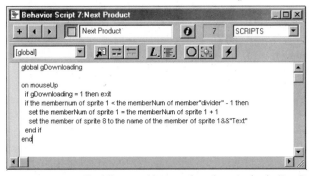

**FIGURE 10.38** *The following addition made to the script for the Next Product behavior.*

```
global gDownloading

on mouseUp
  if gDownloading = 1 then exit
  if the memberNum of sprite 1 < the memberNum of member
  "divider" - 1 then
    set the memberNum of sprite 1 = the memberNum of sprite 1+1
    set the member of sprite 8 to the name of the member of
    sprite 1&&"Text"
  end if
end
```

11. Select the Quit button on the Stage, then return to the behavior inspector. We will modify the Quit Button behavior.

12. Select the Quit Button behavior in the behavior inspector, then click the Script Window button at the top of the behavior inspector. Currently this behavior uses the *go to* command to send the playback head to the Quit area of the Score. This sufficed when the Quit button could only be activated from a single location because we would only need to use the command *go to marker ("Shop")* to send the playback head back to its original location. However, if there is an update occurring, the playback head will be in frame 158, which is the Download area of the Score. We can use another command, the *Play* command, to send the playback head to the Quit area of the Score. The *Play* command only requires the command *Play Done* to send the playback head back to where ever the playback head originated.

**FIGURE 10.39** *The script for the Quit Button behavior.*

```
on mouseUp me
  go to marker ("quit")
end
```

We will need to make just one more adjustment before testing this movie.

13. **Make the following modification to the script for the Quit Button behavior.**

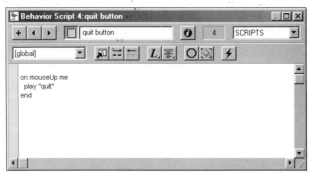

**FIGURE 10.40** *The Script for the Quit Button behavior with the changes in place.*

```
on mouseUp me
  play "quit"
end
```

14.   **Close the Script window. Now we will add the** *Play Done* **command to the No button in the Quit area of the Score.**

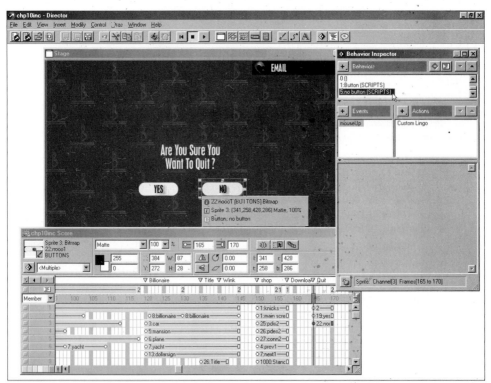

**FIGURE 10.41** *The No button selected on the Stage in the Quit area of the Score. The behavior inspector is visible.*

15. Move the playback head to the Quit area of the Score and select the No button on the Stage, then return to the behavior inspector. We will modify the No Button behavior in the behavior inspector.

16. Click the Script Window button at the top of the behavior inspector. This will display the script for the No Button behavior.

```
on mouseUp me
  go to ("Shop")
end
```

**FIGURE 10.42** *The script for the No Button behavior.*

17. Make the following adjustment to the script for the No Button behavior. This script will now return the playback head to where ever it originated when the Quit button is clicked. Now we can test the movie.

```
on mouseUp
  play done
end
```

**FIGURE 10.43** *The following modifications made to the script for the No Button behavior.*

18. Close the Script window. Now comes the big test.

19. Make certain that you are currently connected to the Internet. You must have a live connection for the Download scripts to work properly.

20. Rewind and play the Movie. Navigate to the Shop area of the Score. Does it indicate that a download is available? If it does, then the movie is working. Now you can click to scroll through the new products. The first five products are the same as the previous inventory, with three new additions. The first update for The Billionaire's Shop is a simple one, so that it happens as quickly as possible while we are working with the lessons in these chapters. Other updates will include products that animate and are interactive, along with tutorials about how to add these features to other projects. Be patient; if the movie doesn't work immediately, review the scripts to be certain that everything is typed correctly.

21. Stop the movie. The stopMovie handler will switch the file that is used for the Products Cast back to the original file. This will allow us to reuse the Download scripts as we continue. The stopMovie handler is not executed when the movie is stopped accidentally or if the *Halt* command is executed. To prevent any potential error messages, we must force the stopMovie handler to execute when the *Help* command is executed when a user chooses to quit out of The Billionaire's Shop.

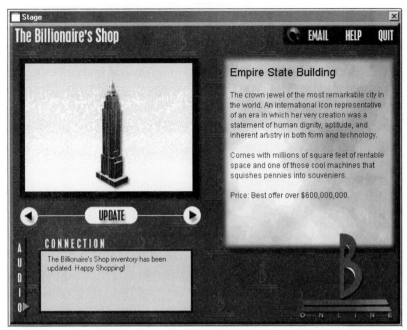

**FIGURE 10.44** *The Billionaire's Shop interface with one of the new products displayed.*

22. Move the playback head to the Quit area of the Score. We will change the behavior on the Yes button that would be clicked to confirm that we would like to quit out of The Billionaire's Shop.

23. Select the Yes button on the Stage and click the Behavior Inspector button on the sprite overlay. This will open the behavior inspector, where we can open the script we would like to change.

24. Select the Yes Button behavior in the behavior inspector, then the click the Script Window button at the top of the behavior inspector. This will display the Halt script.

**FIGURE 10.45** *The Yes Button behavior.*

```
on mouseUp me
  halt
end
```

25.  **Make the following modifications to the script for the Yes But-
     ton behavior. This change will force the stopMovie handler to
     execute when the Yes button is clicked.**

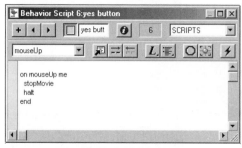

**FIGURE 10.46** *The Yes Button Behavior script with changes in place.*

```
on mouseUp me
  stopMovie
  halt
end
```

26.  **Close the Script window.**

Now we will add scripts that will allow updates that include multiple files.

**NOTE**  If the movie stops in any way other than activating the *Stop* command from
the Control Panel menu—or by using a keyboard shortcut—the *stopMovie*
command will not be activated, and a scripting error in The Billionaire's
Shop will result during authoring. A scripting error is an example of what
can stop a movie and not activate the stopMovie handler.You can cause
the scripts in the stopMovie handler to activate by forcing the stopMovie
handler to execute through the Message window. This is the window that
can be used to trace scripts and test Lingo commands. We can also use
this window to activate Lingo handlers in our movies by typing the name of
the handler and pressing the Return key on the Macintosh keyboard or the
Enter key on the Windows keyboard.

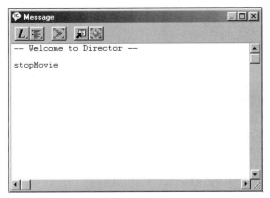

**FIGURE 10.47** *The Message window with stopMovie typed into it.*

## EXPANDING THE SCRIPTS TO DOWNLOAD MULTIPLE FILES

Currently the Download scripts will only download a single file. This might satisfy the majority of inventory downloads that we will add to The Billionaire's Shop, but in the future we will want to download more than one file. To accomplish this we will need to modify the scripts to accommodate the download of more than one file. This will require a modification to the exitFrame handler in frame 158 of the script channel in the Score.

1.  **Double-click in frame 158 of the script channel. This will display the Track Download behavior, which is the script that we want to change.**

```
global  gCurrentProduct, gFilename, gDownloading

on exitFrame
  if the timer < 18000 then
    if netDone() = 1 then
      if netError() = "OK" then
        set the filename of castLib "Products" = the
        pathName&gFileName
        put "The Billionaire's Shop inventory has been updated.
        Happy shopping!" into field "Connection"
      else
        netAbort()
        if netError() = "" then
          put "No update attempted" into field "Connection"
        else
          put "There was an error in the transmission of the file
          you requested." into field "Connection"
        end if
```

```
    end if

    set gCurrentProduct = 1

    set gDownLoading = 0

    set the member of sprite 1 to member (1, "products")
```

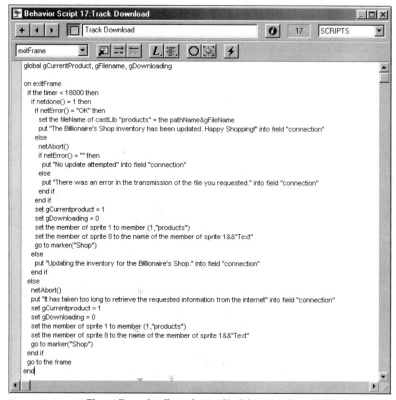

FIGURE 10.48 *The exitFrame handler in frame 158 of the script channel of the Score in Cast position 17 of the Scripts.cst.*

```
    set the member of sprite 8 to the name of the member of
    sprite 1&&"Text"

    go to marker ("Shop")

  else

    put "Updating the inventory for The Billionaire's Shop."
    into field "Connection"

  end if

else

  netAbort()

  put "It has taken too long to retrieve the requested
  information from the Internet" into field "Connection"

  set gCurrentProduct = 1
```

```
        set gDownLoading = 0
        set the member of sprite 1 to member (1, "products")
        set the member of sprite 8 to the name of the member of
        sprite 1&&"Text"
        go to marker ("Shop")
    end if
    go to  the frame
end
```

2.  **Make the following modifications to the script in frame 158 of the
    Score. Note that we are adding two new global variables to this
    window that must be included at the top of the Script window.**

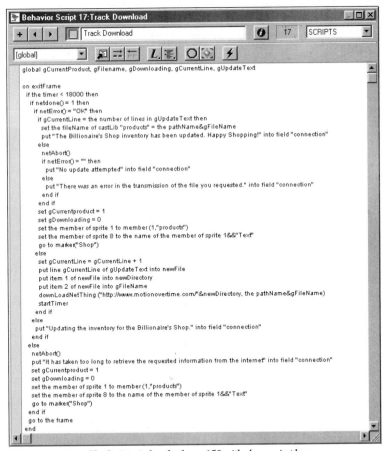

**FIGURE 10.49** *The Script window for frame 158 with changes in place.*

```
global  gCurrentProduct, gFilename, gDownloading,
gCurrentLine, gUpdateText
on exitFrame
  if the timer < 18000 then
    if netDone() = 1 then
      if netError() = "OK" then
        if gCurrentLine = the number of lines in gUpdateText
        then
          set the filename of castLib "Products" = the
          pathName&gFileName
          put "The Billionaire's Shop inventory has been
          updated. Happy shopping!" into field "Connection"
        else
          netAbort()
          if netError() = "" then
            put "No update attempted" into field "Connection"
          else
            put "There was an error in the transmission of the
            file you requested." into field "Connection"
          end if
        end if
        set gCurrentProduct = 1
        set gDownLoading = 0
        set the member of sprite 1 to member (1 , "products")
        set the member of sprite 8 to the name of the member of
        sprite 1&&"Text"
        go to marker ("Shop")
      else
        set gCurrentLine = gCurrentLine + 1
        put line gCurrentLine of gUpdateText into newFile
        put item 1 of newFile into newDirectory
        put item 2 of newFile into gFileName
        downLoadNetThing ("http://www.motionovertime.com/
        "&newDirectory, the pathName&gFileName)
        startTimer
      end if
    else
      put "Updating the inventory for The Billionaire's Shop."
      into field "Connection"
    end if
  else
    netAbort()
    put "It has taken too long to retrieve the requested
    information from the Internet" into field "Connection"
    set gCurrentProduct = 1
```

```
        set gDownLoading = 0
        set the member of sprite 1 to member (1,"products")
        set the member of sprite 8 to the name of the member of
        sprite 1&&"Text"
        go to marker ("Shop")
    end if
    go to the frame
end
```

Updates for The Billionaire's Shop will always be contained in an external Cast file, which we will connect to the Products Cast file in the Shop. Any additional files that we will download will be external files that will be connected to the new Cast file. For example, we might want to include an external Director movie that will add new interactivity to The Billionaire's Shop. We have designed these scripts so that they will download all of the extra files first, then download the new Cast file. When this new Cast file has been downloaded, then we will connect it to the Products Cast.

Let's take a closer look at the new scripts:

```
if gCurrentLine = the number of lines in gUpdateText then
```

The number of lines in gUpdateText gives us the total number of lines in the Billshop.txt file that is stored in the gUpdateText global variable. The last line of this file will always be the name of the new Cast file; so by checking to see if we have reached the last line in the file we are also checking to see if the entire download is complete. This will work for any number of files in a single update because if there is even only one file, it will still be the last line in gUpdateText and will therefore be the equivalent of the number of lines in gUpdateText.

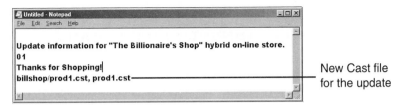

New Cast file
for the update

**FIGURE 10.50** *The content of Billshop.txt. The arrow indicates the name of the new Cast file to be used in the update.*

```
Update information for "The Billionaire's Shop" hybrid on-line store.
01
Thanks for Shopping!
billshop/prod1.cst,prod1.cst
```

If we have not yet reached the end of the text that is stored in the gUpdateText global variable; this will be a signal that there is more that needs to be downloaded. Our first step is to advance to the next line in the gUpdateText global variable, which is accomplished by the following three lines:

```
else
  set gCurrentLine = gCurrentLine + 1
  put line gCurrentLine of gUpdatetext into newFile
```

Next we must separate the directory name and the file name so that we can prepare the appropriate parameters for the *downloadNetThing()* command.

```
put item 1 of newFile into newDirectory
put item 2 of newFile into gFileName
```

The next step is to download the file that is listed at this new location, which occurs in this line:

```
downLoadNetThing ("http//www.motionovertime.com/
"&newDirectory, the pathName&gFileName)
```

Because this will trigger another download, we will want to extend the time limit, which is accomplished in the last lines:

```
  startTimer
end if
```

This will reset the timer and give the script another five minutes to download the new file. With the addition of these scripts, The Billionaire's Shop will be capable of downloading multiple files.

3.    **Close the Script window.**

## USING THE PRELOADNETTHING COMMAND

In this lesson we used the *downloadNetThing()* command to retrieve the new inventory from the Internet for The Billionaire's Shop. This technique will directly create a new file on the hard drive, which we can then use in a Director presentation. Another alternative is to download files into memory in the background while a user is performing other actions, then present the files when it is appropriate. We can use *downloadNetThing()* to download files to the hard drive in the background, or we can use *preload-NetThing*—which does not create a new file, but stores the new files in memory alone. This permits faster access and also leaves the hard drive untouched after the download is completed. We chose *downloadNetThing()*

because we will later remove the Update Every Time feature of The Billionaire's Shop and have it only update when there are new files available. This will require that any files that were previously downloaded remain available on the hard drive for later viewing. With *preloadNetThing* we will lose any downloaded files when the application is exited.

Here is an example of how the *preloadNetThing* command is used in a Lingo Script:

```
preloadNetThing "www.motionovertime.com/(file to be downloaded)"
```

Note that this command does not require the second argument that identifies the location for the downloaded file on the local hard drive, as the *downloadNetThing()* command does. The information included in the quotation marks is the URL where the desired document is located.

## SUMMARY

Using the *downloadNetThing()* command, we are able to retrieve images and other non-text files from the Internet just as if we were downloading a file from a Web site or through email. The *downloadNetThing()* command requires two arguments to work: the first is the URL that leads to the file at its location on a network or on the Internet, and the second is the location and name that the file should assume on the local hard drive. We used this command to update the inventory of The Billionaire's Shop by downloading a new Cast file that contained new product images.

To produce the fastest results from the Hybrid Lingo that we used to download media from the Internet, we used the information provided in the text file that we retrieved using the *getNetText()* command that we added in chapter 9. This text file contains the most current version number of the inventory for The Billionaire's Shop, which we compared to the version number stored in the Products Cast. If the number in the retrieved text file was greater than the number in the Cast file, then we initiated the scripts that produced the download. The *getNetText()* command is capable of retrieving information from the Internet faster than the *downloadNetThing()* command, so we can more readily identify whether it is necessary to take the time to download new files before we choose to do so.

The current update for The Billionaire's Shop consists of a single file; future updates might require the download of more than one file. This will be indicated by the number of files that are named in the text file that we retrieve using the *getNetText()* command. By checking to see that we have downloaded all of the files named in the text file line by line, we can make certain that we have downloaded everything needed for the new update before we make any changes to The Billionaire's Shop.

When the new file was downloaded, we used the *fileName of castLib* command to switch the external file used for the Products Cast to the Cast file that was just downloaded. We identified the Cast file that we wanted the new file to replace by using the name of the Cast as it appears in the Director file. In this case we replaced the Products Cast. Although in this we used the *fileName of CastLib* command to switch an entire Cast file, we can also use this command to switch the files used for individual external Cast members by using the *fileName of member* command.

Another method for changing the media in a Director file is to import new media using the *importFileInto* command. This command requires that we identify the file we would like to import and the location in the Cast where we would like it to appear. Although we did not use this command for The Billionaire's Shop, it is a remarkably useful command for extending the flexibility of Director presentations.

An alternative to the *downloadNetThing()* command is the *PreloadNetThing* command, which will retrieve a file from the Internet, but will not create a new file on the hard drive. This allows a Director presentation to be updated with new media from the Internet but will not produce any permanent changes to the movie. This is a useful command to use in cases where changes and updates occur more frequently than in The Billionaire's Shop because it requires that the download commands be executed each time new media files are required, as opposed to creating a permanent copy on the hard drive that can be used multiple times after being successfully downloaded once.

## QUESTIONS

1. In this lesson, why was it necessary to use the *fileName of castLib* command instead of the *fileName of member* command?

2. What are the two arguments that are required for the *downloadNetThing()* command?

3. Why does the *PreloadNetThing* command only require a single argument?

4. Why did we use the *getNetText()* command to determine if a download is required?

5. What would be the best Hybrid Internet command to use for an online news magazine that has articles that change frequently? Which would be best for a digital art gallery that changes only once a month? Explain.

## EXERCISES

1. Using the Message window, use *downloadNetThing()* to download the file named sample.bmp from the Web site. Remember that the URL for this bitmap is http://www.motionovertime.com/billshop/sample.bmp. Remember that you must have an open connection to the Internet to successfully use *downloadNetThing()*. Download the file to any location on your hard drive.

2. Using the same script that you used in exercise 1, download sample.bmp again. This time, change the name of the file that is created on your hard drive to another name of your choice.

3. Create a movie that has a linked bitmap Cast member. Now use the script that you used in exercise 2 to download, and replace this external graphic with sample.bmp. Be certain to rename the downloaded bitmap with the name of the current linked bitmap. This should replace the Cast member with the sample.bmp file if done correctly.

# CHAPTER 11

# PACKAGING AND DELIVERY

# 11 Packaging and Delivery

**In this chapter, you will learn how to:**

- Create a projector
- Use a stub projector
- Create protected Director movie and Cast files
- Discern between playback through Director and playback through a projector using Lingo
- Comment out Lingo scripts so that they are not activated
- Add an email feature to The Billionaire's Shop
- Create a Shockwave movie
- Create an HTML document with an embedded Shockwave movie

Once a Director presentation has been completed, it must be converted into a file format that can be delivered to other computers for playback. One method is to convert the movie into a projector, which is a self-contained application that can be activated by double-clicking. Another method is to convert the movie into a Shockwave file, which can be played through a Web browser such as Netscape Navigator or Microsoft Internet Explorer.

A projector contains all of the data that is necessary to play a movie back on any machine. The only major consideration is that a projector for Macintosh must be created with the Macintosh version of Director, and a projector for PC must be created with the Windows version of Director. Projectors can only be played on the platform that they were created on.

Shockwave files are Director files that have been compressed and prepared for playback through the Web. The browser must have the Shockwave extensions installed in order to be capable of playing back Shockwave files. This is because, unlike projectors, Shockwave files do not contain the code that permits their playback. This is one of the reasons that Shockwave files are much smaller then the original files and the projector versions of the original files. In this chapter we will create a projector and use other preparation methods for delivery of The Billionaire's Shop. We will also go through the process of creating a Shockwave movie that we will embed into a Web page.

Now that we have completed the development of The Billionaire's Shop, we can prepare it for delivery to the public. To do this, we must take into consideration that most people we would like to deliver this project to will not own or know how to use Director, so we must have an alternative method of playback. This alternative method is called a projector, which is a self-contained application that allows Director presentations to be played without the presence of Director software.

A projector contains the parts of Director that play back a movie, but does not contain the intricacies of the rest of the application. The Score, Cast, and rest of Director's interface are left behind. The only part of the interface that is included is the Stage, which is the display area of the presentation area as described in chapter 2.

Any Director movie can be converted into a projector, allowing any movie to be played outside of the Director application. Projectors cannot be opened in Director, so you must always retain a copy of the original movie if any changes need to be made later. Creating a projector will not overwrite the original file, so we just need to be certain that we don't delete the original file accidentally.

Many projects developed in Director require the presence of multiple Director files. A game that presents the user with multiple rooms to explore can be developed by using a separate movie for each room. Clicking on a door that leads from one room to another actually activates a script that jumps from one movie to another using the script *go to movie moviename*. This design allows for greater organization, because the elements of each room can be isolated into their own environments. A design like this would require the delivery of a single projector that launches the first room that is entered; the rest of the rooms would be delivered in their original form as Director movies. The one projector serves the role of launching and permitting the playback of all of the movies.

## USING A STUB PROJECTOR

During the development process, it is usually necessary to test how a presentation will run from a projector as opposed to running through the Director application. This is useful for determining memory requirements for your application. In this session we will create a *stub projector*, which is a projector created with a Director movie that contains little more than a script that jumps to the first movie of our presentation.

1.   **If it is not already open, launch Director. We are going to create the movie that we will use to create a projector.**

2. Chose File>New>Movie. This is to make certain that we are working with a completely empty file.

3. Double-click in frame 1 of the Score in the script channel. This will open the Script window for frame 1.

4. Type the following script in the Script window for frame 1. This script will cause this movie to jump over to the main movie for The Billionaire's Shop.

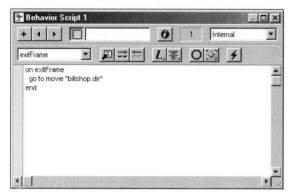

**FIGURE 11.01** *The Script window for frame 1.*

```
on exitFrame
  go to movie "billshop.dir"
end
```

> The name of the Director file that contains The Billionaire's Shop is called **NOTE** billshop.dir in this chapter. This is different from earlier chapters, where we used the chapter number followed by cmp or inc. This is because this is the last lesson chapter; it is where we will create the final version of The Billionaire's Shop.

5. Close the Script window. This movie is ready to be saved.

6. Choose File>Save. This will present the dialog box that we can use to name the movie. Navigate to the Billshop Director application on the hard drive.

7. Name the movie Launcher.dir. Make certain that the file will be placed in the Billshop directory.

8. Click Save. Now we can create the stub projector.

## CREATING THE PROJECTOR

Creating a projector is a very simple process that begins with a selection from the File menu. Then we can choose the file that we would like to convert into a projector. It is not necessary to open the file that is to be converted into a projector.

We have included a completed projector in the following directory on the CD-ROM: ...Lessons/Chaptr11/BackUp. Locate this file and copy it to the Billshop directory on the hard drive.

1.   **Choose File>Create Projector. This will open the Create Projector dialog box.**

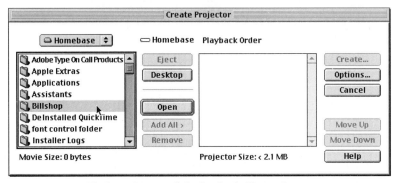

**FIGURE 11.02** *The Create Projector dialog box for the Macintosh.*

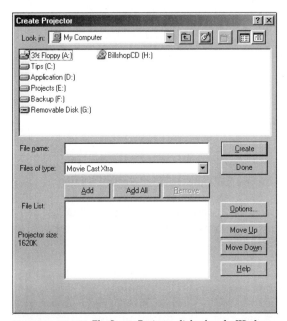

**FIGURE 11.03** *The Create Projector dialog box for Windows.*

2. Locate and select the file named Launcher.dir that we created earlier in the Billshop directory.

3. Click the button labeled Add in the center of the Create Projector dialog box. This will add the file named Launcher.dir to the list of files to be included in the projector on the right side of the dialog box. Multiple files can be added to a projector, but this is not necessary because we can have one movie jump to another using Lingo. Later we will learn how to protect Director movies so that they cannot be opened by other Director users.

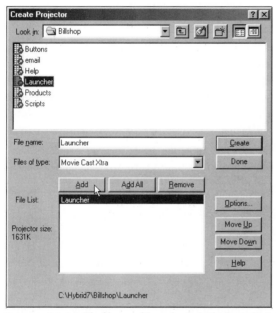

**FIGURE 11.04** *The file named Launcher.dir in the Create Projector dialog box.*

4. Click the button labeled Options. This will open the Projector Options dialog box, where we can make additional settings for the new projector.

> Projectors for Windows can only be created using Director for Windows, **NOTE**
> and Macintosh projectors can only be created through the Macintosh
> version of Director.

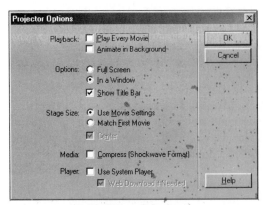

**FIGURE 11.05** *The Options dialog box.*

5.  Choose the checkbox beside the words "Animate in Background" in the Playback options area. This prevents the presentation from being paused if the user chooses to jump to another application while the movie is playing. If we initiate an update while the movie is playing, we can move to another application while we wait for the update to complete.

    We do not need the setting Play Every Movie because our projector will only have one movie in it.

6.  Choose the checkbox beside the words "Full Screen" in the Options area. This will cause Director to cover the entire desktop of the computer screen, even on screens that are larger than the Stage area of the movie we are playing. Areas of the screen that are not covered by the Stage will be colored with our color selection for the Stage. In the Windows version of Director, we have a second option here called "In a window"; this will play the presentation in a window complete with a Close box and the ability to minimize and maximize.

7.  Choose the Use Movie Settings radio button and the Center checkbox in the Stage Size area. The first options here—Use Movie Settings and Match First Movie—only have an effect if the size of the Stage changes from movie to movie. This isn't the case here, so we will just leave these settings at the default. The second setting, Center, will make certain that the presentation will always play at the center of any screen that it plays on. There is one extra option available on Macintosh computers, "Reset Monitor To Match Movie's Color Depth"; this will cause the user's monitor settings in their control panels to change to the movie's settings. It isn't necessary to cause any change to

the user's computer for The Billionaire's Shop, so we will leave this setting unselected.

Another option on the screen is Compress, which will apply Shockwave compression to the files in the projector to reduce file size. Projectors created with Shockwave compression take a little longer to produce because the compression is added to the file as the projector is being compiled. There is also some additional time required for the launching of Shockwave projectors because the files need to be decompressed before they can be viewed. The compression and decompression is controlled by an Xtra that is included in Director's Xtras folder.

8.    **Choose the checkbox beside "Use System Temporary Memory" (Macintosh only). This option will use the available system memory that is left in the computer if the partition that has been allocated to the projector is full. This will help ensure optimum performance for the projector. This option will not work if Virtual Memory is turned on. Memory is already managed this way on Windows machines, so this option is unnecessary.**

These are all of the options that we will select for this projector. You may have noticed that we chose not to apply Shockwave compression to the media in the movie. This is useful for reducing the size of a presentation by using the same compression methods that Director uses for Shockwave movies to be played over the Internet. We do not need this option here because the projector we are creating uses a Director movie that contains no images or sounds, so applying Shockwave compression will have no effect. If we were working with a file that contained media, we would have selected this option.

**FIGURE 11.06** *The Projector Options window with the above options for the Macintosh.*

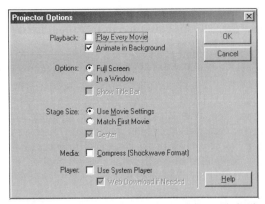

**FIGURE 11.07** *The Projector Options window with the above options for Windows.*

9.  **Click the button labeled OK. We're ready to take the final step to create the projector.**

10. **Click the button labeled Create in the Create Projector dialog box. This will produce a dialog box in which we can choose where to save the projector.**

11. **Name the projector MyShop in the text entry area labeled Save Projector as... on the Macintosh or Filename on the PC. Make certain that you are currently in the Billshop directory on your hard drive.**

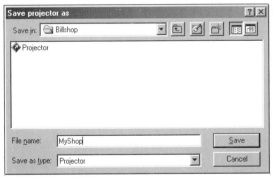

**FIGURE 11.08** *The Save Projector dialog box with the name MyShop in the text entry area.*

12. **Click the button labeled Save.**

    A progress bar will appear indicating that the projector is being created and the Network Xtras are being included. After the progress bar completes its cycle, you will see that there is a new file in the

Billshop directory named MyShop. This is the new executable that can be used to play The Billionaire's Shop on other computers.

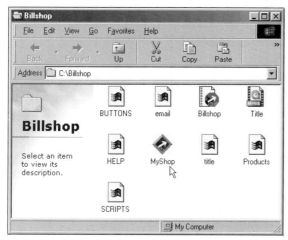

**FIGURE 11.09** *The MyShop projector in the Billshop directory on the hard drive.*

## ABOUT THE SHOCKWAVE PLAYER

The Shockwave player is software that will allow a Shockwave movie to be played without the use of a browser or the Shockwave plug-in. This makes it possible to create and deliver small Shockwave projector files in place of a standard projector on other machines. Because a Shockwave movie requires either a browser with plug-ins or the Shockwave player, it might be necessary for an end user to download the player from Macromedia's Web site before they can view your movie.

To accommodate this, the Projector Options window has a checkbox, Use System Player, that will indicate that you would like to create a projector that will use the Shockwave player instead of creating the larger file that a standard projector results in. This will cause the file to look for the Shockwave player when it is launched. A second checkbox, Web Download If Needed, will cause the file to launch a browser and download the Shockwave player if it is not readily available. Projectors created with the Shockwave Player option will not play without the Shockwave player.

## TESTING THE NEW PROJECTOR

Playback of a Director presentation through a projector is identical in appearance to playback through the Director application. The primary difference is that projector playback does not permit access to the menus and other interface features that allow the modification of the presentation. We can observe this difference in playback by double-clicking on the projector that we have created.

**NOTE**   Playback through a projector is called Runtime mode; playback through the Director application is called Authoring mode.

1.   **Quit Director. Doing this will free up the memory that Director is currently using and will help make certain that our test would work even while Director is inactive. You can quit out of Director by choosing File>Quit (Mac) or File>Exit (Windows).**

2.   **Make certain your connection to the Internet is active. This will be necessary to test all of the features in The Billionaire's Shop. If you are not connected to the Internet, then click the No button on the first screen when you are asked if you are currently connected to the Internet.**

3.   **Locate and double-click on the projector we created earlier and named MyShop. The executable file will be in the directory named Billshop on the hard drive. When the executable file is double-clicked, The Billionaire's Shop will begin playback.**

     If your screen is larger than the display area of the Stage, the area around the Stage will become black, blocking out any background images on your computer. The only functionality available here will be the features that we programmed into The Billionaire's Shop. We can see that the interface will check for an update to the inventory, download the new file, and provide us with access to the new products. All other functionality will also be active: the rollover activity of the buttons; the Help feature; and clicking on the Quit button will now quit completely out of The Billionaire's Shop. (In Authoring mode the Halt command that we programmed into the Quit button only stopped Director, but did not quit out of the Director application.)

4.   **When you are finished playing The Billionaire's Shop, click the Quit button on the main screen of the shop.**

     This will quit out of The Billionaire's Shop. We can also press Command/Control + Period (.). Now we will add some finishing touches.

## ACCELERATING DOWNLOAD TIMES USING SHOCKWAVE

We can speed up the rate of download for updates to The Billionaire's Shop by downloading Shockwave files instead of Director files. Shockwave files have compression applied to them that dramatically reduces file size. The smaller file sizes will take less time to download from the Internet. We will work more with Shockwave later in this chapter and examine how Shockwave files are incorporated into Web sites.

Although Shockwave files are created within the Director application, they cannot be reopened in Director. This is because part of a Director movie is removed when it is converted to a Shockwave movie (one of the ways in which Shockwave reduces file size). For this reason, Shockwave movies cannot be edited in Director. Any new changes to a Shockwave movie will need to be made in the original Director movie and then re-shocked, replacing the old Shockwave movie. Once a Shockwave movie is created, it can be played through a Web browser using the Shockwave plug-in, or it can be played through a projector. Now that we are using a projector for The Billionaire's Shop, we can use Shockwave files to update the inventory instead of the full and editable Cast files that we have been using. This will mean that the inventory will be much smaller and therefore will require less time to download.

We will be adding a Script to the billshop.dir file that will download Shockwave files for the inventory in The Billionaire's Shop. We can drag the completed version of this file to the Billshop directory on the hard drive from Lessons/chaptr11/Starter/Billshop.dir on the CD-ROM. The other files in The Billionaire's Shop are also in this directory, so we can choose to copy the entire directory over. It is only necessary to copy the billshop.dir file if you have not followed all of the steps in this book up to this point. After you have copied the file you can follow the steps in this section to view the new scripts, then continue from the section titled "Testing for Accelerated Download Times."

**FIGURE 11.10** *The directory on the CD-ROM: Lessons/chaptr11/Starter/Billshop.dir.*

1.  Launch Director and open the billshop.dir movie. You can locate
    the Billshop.dir file along the following path on the Billshop CD:
    Lessons/chaptr11/starter/Billshop.dir.

2.  Open the Score. The scripts we will modify are located on the
    Yes button in the first screen and on the Update button.

3.  Move the playback head to frame 2 of the Score. This frame con-
    tains the sprites used for the screen that asks for a confirmation
    of a connection to the Internet.

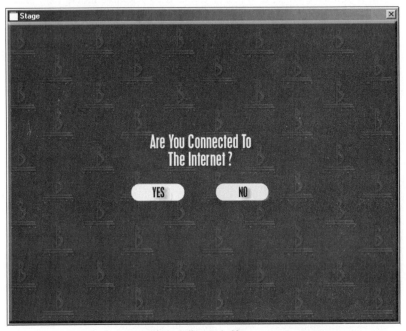

**FIGURE 11.11** *The first screen of The Billionaire's Shop.*

4.  Select the Yes button on the Stage. We will access the Request
    Text behavior from the behavior inspector.

5.  Click the Behavior Inspector button on the sprite overlay for the
    Yes button. This will open the behavior inspector.

6.  Select the Request Text behavior in the Behavior Inspector win-
    dow.

7.  Click the Script Window button at the top of the behavior inspec-
    tor. This will open the Script window and display the script that
    was used to create the Request Text behavior.

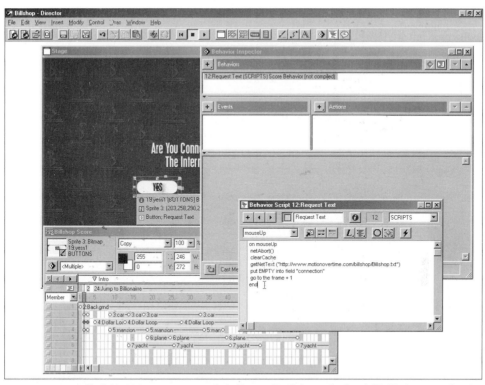

**FIGURE 11.12** *The behavior inspector open, with the Request Text behavior displayed. The Yes button is selected on the Stage, with its sprite overlay visible. Also visible on the Stage is the open script window, with the Request Text behavior script.*

```
on mouseUp
  netAbort()
  clearCache
  getNetText ("http://www.motionovertime.com/billshop/Billshop.txt")
  put EMPTY into field "connection"
  go to the frame + 1
end
```

**8.    Modify the script for the Request Text behavior as follows.**

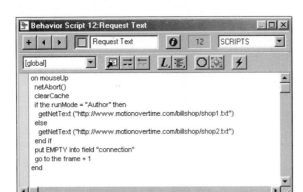

**FIGURE 11.13** *The Request Text behavior with changes in place.*

```
on mouseUp
  netAbort()
  clearCache
  if the runMode = "Author" then
    getNetText ("http://www.motionovertime.com/billshop/
    shop1.txt")
  else
    getNetText ("http://www.motionovertime.com/billshop/
    shop2.txt")
  end if
  put EMPTY into field "connection"
  go to the frame + 1
end
```

This change will cause the *getNetText()* command in the Request
Text behavior to download different text files from the Internet,
based upon how the Director movie is playing. The script will be able
to tell how the movie is being played by using the *RunMode* function,
which can distinguish between playback through a projector, as a
Shockwave movie, or through the Director application. If the movie
is playing through the Director application (*RunMode = Author)*, then
*getNetText()* will request a file named Shop1.txt, which contains file
names that can be played from within Director for the shop's inventory. If the Director movie is played through a projector (*RunMode =
Projector*), then *getNetText()* will request a file named Shop2.txt,
which contains the file names of the Shockwave versions of the files
for the shop. Because only projectors and Internet browsers are
capable of playing Shockwave files, this script will make certain

that the only time Shockwave files will be used is when The Billion-aire's Shop is playing as a projector or as a Shockwave movie.

9. **Close the Script window. Now that we have modified the Request Text behavior, we can change the behavior that is on the Update button.**

10. **Open the Score if it is not currently open. We will access the Update button in the Shop area of the Score.**

11. **Move the playback head to the Shop area of the Score.**

12. **Select the Update button on the Stage (sprite 9). The Update behavior is listed on the sprite overlay for the Update button. If the behavior inspector is still open, it will list the two behaviors that are currently on the Update button.**

13. **Open the behavior inspector if it is not currently open. Make certain that the Update button is still selected so that the behavior inspector lists the Update behavior.**

14. **Select the Update behavior in the behavior inspector. We will make the change to the script that was used to create the Update behavior**

15. **Click the Script Window button at the top of the behavior inspector. We will add the same script here that distinguishes between playback from a projector and playback though the Director application.**

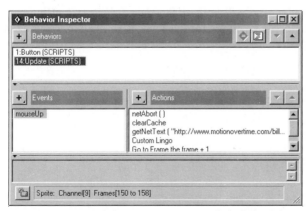

**FIGURE 11.14** *The behavior inspector open, with the Update behavior displayed.*

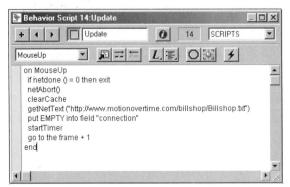

**FIGURE 11.15** *The Script window open showing the current Update behavior scripts.*

```
on mouseUp
  if netDone() = 0 then exit
  netAbort()
  clearCache
  getNetText ("http://www.motionovertime.com/billshop/
  Billshop.txt")
  put EMPTY into field "connection"
  startTimer
  go to the frame + 1
end
```

16. **Make the following modifications to the script for the Update behavior. Now the Update button will cause The Billionaire's Shop to download Shockwave files if it is played through a projector. Besides adding the scripts that will distinguish between playback through Director and the Director application, we are also replacing the line *if netDone() = 0 then exit* with a script that used the gDownloading global variable. This achieves the same result, but conforms to the standard that we have set in other scripts.**

**FIGURE 11.16** *The script for the Update behavior with changes in place.*

```
global gDownLoading

on mouseUp
  if netdone () = 0 then exit
  if gDownLoading = 1 then exit
  netAbort()
  clearCache
  if the runMode = "Author" then
    getNetText ("http://www.motionovertime.com/billshop/shop1.txt")
  else
    getNetText ("http://www.motionovertime.com/billshop/shop2.txt")
  end if
  put EMPTY into field "connection"
  startTimer
  go to the frame + 1
end
```

## 17.   Close the script window.

Now we will test the new scripts to see if there is a noticeable difference in download times.

## TESTING FOR ACCELERATED DOWNLOAD TIMES

To test the difference in time between downloading the Shockwave version
of the inventory files and the standard Director files, we need to play The
Billionaire's Shop from a projector. This will allow the new scripts that we
have added to choose the Shop2.txt file, which contains the Shockwave
file names.

1.  Quit Director.

2.  Establish a connection to the Internet.

3.  Locate and open the Billshop directory.

4.  Launch the file named MyShop.

5.  When you are presented with the first screen, click the Yes button to indicate a live connection to the Internet and allow for file downloads.

    When the presentation reaches the end of the opening animation, the Shop will download the Shockwave version of the inventory. The Shockwave version of the inventory is less than half the size of the original file, so it takes less than half the time to download. The speed of your connection to the Internet has a direct bearing on how long it takes for the download to occur, so the time can vary on different machines. When the download is complete, you will see that the presentation is identical to the non-Shockwave version. As mentioned earlier, Shockwave files cannot be opened within Director, so the only time that we will be able to see the Shockwave version is when we are using the projector version. When the movie is stopped, the stopMovie handler will switch the file that is used for the Products Cast back to the sample Cast file that we have been using in earlier lessons.

6.  Click the Quit button.

We are almost finished developing The Billionaire's Shop. Our next step is to add an email feature.

## ADDING AN EMAIL FUNCTION TO THE BILLIONAIRE'S SHOP

Director's Hybrid Internet Lingo functions are designed to only request and download information from the Internet along with the functions that track the progress and status of a network request. Besides calling on text, the *getNetText()* command can be used to activate text-based programs that are located on servers, such as CGI scripts and active server pages, which are the same scripts that are used by Web developers to incorporate the ability of sending email messages from Web pages. Using this capability, we can use *getNetText()* to activate an email script from The Billionaire's Shop. Information from Director, such as text, can be sent to a CGI script or an active server page in this manner. The CGI script or active server page can then be used to re-route the text to another location as an email message. In this session we will add the screen to The Billion-aire's Shop that we saw in the completed version in chapter 1, which will allow you to send a message to us here at Motion Over Time.

1.    Locate and open the folder named Starter on the CD-ROM that is located in the directory Lessons/chaptr11/. This directory contains the entire Shop. We only need to transfer two of the files to work with what we have developed so far.

2.    Copy the files named email.cst and billshop.dir from the CD-ROM to the directory named Billshop on the hard drive. These are the only new files that we need, although we can also copy and replace all of the files on the hard drive with the files in this directory.

### ADDING THE EMAIL CAST FILE

We will link the file named email.cst file to the billshop.dir file. Then we will add the new screen along with the buttons that will give the new screen functionality.

1.    Launch Director if it is not already open.

2.    Locate and open the file named billshop.dir in the Billshop directory on the hard drive.

3.    Choose Modify>Movie>Casts. All of the current Cast will be listed here. We will add the email.cst file.

4.    Click the button labeled Link.... We can use this window to locate the email.cst file.

5.    Locate and select the file named email.cst in the Billshop directory on the hard drive.

6.    Click the button labeled Open. This will add the email.cst file to the list of Cast files used in The Billionaire's Shop.

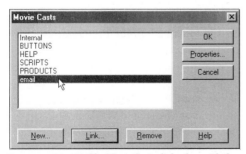

**FIGURE 11.17** *The Movie Casts dialog box with the email.cst file added.*

**7.  Click the button labeled OK.**

Now we can construct the new email screen.

## CREATING THE EMAIL AREA OF THE SCORE

The email area of the Score will consist of only a single screen. We will
create a new area of the Score to assemble this screen.

1.  **Open the Score. We will add a new marker to frame 175 of the
    Score.**

2.  **Add a new marker to frame 175 of the Score and name it email.
    This is the target that we will use to branch to the email area of
    the Score.**

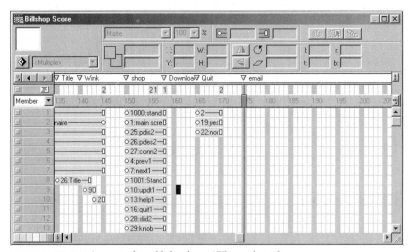

**FIGURE 11.18** *A new marker added to frame 175 named email.*

3.  **Open the email Cast window. This Cast file contains most of the
    media that we will need for the new screen.**

4.  **Drag Cast member 1 of the email Cast to frame 175 of channel 1
    in the Score. This is the background for the email area of the
    Score.**

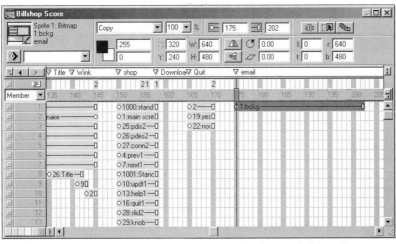

**FIGURE 11.19** *Cast member 1 of the email Cast dragged to frame 175 of channel 1.*

5.   Drag Cast members 2, 3, 4, 5, and 6 of the email Cast to chan-
     nels 2, 3, 4, 5 and 6 of frame 175 in the Score. Set the ink effect
     for each of these new sprites to background transparent. These
     are the Name, Address, Email Address, and Questions/Com-
     ments text entry fields that we will use to create email files, as
     well as the connection text field that we will use to display the
     status of the email transmission.

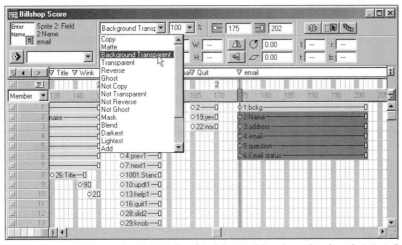

**FIGURE 11.20** *Cast members 2, 3, 4, 5, and 6 of the Email Cast dragged to channels 2, 3, 4, 5
and 6 of frame 175 in the Score.*

6.  Position and resize the sprites in channels 2 to 6 of frame 175
    on the Stage as they appear in figure 11.21. This will place the
    text entry sprites in the appropriate areas on the Stage.

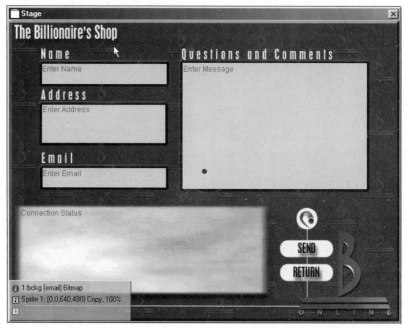

**FIGURE 11.21** *The sprites in channels 2 to 6 of frame 175 positioned and resized to fit in the display areas defined in the background.*

7.  Open the Buttons Cast. This Cast window contains the buttons
    we will place on the email screen.

8.  Drag Cast member 31 (the Return1 button) and Cast member 34
    (the Send1 button) from the Buttons Cast to channels 7 and 8 of
    frame 175 in the Score. We will later add the button that will
    jump to this screen. We will program the Return button to go
    back to the shop, and the Send button to send the email file.

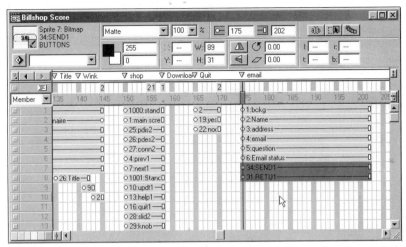

**FIGURE 11.22** *Cast members 31 and 34 of the Buttons Cast dragged to channels 7 and 8 of frame 175.*

9.  Position sprite 7 and 8 on the Stage as they appear in figure 11.23 and select Matte from the Ink menu. This will complete the placement of all of the sprites in the email screen.

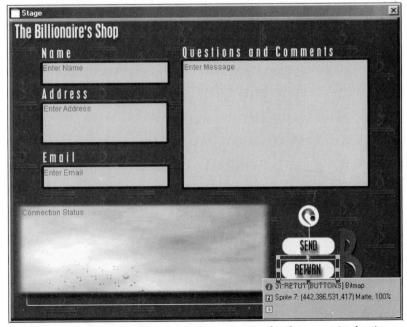

**FIGURE 11.23** *Sprites 7 and 8 on the email screen positioned in their appropriate locations.*

10. Drag the endpoints for the sprites in channels 1 to 8 in the email area of the Score to frame 180. This will have the sprite objects here span only 6 frames. Now we will place the scripts for this area of the Score.

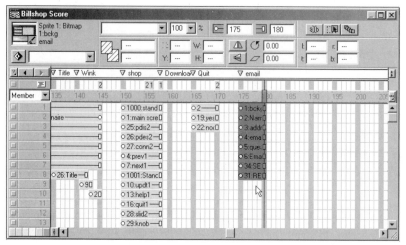

**FIGURE 11.24** *The endpoints for the sprites in channels 1 to 8 in the email area of the Score dragged to frame 180.*

11. Open the Scripts Cast. This Cast contains the script that we will use to program the buttons.

12. Drag Cast member 1 (the Button behavior) directly onto the Return and Send buttons on the Stage. These buttons will now react to mouse activity just like the others in the interface.

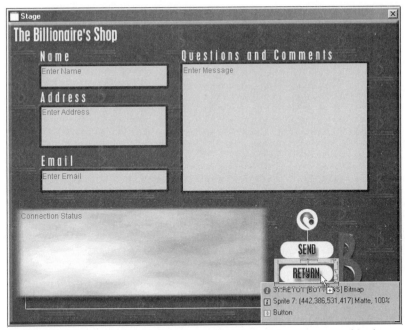

**FIGURE 11.25** *Cast member 1 (the Button behavior) dragged onto the Return and Send buttons on the Stage.*

13. Open the Internal Cast. This is where the Loop in Frame behavior is located.

14. Drag Cast member 23 of the internal Cast (the Loop in Frame behavior) directly into frame 179 of the script channel. This behavior will keep the playback head in frame 179 until the playback head is sent elsewhere. The rest of the scripts we will need are located in the email Cast window.

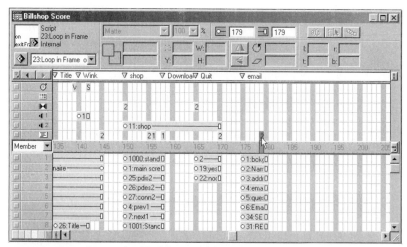

**FIGURE 11.26** *Cast member 23 of the internal Cast (the Loop in Frame behavior) dragged into frame 179 of the script channel.*

15. **Open the Email Cast window.**

16. **Drag Cast member 7 from the Email Cast (the Return behavior) directly onto the Return button on the Stage. This behavior will send the playback head back to the Shop from the email screen.**

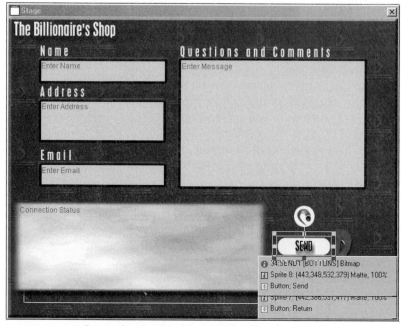

**FIGURE 11.27** *Cast members 7 and 8 of the Email Cast (the Return and Send behaviors) dragged onto the Return and Send buttons on the Stage.*

17. Drag Cast member 8 from the Email Cast (the Send behavior) directly onto the Send button on the Stage. This behavior will activate the script that will send the information on the email screen as an email message using *getNetText()*. This behavior will then send the playback head to the next frame where we are about to place a script to track the progress of the email's transmission.

18. Drag Cast member 9 from the Email Cast (the email Track behavior) directly into frame 180 of the script channel. This behavior will track the progress of the email transmission and will display information about the transmission in the connection field on the email screen. Next we will add a transition to the beginning of the email area of the score to make the jump to it more interesting. We can use the transition Cast member in position 12 of the Email Cast window.

19. Drag Cast member 12 from the Email Cast window to frame 175 of the transition channel in the Score. We will see this transition now when the playback head enters this frame. We have completed the development of the email screen. Our first step is to add the Logo button, which will be used to send us to the email area of the Score. Our second step is to extend the background sound for the Shop to the email area of the Score.

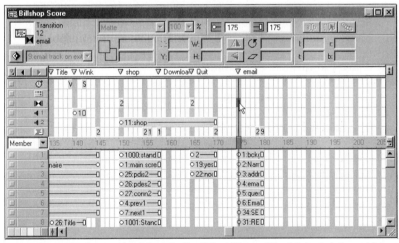

**FIGURE 11.28** *Cast member 9 from the Email Cast (the email Track behavior) dragged into frame 180 of the Script channel, and the transition in Cast position 10 of the Email Cast dragged into frame 175 of the Transition channel.*

20.  Drag the endpoint for the sound in sound channel 2 of the Score from frame 170 to frame 180. This will extend the sound to the email area of the Score.

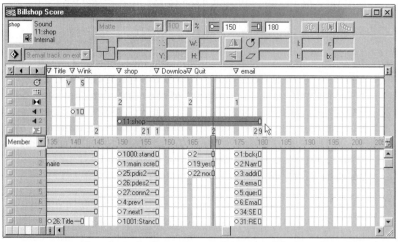

**FIGURE 11.29** *The endpoint for the sound in sound channel 2 of the Score dragged from frame 170 to frame 180 of the Score.*

### ADDING THE LOGO BUTTON

Now that we have created the email screen, we can add the button that we will use to access it from other areas of The Billionaire's Shop. The button we will use is the Motion Over Time logo, which is Cast member 37 in the Buttons Cast.

1.  Open the Buttons Cast window.

2.  Drag Cast member 37 from the Buttons Cast window (the Logo1 graphic) to frame 150 of channel 15 in the Score. This will place the logo button in the last channel of the Shop area of the Score.

3.  Place the Logo1 image on the Stage as it appears in figure 11.30 and set the sprite duration to frames 150 to 158. Our next step is to program the Logo1 button.

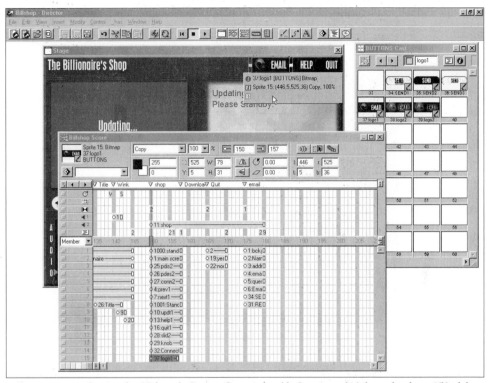

**FIGURE 11.30** *Cast member 37 from the Buttons Cast window (the Logo1 graphic) dragged to frame 150 of channel 15 and positioned in the appropriate location on the Stage.*

4.    Open the Scripts Cast window. We will use the Buttons behavior for this button.

5.    Drag Cast member 1 from the Scripts Cast window (the Button behavior) directly onto the Logo1 image on the Stage. Now this button will react to mouse activity just as the other buttons in our interface do. It will even react to the Help feature by producing a Help Balloon image when the Help feature has been activated. Next we will add the script that will cause the logo button to jump to the email area of the Score. For convenience we have already included this behavior in the Email Cast window.

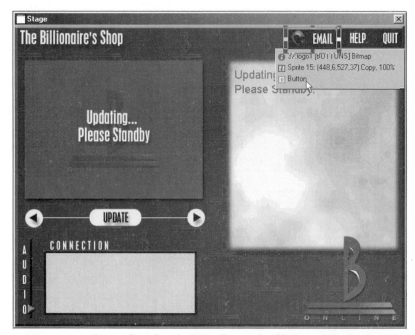

**FIGURE 11.31** *Cast member 1 from the Scripts Cast window (the Button behavior) dragged onto the Logo1 image on the Stage.*

6.   Open the Email Cast window.

7.   Drag Cast member 11 from the Email Cast window (the Email behavior) directly onto the Logo1 image on the Stage. This script will send the playback head to the email area of the Score. Now that the new button is programmed we will make it available in all appropriate areas in The Billionaire's Shop.

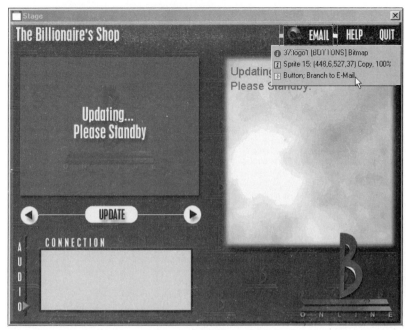

**FIGURE 11.32** *Cast member 11 from the Email Cast window (the Branch to Email behavior) dragged directly onto the Logo1 image on the Stage.*

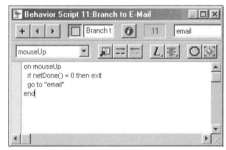

**FIGURE 11.33** *The Open Script window displaying the Lingo script for the Branch to Email behavior.*

8.  Drag the endpoint for the sprite located in channel 15 from frame 158 to frame 170. This will make the Logo1 button available in the Shop and Quit area of the Score. Now we can test the new email feature.

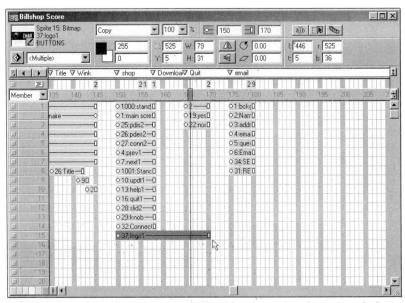

**FIGURE 11.34** *The endpoint for sprite 15 dragged from frame 158 to frame 170 in the Score.*

## TESTING THE NEW EMAIL FEATURE

The email feature that we have added to The Billionaire's Shop uses the *getNetText()* command to activate a CGI script that is located on the Motion Over Time server. This CGI script will then reroute the information that has been sent to it from Director to the Motion Over Time email account, the same email account that can be accessed from our Web site. Although this feature is not built into Director, it is a testament to Director's capability for endless growth and flexibility. Let's test the new feature.

1.  Log on to the Internet. As with the other Hybrid scripts that we have worked with, the email scripts that we have added require a live connection to the Internet to function properly.

2.  Rewind and play The Billionaire's Shop. We will go through the opening animation, the Shop will update its inventory, and then we will come to the Shop screen.

3.  Click the Email button on the Stage. This will send us to the email area of the Score.

4.  Type your information into the text entry fields. Under Questions and Comments, feel free to send us any questions you have about Director. Be certain to include your email address so that we can respond to you.

5.   When you have finished your entries, click the Send button. The connection field will display the progress of the email transmission and will eventually display the information "Your email has been sent!"

The new email feature works. Now we can add the finishing touches that will complete The Billionaire's Shop.

## PREPARING THE BILLIONAIRE'S SHOP FOR FINAL DELIVERY

We have successfully completed The Billionaire's Shop; however, there are certain features that we must change before the Shop is ready for delivery. One feature to change is the names of the text files that are requested with the *getNetText()* command, which are test files that always result in the same update files for instructional purposes. We will change these names to the files that are regularly updated, so that we can see new updates to The Billionaire's Shop as they are added. The other feature that we will change is the script in the stopMovie handler, which will always revert the inventory Cast file back to the original Cast file. If this file is not changed, it will result in a download every time the movie is played because there will always be an update available. This was also for instructional purposes. By removing this script we will cause The Billionaire's Shop to only update when there is actually a new file to be updated. If the shop is current, then it will continue to use the current inventory until a different inventory is introduced. There are some other modifications that we will make to the *stopMovie* handler that will allow it to be used when we protect the files later in this chapter. Protecting Director movie files and Casts prevents other Director users from changing your files and is usually one of the last things performed to prepare a project for delivery.

1.   Launch Director.

2.   Locate and Open the file named Billshop.dir. If you have copied your files to your hard drive, then locate the Billshop.dir file where you have placed it; otherwise, continue using the file in the following directory on the CD-ROM: Lessons/Chaptr11/ Starter.

3.   Move the playback head to frame 2 in the Score. This is the first screen in The Billionaire's Shop.

4.   Select the Yes button on the Stage. This is the button that uses the Request Text behavior.

5.  Click the Behavior Inspector button on the sprite overlay for the
    Yes button. This will open the behavior inspector where we can
    access the Request Text behavior.

6.  Select the Request Text behavior in the behavior inspector, then
    click the Script Window button at the top of the behavior inspec-
    tor. This will open the script window and display the script that
    is used to create the Request Text behavior.

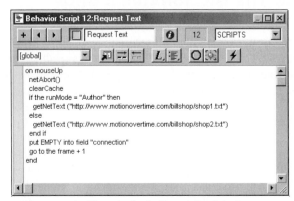

**FIGURE 11.35** *The script for the Request Text behavior.*

```
on mouseUp
  netAbort()
  clearCache
  if the runMode = "Author" then
    getNetText ("http://www.motionovertime.com/billshop/
    shop1.txt")
  else
    getNetText ("http://www.motionovertime.com/billshop/
    shop2.txt")
  end if
  put EMPTY into field "connection"
  go to the frame + 1
end
```

7.  Modify the script for the Request Text behavior as follows.
    This change will cause the Request Text behavior to download
    text files that contain the most current updates of The Billion-
    aire's Shop.

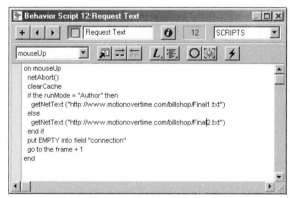

**FIGURE 11.36** *The script for the RequestText behavior with changes in place.*

```
on mouseUp
  netAbort()
  clearCache
  if the runMode = "Author" then
    getNetText ("http://www.motionovertime.com/billshop/
    Final1.txt")
  else
    getNetText ("http://www.motionovertime.com/billshop/
    Final2.txt")
  end if
  put EMPTY into field "connection"
  go to the frame + 1
end
```

8.  Close the Script window. Our next step is to make a similar change to the Update behavior.

9.  Move the playback head to the Shop area of the Score. We can access the Update button in this frame.

10. Click directly on the Update button. The sprite overlay for this button will appear, and the behavior inspector will display the two behaviors that are currently applied to this sprite.

11. Choose the Update behavior in the behavior inspector, then click the Script Window button at the top of the behavior inspector. This will display the script that is used to create the Update behavior.

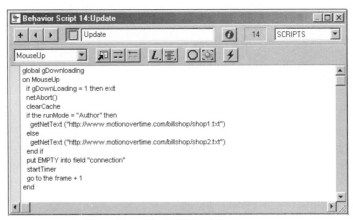

**FIGURE 11.37** *The script used for the Update behavior.*

```
global gDownLoading

on mouseUp

  if gDownLoading = 1 then exit

  netAbort()

  clearCache

  if the runMode = "Author" then

    getNetText ("http://www.motionovertime.com/billshop/
    shop1.txt")

  else

    getNetText ("http://www.motionovertime.com/billshop/
    shop2.txt")

  end if

  put EMPTY into field "connection"

  startTimer

  go to the frame + 1

end
```

12. **Make the following modifications to the Update behavior. These changes will cause the Update behavior to request the same final text files. Our last step is to remove the script in the stopMovie handler.**

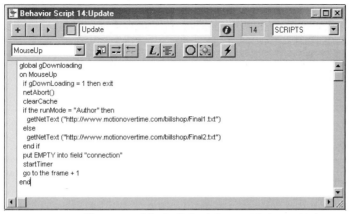

**FIGURE 11.38** *The script used for the Update behavior with changes in place.*

```
global gDownLoading
on mouseUp
  if gDownLoading = 1 then exit
  netAbort()
  clearCache
  if the runMode = "Author" then
    getNetText ("http://www.motionovertime.com/billshop/
    Final1.txt")
  else
    getNetText ("http://www.motionovertime.com/billshop/
    Final2.txt")
  end if
  put EMPTY into field "connection"
  startTimer
  go to the frame + 1
end
```

**13.  Close the Script window.**

With this change we can complete the development of The Billionaire's Shop.

## PROTECTING MOVIE AND CAST FILES

As we have seen in the development of The Billionaire's Shop, there is plenty of room to develop personal style, such as how you organize your Cast files or how you use naming conventions in scripts. Planning, design, and development of a project comprise an art-form that developers might want to keep confidential. One way to accomplish this is to *protect* the files that are used in the presentation. This is the process of converting the files in your project into files that cannot be opened with Director. In this session we will protect the movies and Casts of The Billionaire's Shop.

> **NOTE**  Protected files can only be opened and played through projectors. They will lose all capability of being viewed through the Director applications. This rule applies to files that have Shockwave compression applied to them.

**TABLE 11.01** *Table showing which format can open different Director files.*

| Format | Unprotected Files | Protected Files | Shockwave Files |
|---|---|---|---|
| Director | Yes | No | No |
| Projector | Yes | Yes | Yes |
| Shockwave | No | No | Yes |

1.  Locate and open the Billshop directory on the hard drive. When we protect the files in The Billionaire's Shop, we will need to back up our original files so that they are not overwritten by the locked versions that we will create when they are protected. Our first step is to create a new directory where we will back up the original files.

2.  Create a new directory in the Billshop directory and name it Back Up. This is where we will back up our original files.

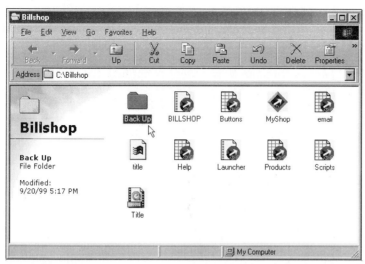

**FIGURE 11.39** *The Back Up directory in the Billshop directory on the hard drive.*

3. Drag the file named Launcher.dir into the directory named Back Up. This is the only file we will not be converting into a protected file. The MyShop projector will not be affected, because it is not a Director movie or Cast file.

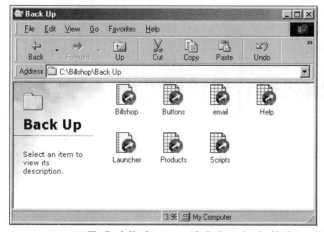

**FIGURE 11.40** *The Back Up directory, with the Launcher.dir file dragged into it.*

4. Drag a copy of the Title.mov movie into the Back Up directory. This is the digital video file that we added to the project in an earlier lesson. We need a copy of it in every directory that the Shop will play in; otherwise, the movie will ask for it when it is launched. You can copy the file over by holding down the Option

key(Macintosh)/Ctrl key (Windows) while you drag the file over. We will not be protecting this file, but we will need it to play the files in this directory (see figure 11.40).

5.    **Launch Director.** Now we will go through the steps of protecting the files in The Billionaire's Shop. It is not important to open a specific Director file for this process.

6.    **Choose Xtras>Update Movies... This will open the Update Movies dialog box.**

7.    **Choose the Protect radio button in the Action area.** This will indicate that we are interested in protecting the files that we will choose. This dialog box can also be used to convert files created in earlier versions of Director into Director files by selecting the Update radio button. The last option, Convert to Shockwave Movie(s), can be used to apply Shockwave compression to multiple files. Shockwave files can be played through projectors just as protected files can; we will demonstrate this later in this lesson. Our next step is to choose the directory where we will back up the original files.

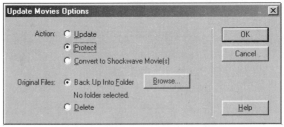

**FIGURE 11.41** *The Update Movies dialog box, with Protect selected. No backup folder has been selected yet.*

8.    **Locate and open the directory we created earlier and named Back Up.** This directory should be located in the Billshop directory on your hard drive.

9.    **Click the button labeled Select Folder.** This will select the directory named Back Up for the original files. You will see that the selection is reflected in the area labeled Back Up Into Folder.

**NOTE**  You will only see the beginning and end parts of the directory to your selected backup folder, because the area available for displaying the directory in the dialog box is limited.

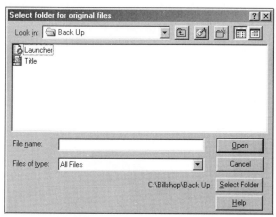

**FIGURE 11.42** *The Select Folder for Original Files dialog box, with the Back Up directory open.*

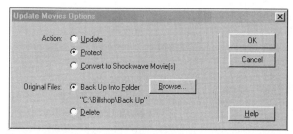

**FIGURE 11.43** *The Update Movies dialog box, with the Back Up directory selected for the original files.*

10. Click the button labeled OK. This will open the Choose Files dialog box, where we can select the files that we would like to protect.

11. Locate and open the Billshop directory on your hard drive. If you have been working with the files directly on the CD-ROM, then locate the files in chaptr11/Starter. We want to convert all of the files that remain in this directory.

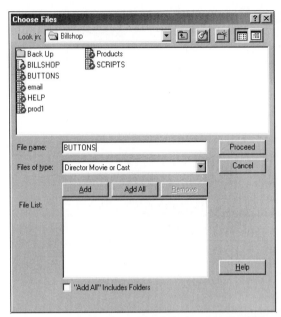

**FIGURE 11.44** *The Choose Files dialog box, with the Billshop directory selected.*

12.   **Click the button labeled Add All. All of the remaining files in the
      Billshop directory will be added to the lower half of the dialog
      box. We can also choose to select each file individually and
      select the button labeled Add. As the files are added, they will be
      removed from the upper area of the dialog box and added to the
      Selected Files: (Macintosh) File List: (Windows) area at the bot-
      tom of the dialog box.**

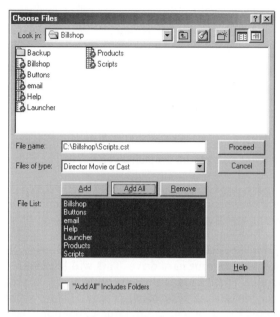

**FIGURE 11.45** *The Choose Files dialog box, with the files in the Billshop directory added to the File List section.*

13.  Click the button labeled Proceed in the Choose Files dialog box. We will be presented with a warning window that reminds us that we are about to create protected files that cannot be edited. We are also reminded that the original files will be saved into the Back Up directory.

14.  Click the button labeled Continue. The will produce the Updating Movies and Casts dialog box. A progress bar will show the status of the entire update. All of the files in The Billionaire's Shop will be protected through this process.

---

The extension at the end of the file names of protected files is .dxr for **NOTE** movies and .cxt for Cast files. By default, any Lingo script in a projector that references another movie will look for and open the unprotected/ non-Shockwave version of the movie if it is available (this is the editable, or Authoring, version). Specific Lingo scripts need to be added to a projector to force it to open a protected movie. Once a movie is protected, it can no longer be opened and edited using the File>Open menu command.

---

15.  Choose File>Quit (Macintosh) File>Exit (Windows) to exit Director.

We will now play The Billionaire's Shop with the newly protected files, using the projector that we created earlier.

## PLAYING THE PROTECTED VERSION OF THE BILLIONAIRE'S SHOP

Once Director movies are converted into protected files, they can no longer be played through the Director application. Protected files can, however, be played through a projector. In this session we will use the projector we created earlier, MyShop, to play the protected version of The Billionaire's Shop.

1.  **Make certain your connection to the Internet is active. This will allow us to test the Hybrid functions of the protected files.**

2.  **Locate and double-click the projector named MyShop in the Billshop directory on your hard drive. This will launch the protected version of The Billionaire's Shop because the unprotected version is not in the same directory any more. (More about this in the sectioned titled "About the runMode Function," later in this chapter.)**

3.  **When you have finished playing The Billionaire's Shop, click the Quit button, then exit The Billionaire's shop.**

Congratulations! We have completed our journey to build The Billionaire's Shop. New updates to the inventory will be added from time to time, and we will be certain to make other interesting lessons available soon at **http://motionovertime.com.**

## MORE ON THE runMode FUNCTION

Earlier in this chapter we used the *runMode* function in our update scripts to determine if The Billionaire's Shop was playing through a projector or through the Director application. The *runMode* function is an excellent tool to use for authoring and testing your projects in different playback environments. The basic description of the *runMode* function is that it checks for how director movies are played: Author = Director, Projector = Projector, and Plugin = Shockwave or other plug-in method (such as ActiveX). The example in figure 11.46 uses the *runMode* function to check to see if we are using Director as a playback method, in which case it will open MyGame.dir. Otherwise the script will check to see if a projector is the playback method, in which case the protected version of MyGame will play. In the final case, *plugin*, the Shockwave version of the movie, will be

> The protected version of The Billionaire's Shop behaves precisely as the editable version does. Although the Lingo in the projector that we created is written to open the file named billshop.dir, it will still open the movie named billshop.dxr. This is because, although the .dir version of the movie is not available in this directory, the projector found another Director file type named Billshop and took this option. Although this might be convenient for most instances, there might be times when you will want to have the unprotected and protected versions of the same movies share the same directory. In this case, the projector will always open the .dir version of the movies first, unless we add Lingo that tells it to do otherwise. This is not an issue for The Billionaire's Shop, so we will not need to change these scripts in the Launcher.dir movie.

**NOTE**

played. Another playback method and value for the *runMode* function is Java, which is a Director movie converted into a Java applet.

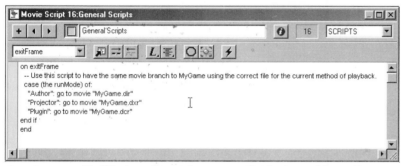

**FIGURE 11.46** *The following script contains a comment line that is not a Lingo script.*

```
on exitFrame
    -- Use this script to have the same movie branch to MyGame
    using the correct file for the current method of playback.
    case(the runMode) of:
      "Author": go to movie "MyGame.dir"
      "Projector": go to movie "MyGame.dxr"
      "Plugin": go to movie "MyGame.dcr"
    end if
end
```

## ABOUT SCRIPT COMMENTS

As you advance in your Lingo programming, you will write very detailed scripts that might become difficult to keep track of. One way to help you keep your scripts organized is to add *comments* to your scripts (figure 11.46). Comments are lines of text added anywhere within a script window. These lines of text are not Lingo scripts and are not intended to perform any function other than simply presenting information within the Script window.

Text is commented within the Script window by adding two dashes (--) to the beginning of the line of text. It is important that these two dashes be added to the beginning of the line; otherwise, Director will attempt to activate the text as a script and will likely return an error message. Text in the script window can be commented by typing directly, or you can use the Comment and Uncomment buttons at the top of the Script window.

Another useful purpose for comments is experimentation within your scripts. If you write scripts that are not working quite the way you expect, you can comment out the scripts that are not performing properly while you try different versions of the script. You can also comment out parts of scripts that you would like to temporarily deactivate without needing to completely rewrite your scripts.

Uncomment

Comment

**FIGURE 11.47** *The top of the script window, with arrows identifying the Comment and Uncomment buttons.*

### USING SHOCKWAVE

Shockwave is a method of compressing and playing Director movies so that they are smaller and can be viewed over the Internet. It works by adding a plug-in extension to the browser that you use for the Web, which serves as the software to play Shockwave files. The compressed Shockwave files themselves only contain the content of the movie, they do not contain a method for playback like a projector; as a result, the Shockwave plug-in must be present in the browser's Plug-ins folder in order to be able to view Shockwave files on the Web. In this session we will cover information about the technology behind Shockwave, and we will present a tutorial for creating a Shockwave movie and playing it through a browser.

There are different categories of Shockwave files that are created with other Macromedia products. Freehand, Flash, and Authorware are all capable of creating Shockwave files that require their own Shockwave plug-in to be viewed. Because all of the software that is used for the Web is constantly evolving, it is best to download the latest version of Shockwave from Macromedia's Web site at **www.Macromedia.com**. You can also visit our Web site at **www.motionovertime.com** and use the link on our home page that will send you directly to the Shockwave download area of Macromedia's Web site. This will save you some time navigating to Shockwave through Macromedia's site.

## WHAT IS STREAMING SHOCKWAVE?

Shockwave files must be downloaded to be viewed on a browser. This will take as much time as it would take to actually download a file of equal size to your hard drive; as a result, Shockwave files must be created with small file size as a requirement. *Streaming Shockwave* is a technology that helps to bypass the wait time associated with the Shockwave download by permitting the Shockwave movie to begin playback while it is downloading. Lingo can be used to detect if an area of the Score has been downloaded, then begin playback of that area until the following areas have been downloaded. This facilitates users being willing to download larger Shockwave movies.

One of the Lingo commands that can be used for this progressive playback is *frameReady()*, which will determine if the media used in the frame indicated in the parentheses has all been downloaded. If so, then you can begin playback. Another useful Script is the mediaReady of member property, which can be used to detect the download status of individual Cast members. Used properly, the download times for Shockwave files can be made almost imperceptible to the user.

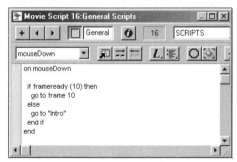

**FIGURE 11.48** *An example of a script that used the frameReady() command.*

```
on mouseDown

    if frameready(10) then
      go to frame 10
    else
      go to "Intro"
    end if
end
```

## WHAT IS SHOCKWAVE AUDIO?

Audio files can be played through a Web page just as animations can. It is not necessary to include them in movies that contain images and interactivity. Macromedia's SoundEdit 16 (Macintosh) can be used to create Shockwave audio files that can be played on a Web page. The addition of sound can make a Web page far more interesting. Shockwave audio files typically also take less time to download and can be streamed so that playback begins as soon as the audio file reaches the user's browser. You can also use Shockwave audio files in a Director movie. This helps to keep file sizes small.

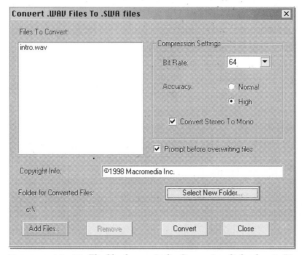

**FIGURE 11.49** *The Shockwave Audio Conversion dialog box in Director for Windows.*

## SHOCKWAVE TUTORIAL

Creating Shockwave files is as easy as saving the Director movie in a different format. The detailed issues are how to add that Shockwave movie to a standard HTML document and how to prepare the browser for playback of Shockwave files. In this session we will address all of these issues as we create a Shockwave movie and play it through a browser.

**NOTE**   Director for Windows comes with an Xtra that will convert .wav files to shockwave audio.

**NOTE**   To create and view the files in this lesson, you must have a network browser—such as Microsoft Internet Explorer or Netscape Navigator. You must also have a standard word processor application, such as ClarisWorks or Microsoft Word, to create the HTML document.

## ADDING THE SHOCKWAVE PLUG-INS TO YOUR BROWSER

If you do not already have the Shockwave plug-ins available in your browser, you will need to visit Macromedia's Web site to download them (**www.macromedia.com**). You can visit our Web site at **www.motionover-time.com** for a direct link to the Shockwave download area on Macromedia's site. The file that is downloaded is an installer application that will allow you to specify the browser that you would like to add the Shockwave plug-ins to. The plug-ins will be located in the Plug-ins folder in your browser application folder. Once you have installed the Shockwave plug-ins, you will be able to view Shockwave files. A quick way to determine if you have the Shockwave plug-in is to run the completed version of the upcoming tutorial. If the Shockwave movie in the example file plays, then you already have Shockwave installed; if not, you need to download Shockwave from Macromedia's Web site.

We did not include the Shockwave plug-ins on the Billshop CD because the technology is constantly evolving. One of the features that change frequently is the efficiency of downloads, so it is always best to be certain that you are using the most current version from Macromedia. **NOTE**

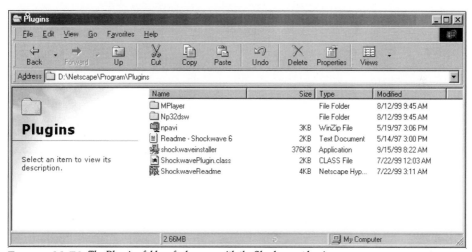

**FIGURE 11.50** *The Plug-ins folder of a browser with the Shockwave plug-ins.*

## VIEWING THE COMPLETED FILE

With Shockwave installed in our browsers, we can now view the completed version of this lesson.

1.  **Launch your browser of choice. Remember, you must use a browser that has the Shockwave plug-in installed.**

2.  **Choose File>Open Page in the browser.**

    The command might be different on different browsers or in different versions of the browser. Be certain that you are making the selection that allows you to view Web pages that are on your hard drive, and not on the Internet.

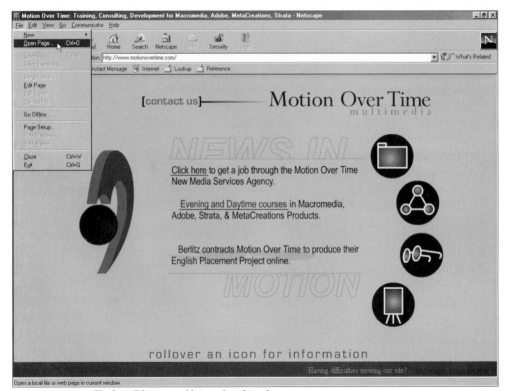

**FIGURE 11.51** *The Open File command being selected in a browser.*

3.  **Locate and open the file named MyShock.html in the following directory on the Billshop CD: Lessons/chaptr11/Shockwv/Complete/. When the file opens, you will see a Web page that will load and then play back an interactive Shockwave movie. You**

can click on the arrow buttons in the lower right corner to move the spaceship and crash into the aliens. The aliens explode on impact and your score will go up 1 point. You can click the Reset button to start the movie over again. The Motion Over Time logo in the upper left corner has a script on it that uses the *GotoNetPage* command to open the Motion Over Time Web site. If you have an active connection to the Internet, you can click on the logo to jump to the Web site in a separate window. You can still view the lesson Web page without an active connection to the Internet, but the script on the logo will not work.

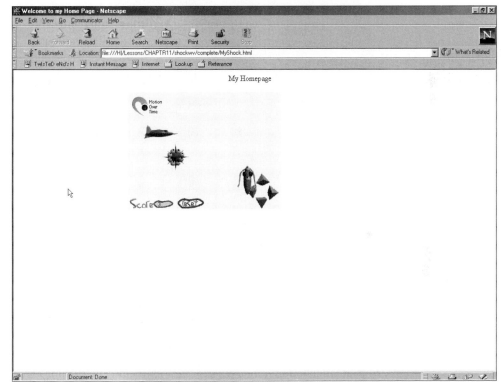

**FIGURE 11.52** *The MyShock.html page loaded and playing in a browser.*

4.  **Quit out of the browser.**

We will now create this Web page.

## CREATING THE SHOCKED WEB PAGE

In this lesson we will save a Director movie as a Shockwave file and create the HTML document that will allow us to view the page. Our first step is to create a directory for this lesson.

1.  **Create a new directory on your hard drive and name it Shock. This is where we will locate the files for this lesson. Our next step is to copy the Director file that we will be working with to the new directory.**

**FIGURE 11.53** *The new Shockwave directory.*

2.  **Copy the file named game.dir to the new Shock directory. You can locate the file named game.dir along the following directory on the Billshop CD: Lessons/chaptr11/ShockWV/Starter.**

## CREATING A SHOCKWAVE MOVIE

With the file that we will work with now copied to the hard drive, we can create our Shockwave movie.

1.  **Launch Director.**

2.  **Locate and open the file named game.dir in the directory we created named Shock on the hard drive.**

3. Play the movie. You can see that this is the same movie that we viewed earlier through a browser. This is how it appears in Director prior to Shockwave compression.

4. Stop the movie.

5. Choose File>Save As Shockwave Movie. This will present us with a dialog where we can choose the location for the new Shockwave movie. Notice that the file is automatically renamed with the extension .dcr at the end. We will save it in the Shock directory on the hard drive.

6. Locate the directory named Shock on the hard drive. This will maintain all of the files in the same place.

7. Make sure that the file's name is game.dcr, then click the button labeled Save. This will save the game file as a Shockwave movie. We are finished with Director, so we can quit out of the application to conserve system memory.

8. Choose File>Quit (Macintosh)/ File>Exit (Windows).

Now we are ready to create the HTML document.

The Save As Shockwave Movie command will convert only the file that is currently open in Director as a Shockwave movie. We can convert multiple files simultaneously by choosing Xtras>Update Movies, as we had earlier in this chapter to protect the files in The Billionaire's Shop. One of the options available to us in this dialog box is to convert Director files into Shockwave files.  **NOTE**

## CREATING AN HTML DOCUMENT THAT WILL DISPLAY THE SHOCKWAVE MOVIE

To create an HTML document, we need to use a standard text editor, such as Microsoft Word or ClarisWorks. Select your text editor of preference for this lesson.

1. Launch your text editor application.

2. Type the text in figure 11.54 into a new text document window. This text will create an HTML page that has the header Welcome to my homepage at the top and the Shockwave movie we created earlier at the bottom. The line that is critical to this lesson is the line that indicates the Shockwave movie to be played.

**FIGURE 11.54** *The HTML document that will display the Shockwave movie with the header Welcome to my homepage.*

3.    Choose File>Save As. We will save the document as a text only file.

4.    Name the file MyShock.HTML.

5.    Choose Text from the Format menu in your text editor. Some applications use the words Text Only for this option.

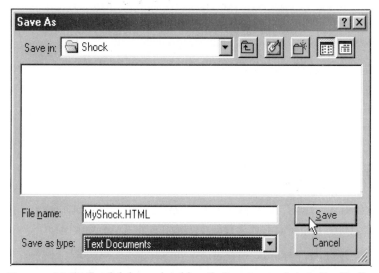

**FIGURE 11.55** *Text Only being selected from the Format menu of a text editor. The file is named MyShock.HTML.*

6.    Locate the directory named Shock on the hard drive, then click the button labeled Save. We have completed the development of our shocked Web page.

7.    Quit out of the text editor.

Now we can preview our new Web page with a browser.

## VIEWING THE NEW WEB PAGE

HTML documents are essentially just text files that follow a certain format that can be understood by a browser. The file that we created with the text editor follows this format and can therefore be opened as a Web page. Let's take a look at what we have accomplished:

1.  **Launch your Web browser. Once again, remember that you must be using the browser that has the Shockwave plug-in installed.**

2.  **Choose File>Open File.**

3.  **Locate and open the file we created named MyShock.HTML in the directory named Shock on the hard drive.**

The file will load, we will see the header in the HTML document, and finally the Shockwave movie will load. Notice that the progress area in the browser indicates that the Shockwave movie is loading; it will also indicate that the Shockwave plug-in is being loaded. The plug-in serves as the playback mechanism. We have successfully created a shocked Web page!

## DOWNLOAD TIMES FOR SHOCKWAVE FILES

The time that is required for a Shockwave movie to download is dependent upon the size of the file and the speed of your Internet connection. Table 11.02 gives you an idea of how this correlation will affect download times.

**TABLE 11.02** *Table showing the number of seconds needed to transfer a file, based on the size of the file and the speed of the Internet connection.*

| | Connection Speed (in Kilobytes per second) | | | | |
|---|---|---|---|---|---|
| **File size** | 14.4 | 28.8 | 56 | 128 | T1 |
| 1k | * | * | * | * | * |
| 10k | 6 | 3 | 1 | * | * |
| 25k | 14 | 7 | 3.5 | 2 | * |
| 50k | 28 | 14 | 7 | 4 | * |
| 100k | 56 | 28 | 14 | 8 | * |
| 500k | 280 | 140 | 70 | 45 | 3 |
| 1MB | 560 | 280 | 140 | 90 | 6 |

k = kilobyte    MB = megabyte
Connection data rates are measured in kilobytes per second.
* Less than 1 second.

**NOTE**   These download rates are approximate and can differ based upon the activity on the network that the files are traveling along. These figures assume that there is no activity occurring other than the download of the file.

## LINGO FOR SHOCKWAVE FILES

Shockwave files can be fully interactive, so there are several Lingo commands that are available specifically for Shockwave files. Many of these commands are used to track the download status of the Shockwave movie itself and other non-interactive elements, but two in particular are used to add interactivity to a Web page (either to jump to another Web page, or to another Shockwave movie on the same page): *gotoNetPage* and *gotoNetMovie*. Here are examples of how these two commands are used.

**NOTE**   Shockwave is capable of using all of the NetLingo Hybrid scripts that we used in earlier chapters, with the exception of *downloadNetThing*. This is designed to protect users from having files unintentionally downloaded to their hard drives from Shockwave files.

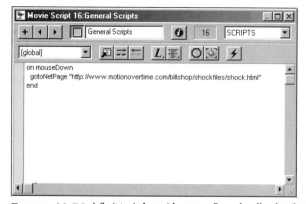

**FIGURE 11.56** *A Script window with a mouseDown handler that demonstrates the syntax of gotoNetPage.*

```
on mouseDown

  gotoNetPage"http://www.motionovertime.com/billshop/
  shockfiles/shock.html"

end
```

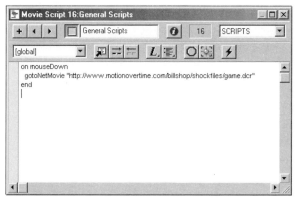

**FIGURE 11.57** *A Script window with a mouseDown handler that demonstrates the syntax of gotoNetMovie.*

```
on mouseDown
  gotoNetMovie"http//:www.motionovertime.com/billshop/
  shockfiles/game.dcr"
end
```

This script will load the Shockwave movie named game.dcr in the same location on the Web page as the current Shockwave movie. *GotoNetMovie* will only work when it is calling a Shockwave movie that is located on a local hard drive, or when it is activated from one movie on the Internet that is calling another movie that is also on the Internet. This is the same file that we will later use to create a simple Web page with Shockwave.

**NOTE**

The *gotoNetPage* command can be tested from the Director application. You will need an active connection to the Internet as well as an Internet browser, such as Netscape Navigator or Microsoft Internet Explorer, for *gotoNetPage* to work properly. *GotoNetMovie* will only work within the Director application when the file that is being called upon is located somewhere on your hard drive and not on the Internet.

Using these commands, it is possible to create almost an entire Web site with Shockwave. We will always need the HTML document to be recognized by a browser, but we can limit the use of HTML to simply the display of the first Shockwave movie on the site. From that point on, we can use Shockwave and Lingo to jump between movies that contain the information we want to deliver on the site in full multimedia.

**NOTE**   Shockwave files can send messages directly to a browser using scripting languages that are understood by the browser. For example, a Shockwave movie can use the *on externalEvent* event handler to send a command using the liveConnect scripting language, which is supported by Netscape. This is a fairly advanced method of Web site development that requires a good amount of testing on different browsers to be certain it will be available to the largest number of users. This is mainly because all browsers can read HTML, but not necessarily understand the scripting language that you are using with the *on externalEvent* command. There is more information on this type of scripting in the Lingo Dictionary and the Using Lingo manual that are included with Director.

## SUMMARY

By converting a Director movie into a projector, we make it possible to play that movie on most other computers. Projectors can only be played back on the computer platform they were created on, although the same Director file can be used in Director for both Windows and Macintosh. Once a movie has been converted into a projector, it can no longer be opened with Director, so it is important to always retain a backup copy of the movies you work with.

As mentioned above, Director movies cannot be edited once they are converted to projectors. This can be cumbersome if we want to edit the movie within the projector at a later date. One way of avoiding this problem is to create a *stub* projector, which is a projector created with a movie that contains a script that launches the first movie of the presentation as an external file. The stub projector serves as a container for the resources that are needed to play the presentation. The other Director movies remain unconverted; therefore they can be reopened and edited at a later date.

Many Director presentations are created with multiple external movie and Cast files. These files contain the media and scripts that are used in the presentation and can be opened by anyone who has Director installed on their computer. We can protect our movies from being opened by other people, by saving them as protected files. This process strips the Director movies and Casts of the information that allows them to be opened in Director, but leaves the information that allows them to be opened by a projector. To use this technique properly, you need to retain a backup copy of the files in the presentation, in the event that you want to edit them later.

During the development process, it is common to switch between versions of a presentation that use protected files and versions that use unprotected files. During this process, it is important to program the files so that the Director application will only open the files that are unprotected; otherwise, we will receive an error message and the movies will not open and play properly. The Lingo script `runMode` allows us to discern between playback through Director and a projector, so we can write scripts that will steer Director to the appropriate files when the movies are playing through Director.

As we write Lingo scripts, we will want to experiment with versions of the same scripts. To allow us to add scripts and render them inactive as needed, we can *Comment Out* the scripts by adding two dashes to the front of the line of script. This will prevent those scripts from being activated as the movie plays. We can also use commented text in the script window to add support notes in the script window.

Although Director's Hybrid scripts are designed to retrieve information and not to send information, we can use the *getNetText()* command to activate scripts on a network server. The *getNetText()* command is also capable of sending information from Director to a server-side script, such as a CGI script. The CGI script can then be programmed to reroute the information to send it to other applications, such as email systems or databases. To add this capability to a Director presentation, you need to create custom applications in a programming language, such as CGI scripts or ASP documents.

Another method for delivery and playback of Director presentations is as Shockwave files, which can be played across networks or the Internet through network browsers. The process of developing a movie for Shockwave conversion is the same as the process for developing for delivery as a projector. The only additional concern is that a Shockwave movie is best developed as small as possible to reduce download times through the network. Director movies and Cast files are converted into Shockwave files simply by saving the files in the Shockwave format. Besides playback through a Web browser, Shockwave files can also be played through a projector.

Shockwave files can be added to Web pages using Web scripting methods, such as HTML, in a manner similar to how images are added to Web pages. To view Web pages that use Shockwave files, you need to install the Shockwave plug-ins into the browser that you are using. You can download the latest versions of Shockwave from Macromedia's Web site at **http:// www.macromedia.com**.

## QUESTIONS

1. Why is it useful to create and work with a stub projector?

2. Why is it important to retain a copy of your original files when converting Director Cast and movie files into protected files?

3. Can the Director application open Shockwave files? Protected files? Which file types can a projector open?

4. Why is it helpful to use Shockwave files to update The Billionaire's Shop instead of unconverted Director files?

5. Why do Web pages that include Shockwave files require the presence of the Shockwave plug-in in the browser where they are viewed?

## EXERCISES

1. Using one of the movies you created in an earlier lesson, create a projector. Confirm that you created it properly by running it on your computer.

2. Create a new movie, which we will use to create a stub projector. This new movie should contain a script in a *startMovie* or *exitFrame* handler that will launch another movie. You can use a movie that you created in an earlier lesson as the target movie. Confirm that you were successful by launching the new stub projector on your computer.

3. Create a Shockwave movie using one of the files that you created in an earlier lesson. Run the file through an Internet browser to confirm that it works. If you have more than one browser, run it in the different browsers. You should see that there is no difference in the performance of the Shockwave movie playing through different browsers.

4. Using the files that you created in chapters 4 and 7 with the storyboards and logic flowchart you created in chapter 1, create a projector that will run your project without using the Director software. When you have done this, run the new application to make sure it works.

5. Save the original files from exercise 4 as Shockwave movies and play them through a browser with the Shockwave plug-in.

# Index

# Technical Documentation for The Billionaire's Shop CD

## Minimum Hardware System Requirements

Windows - IBM compatible computer (Pentium II or later, or equivalent), Windows 95, 98, NT, or later, CD-ROM Drive (4X or greater), Soundblaster or compatible sound card, 16 MB RAM or greater (32MB recommended), External or built-in speakers, 8 bit or greater Color Display (640X480 resolution or greater)

Macintosh - PowerPC, System 8.0 or later, CD-ROM Drive (4X or greater), 16 MB RAM or greater (32MB recommended), 8 bit or greater Color Display (640X480 resolution or greater)

## Software Requirements*

Macromedia Director version 7.0 or later, Apple QuickTime Version 3.0 or later, Macromedia Shockwave version must be compatible with current version of Director

* No software is included on the CD-ROM other than lesson files. Please refer to section titled Other Software Needed for further information.

## CD-ROM Contents

Lesson Files (11 directories) and all related media for Chapter 1 to 11 of The Billionaire's Shop project. All lesson files are created with Macromedia Director. Each lesson directory contains file and sub-directory structures that may vary from lesson to lesson. Chapter text describes the contents of each respective chapter lesson. See chapter 1 of text for CD-ROM directory structure.

## Other Software Needed

Macromedia Director - Director is the authoring software that was used to create The Billionaire's Shop. The commercial version of Director is available through mail order, software resellers, and Macromedia Value Added Resellers (VAR). The Trial version of Director is available for free download from Macromedia's web site at http://www.macromedia.com. Follow installation instructions that are downloaded with the Trial version of Director or that are included on the installation CD-ROM for the commercial version of Director. Visit Macromedia's web site for further information about Macromedia software resellers. Motion Over Time, Inc. is a Macromedia software reseller.

Apple QuickTime - QuickTime is the software extension for both Macintosh and Windows that is used to play digital video files that are generated using the QuickTime format. QuickTime can be downloaded from Apple's web site at http://www.apple.com. Follow the instructions for installation that are downloaded with the software. QuickTime is required for the playback of the completed version of The Billionaire's Shop project in chapter 1 and in all lessons from chapter 5 to 11.

Macromedia Shockwave - Shockwave is the extension that is used to play Macromedia Director movie files through a web page. The shockwave extension must be installed in the extensions folder of a browser such as Netscape Navigator or Microsoft Internet Explorer. Shockwave is available for download from Macromedia's web site at http://www.macromedia.com. Follow the instructions for installation that are downloaded with the software. Shockwave is required for the Shockwave lesson in chapter 11.

## Installation Instructions

After installing Director, QuickTime, and Shockwave per the instructions in the section titled Other Software Needed, remove the CD-ROM from the rear cover of the book and insert into your computer's CD-ROM drive. Windows: Double click on your CD-ROM drive icon to access the directories on the disc. Macintosh: Double click on the CD-ROM image that appears on your desktop. Follow the instructions provided with each lesson chapter for information about which files to access on the CD-ROM for each lesson.